THEORIES OF MEMORY II

Theories of Memory
Volume II

edited by

Martin A. Conway
Susan E. Gathercole
&
Cesare Cornoldi

Psychology Press
a member of the Taylor & Francis group

Copyright © 1998 by Psychology Press, Ltd.,
a member of the Taylor & Francis Group

Psychology Press Ltd., Publishers
27 Church Road
Hove
East Sussex, BN3 2FA
UK

British Library Cataloguing in Publication Data

A catalogue record for this book is available from the British Library

ISBN 0-86377-805-4

Typeset by GCS, Leighton Buzzard
Printed and bound in the UK by Biddles Ltd, Guildford and King's Lynn

Contents

List of Contributors

Nicole D. Anderson, Rotman Research Institute of Baycrest Centre, 3560 Bathurst Street, North York, Ontario, M6A 2E1, Canada

Jackie Andrade, Department of Psychology, Western Bank, University of Sheffield, Sheffield, S10 2TN, UK

Alan D. Baddeley, Department of Psychology, University of Bristol, 8 Woodland Road, Bristol BS8 1TN, UK

Gordon H. Bower, Department of Psychology, Stanford University, Stanford, CA 94305, USA

Cesare Cornoldi, Università degli Studi di Padova, Dipartimento di Psicologia Generale, Via Venezia 8, 35131 Padova, Italy

Fergus I.M. Craik, Department of Psychology, University of Toronto, Toronto, Ontario, Canada M5S 3G3

Rossana De Beni, Università degli Studi di Padova, Dipartimento di Psicologia Generale, Via Venezia 8, 35131 Padova, Italy

Ray Dolan, Wellcome Department of Cognitive Neurology, Institute of Neurology, Queen Square, London, WC1N 3BG, UK

Paul Fletcher, Wellcome Department of Cognitive Neurology, Institute of Neurology, Queen Square, London, WC1N 3BG, UK

Fiorella Giusberti, Università di Bologna, Dipartimento di Psicologia, Viale Benti Pichot, Bologna, Italy

Janine F. Hay, Department of Psychology, McMaster University, 1280 Main Street West, Hamilton, Ontario, Canada L8S 4K1

Larry L. Jacoby, Department of Psychology, McMaster University, 1280 Main Street West, Hamilton, Ontario, Canada L8S 4K1

Elizabeth F. Loftus, Psychology Department, University of Washington, Seattle, WA 98195-1525, USA

Jean M. Mandler, Department of Cognitive Science, University of California, San Diego, La Jolla, CA 92093-0515, USA

Manfredo Massironi, Università di Verona, Istituto di Psicologia, Via S. Francesco 22, 37129, Verona, Italy

Kathleen B. McDermott, Departments of Radiology and Psychology, Box 1125, Washington University, St Louis, MO 63130-4899, USA

Moshe Naveh-Benjamin, Department of Behavioral Sciences, Ben-Gurion University of the Negev, Beer-Sheva 84120, Israel

Ulric Neisser, Department of Psychology, Cornell University, Ithaca, NY 14853, USA

Henry L. Roediger III, Department of Psychology, Box 1125, Washington University, St Louis, MO 63130-4899, USA

Kerry J. Robinson, Department of Psychology, Box 1125, Washington University, St Louis, MO 63130-4899, USA

Tim Shallice, Institute of Cognitive Neuroscience, University College London, Gower Street, London WC1E 6BT, UK

Barbara Tversky, Department of Psychology, Bldg 420, Stanford University, Stanford, CA 94305-2130, USA

Preface

The Second International Conference on Memory (ICOM-96) was held from the 14th to the 19th of July 1996, at the Centro Congressi, in the spa town of Abano Termie, Italy. The conference was supported by the Departments of Psicologia Generale and Psicologia dei processi di sviluppo e di socializzazione of the University of Padova, by the Italian 'Consiglio Nazionale delle Ricerche' (CNR), and by the Department of Psychology and Faculty of Social Sciences of the University of Bristol. Erlbaum (UK) Taylor & Francis (now Psychology Press) also provided support for advertising and dissemination of conference materials and we thank them for their assistance. The Cognitive Section of the British Psychological Society also sponsored the meeting. This ICOM was undoubtedly the largest single conference devoted solely to the study of human memory: the programme had six parallel sessions for each of the five days with 35 symposia and over 400 individual presentations, 80 poster presentations, and 10 keynote addresses. Over the whole period of the ICOM 500 to 600 delegates (including speakers) attended the meeting and a large group of 300 to 400 were present for the entire duration.

Given this concentration of international memory researchers at the meeting, the contents of the programme provide an interesting snapshot of the current terrain of memory research. Areas of memory research particularly strongly represented throughout the conference programme were working memory, autobiographical memory, memory and consciousness, imagery, amnesia, age-related changes in memory, and eye-witness testimony. Other significant topics which featured more strongly in ICOM-96 than in the first conference of the series, ICOM-91, were impairments to semantic memory, neuroimaging studies of human memory, reasoning and memory, inhibition, and the rehabilitation of memory following brain injury.

The present volume contains invited chapters based ICOM-96 presentations and includes papers by the keynote speakers. As with the previous volume, *Theories of memory I*, we have not imposed any editorial organisation on the order of presentation of the chapters which are listed alphabetically by first author. Our aim in producing this volume has been to provide the reader with a feeling for the diversity of research themes in the study of human memory and also for the undoubted maturity of some of these themes, which currently rest on several decades of research findings. The authors appraise current theories and evaluate their standing while considering alternative formulations, and at the same time review recent empirical findings. We hope that the volume will provide a source book for most current aspects of memory research.

Organising a conference is a joint enterprise and there were a number of individuals who made crucial contributions to ICOM-96. In so doing they increased their workload, often by taking on rather tedious but essential tasks. In Bristol the secretarial staff of the Department of Psychology, Mary Pope, Hazel Carrington, and Louise Stoney, all contributed to the unenviable task of constructing the provisional and final programmes. Especially important to the success of the ICOM were the efforts of Hazel Carrington who both compiled the programme and answered all queries from delegates. We take this opportunity to thank Hazel and Mary and Louise for their excellent work. The day-to-day running of the conference was brilliantly conducted by a team of doctoral students from the Department of General Psychology, University of Padova. They quietly took over the daily business of the conference, which was considerable, and with a very high degree of efficiency and friendliness ran a trouble-free academic and social programme, and we are especially grateful to them. Finally, we thank Mr Sbalchiero, the manager of the Centro Congressi, for his friendly and efficient management.

Martin Conway
Sue Gathercole
Cesare Cornoldi

June 1997, Bristol, UK
Padova, Italy

1 Working Memory and Consciousness: An Empirical Approach

Alan D. Baddeley
Centre for the Study of Memory & Learning, University of Bristol, UK

Jackie Andrade
Department of Psychology, University of Sheffield, UK

After almost a century in the wilderness, the study of consciousness has, in the last decade, become not only respectable, but also highly fashionable. New journals have been created, and many books edited, with contributions not only from the traditional sources of philosophy and psychology, but from many other disciplines. While much of this work is based on an empirical core, typically derived from neuropsychology or cognitive psychology, much of it still represents armchair speculation from philosophers, mystically inclined physicists, and religiously inspired biologists. Although the armchairs available for speculation may be of a better quality than a hundred years ago, our own view is that if the study of consciousness is to avoid returning to the intellectual morass that engulfed it in the middle years of this century, it is important that the speculations are based on empirical evidence, and that this in turn depends on the development of a suitable theoretical framework, and adequate empirical tools. A framework based on the concept of working memory was presented at the first meeting of this group (Baddeley, 1993; see also Baddeley, 1997). The present chapter outlines three areas in which the framework has been applied, beginning with research using anaesthetics to alter level of consciousness, then describing experiments on mind-wandering and the control of conscious awareness, and concluding with an account of an experimental programme concerned with the qualitative aspects of consciousness as reflected in the analysis of the subjective vividness of imagery.

A THEORETICAL FRAMEWORK

Bisiach (1988) distinguishes three aspects of consciousness. The first of these is consciousness as a mysterious entity or property, which typically resembles the concept of the soul in differentiating man from the beasts. We regard such a quasi-theological concept as neither necessary nor desirable, and as having little or no relevance to the empirical study of conscious awareness.

The second aspect, phenomenal consciousness (see also Block, 1995), refers to our sensory experience of the world. The basic units of this experience are termed *qualia*; the taste of chocolate, the smell of woodsmoke, the sound of rain, the feel of pain, are examples of qualia. Regarding qualia as the essence of conscious experience raises important questions about how physical events transform themselves into mental events, why we experience those events in the way we do, and whether our experience is the same as someone else's experience. Why, for instance, does light with a wavelength of 660nm falling on the retina result in the experience of seeing red rather than green? When I stub my toe, is my pain the same as the feeling you have when you stub your toe? The problem of answering questions such as these, of explaining conscious experience even with a perfect understanding of the underlying brain processes, has been termed the explanatory gap (Levine, 1983). While some authors have claimed that "at present the gap remains dauntingly large" (Young & Block, 1996, p.150), others argue that it arises only from the mistaken assumption that consciousness is based on irreducible, private experiences (Baddeley, 1993, 1997; Dennett, 1988) and from our current lack of knowledge about how the brain works (Churchland, 1995; Dennett, 1991).

Bisiach's third aspect of consciousness refers to the availability of mental representations for use in other cognitive processes. Mental states are conscious if they can be reported, reasoned about, voluntarily acted on, or recollected. Block (1995) describes such states and their contents as access-conscious, i.e. other cognitive processes have access to them. This aspect of consciousness presents a more fruitful area for empirical research, as illustrated by recent studies of topics as diverse as the neurobiological basis of visual perception (Crick & Koch, 1990), the anatomical regions important for conscious or explicit memory (Shallice et al., 1994), and the cognitive processes needed for the voluntary control of action (Norman & Shallice, 1986). This research treats consciousness as an empirical, biological, and psychological phenomenon; a solution that has evolved to cope with certain problems. We share this approach and believe that it may also lead the way to explaining phenomenal consciousness.

We introduce our account through a quasi-biological speculation concerning the problems facing an evolving organism and the solution offered by consciousness. Although we regard biological plausibility as an ultimately necessary feature of any model of consciousness, such plausibility is not of course in and of itself evidence for any given view. In the present instance, it is used primarily as an expository device. We suggest furthermore that the value, if any, of our model does not lie in the ultimate validity, or indeed testability, of the biological speculation, but in its capacity to provide a framework for conceptualising existing evidence, and a platform for making further empirical progress.

A Quasi-biological Speculation

Suppose we were trying to develop an organism that could flourish in the ordered but far from predictable world that we live in, what capacities would it find useful? Our organism should clearly have some sensory channels to tell it about the surrounding environment. Given that many objects are detectable by a number of different sensory channels, vision, touch, smell, and often sound, then it makes sense to have a system that is capable of registering the fact that these many channels have a common source. This task is sometimes known as the *binding* problem, and is currently the focus of intensive neurobiological research activity (e.g. Crick & Koch, 1990; Pöppel & Schwender, 1993; Singer, 1996).

If our organism is to interpret the source of this incoming sensory information as dangerous or safe, learn whether it is edible or poisonous, or decide to flee from it, then the bound information must persist for long enough to influence other cognitive processes. We suggest that working memory is the mechanism that achieves this persistence of representations, making them available to other cognitive processes (see also Baars, 1988), and also that it is the mechanism for focusing on, selecting, and if necessary manipulating selected aspects of the representation (for a more detailed discussion see Baddeley, 1997, Chapters 18, 19, and 20).

We are of course well aware that the proposed link between consciousness and the binding problem is far from novel. The particular virtue, if any, of our approach lies in our linking it with a relatively well-developed model of working memory. This makes available a ready-made conceptual framework, together with a range of empirical techniques that provide ways of investigating the multifarious aspects of conscious awareness. For example, research has already considered the role of the central executive in encoding and retrieving information in long-term memory (Baddeley, Lewis, Eldridge, & Thomson, 1984), the nature of articulatory and visuo-spatial maintenance or rehearsal processes (Baddeley, 1986; Logie, 1995) and the role of the executive in selective attention (Baddeley, 1996).

The working memory model has guided research into diverse areas of everyday cognition such as language learning (Ellis & Sinclair, 1996; Gathercole & Baddeley, 1993), comprehending speech (Vallar & Baddeley, 1984), and doing two things at once (Baddeley et al., 1991, 1997). We aim to continue this approach, looking at a broad range of everyday conscious behaviour rather than attempting a fine-grained analysis of one aspect of conscious awareness. The remainder of this chapter describes three strands of our research into consciousness. The first strand uses general anaesthetic agents to impair consciousness and addresses issues such as how can we measure global changes in level of conscious awareness and what is the role of consciousness in other aspects of cognition? The second strand, on mind-wandering, seeks to characterise normal, conscious mental life as a state in which cognitive processes are driven internally as well as by external stimulation. This research explores the role of working memory in daydreaming, concentration, and focused attention, i.e. the control of conscious awareness. The third strand investigates the role of working memory in mental imagery, attempting to elucidate the cognitive processes associated with the subjective experience of vivid imagery.

ANAESTHESIA AS A TOOL FOR RESEARCHING CONSCIOUSNESS

General anaesthetics are a chemically diverse group of drugs that have in common the effect of temporarily abolishing consciousness. Brain imaging studies of anaesthesia (e.g. Alkire et al., 1995) show a global depression of cerebral metabolism. Single-cell electrophysiological recordings suggest this may be caused by inhibition of information flow through the thalamus to the frontal cortex (Angel, 1993). The cognitive effects of anaesthetics are consistent with reduced frontal activity (Caseley-Rondi, 1996). For example, even very small doses of anaesthetics have been shown to impair attention (Bruce & Bach, 1975, 1976) and decision making (Bentin, Collins, & Adam, 1978). Functionally, therefore, anaesthetics seem to impair the executive processes, such as focusing attention and selecting responses, that we associate with conscious awareness.

At first sight, anaesthetics appear to offer a useful tool for researching cognition in the absence of consciousness. Of particular interest has been the issue of whether people continue to learn new information during surgery under general anaesthesia. There have been many demonstrations of implicit memory for intra-operative events (see Andrade, 1995, for review). Jelicic, de Roode, Bovill, and Bonke (1992), for example, played a tape of fictitious names to one group of patients and answers to Trivial Pursuit-type questions to another group during surgery. Memory test performance on recovery suggested that some of this information had been encoded during surgery—thus the first group was more likely to incorrectly identify the fictitious names as famous (the false fame effect) and the second was more likely to answer the Trivial Pursuit questions correctly. Findings such as these raise concerns about the effects of operating theatre conversations on patients' recovery from surgery. However, there are also many studies that failed to show learning during surgery, including an attempt by Jelicic to replicate his own findings (Jelicic, Asbury, Millar, & Bonke, 1993). The methodology of these studies varies widely, but no single factor such as anaesthetic technique or type of memory test is sufficient to distinguish the studies that found intra-operative learning from those that did not (Andrade, 1995).

One important variable, depth of anaesthesia or level of unconsciousness, was not measured in the majority of these studies, leaving open the possibility that patients who learned the intra-operative stimuli were more lightly anaesthetised—or more conscious—than those who did not. Depth of anaesthesia fluctuates during an operation even if the dose of anaesthetic remains constant because there is a trade-off between the sedative effects of the anaesthetic and the arousing effects of surgery. A good measure of depth of anaesthesia must therefore reflect changes in cognitive function and not simply the amount of anaesthetic in the patient's bloodstream. There is not yet agreement on how best to measure depth of anaesthesia, hence the absence of information about level of unconsciousness in the reports of studies of learning during surgery. Several potential measures of depth of anaesthesia are currently under investigation, including various aspects of the raw and processed EEG (see Andrade & Jones, 1997, for review), but none is routinely used in operating theatres.

A recent study (Andrade, Munglani, Jones, & Baddeley, 1994) suggests that a measure of steady state auditory-evoked responding called the coherent frequency provides an objective measure of cognitive function during sedation with anaesthetic drugs. Volunteers in this study received varying subclinical doses of a volatile anaesthetic, isoflurane. At each dose of isoflurane, we assessed cognitive function in two ways, first by asking participants to raise their hand whenever they heard an example of a particular category in a spoken list of common nouns, and second by a within-list recognition test. This memory test required participants to listen to a sequence of words and raise their hand every time a word was repeated, with the repetitions occurring after delays ranging from 0 to 16 intervening words. This test therefore relies on participants' working memory function, both in terms of their ability to maintain words in memory over short intervals and in terms of their ability to sustain attention throughout a supra-span list. If we are correct in our assumption that consciousness depends on working memory function, then performance on this task should be very sensitive to the effects of anaesthetics.

Performance on both the within-list recognition and category judgement tests declined as the dose of isoflurane increased, and so did the coherent frequency in the EEG recording. Scores on all three measures returned gradually to baseline as the dose of anaesthetic decreased again. Performance on the category judgement task is instructive: when participants were inhaling 0.4% isoflurane (the higher dose at which cognitive tests were attempted), they correctly responded to a mean of 4 of the 10 category exemplars. Electrical stimulation of the ulnar nerve, intended to mimic the arousing effect of surgery, improved performance to 6 of 10 exemplars identified even though the dose of isoflurane remained constant.

On recovery from the anaesthetic, participants performed at chance on a test of recognition of the exemplars presented at this dose (pre-stimulation).

This study shows that cognitive function declines gradually as the dose of anaesthetic increases, and that this decline can be measured by recording the brain's electrical responses to auditory stimuli. The finding that words could be heard, understood, and responded to, without later being recognised, suggests that conscious awareness during anaesthesia is not sufficient for explicit memory formation.

Using a measure such as coherent frequency in studies of learning during surgery would help to answer the question of whether learning occurs only during periods of light anaesthesia. However, it would not conclusively reveal whether this learning were explicit or implicit because coherent frequency, like most other potential measures of anaesthetic depth, indicates only the relative level of cognitive function and not awareness of a particular stimulus. We believe the advantage of anaesthetics as a tool for psychological research lies less in their potential for proving that we can learn without awareness, than in their ability to gradually impair the executive processes that contribute to conscious awareness. Studies of the effects of small doses of anaesthetics suggest that impairing these processes has a similar effect on implicit memory as on explicit memory. This contrasts with studies of, say, subliminal perception, where implicit memory is relatively unimpaired by manipulations that abolish explicit memory. One interpretation of these findings is that executive processes associated with consciousness, and impaired by low doses of anaesthetic, are essential for implicit memory formation even if conscious awareness of the stimulus is not (see Andrade, 1996, for further discussion). Future volunteer studies of anaesthesia may reveal the role of consciousness in other aspects of cognition— not, that is, the function of conscious *awareness,* but more simply the effect on general cognitive function of the processes that we associate with consciousness.

MIND-WANDERING AND THE CONTROL OF ATTENTION

One of the most important aspects of conscious awareness is the way in which it may be focused and controlled. Indeed, the question of attentional control was the first aspect of the study of consciousness to regain respectability through the study of selective attention (Broadbent, 1958). There are, however, occasions on which active control is relinquished, as in daydreaming, or indeed dreaming, while in other circumstances our attention may be seized by an intrusive thought or stimulus despite our attempts to focus attention elsewhere. In some instances, such as feeling pain or hearing a loud noise, the capacity of the attentional system to break away from control is clearly of considerable potential survival value. In other situations, however, the domination of attention by memories, thoughts, or potential threats may be pathological, resulting from and maintaining levels of anxiety or depression and interfering with the capacity to work or relax (Williams,

Watts, MacLeod, & Mathews, 1997). For example, an important component of depression is the tendency to ruminate, a process that tends to be biased in the direction of accessing negative and self-denigratory memories, which in turn tend to increase the level of depression. In the case of post-traumatic stress disorder, intrusive thoughts again form an important and highly disruptive symptom, with patients experiencing involuntary and vivid memory "flashbacks" of the traumatic event. Finding methods of controlling such unwanted recollections is an important problem within clinical psychology.

Antrobus (1968), using a simple channel capacity model of cognition, proposed that irrelevant thoughts could be banished by requiring the subject to perform concurrently a demanding intellectual task. He showed that mental arithmetic successfully suppressed unwanted thoughts, a result that was consistent with the model, but whose practical value was limited by the likelihood that a lifetime of concurrent mental arithmetic might be even less attractive than one plagued with depressive ruminations. In the previous account of our approach to consciousness (Baddeley, 1993) the beginning of an attempt to use the working memory model to tackle this problem was described. This will be recapitulated and some subsequent work described.

As the ruminations appear to be verbal in nature, Teasdale, Proctor, Lloyd, and Baddeley (1993) speculated that it might be possible to disrupt them by blocking the articulatory loop component of working memory through verbal suppression. Verbal or articulatory suppression typically involves repeating a single word or phrase, blocking the operation of the articulatory rehearsal process, while placing relatively little load on the remainder of working memory. This can be contrasted with concurrent immediate serial recall in which a subject is required to remember and rehearse a string of numbers approaching span, a task that places substantial demands on executive resources as well as suppressing articulation (Baddeley & Hitch, 1974). A series of experiments demonstrated first of all that a range of concurrent verbal tasks were capable of substantially reducing the extent to which self-reported mind-wandering occurred. Furthermore, it did not prove necessary to impose a heavy load on the subject's working memory in order to achieve a substantial degree of suppression of irrelevant thoughts. Indeed, the need to retain a single digit was sufficient to disrupt mind-wandering, provided that the digit kept changing, preventing the process from becoming automated. However, a spatial tapping task proved just as disruptive of irrelevant thoughts as the phonological tasks, suggesting that the crucial controlling factor was the operation of the attentional control system of working memory, namely the central executive. This was investigated directly in two further experiments.

The first experiment capitalised on the observation that the capacity to generate sequences of numbers at random is one that depends heavily on the central executive component of working memory (Baddeley, 1986). Teasdale et al. (1995) required subjects to generate sequences of numbers at random and interrupted them from time to time with the request to report the content of their thoughts. Those occasions on which an instance of mind-wandering occurred were noted, and the randomness of the numbers during the preceding seconds was compared with the equivalent numbers preceding an occasion on which attention was reportedly concentrated on the task in hand. As predicted, the number sequences preceding an instance of mind-wandering were less random and more stereotyped than those preceding an instance of more focused attention.

A further experiment was based on the assumption that practice on a given task will systematically reduce the extent to which it is dependent on the central executive. Teasdale et al. (1995) therefore tested the disrupting effect of concurrent pursuit tracking and a simple single-digit memory task on the frequency of the occurrence of irrelevant thoughts. Performance was assessed before and after a period of practice on the concurrent tasks. On the second occasion, after secondary task practice, substantially more irrelevant thoughts were reported, as predicted. Finally, a more qualitative analysis of the irrelevant thoughts reported by subjects showed that a minimal task involving the central executive was sufficient to reduce the incidence of irrelevant thoughts and particularly disrupted coherent and continuous streams of thought. It is of course these coherent thought-streams that are likely to form the disruptive component of the ruminations of depressed patients.

What, then, is the practical outcome of this series of experiments? It clearly does not in and of itself comprise a method of treatment. What it does, however, is to provide a carefully evaluated tool which may be used as one part of the armoury available to the cognitive therapist attempting to develop a treatment procedure. We will return to this point briefly after the next section.

WHAT MAKES AN IMAGE VIVID?

In the days when introspection was regarded as the royal road to the analysis of cognition, the nature of imagery formed one of the central topics of psychology. When the introspective method became discredited because of difficulty in deciding between the claims of different schools of thought, imagery disappeared as a respectable subject of study. Psychology was concerned with behaviour, not experience. The rehabilitation of imagery as a proper psychological study began with Paivio's (1969) demonstration that ratings of the imageability of words was the most powerful predictor of the ease with which they could be learned as paired associates or in free recall experiments. The topic of imagery gained further ground with the demonstration by Shepard and colleagues that when presented with a pair of rotated figures, the time to judge whether they were equivalent was a linear function of their angular separation, a result that was consistent with the idea of a process whereby one object was internally rotated to the same orientation as the other, before a judgement was made (Shepard & Metzler, 1971). The analogy between the physical scanning of the scene and the "mental scanning" of a mental image formed an important part of the model of imagery proposed by Kosslyn (1980) who proposed a complex set of mechanisms whereby images were conceived as internal representations which utilised much of the same mental equipment as did vision. By the 1980s therefore, any self-respecting cognitive psychology textbook was likely to have a chapter on imagery. Despite this, however, Paivio, Shepard, and Kosslyn were all at pains to deny that they were studying the experience of the subject, even though in Paivio's case his work was based on subjective ratings of the imageability of words, in which subjects were explicitly invited to comment on the extent to which a given word could evoke a quasi-sensory experience. The problem was not that people denied the existence of such experience. For example, Pylyshyn (1973, p.2), a noted critic of some of the claims for the study of imagery, points out that "Imagery is a pervasive form of experience and is clearly of utmost importance to humans. We can not speak of consciousness without, at the same time, implicating the existence of images". As Marks (1977) observed "The mental image has been allowed to re-enter the arena of scientific psychology on condition that it be stripped of its mental and phenomenological aspects."

However, it is not true to say that there was no interest in the subjective experience of imagery. There has for many years been an interest in individual differences in the vividness of imagery that people report. As early as 1883 Galton wrote to a range of eminent contemporaries inviting them to reflect on their capacity to image their breakfast table, rating the vividness of the image from totally absent to as vivid as if they were seeing it. He observed huge individual differences, a finding that has been replicated many times since, and which has resulted in the development of a series of questionnaire measures of the vividness of imagery, of which the Vividness of Visual Imagery Question-naire (VVIQ; Marks, 1972) is one of the more prominent. However, although large differences exist in subjective ratings of vividness, there is little evidence to suggest that these have clear implications for performance. Many studies have attempted to relate subjective vividness to memory performance, including for example an early study by DiVesta, Ingersoll, and Sunshine (1971) that found no correlation between vividness ratings and memory performance. Subsequent studies have broadly replicated this finding of no major effect of rated vividness of imagery on memory performance, although one or two studies have found a positive effect (e.g. Hanggi, 1988), while rather more have found a small negative correlation (e.g. Dobson & Markham, 1993; Heuer, Fischman, & Reisberg, 1986; Reisberg & Leak, 1987).

The situation on the qualitative aspects of visual imagery therefore does not look particularly encouraging. Although we have some clear and highly reliable experimental phenomena, those investigating such phenomena typically deny that they have any link with conscious experience, and very clear individual differences in rated experience of imagery appear to have small, inconsistent, and somewhat puzzling links with performance.

One response to this state of affairs is to suggest that phenomenological data are inherently unreliable and to be avoided. To exclude subjective experience from the domain of empirical psychology does, however, seem unduly defeatist.

This is particularly the case in view of the contribution that has already been made to our understanding of cognition from the study of phenomena such as blindsight (Weiskrantz, 1986) that are themselves inherently phenomenological. In the area of memory, Tulving (1985) has argued that the phenomenological experience of recollection lies at the heart of the important concept of episodic memory, a concept that has derived further support from studies in which subjects were explicitly required to make phenomenological judgements as to whether a recognised item in a memory study was adjudged to be "remembered", with associated information about the conditions under which it was acquired, or simply "known", a condition under which the subject is fairly certain that the item was presented, but cannot provide any supplementary recollective data. Although such a judgement might appear to be somewhat arcane for the average subject, in fact this manipulation has proved to be readily useable with an in-creasingly wide range of subject groups, producing highly consistent data (see Gardiner & Java, 1993; Baddeley, 1997, Chapter 20 for reviews).

We were encouraged by such findings as these, together with those of Teasdale et al. (1993, 1995), to attempt to study the qualitative aspects of visual imagery using phenomenological judgements. We opted to study subjective assessments of vividness, because, as just discussed, this appears to be a phenomenon that yields large individual differences, which mysteriously appear to have little practical significance. We proposed to use the working memory model to explore this apparent paradox.

Since the inception of the model, we have tended to identify the visuo-spatial sketchpad sub-component of working memory with the manipulation of visual imagery, and more recently, the phonological loop with its auditory equivalent (Baddeley & Logie, 1992). However, despite the implicit association between the subjective experience of an image and the utilisation of the relevant slave system, at no point had we explicitly questioned our subjects about their experiences. We decided to do so in a series of experiments, most of which used the same broad design. We made the assumption that if the visuo-spatial sketchpad played an important role in the experience of a visual image, then interfering with the operation of that sub-system by means of a secondary task should interfere with the experience of the image and lead to lower ratings of image vividness. It is of course the case that virtually all secondary tasks involve placing some load on the central executive. How then could we be sure that the effects were due to the relevant slave system, and not to the demand on executive processing? We attempted to tackle this problem by studying both visual and auditory imagery simultaneously, combining each with both a visuo-spatial and an auditory verbal distractor. If our hypothesis were supported, then we would expect an interaction such that the visuo-spatial distractor should interfere more with visual imagery, while the audio-verbal one should preferentially disrupt auditory imagery. If, on the other hand, interference effects are primarily the result of executive disruption, then each task should cause a broadly equivalent degree of disruption to both visual and verbal imagery. Our experiments fell into three groups, the first being concerned with the short-term maintenance of images of recently presented meaningless material, the second with images evoked from long-term memory by verbal cues, while the third tested a specific hypothesis about the nature of the image.

We tried to make the judgement of vividness as simple as possible, requesting the subject to hold the image in mind over a five- or six-second period, and then rate its vividness on a scale ranging from 0, "no image at all", to 10, "image as vivid as if perceived directly". We anticipated that at least some subjects would complain that they had no image and could therefore not perform the task, but all subjects appeared to find the task meaningful and readily complied with our instructions.

STM-based Imagery

Our first experiment involved presenting the subject with either an array of five shapes for a five-second period, or a sequence of five tones at a mean rate of one second per tone (see Fig. 1.1). After a six-second delay, during which the subjects were encouraged to maintain the visual or auditory image, the rating scale appeared and prompted the subject to make a response. During each trial, subjects were either left unencumbered by a secondary task (the control condition), or performed a visuo-spatial or auditory verbal distractor task. The visuo-spatial task involved tapping a 3×4 array of buttons in a boustrophedon pattern, starting in the top left-hand corner, proceeding to the end of the row, moving down to the next row and so forth. This has been shown to disrupt the utilisation of the visuo-spatial sketchpad (see Logie, 1995, Chapter 4). Equivalent disruption of the phonological loop was provided by requiring the subject to count repeatedly from one to ten; such articulatory suppression is known to interfere with verbal rehearsal (Murray, 1965). In the first experiment, subjects were instructed to try to remember the pattern or sequence, and were subsequently required to recognise whether a subsequent pattern or sequence was identical or changed. Experiment 2 abandoned this requirement on the grounds that subjects might be using their memory performance as a clue to the vividness rating. Both studies gave broadly equivalent results; those from Experiment 2 are shown in Fig. 1.2. Both experiments showed a highly significant interaction, indicating that auditory imagery was indeed disrupted more by articulatory suppression than by spatial tapping, whereas for visual imagery the reverse occurred. Although this clearly supported our initial hypothesis, it could be argued that images that are based on information that must be held in working memory represent a special case, whereby the very information on which the image is based is dependent on the relevant slave system. It may be the case that imagery of meaningful material and material that is available in long-term memory will behave quite differently. Experiment 3 continued to use an immediate memory paradigm, but used meaningful material to test whether the modality-specific interference with vividness occurred even when long-term memory support was available.

Experiment 3 involved presenting subjects with either meaningful coloured pictures and scenes cut from magazines, or sentences uttered by a range of different speakers, some male and some female. In order to vary the degree of meaningfulness we introduced a further condition in which pictures were cut into four rectangles, with the rectangles rearranged in location and orientation, while the sentences were cut into four segments which were then presented in random order. If our previously observed interaction was dependent on using meaning-less material, then we would expect it to disappear in the nonfragmented cases, possibly being present in an attenuated form for the rearranged stimuli. Presentation conditions and judgement instructions were as in Experiments 1 and 2. The results are shown in Fig. 1.3. The largest effect on rated vividness resulted from the nature of the stimulus material, with images of scrambled stimuli being

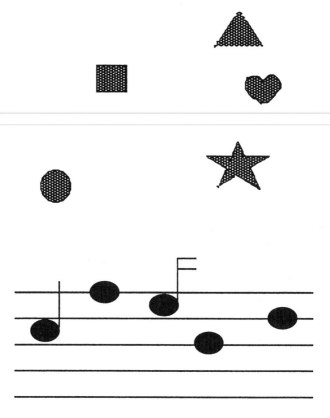

FIG. 1.1.   Examples of the visual and auditory imagery stimuli used in Experiments 1 and 2.

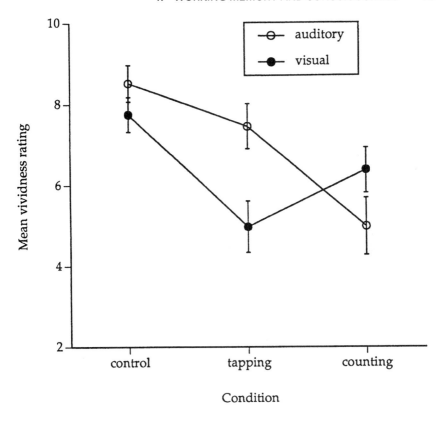

FIG. 1.2. Mean vividness of auditory and visual imagery in Experiment 2, as a function of secondary task condition (with standard error bars).

rated as less vivid. However, there was also a significant interaction between the modality of the image and the nature of the interfering task. The magnitude of this interaction was unaffected by whether or not the stimulus was scrambled.

We interpreted our results as suggesting that the dependence of an image on the relevant slave system of working memory is not limited to meaningless material. However, the large effect of scrambling the stimulus material suggested an additional and separate effect, possibly based on the contribution of long-term memory, with meaningful material being more readily maintained. We therefore decided to move on to a series of studies in which the images were based on the subject's prior experience, and hence on long-term memory. In each we included a further variable that might be expected to influence this long-term component.

LTM-based Imagery

The next two experiments involved presenting subjects with a cue written on a card which the experimenter presented to the subjects and read out loud. In

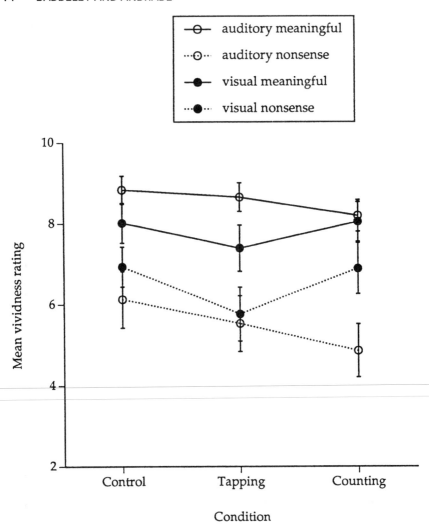

FIG. 1.3. Mean vividness of auditory and visual imagery in Experiment 3, for meaningful and nonsense (scrambled) stimuli in the three interference conditions (with standard error bars).

Experiment 4, the cues were either for relatively static or repetitive images such as *King's College Chapel* (a well-known Cambridge landmark) or *a telephone ringing*, or were comparatively dynamic such as *a cat chasing a mouse* or *two people arguing*. In Experiment 5, we used either the dynamic images from Experiment 4, or dynamic but bizarre images such as *a swan shopping* or *the sound of someone walking on tin foil*. The instructions and rating procedure were as before. For both studies, the results were clear in showing major effects of the

LTM manipulations, with dynamic images being rated as less vivid than static, and bizarre as less vivid than familiar. In addition, we once again obtained the significant interaction between modality of image and type of secondary task, suggesting an involvement of the relevant slave systems. Again the magnitude of the slave system effect appeared to be substantially less than that of the LTM variables. Before going on to discuss this, however, we need to consider one further point.

The task that we had consistently used to disrupt visual imagery was pattern tapping. Although this certainly interferes with some aspects of the sketchpad, it could be argued that it is primarily a spatial disruptor. As there is abundant evidence to suggest that the sketchpad has two components, one visual and the other spatial (Farah, 1988; Logie, 1995), it is arguable that we may have been using an inappropriate suppression task, if imagery proves to be visual rather than spatial in nature. Experiment 6 checked this by replacing our visuo-spatial tapping task with a task that has recently been shown to interfere specifically with the visual component of the sketchpad. Quinn and McConnell (1996) have demonstrated that watching a pattern of flickering dots on a VDU specifically disrupts the visual component of imagery, while having no apparent effect on executive processing. We therefore investigated the effect of this visual noise on image vividness. Subjects were asked to form visual images of the novel arrays of shapes used in Experiments 1 and 2 and of the verbally cued dynamic scenes from Experiments 4 and 5. Three conditions were compared, namely a control condition in which subjects looked at a blank VDU screen, an articulatory suppression condition in which the subject counted repeatedly from one to ten during the maintenance and rating of the image, and a visual suppression condition in which the subject looked at the flickering pattern.

Results are shown in Fig. 1.4, from which it is clear that the interaction between condition and secondary task again occurs. Interestingly, however, the effect appears to be rather more clear-cut for the LTM- than the STM-based images. It seems likely that this reflects the essentially spatial nature of the pattern array, in contrast to the much richer visual component of the LTM-based scenes. The main point to be derived from this experiment, however, is that reduced vividness of imagery can be obtained with both visual and spatial distractor tasks.

To summarise, we consistently found an interaction between the modality of the image and the nature of the secondary task, supporting our prediction that the slave systems of working memory play a role in vivid imagery. In addition, however, we found substantial, and typically more marked, effects from a range of variables that could plausibly be associated with the availability of information in LTM. These included whether the image was static or dynamic, whether familiar or bizarre, and whether whole or fragmented. One way of conceptualising this pattern of results is to suggest that one determinant of an image is the amount of

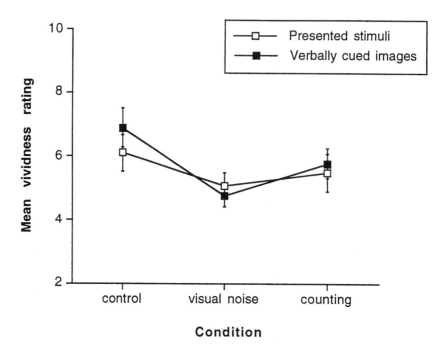

FIG. 1.4. Mean vividness of visual imagery in Experiment 6 for presented stimuli (arrays of shapes) and verbally cued dynamic images (with standard error bars).

quasi-sensory information available. In the case of the STM studies, this would be limited by the capacity of the slave systems to maintain the novel information, but in the case of LTM-based images, availability of information might reasonably be assumed to depend on long-term knowledge, based on prior experience. It is plausible that more information is needed to form a dynamic image that is "as vivid as perception" than is needed to form a vivid static image. Vividness of dynamic images is therefore limited by the rate at which information can be retrieved from LTM. In the case of bizarre images, vividness is limited by the availability of relevant information in LTM. We can create an image of a swan shopping by putting together a series of components of earlier experience of swans and shops, but much of the detail, such as how the swan picks up the items or pays for them, is likely to be either absent or based on events we have rarely if ever experienced. Similarly, a whole image or an entire sentence is likely to map much more compatibly onto our earlier experience than a randomly arranged set of fragments of the scene or phrase.

The concluding two-part experiment tested our hypothesis by manipulating the amount of information available and studying the effect on the rated vividness of imagery. One part used the arrays of shapes from the STM experiments, varying the amount of information available by presenting the array for either one or five seconds. The longer exposure should enable more information to be encoded and lead to a higher vividness rating. The other part used more naturalistic materials, namely coloured pictures of British birds, an area of knowledge in which substantial individual differences typically occur. Subjects were asked to rate their knowledge of British birds as poor, moderate, or good. Of the 24 subjects, 13 rated their knowledge as poor, 9 as moderate, and 2 as good. For the purpose of analysis, the moderate and good groups were combined to provide two sub-groups differing in knowledge. Subjects were shown a series of blank pictures, each one accompanied by the name of the bird, and a few sentences about its characteristics or habits. Each bird was then named, and subjects were invited to form an image and rate its vividness.

As predicted, longer exposure to the arrays of shapes led to a significantly higher rating of the vividness of the subsequent images, and the more knowledgeable subjects rated the vividness of their images of birds as significantly more vivid than did those who rated their knowledge as poor. Although this latter result is consistent with the prediction that a vivid image stems from relatively abundant knowledge of the sensory characteristics of the object being imaged, it could be argued that it simply reflected a response bias, with subjects who tended to rate their knowledge as high also tending to rate their imagery as vivid. This was not the case; although rated knowledge of birds correlated strongly with rated vividness of bird images ($r = .76$), it did not correlate with the rated vividness of images of the arrays of shapes ($r = -.04$).

We began with the proposal that the two slave systems of working memory play a crucial role in the experience of imagery, predicting that disruption of the sketchpad would impair the rated vividness of a visual image substantially more than it would an auditory image, whereas articulatory suppression was predicted to do the opposite. Our results consistently supported this prediction across a range of experiments involving imagery of meaningful and meaningless material cued from both STM and LTM. In addition, however, we found a number of LTM variables that have at least as great an effect on rated vividness. We suggest that a vivid image is one that comprises a rich array of quasi-sensory information. Maintenance of this information in working memory contributes coherence and continuity to the image, increasing its lifelikeness. Working memory also provides a workspace in which information from LTM may be recombined and manipulated to create images that are more vivid than our recollections of experienced events, or which are completely novel.

We do not wish to claim that images are like pictures, in which everything is simultaneously present. When we say for example that we have a vivid image of Cambridge market, we suggest that our experience is not one of looking at a picture, but of evoking specific sensory detail, for example, the flower stall at the corner, together with its typical array of flowers. This information is almost certainly not veridical, but rather represents knowledge of flowers and of that particular stall acquired over many different experiences. In short, it is part of our knowledge of the world. Such quasi-visual information is of course potentially useful, in this particular case if you want to buy a particular sort of flower at a given time of year. In an evolutionary context, such quasi-sensory semantic information could be of considerable importance in indicating for example whether a particular area of country was likely to be a good place to hide from an enemy, or whether it might be a good place to search for a particular kind of fruit.

In the case of autobiographical memory, the capacity to evoke specific sensory detail about a particular memory appears to provide an important cue in deciding whether the event was indeed experienced directly and is being "remembered", rather than representing information that is "known", but may have been acquired indirectly. In a recent diary study, for example, Conway, Collins, Gathercole, and Anderson (1996) observed that those events taken from an earlier diary that were associated with specific sensory detail were correctly categorised as accurate with a greater degree of confidence than those for which such detail was absent. In general therefore, the presence of detail tends to form a useful and valid cue. It is not, however, invariably valid, and when it accompanies an erroneous response, subjects tend to have a higher confidence in their false judgements than if the judgement was unaccompanied by such sensory detail. This effect can be particularly problematic under a condition such as that facing an eye-witness, when accurate recall of detail may be of great importance. Anything that tends to conjure up the associated sensory characteristics of an event will potentially increase the likelihood that the material that is introduced, either by suggestion or spontaneously from prior knowledge, will be endowed with a stronger feeling of veridical recollection, as a result of its associated sensory characteristics, leading to a situation in which confidence becomes dissociated from accuracy.

Whereas the tendency to import sensory detail from long-term knowledge represents a potentially dangerous problem for the eye-witness, in other situations the process may be entirely benign. Consider for example the process of reading a novel, or indeed hearing someone tell a story. An important component of the enjoyment of such activity comes from the capacity to identify with the narrator sufficiently to "experience" the event being told. A good descriptive writer will provide specific sensory cues, relying on the reader to interpret these through his or her own experience. Consider for example the following passage (Brontë, 1847, p.262):

On an October afternoon, or the beginning of November—a fresh, watery afternoon, when the turf and paths were rustling with moist, withered leaves, and the cold, blue sky was half hidden by clouds—dark grey streamers, rapidly mounting from the west, and boding abundant rain—I requested my young lady to forego her ramble because I was certain of showers.

The capacity of an author to transmit a scene or experience appears to depend very heavily on the utilisation of prior knowledge, so that a reader who has always lived in a desert or the tropics might be expected to find such a scene less vivid than someone familiar with autumn in England.

What are the implications of our simple model for interpreting individual differences in rated vividness of imagery? We suggest that the capacity to accompany a given word, phrase, or recollection with plausibly associated sensory detail is under direct attentional control. We suggest that high imagers are habitually more likely to provide such sensory default data than are those who rate their imagery as low. However, the two groups do not differ in the amount of information that they acquire, simply in their strategic use of supplementary default data. Consequently, under most circumstances, where performance is determined by the information that has been acquired, no difference between the two groups will be observed. However, under certain circumstances, when operating at the limits of performance, subjects with vivid imagery may be more inclined to import irrelevant sensory detail from semantic memory. The presence of such detail is likely to signal a higher degree of veracity than is appropriate, leading them to make more false alarm responses and hence perform somewhat more poorly, as indeed typically occurs in those studies where a difference is observed (Heuer et al., 1986; Reisberg & Leak, 1987).

CONCLUSION

We have presented a framework for the study of consciousness. It comprises first of all a set of basic theoretical assumptions, proposing that consciousness represents a complex and elegant biological solution to some practical evolutionary problems. We demonstrate that the concept of working memory can be used within this framework to investigate a range of problems including those concerned with levels of consciousness, with mind-wandering, rumination, and the control of conscious awareness, and finally with its qualitative or pheno-menological characteristics. How important are our findings? In terms of explaining consciousness, we have described some of the cognitive processes underlying everyday conscious experiences such as daydreaming and imagery, but this is clearly a long way from bridging the explanatory gap. However, if like Dennett (1991) and others, one takes the view that explaining phenomenal experience is a matter of understanding the underlying brain processes, then our research is at least heading in the right direction.

In terms of practical relevance, we feel our findings directly help to understand conditions such as depression, insomnia, and post-traumatic stress disorder. Here there seems to be a clear and indeed defining role of conscious experience, where people's subjective reports of, say, feeling miserable or tired are crucial to the clinical diagnosis. People with depression or insomnia are also likely to be aware of their ruminations, even if they are unable to control them. In the case of post-traumatic stress disorder, a frequent and distressing symptom is the experience of intrusive images of the traumatic event. Shapiro (1989) has claimed that this and other symptoms can be reduced by asking the client to visualise the traumatic event while tracking the therapist's finger, which moves rapidly to and fro. Although there have yet to be rigorous clinical trials of this potential therapy (known as Eye Movement Desensitisation and Reprocessing, or EMD-R), our imagery research suggested to us that the crucial feature of this tracking task might be its interference with visuo-spatial sketchpad function. We hypothesised that this interference would, like our spatial tapping task and Quinn and McConnell's (1996) visual noise, reduce the vividness of visual images and thereby make them temporarily less distressing. This reduction in level of distress may make it easier for the client to participate in other aspects of cognitive therapy. A series of studies (Andrade, Kavanagh, & Baddeley, 1997), in which nonclinical volunteers were asked to image distressing and neutral scenes under dual task conditions, supported our hypothesis that saccadic eye movements make visual images less vivid. The effects of spatial interference on rated emotion were somewhat smaller and less consistent than the effects on vividness, but were still in the predicted direction. These findings encourage us to believe that empirical research into conscious experience contributes to the understanding of psychological disorders and to developing treatments for them.

Although there is still clearly a huge amount of work to be done, we hope that the examples given provide support for the view that the study of consciousness provides a tractable and fruitful area of empirical cognitive psychology.

REFERENCES

Alkire, M.T., Haier, R.J., Barker, S.J., Shah, N.K., Wu, J.C., & Kao, J. (1995). Cerebral metabolism during propofol anesthesia in humans studied with positron emission tomography. *Anaesthesiology, 82*, 393–403.

Andrade, J. (1995). Learning during anaesthesia: A review. *British Journal of Psychology, 86*(4), 479–506.

Andrade, J. (1996). Investigations of hypesthesia: Using anesthetics to explore relationships between consciousness, learning, and memory. *Consciousness and Cognition, 5*, 562–580.

Andrade, J., & Jones, J.G. (1997). Awareness in anaesthesia. In G. Hall & M. Morgan (Eds.), *Short practice of anaesthesia* (pp. 753–763). London: Chapman & Hall.

Andrade, J., Kavanagh, D., & Baddeley, A. (1997). Eye-movements and visual imagery: A working memory approach to the treatment of post-traumatic stress disorder. *British Journal of Clinical Psychology, 35*, 209–223.

Andrade, J., Munglani, R., Jones, J.G., & Baddeley, A.D. (1994). Cognitive performance during anaesthesia. *Consciousness and Cognition, 3*(2), 148–165.

Angel, A. (1993). Central neuronal pathways and the process of anaesthesia. *British Journal of Anaesthesia, 71*, 148–163.

Antrobus, J.S. (1968). Information theory and stimulus-independent thought. *British Journal of Psychology, 59*, 423–430.

Baars, B.J. (1988). *A cognitive theory of consciousness*. Cambridge: Cambridge University Press.

Baddeley, A.D. (1986). *Working Memory*. Oxford: Oxford University Press.

Baddeley, A.D. (Ed.). (1993). Working memory and conscious awareness. In A.F. Collins, S.E. Gathercole, M.A. Conway, & P.E. Morris (Eds.), *Theories of memory* (pp. 11–28). Hove, UK: Lawrence Erlbaum Associates Ltd.

Baddeley, A.D. (1996). Exploring the central executive. *Quarterly Journal of Experimental Psychology*, *49A*(1), 5–28.

Baddeley, A.D. (1997). *Human memory: Theory and practice*. Hove, UK: Psychology Press.

Baddeley, A.D., Bressi, S., Della Sala, S., Logie, R., & Spinnler, H. (1991). The decline of working memory in Alzheimer's Disease: A longitudinal study. *Brain*, *114*, 2521–2542.

Baddeley, A.D., Della Sala, S., Papagno, C., & Spinnler, H. (1997). Dual task performance in dysexecutive and non-dysexecutive patients with a frontal lesion. *Neuropsychology*, *11*(2),187–194.

Baddeley, A.D., & Hitch, G. (1974). Working memory. In G.A. Bower (Ed.), *The psychology of learning and motivation* (pp.47–89). New York: Academic Press.

Baddeley, A.D., Lewis, V.J., Eldridge, M., & Thomson, N. (1984). Attention and retrieval from long-term memory. *Journal of Experimental Psychology: General*, *113*, 518–540.

Baddeley, A.D., & Logie, R.H. (1992). Auditory imagery and working memory. In D. Reisberg (Ed.), *Auditory imagery* (pp.171–197). Hillsdale, NJ: Lawrence Erlbaum Associates Inc.

Bentin, S., Collins, G. I., & Adam, N. (1978). Decision-making behaviour during inhalation of subanaesthetic concentrations of enflurane. *British Journal of Anaesthesia*, *50*, 1173–1177.

Bisiach, E. (1988). The (haunted) brain and consciousness. In A.J. Marcel & E. Bisiach (Eds.), *Consciousness in contemporary science* (pp.101–120). Oxford: Clarendon Press.

Block, N. (1995). On a confusion about a function of consciousness. *Behavioural and Brain Sciences*, *18*, 227–287.

Broadbent, D.E. (1958). *Perception and communication*. London: Pergamon Press.

Brontë, E. (1847). *Wuthering Heights* (1974 edn.). Harmondsworth, UK: Penguin Books.

Bruce, D.L., & Bach, M.J. (1975). Psychologic studies of human performance as affected by traces of enflurane and nitrous oxide. *Anaesthesiology*, *42*, 871.

Bruce, D.L., & Bach, M.J. (1976). Effects of trace anaesthetic gases on behavioural performance of volunteers. *British Journal of Anaesthesia*, *48*, 871.

Caseley-Rondi, G. (1996). Perceptual processing during general anaesthesia reconsidered within a neuropsychological framework. In B. Bonke, J. Bovill, & N. Moerman (Eds.), *Memory and awareness in anaesthesia* (pp.102–107). Assen: Van Gorcum.

Churchland, P.S. (1995). Can neurobiology teach us anything about consciousness? In H. Morowitz & J. Singer (Eds.), *SFI Studies in the science of complexity*. Reading, MA: Addison-Wesley.

Conway, M.A., Collins, A.F., Gathercole, S.E., & Anderson, S.J. (1996). Recollection of true and false autobiographical memories. *Journal of Experimental Psychology, General*, *125*, 69–95.

Crick, F., & Koch, C. (1990). Towards a neurobiological theory of consciousness. *The Neurosciences*, *2*, 263–275.

Della Sala, S., Baddeley, A.D., Papagno, C., & Spinnler, H. (1997). Dual-task paradigm: A means to examine the control exeuctive. In J. Grafman, K.J. Holyoak & F. Boller (Eds.), *Strcuture and functions of the human prefrontal cortex. Annals of the New York Academy of Sciences*, *769*, 161–171.

Dennett, D.C. (1988). Quining Qualia. In A.J. Marcel & E. Bisiach (Eds.), *Consciousness in contemporary science* (pp.42–77). Oxford: Clarendon Press.

Dennett, D.C. (1991). *Consciousness explained*. London: Penguin.

Di Vesta, F.J., Ingersoll, G., & Sunshine, P. (1971). A factor analysis of imagery tests. *Journal of Verbal Learning and Verbal Behavior*, *10*, 471–479.

Dobson, M., & Markham, R. (1993). Imagery ability and source monitoring: Implications for eye-witness memory. *British Journal of Psychology, 84*, 111–118.

Ellis, N.C., & Sinclair, S.G. (1996). Working memory in the acquisition of vocabulary and syntax: Putting language in good order. *Quarterly Journal of Experimental Psychology, 49(A)*, 234–250.

Farah, M.J. (1988). Is visual memory really visual? Overlooked evidence from neuropsychology. *Psychological Review, 95*, 307–317.

Galton, F. (1883). *Inquiries into human faculty and its development.* London: Dent.

Gardiner, J.M., & Java, R.I. (1993). Recognising and remembering. In A.F. Collins, S.E. Gathercole, M.A. Conway, & P.E. Morris (Eds.), *Theories of memory* (pp.163–188). Hove, UK: Lawrence Erlbaum Associates Ltd.

Gathercole, S.E., & Baddeley, A.D. (1993). *Working memory and language.* Hove, UK: Lawrence Erlbaum Associates Ltd.

Hanggi, D. (1988). Differential aspects of visual short- and long-term memory. *European Journal of Cognitive Psychology, 1*, 285–292.

Heuer, F., Fischman, D., & Reisberg, D. (1986). Why does vivid imagery hurt colour memory? *Canadian Journal of Psychology, 40*, 161–175.

Jelicic, M., Asbury, A.J., Millar, K., & Bonke, B. (1993). Implicit learning during enflurane anaesthesia in spontaneously breathing patients. *Anaesthesia, 48.* 766–768.

Jelicic, M., de Roode, A., Bovill, J.G., & Bonke, B. (1992). Unconscious learning during general anaesthesia. *Anaesthesia, 47*, 835–837.

Kosslyn, S.M. (1980). *Image and mind.* Cambridge, MA: Harvard University Press.

Levine, J. (1983). Materialism and qualia: The explanatory gap. *Pacific Philosophical Quarterly, 64*, 354–361.

Logie, R.H. (1995). *Visuo-spatial working memory.* Hove, UK: Lawrence Erlbaum Associates Ltd.

Marks, D.F. (1972). Individual differences in the vividness of visual imagery and their effects on function. In P.W. Sheehan (Ed.), *The function and nature of imagery.* New York: Academic Press.

Marks, D.F. (1977). Imagery and consciousness: A theoretical review from an individual differences perspective. *Journal of Mental Imagery, 1*, 275–290.

Murray, D.J. (1965). The effect of white noise upon the recall of vocalized lists. *Canadian Journal of Psychology, 19*, 333–345.

Norman, D.A., & Shallice, T. (1986). Attention to action: Willed and automatic control of behaviour. In R.J. Davidson, G.E. Schwarts, & D. Shapiro (Eds.), *Consciousness and self-regulation. Advances in research and theory* (pp.1–18). New York: Plenum Press.

Paivio, A. (1969). Mental imagery in associative learning and memory. *Psychological Review, 76*, 241–263.

Pöppel, E., & Schwender, D. (1993). Temporal mechanisms of consciousness. In J.G. Jones (Ed.), *Depth of anesthesia, International Anesthesiology Clinics, Vol 31*, Number 4, pp.27–38.

Pylyshyn, Z.W. (1973). What the mind's eye tells the mind's brain: A critique of mental imagery. *Psychological Bulletin, 80*, 1–24.

Quinn, G., & McConnell, J. (1996). Irrelevant pictures in visual working memory. *Quarterly Journal of Experimental Psychology, 49*A, 200–215.

Reisberg, D., & Leak, S. (1987). Visual imagery and memory for appearance: Does Clark Gable or George C. Scott have bushier eyebrows? *Canadian Journal of Psychology, 41*, 521–526.

Shallice, T., Fletcher, P., Frith, C.D., Grasby, P.M., Frackowiak, R.S.J., & Dolan, R.J. (1994). Brain regions associated with acquisition and retrieval of verbal episodic memory. *Nature, 368*, 633–635.

Shapiro, F. (1989). Eye movement desensitization: A new treatment for post-traumatic stress disorder. *Journal of Behavior Therapy and Experimental Psychiatry, 20*, 211–217.

Shepard, R.N., & Metzler, J. (1971). Mental rotation of three-dimensional objects. *Science, 171,* 701–703.

Singer, W. (1996). Time as coding space in neocortical processing. In M.S. Gazzaniga (Ed.), *The cognitive neurosciences* (pp. 91–104). Cambridge, MA: MIT Press.

Teasdale, J.D., Dritschel, B.H., Taylor, M.J., Proctor, L., Lloyd, C.A., Nimmo-Smith, I., & Baddeley, A.D. (1995). Stimulus-independent thought depends on central executive resources. *Memory and Cognition, 23,* 551–559.

Teasdale, J.D., Proctor, L., Lloyd, C.A., & Baddeley, A.D. (1993). Working memory and stimulus-independent thought: Effects of memory load and presentation rate. *European Journal of Cognitive Psychology, 5,* 417–433.

Tulving, E. (1985). How many memory systems are there? *American Psychologist, 40,* 385–398.

Vallar, G., & Baddeley, A.D. (1984). Phonological short-term store, phonological processing and sentence comprehension: A neuropsychological case study. *Cognitive Neuropsychology, 1,* 121–141.

Weiskrantz, L. (1986). *Blindsight: A case study and implications.* Oxford: Oxford University Press.

Williams, J.M.G., Watts, F.N., MacLeod, C., & Mathews, A. (1997). *Cognitive Psychology and emotional disorders* (2nd edn.). Chichester, UK: Wiley.

Young, A.W., & Block, N. (1996). Consciousness. In V. Bruce (Ed.), *Unsolved mysteries of the mind.* Hove, UK: Psychology Press.

2 An Associative Theory of Implicit and Explicit Memory

Gordon H. Bower
Stanford University, CA, USA

A central focus of memory research for the past 15 years has been implicit memory—its varieties of forms and their inter-correlations, its properties and functional relationships to experimental variables, and especially the relation of implicit to explicit memory. The amount of information collected around these topics has been immense, even staggering, and the research literature has grown far beyond the limits of our capacities to read it all, to catalogue and comprehend it all.

In such situations of information overload, a useful strategy for reducing cognitive strain is to examine simple theories of the psychological processes involved, and see to what extent the major generalisations within the field can be captured by a simple theory. We understand at the outset that the phenomena are probably far too complex to be fully explained by a simple theory; nonetheless, a theory that explains, say, 80% of the major generalisations can still serve a useful function as a mnemonic device, to catalogue and organise the major findings for teaching purposes, and to identify situations in which the processes operating are more complex than the mechanisms postulated in the simple theory.

Although I have personally contributed very little to the literature on implicit memory, I would like to propose such a simple theory. I will proceed by bringing out of the closet a hoary old dinosaur of a theory of implicit memory. This is one I proposed over 12 years ago in a little noticed speech I gave at an obscure conference of European Behavior Therapists meeting in Brussels (Bower, 1984). I presented the theory again with more illustrations in a recent paper in the journal *Consciousness and Cognition* (Bower, 1996) that may serve as a reference for the

25

present article. I have since discovered that my ideas about priming set forth in that 1984 paper were very similar to those of Mandler (1980) and of Graf and Mandler (1984; see also Mandler, Graf, & Kraft, 1986). They used the term "intra-unit integration" (or "organisation") to characterise what in my theory are bundles of associations amongst sensory elements comprising a word or memory unit.

THE BASIC FRAMEWORK

The framework of the theory is that which was common to cognitive psychology in the 1970s, namely, John Morton's (1969, 1979) logogen theory of word identification, Anderson and Bower's (1973) HAM associative network theory about lexical and conceptual structures, and their view of how event memories are recorded therein. To characterise the arousal of ideas within the model, I use the idea of spreading activation from Anderson's (1976) ACT model, also found in McClelland and Rumelhart's (1981) connectionist models.

The framework assumes that words have corresponding internal representations in memory as units called *logogens* or *lexical* units. Each unit serves to collect together a variety of associations, and provides a switching juncture to pass activation from one unit to another in the associative network. A word logogen would have associations to visual letter patterns which comprise its appearance, the phonemes that comprise its sound, its part of speech, its various conceptual meanings, possibly a perceptual description of the appearance of a canonical referent, and procedures for identifying the object, action, or property. In learning a word, we set up in memory a perceptual unit for it along with many different associations arising from multiple experiences with the contexts of its use.

Figure 2.1 shows some of the associations between visual letters-in-position and the lexical entry for the English word HARE, which I will use for my illustrations. Only positive associations are shown; each letter-in-position also has associations to the many other logogens which also have that letter in that position. This associative diagram could be complicated in several ways: we could augment the letter-in-position cues with more graphemic features such as bigram or spelling patterns or intermediate morpheme cues such as frequent prefixes (un-, dis-), suffixes (-ion or -ness), or syllables (see Dorfman, 1994); we could add inhibitory links between levels, so that the final letter E would rule out HARM; and we could add inhibitory links among logogens at a given level that engage in a "winner-take-all" battle to identify the external stimulus. Finally, the graphemic input probably needs to be augmented by a parallel automatic route of phonological encoding that intervenes between the visual orthography and the logogen units. Strong evidence indicates that mature readers have highly practised productions that convert graphemes into covert phonemes and these productions fire automatically to create phonological influences on reading—for

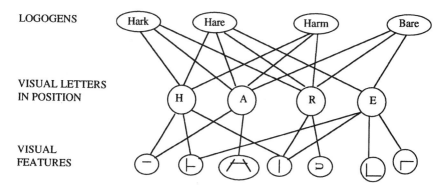

FIG. 2.1.   Schematic representation of several memory units ("logogens") in the neighbourhood of the logogen for the word HARE. Associations from visual features to letters are shown, as are associations from visual letters-in-position to logogens. Units are depicted as circles, and associations by lines between circles. (Figure 1, p.29 from "Reactivating a reactivation theory of implicit memory" by G.H. Bower, 1996, *Consciousness and Cognition, 5*, 27–72. Copyright by Academic Press Inc. Reprinted by permission.)

example, slowing decisions that pseudo-homophones like BRANE are not words or that the grapheme BARE does not designate an animal (e.g. McCann & Besner, 1987; Seidenberg, Petersen, MacDonald, & Plaut, 1996).

My point here is that the framework in Fig. 2.1 is minimal but could be greatly complicated to make a more adequate model of word identification. However, these amendments would not alter the general points made later regarding implicit and explicit memory.

In these connectionist theories, the mechanism for word retrieval is spreading activation. Presentation of a visual word causes activation of the sensory features corresponding to its letters-in-position. These feature nodes pass along their activation to the word nodes. The activation transmitted along a given input line is the product of the activation of the sensory element times the strength of its association to the logogen; the activation accumulated at a given logogen is the sum of the activations of its incoming associations. It is assumed that the model subject will perceive that lexical unit whose activation is both above an aware-ness threshold and highest among all those units activated by the stimulus. If none of the logogens is activated above threshold, then no word will be con-sciously perceived, although the model subject may be able to guess the target above chance based on partial information about letters-in-position.

THE FAST STRENGTHENING ASSUMPTION

To explain priming, this theory makes one assumption: whenever a pre-existing or old association is successfully re-aroused or reactivated by a perceptual or conceptual stimulus, that association is greatly strengthened, and this elevated strength of association will be maintained for a significant duration. The elevated strength will decay over time, fading more rapidly the more often that sensory element participates in the arousal of competing and interfering logogens. This strengthening assumption is presumed to apply to any pre-existing association—not only those from sensory features to logogens but also those between logogens and their concepts, those between two concepts, and those between pictures and other nonverbal stimuli and their names. It is also intended to apply to the establishment and strengthening of associations to memory units that encode novel perceptual, unitary configurations ("gestalts") such as pseudo-words and novel geometric patterns. For convenience, let us call this entire collection "Type-l" associations: it includes not only all old associations but also those encoding novel, integrated perceptual patterns. Later I will introduce a second type of association to characterise episodic memories.

These strengthened sensory feature-to-logogen associations are my rendition of the process of "intra-item integration" identified in Mandler's (1980) two-factor theory of recognition memory and in Graf and Mandler's (1984) theory of repetition priming. My theory differs from Mandler's earlier one in that he supposed that such intra-item integration was sufficient for recognition memory, whereas in my theory recognition memory of well-integrated units often requires something more than this.

Priming Visual Word Recognition

For priming of visual word recognition, the visual letter-to-logogen associations play a critical role. Earlier visual presentation of HARE will strengthen the four associations in Fig. 2.1 from the letters-in-position H, A, R, E to the logogen for the word HARE. Consequently, that logogen will compete more effectively in the future with similar alternatives such as HARK, HARM, or BARE. Thus, these strengthened associations from sensory features to the logogen underlie repetition priming. A second presentation of the word HARE will be read more quickly because the word node will accumulate winning activation and pass threshold for perception more rapidly than before priming. Thus, the word would be more likely to be seen in a brief tachistoscopic flash or when presented in a degraded, fuzzy fashion.

We can also expect that decisions that rely on retrieving the word node would be speeded as well. This includes lexical decisions in which subjects decide that a letter string such as HARE is an English word whereas HURE is not. The model also expects that decisions regarding nonwords will be especially slowed by priming words similar to them. Thus, presentations of HARE, HIRE, and HURT will substantially slow down later rejection of HURE as a word, because it reminds the model of so many highly available words.

Such models explain word-frequency effects in lexical decision and perceptual identification. The pre-existing associations from letters to logogens in Fig. 2.1 will reflect the accumulated joint frequency in the language of that sensory feature with that word. Thus, perceptual identification will be easier for high-frequency words and for those that follow regular grapheme–phoneme rules. Moreover, due to limits on strength, facilitation due to priming should be less for high-frequency than for low-frequency words—and that accords with the facts of the matter. In addition, Logan (1990) and Kirsner and Speelman (1993) reported a power-law speed-up in lexical decisions with practice on repeated words, although there was some later question to what extent the speed-up was associated with specific recurring stimuli as opposed to a general effect of practising the lexical decision task (Kirsner & Speelman, 1996).

Perceptual identification, reading speed, and lexical decision are indirect tasks that do not require subjects to refer to past experiences. Nor does the model need to refer to past experiences to exhibit priming. Rather, due to strengthened letter-to-word associations, the model simply "perceives" the primed word more quickly. It may only be aware of that perceptual experience and not aware that the item had been presented earlier nor that its perceptual clarity is due to that earlier presentation. Later I will discuss how awareness enters into the model's account of explicit memories.

Other Indirect Measures

Besides indirect measures such as perceptual identification, reading speed, and lexical decision, the model may also be applied to several other indirect memory tasks. An example is word-stem or word-fragment completion. Presentation of the grapheme HARE will strengthen the visual letter-in-position associations in Fig. 2.1 to that logogen, so that it will be more likely to win out in competition with other words evoked by an appropriate stem (HA_ _) or fragment cue (H_R_).

A second example is the letter insertion and letter deletion measures of priming introduced by Reingold (1995). In the insertion task, subjects are shown a test string of letters plus two extra letters, and must decide which of the two could be inserted into the test string to make a word. Thus, given the test string CRAH and the extra letters R and S, the subject should insert S to spell CRASH. Reingold found that compared to unprimed controls, subjects primed with CRASH were speeded in finding that solution. This would be expected by the theory in Fig. 2.1 because earlier presentation of CRASH would strengthen the letter-in-position associations that are also evoked by the test string CRAH, thus readily bringing CRASH to mind as a candidate target for insertion. Reingold also found that if the test string was a familiar word, such as CASH into which R or S was to be inserted, subjects took longer to solve the problem. The model expects this, because the test string strongly activates its own logogen that will then compete with and retard finding the solution.

In Reingold's deletion task, two letters in a test string are underlined (e.g. C H A S H) and subjects decide which underlined letter should be deleted to make a word. Here, priming with the solution word (CASH) speeds performance. Reingold found again that a test string that made a familiar word (C R A S H) caused delay in subjects' solution times. This would have the same competing-response explanation as given before.

Priming Interfering Words

As the last remark indicates, priming of competing responses is a natural implication of this associative account. One simply strengthens an alternative response to cues similar to those used in the indirect memory test.

An example of interference in perceptual identification was provided by Ratcliff, McKoon, and Verwoerd (1989). In one condition of their experiments, a brief flash of a target word (e.g. DIED) would be followed by a forced choice against a similar alternative (DIED or LIED). Prior presentation of the target word (or the distractor) in a study list increased choice of the target (or the distractor) on the later test trial, thus either facilitating (or interfering with) identification of the target word.

Strong interference was also reported by Reingold (1995) for the letter-deletion task after priming a competing response. For example, after being asked during study to delete the E or D in PEDARL (to get PEARL), subjects are considerably slowed when later asked to delete A or R in PEDARL (to get PEDAL). Presumably, the study episode strengthened the letter-in-position associations to PEARL, and that response was evoked by the altered test stimulus, thus interfering with finding the solution to the test string.

Interference has also been reported by Smith and Tindell (1997) who primed competitors to completing test word fragments. Fragments like A_L_ _ GY, T_NG_ _T, and C_U_TR_ when unprimed were completed an average of 59% successfully within five seconds (as ALLERGY, TANGENT, COUNTRY), and when primed were completed 75% successfully. In contrast, the fragment was completed successfully only 18% of the time after a similar word had been primed (ANALOGY, TONIGHT, CLUSTER). Because presentation of a competitor such as ANALOGY strengthens those letters-in-position to that word, the similar fragment A_L_ _GY will activate that competitor. Because it almost but not quite fits the fragment, ANALOGY serves to block and delay the search for a successful completion, thus allowing the brief test time to be exceeded.

As a further illustration, Wolters (1996) in a talk given at the Padua conference described several experiments demonstrating strong interference effects from priming competitors in a word-stem completion task.

Modality Effects

Priming also occurs in other sensory modalities. The logogen framework assumes that a spoken word eventually contacts the same logogen unit as does the visual word except that the sensory elements and input associations are acoustic and phonetic rather than orthographic. Figure 2.2 shows the relevant elements, including not only the phonemic elements directly activated by the acoustic wave form but also the parallel route by which visual words cause expert readers to automatically activate the covert sound of the word, at least to a mild degree. The phonemic features have a collection of sensory associations to the word logogens that are used in spoken word identification. For experienced language users, these will be old associations of Type 1. These associations can be strengthened by hearing the word in a study list, so that it will be identified more readily in a later hearing test given against a noisy background. This describes auditory

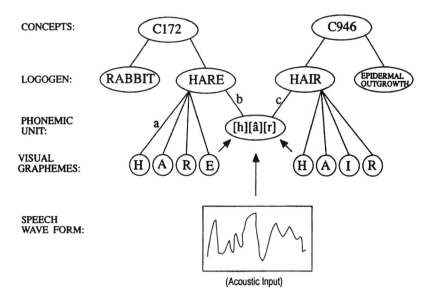

(Acoustic Input)

FIG. 2.2.   Schematic representation of the logogens for HARE and HAIR. The visual graphemes activate their logogens by the direct-route, Type-1, associations (labelled a); automatic application of pronunciation rules creates a weak phonological representation which has pre-existing Type-1 associations (labelled b and c) to the different logogens. The spoken word directly activates the phonemic representation. Type-1 associations also connect the name logogens to their concepts (No. C172 which also has the name *rabbit* and No. C946 which denotes the *hair* on one's head). (Figure 2, p.34, from "Reactivating a reactivation theory of implicit memory" by G.H. Bower, 1996, *Consciousness and Cognition*, 5, 27–72. Copyright by Academic Press Inc. Reprinted by permission.)

priming. These phonetic associations also provide a basis for some phonological priming of similar-sounding words (see later).

Residual Activation of the Logogen

Morton's (1969, 1979) logogen model assumed that once a logogen has been activated, its level of activation persists for a while before decaying to baseline. An alternative formulation is that its threshold is temporarily lowered. In any event, less sensory information will be needed for the logogen to pass its threshold and fire when the word is repeated a short time later.

This residual activation provides an explanation of several observations including the intermediate amounts of *cross-modal priming* that are typically observed. Thus, a visual word prime will leave some residue of activation on that logogen, and in addition may activate and strengthen the indirect phonological route, strengthening the association labelled b in Fig. 2.2. Consequently, the later spoken word HARE in a noisy channel would now be more likely to pass the logogen's threshold of identification.

The theory also expects that cross-modal priming due to residual activation will transfer to a modest degree from a spoken prime to a visually presented target. Cross-modal priming due to residual activation is expected to be much less than same-mode priming because the same-mode route capitalises in addition on reusing the strengthened associations from the specific sensory features to the target logogen.

Enhancing Cross-modal Transfer of Priming

Evidence indicates that cross-modal priming can be augmented by instructing subjects to image the stimulus in the alternate modality. As one example, Roediger and Blaxton (1987) enhanced auditory priming of a visual word-fragment completion task by instructing their subjects to image the printed visual appearance of the spoken words. (Such conversions may be simulated in theory by production rules that the instructions set up in an executive controller that guides the operation of working memory.) The conversion thus causes a spoken word to recapitulate a weakened version of the event of perceiving the visual word and strengthening its letter-to-logogen associations.

Augmentation of cross-modal priming from vision to audition has also been reported. Stuart and Jones (1996) asked subjects to vividly imagine the sound (pronunciation) of a visually presented word. Subjects who imagined the sound of the word later showed more accurate identification when it was spoken softly in a background of white noise. On the other hand, Stuart and Jones found, as the theory expects, that imagining the sound of the referent of a word (e.g. the ticking of a CLOCK, the lowing of a COW) did not prime identification of the sound of the word itself spoken in noise.

Semantic Priming

Residual activation due to associations can also be used to explain semantic and associative priming. Thus, presentation of the word DOCTOR will speed lexical decisions for related words such as NURSE or HOSPITAL. Furthermore, if a text has been discussing rabbits, then residual activation on that concept node will cause the person to more readily perceive the word HARE in a degraded or quick flash, or judge that it is a word. Residual activation will also explain homophone resolution. Thus, the model person would resolve the spoken ambiguous sound HARE/HAIR in terms of the HARE logogen recently activated by mention of rabbits. These expectations accord with well-established facts in this area.

Phonological Priming

Residual activation can also explain the availability of studied words on a later rhyming test. For example, after studying a list containing BUY and BLUE, subjects are more likely later to give those as the first rhymes that come to mind to the test words TRY and THREW (Mandler et al., 1986). A similar kind of phonological priming based on similar-sounding words arises with stem completion. After reading aloud a series of related words such as ARROW, NARROW, and HARROW in a study list, subjects are more likely later to complete a visual word stem SPA_ with a word that sounds like the primers, viz., SPARROW. The result can also arise with dissimilar orthographies, as when overt reading of DARE and HEIR prime later stem completion of CHA_ as CHAIR (Mandler et al., 1986). This outcome is predicted by the model because the common phonemes (e.g. "_air") mildly activate the logogens for words that share those phonemes, thus causing the logogen for CHAIR to be activated above baseline. Thence, the visual stem CHA_ is completed as CHAIR rather than CHANCE or CHAIN.

Priming by Episodic Associations

In healthy subjects (but not amnesic patients) study of novel word–word paired associates will set up a new association between those two concepts. Thus, activation of one member of the pair will spread activation to the other member in an amount and speed depending on the strength of the association. This associative spread provides the basis for priming of a learned response associated to a cue. The critical observation is to show facilitation when one of the items of the studied pair receives an indirect memory test in the presence versus the absence of the other member of its pair.

An example of associative priming was reported by Paller and Mayes (1994). After studying word pairs, their subjects were tested in a sequential perceptual identification task: two words were quickflashed one at a time in succession and subjects tried to identify the second word. They were better able to do so if the second word had been previously associated to the first word shown in the pair of test flashes.

A second example of associative priming arises with stem completion. Graf and Schacter (1985) found that subjects completed word stems with the studied response word at a higher rate when the stem was accompanied by the other member of a studied paired associate. The model's explanation for this is illustrated in Fig. 2.3 which shows the memory trace set up due to studying the pair DRYER–BLOCK. At the test, DRYER is presented beside the stem BLO_ with instructions to complete it with the first word that comes to mind. The model supposes that the cue word (DRYER) sends activation over to the logogen of the associated unit (BLOCK), there to summate with the activation coming into that BLOCK logogen from the strengthened, Type-1 associations from the sensory fragments BLO_. Thus, the model is more likely to complete the stem with the studied item when it is accompanied by the other member of its studied pair. Moreover, and as predicted, the stem-completion rate is greater the stronger is the elaborative encoding of the association from the cue to the response word.

As will be discussed later, Fig. 2.3 is incomplete in that it does not show an association of the studied pair (DRYER–BLOCK) to the experimental context in which it was presented. As explained later, such context associations can be retrieved and used to modulate (or suppress) the expression of a given

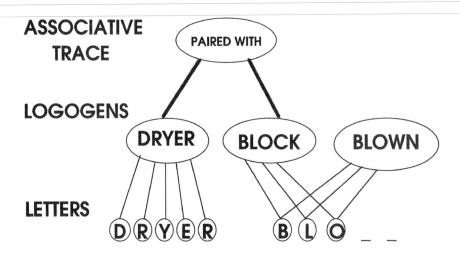

FIG. 2.3.   Diagram of associative priming in stem completion. Study of the pair DRYER–BLOCK establishes an association (trace of the pairing) in memory connecting the two. Subjects are asked to complete the stem BLO_ in the presence of the paired cue (DRYER) or an unassociated cue.

association—for example, for the subject to obey instructions to exclude the studied response word (BLOCK) as a completion to the stem cue (BLO_ _). The presumption that contextual associations can modulate the expression of other, primed associations relates to the question of whether episodic associative priming involves differing degrees of implicit versus explicit memory depending on the nature of the test procedure (e.g. whether or not fast reactions are required). We will revisit this issue later in our discussion of Jacoby's (1991) "Process Dissociation" procedure for estimating automatic versus recollective contributions to performance in various memory tasks.

Picture–Word Priming

Priming is also observed in facilitation of naming or categorising pictures of common objects like *cups* and *horses*. To deal with such data, the present framework must hypothesise some means by which visual objects are recognised. Several approaches are plausible, but for illustration I will use Biederman's (1986, 1987) geon theory which views visual objects as composed of configurations of primitive geometric elements (called "geons"). Each configured-geon description of an object would have Type-1 associations in long-term memory to a canonical object-picture file which Paivio (1978, 1986) has called an *imagen* in analogy to a logogen for words. The imagen would be associated to a concept, which would be associated to one or more names for the concept. Figure 2.4 shows the basic ideas. The lines here denote pre-existing Type-1 associations.

Picture priming follows directly from this associative diagram along with the assumption that associations are strengthened by their use. Presentation of an object-picture will strengthen the Type-1 associations of the geons-in-relations to the corresponding imagen and concept. Thus, on repetition, the picture will be seen more quickly in a tachistoscopic flash, or when unfocused or covered with visual noise, or when shown as a fragmented outline (Biederman & Cooper, 1991). The speed of naming a repeated picture will also be increased, especially if it had been named when it was presented earlier. Similarly, if categorising the object pictured (categorising a *horse* as a *animal*) strengthens Type-1 associations from the object concept to its superordinate category, that should facilitate later categorisation of the same picture.

If activation spreads from the imagen via the concept node to the word unit, then presentation of the picture will produce some modest, cross-modal priming of its name, and that should occur whether the word is presented visually or spoken in noise. This cross-modal priming can be augmented by instructing subjects to imagine what the name of the pictured object looks like, i.e. image the visual grapheme PENCIL when shown a picture of a pencil. Roediger, Weldon, Stadler, and Riegler (1992) found that such graphemic encoding enhanced priming as measured by visual word-fragment completion. Presumably, im-

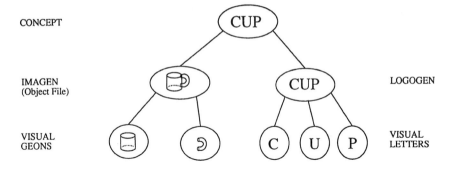

CONCEPT

IMAGEN
(Object File)

LOGOGEN

VISUAL
GEONS

VISUAL
LETTERS

FIG. 2.4.   Representation of two elementary geometric units ("geons" of a cylinder and curved tube that serves as a handle) associated to the object file ("imagen" unit) formed by their structured configuration. The imagen and the logogen for the word *cup* have converging associations to the concept node for cup. (Figure 3, p.40, from "Reactivating a reactivation theory of implicit memory" by G.H. Bower, 1996, *Consciousness and Cognition*, 5, 27–72. Copyright by Academic Press Inc. Reprinted by permission.)

agining the canonical referent to a name should also enhance later perceptual identification of a picture of that canonical referent.

Our associative analysis also implies that presentation of a pictured object will create interference in perceptually identifying a degraded version of a very similar-appearing object. Ratcliff and McKoon (1996) reported such interference in priming of similar-appearing pictures (e.g. a hot-air balloon and a lightbulb; a loaf of bread and a mailbox).

A complete theory will also need some way to represent our knowledge of common sounds that we can identify, such as the sound of footsteps, a motor car, a bird song, Beethoven's Fifth Symphony, and so on. While I have no specific proposals in this respect, the obvious approach is to represent such stimuli in the abstract as a temporal sequence of segmented sound patterns from which acoustic features are extracted which are then associated with the category of the sound. These would be Type-1 sensory associations, so they could be activated and strengthened by an earlier priming experience in an experimental study list. Consequently, on re-hearing the same sound, subjects would be able to identify it accurately faster and with greater certainty. This kind of priming in identification of naturalistic sounds has been reported by Chiu and Schacter (1995).

Learning Novel Patterns

Any learning theory must also deal with the learning and subsequent priming of novel patterns such as nonwords and novel objects. Within associative network theories, a novel pattern is learned by recording into memory a description of its units-in-position and their inter-relationships (e.g. sequence of familiar letters or syllables; or a configuration of geon units). When the pattern is presented as a unitary perceptual gestalt, it causes a memory unit (similar to a logogen or imagen) to be established and its sensory features to be linked into that unit. For example, visual presentation of the letter string TUN will set up sensory associations from the letters-in-position, T then U then N, to a logogen encoding that pattern. Repetition of this pattern will re-arouse and strengthen these associations, and these provide the basis for priming in later identification of this novel letter sequence. As a nonword becomes better learned with repetition, it will be more easily identified at shorter exposure times or under more degraded stimulation (for a more detailed model, see Salasoo, Shiffrin, & Feustal, 1985).

Conceptual Priming

Conceptual priming refers to the fact that having the subject generate or think about a conceptual associate to a stimulus facilitates that response to a second presentation of that stimulus. The experimental demonstrations almost always involve reactivation and strengthening of old, Type-1 associations. An example is shown in Fig. 2.5 for exemplars associated to the category of BIRDS. We suppose that when subjects are presented with exemplars such as OWL and EAGLE, they activate their associations to the corresponding taxonomic category, thus strengthening these associations. Such automatic activation will be stronger for instance-to-category associations that Barsalou and Ross (1986) have described as "context-independent". But even for weak associates, asking subjects during study to engage explicitly in semantic categorisation of the exemplars (a "depth of processing" manipulation) should especially strengthen these associations.

As a consequence, reading these exemplars in a study list will increase their probability of being generated later when the model is asked to retrieve instances of the category. The enhancement in production frequency should be especially large for nontypical exemplars which normally have a low baseline of generation. The enhancement arises for two reasons: first, presentation of the exemplar during study leaves some residual activation on that logogen, causing it to stand out among other exemplars; and second, activation of the exemplar-to-category association during study strengthens the very association that is utilised in the later category generation test.

Such exemplar priming is conceptual because it varies according to activation of the concepts (of BIRD and OWL). Three consequences follow: first, conceptual priming should transfer across presentation-and-test modalities of the stimuli, among auditory or visual word or referent picture modes of presentation. Second, the outcome depends on the studied stimulus evoking the same concept as is evoked during testing. For example, a picture of a baseball *bat* would not be expected to enhance the later probability of generating BAT as an exemplar to the test category of SMALL ANIMALS.

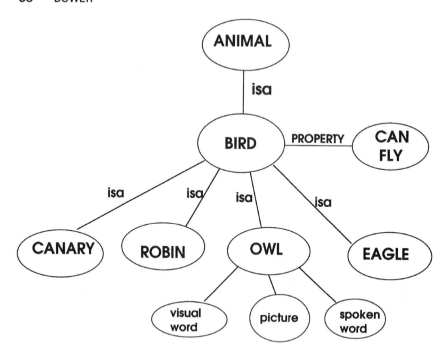

FIG. 2.5. Pre-existing associations from a category (BIRD) to exemplar concepts (*canary, robin,* etc.). Thinking of an exemplar as an instance of the BIRD category will increase the later probability of generating it as an exemplar of the category. The OWL concept can be accessed from either the visual word, the spoken word, or a picture of an owl. Superordinate and property information attached to the BIRD concept is also depicted.

A third consequence is that the conceptual priming should show encoding specificity—that is, it should be specific to the particular associations aroused during initial encoding of a word. This implication was confirmed in experiments by Vriezen, Moscovitch, and Bellos (1995). Their subjects classified the referents of nouns according to one of two criteria—either "Is it man-made?" or "Is it larger than a bread box?". At later testing, a given noun was classified according to either the same or the opposite question. Significant facilitation occurred for same-question judgements but very little for different-question judgements.

This result is expected by the model. Figure 2.6 shows the relevant associations attached to the concept, say, of a TREE. This theory expects facilitation when answering the same question because that reuses the strengthened conceptual association; on the other hand, only slight priming will arise if the questions are changed, because different facts (or associations out of TREE) must be accessed to answer the different questions. That is, retrieving the

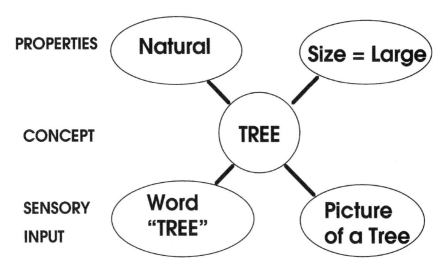

FIG. 2.6.   Conceptual associations to the concept of TREE which can be accessed and strengthened via its name or a picture of a referent. The properties shown are of the size and naturalness of trees.

fact that a TREE is natural (rather than man-made) will not strengthen the association to its size that is needed to answer whether it is larger than a bread box.

This lack of cross-question transfer may be contrasted with strong transfer between verbal versus pictorial routes of accessing the TREE concept when asking the same semantic question. Thus, if during study the subject answers that a picture of a TREE represents an object larger than a bread box, that will strengthen the same conceptual association needed to answer that same question for the word TREE whether it is presented later in either spoken or written form. Although repetition of the same question in the same form will slightly reduce the time to access the logogen, the reduction in time is quite small relative to the much larger time required to retrieve and answer the conceptual question.

EXPLICIT MEMORY

The associative network theory was long ago used to explain results from explicit memory tests such as cued recall, free recall, source memory, and recognition memory (Anderson & Bower, 1972, 1973, 1974). In our theory of human associative memory (HAM: Anderson & Bower, 1973), Anderson and I proposed that one purpose of memory is to record the history of a subject's experiences. And the most elementary autobiographic record is one asserting that I (the subject) witnessed a particular event at a specific time and place. We rendered this as the recording into memory of a bundle of structured associations describing a Fact observed in a given temporal-spatial Context, as in the prototypical assertion "Last night in the park a hippy kissed a debutante".

The way the theory applies to recognition memory, then, differs slightly depending on whether the experimenter's to-be-remembered "items" are already familiar units such as single words or pictures of common objects, or whether they are novel combinations of several familiar units, such as unrelated pairs of words or letters, novel names like Simon Wiesenthal, or novel assertions such as "A hippy kissed a debutante". The model encodes a novel combination by setting up an associative structure that describes it, such as labelled links to the first and second part of a name, or to the three letters of a novel trigram, or to the agent-action-object concepts comprising an assertion. That associative cluster is also linked into the context in which this pattern was presented, such as that I read the name Simon Wiesenthal in one of Larry Jacoby's papers.

Later, when asked to intentionally recognise a specific constellation or pattern of elements, such as a test proposition, we presumed that the model-subject searches for a match of the test probe to a structure in memory having just those elements or concepts in just those relationships. So, the model in one sense can "recognise" that the name Simon Wiesenthal is "familiar"; moreover, if the association to context can be retrieved, the model can "recognise" in addition that it was Larry Jacoby who introduced me to that name. Experimental conditions that create the former association while blocking retrieval of the latter contextual one (e.g. divided attention during testing) will lead to many "false fame" judgements of the sort observed by Jacoby and Kelley (1991).

The theoretical analysis is considerably simplified for the standard item recognition-memory experiments in which subjects are presented with single familiar words or object pictures, and are later asked to indicate whether each of a series of test items had been presented in the study list (are "Old") or not (are "New" lures). The question for the subject in this case is not whether the test item is "familiar" in the standard meaning of that term, as all items are so; rather, the question is whether it had been presented in the study list. I will be dealing with this simple case for the remainder of this paper.

The basic idea is shown in Fig. 2.7a, namely, presentation of a familiar or well-integrated item in a given context sets up an association between the item and the experimental context. I call these Type-2 associations because they are encoding a new association between two arbitrary autobiographic events—one's being in a particular place and time, and witnessing some stimulus event there along with one's reaction to it. The strength of this episodic association will vary with the usual learning parameters, including semantic elaboration.

A later "recognition memory" test presents the studied items along with some new distractors and asks subjects to judge whether or not each appeared in the earlier study context. The model simulates this process by accessing the strength of association between the test item's concept and the earlier experiential context.

(a)

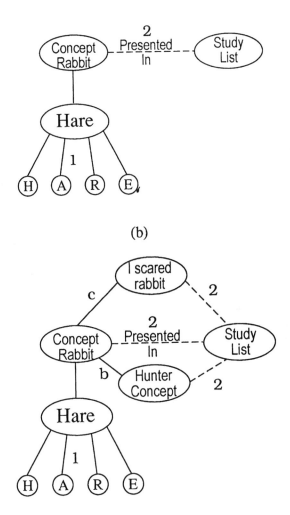

(b)

FIG. 2.7. (a) Schematic representation of the associations from the letters-in-position to the logogen HARE and its concept, along with the new association (labelled 2) encoding the proposition that the word/concept had been presented in a given study context. (b) Elaborated associations relating the presented word/concept HARE to other thoughts occurring during its study. New associations are indicated by dashed lines, and refreshed pre-existing associations by solid lines. (Figure 4, p.44, from "Reactivating a reactivation theory of implicit memory" by G.H. Bower, 1996, *Consciousness and Cognition, 5*, 27–72. Copyright by Academic Press Inc. Reprinted by permission.)

If the strength of this association is sufficiently large, then a positive recognition response is given. With minimal assumptions, this line of theorising leads to the standard "signal detection" theory of recognition memory.

The connection of the studied word to the study-list context may be strengthened through semantic elaboration and inter-item associations. Thus, on studying HARE in the list, the subject might relate it to the word HUNTER which occurred earlier in the list, and it may also trigger a specific memory of a time he scared a rabbit while on a hike (see Fig 2.7b). These elaborations provide redundant routes for connecting the concept to the study context, so that they provide back-up support when the direct association is very weak. These redundant connections help to explain why explicit memory improves with semantic processing of items during study (see Anderson & Reder, 1979).

Explicit recognition-memory tests point backwards in time, asking subjects to retrieve a memory of a past event. I use the concept of "context" to refer inclusively to a variety of external stimuli as well as subjective experiences accompanying earlier presentation of the item. A critical element of the context, of course, is the experiencing person—the self or ego—the internal sense or feel of oneself as a witness to an event, albeit in this case a trivial event (i.e. seeing HARE in a study list). These contextual associations provide the basis for autobiographic memories, for the subjective sense of "being there then". They provide the substrate for the "autonoetic consciousness" described by Tulving (1985a). They are the means by which people's current mental state can be put into informational contact with their prior mental states, providing them with a sense of personal continuity and coherence.

The Independence Assumption

A major assumption of the theory is that on presentation of a word in a study list, the amount of strengthening of the Type-2, concept-to-context association (labelled 2 in Fig. 2.7a) is a random variable that is statistically independent of the amount of strengthening of the sensory letter-to-word associations (those of Type 1, labelled 1 in Fig. 2.7a) caused by that presentation. That is, implicit learning reflected in sensory priming of the item is assumed to be independent of the learning of the Type-2 context associations or inter-item associations that underlie explicit memory tests. This assumption is controversial, but it is motivated by the research showing independence between the subjects' explicit recognition memory for studied words and their priming in perceptual identification (e.g. Jacoby & Dallas, 1981) or in fragment completion (Tulving, Schacter, & Stark, 1982).

An important consequence of this independence assumption is that the theory is not forced to predict that experimental variables that influence indirect measures of memory will necessarily influence direct measures in the same manner. Rather, we know that some variables that primarily involve "data-driven", perceptual processes will influence the Type-1, sensory associations but not the Type-2 contextual associations. On the other hand, other variables such as semantic elaboration, generation, and mnemonic strategies will enhance the Type-2 contextual associations, but not the Type-1, sensory associations.

It is not uncommon for different procedures to affect the two types of associations in different directions. As one example, words that are read during study are identified more easily later when quickflashed, whereas words that are generated to an associated cue during study are remembered more on a recognition memory test (Jacoby & Dallas, 1981). Such interactions are called "dissociations" and are often taken as evidence for different memory systems. The present theory sees them instead as revealing the relative contributions of the two types of associations to the different types of memory tests.

It would be a mistake, however, to strictly align Type 1 and 2 associations with exclusive control of performance on indirect and direct tests, respectively. As a counter-example, consider the fact that reading a category exemplar will increase its perceptual identification more but its category generation less than will generating it to a strong category cue during study (BIRD–E_). This is because actually generating the exemplar during study causes more strengthening of the category-to-exemplar association (used again in the later generation task) than does merely reading the word (see Wagner, Gabrieli, & Verfaellie, 1997). So, that is an example in which a conceptual orienting task influences performance on a memory task often classified as "indirect".

Opposition Procedures

Jacoby (1991) and Mandler (1980; also Atkinson & Juola, 1974) have argued that subjects' judgements in recognition memory tests reflect both an explicit "recollective" component and an implicit "familiarity" or "fluency" component. To separate these two factors, Jacoby proposed "opposition" procedures which instruct subjects to perform under one of two different decision criteria. The "Inclusion" criterion instructs subjects to perform some task in such a manner that the hypothetical "recollection and familiarity" processes will summate in facilitating performance. The "Exclusion" criterion asks subjects to perform in such a manner that the two alleged processes are placed into opposition. The manner in which this is done, and the theoretical analysis, varies somewhat with the task.

Let us first consider the task of word-fragment completion. After study of a list of words, subjects are shown word fragments and asked to give either the first completion that comes to mind ("Inclusion") or to give only completions that exclude any word that appeared on the study list ("Exclusion"). Notice that the Exclusion test places the alleged automatic or familiarity component of memory into opposition to the recollective component. Notice also that in order to mimic the task performance induced by such instructions, a complete cognitive theory needs to postulate executive control routines that operate over and make use of declarative memories. In Anderson's (1983) ACT theory, these control routines are represented as sets of "if–then" rules or productions that (a) encode the instructed goals and action plans, and (b) are loaded into working memory to control the cognitive machinery. For example, Exclusion instruction would be encoded by productions that set as a condition for expressing an associated response (to a cue) that the response must be associated with one designated context (source) but not with the forbidden source.

The present theory provides an account of fragment-completion produced under these Inclusion and Exclusion instructions (see Fig. 2.8). Recall that visual presentation of a word in the study list will both increase the Type-1 sensory associations to its logogen, and possibly (and independently) establish a Type-2 association to the context. So, when given the word fragment along with Inclusion instructions, the model may access the studied logogen either directly from the sensory associations or perhaps by retrieving it from the list context, and confirming that it fits the fragment. (Indeed, Inclusion subjects are often encouraged to use this recollection strategy; even if not so encouraged, they soon discover its utility during the test series.) If A denotes the probability of accessing the target word from the fragment's sensory features, and R denotes the probability of retrieving it from the list cue, then the likelihood that the subject produces the primed word on an Inclusion test will be $I = A + (1–A) R = R + (1–R) A$.

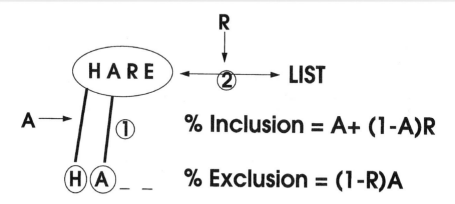

FIG. 2.8. A portion of the associative structure (from Fig. 2.7a) needed to characterise the opposition tests in fragment completion of HA__. With probability A the sensory ("automatic" Type-1) associations from the fragments retrieve the logogen, and with probability R the logogen can be retrieved ("Recollected" by Type-2 associations) from the study-list cue, and then fit onto the fragment.

Turning to the Exclusion task, subjects will give the primed item as a completion only if its logogen is triggered by its strengthened sensory associations but no contextual association is retrieved and used to exclude this completion. The joint likelihood of these events is E = (1–R) A. From these two equations, one can estimate R = I–E and A = E/1–R.

These two equations are those of Jacoby (1991) who has shown their applicability over a range of tasks. Of special importance is his finding that experimental variables that should influence the formation or use of Type-2 associations (such as semantic elaboration, divided attention, ageing) primarily influence estimates of R, the recollective component. In contrast, he finds that variables that should affect the formation or use of Type-1 sensory associations (e.g. modality shifts) are primarily reflected in estimates of the familiarity component, A, rather than the recollective part. Thus, in certain cases the present theory maps neatly onto Jacoby's equations for the opposition procedure. For other cases, the analyses diverge, as we shall show shortly.

Context Associations as Modulators

Our analysis of the Exclusion task shows how retrieval of contextual associates can be used by the subject to suppress or exclude another association. However, such suppression will succeed only if sufficient time is allowed during the test for the subject to bring the contextual associate to mind before the to-be-suppressed associate intrudes and is expressed. Let us consider two cases from the literature, one in which subjects are pressured to respond quickly, the other without time pressure.

Experiments by Reingold and Goshen-Gottstein (1996) may be used to illustrate the situation without time pressure to respond. They examined episodic associative priming using stem completion of the response word in the presence (vs. absence) of the stimulus word following paired associate learning, rather like the DRYER–BLO(CK) materials illustrated earlier in Fig. 2.3. They found that when subjects were instructed to exclude any response word from the studied list as a completion, associative priming was greatly reduced. The present theory explains such findings by assuming that an association to the study context was set up for each pair (say, linked to the "paired with" top node in Fig. 2.3). Under slow, self-paced testing conditions, retrieval of this context tag from either the cue-word or the stem will suffice to enable the learner to exclude the studied completion.

The findings in this case (for the slow, stem-completion task) may be contrasted to those in tasks that emphasise processing speed such as reading speed and lexical decisions for paired words. In these cases, subjects show consistent pair-specific facilitation (compared to scrambled pairs) for both reading speed (Poldrack & Cohen, in press) and for lexical decision (Goshen-Gottstein & Moscovitch, 1995). Theoretically, these performances require no references to past contexts to modulate performance; rather, the subjects' explicit goal is speeded processing. Therefore, the small boost in activation of the response word created by the presented stimulus term (of the prior episodic association) helps to achieve that speed goal.

Experiments by Hay and Jacoby (1996) that were reported at the conference by Jacoby (this volume) illustrate results due to speeded time pressure. In the "incongruent" condition of their experiment, a weakly established associate from a desired list context was pitted against a strongly established associate from a to-be-excluded list context. For example, the association KNEE–BONE might receive three times as many study trials as the association KNEE–BEND in an initial list, making the former much stronger. In their incongruent condition, the weaker pair would then be presented briefly in a second list context, followed by a speeded test with the common cue term (KNEE–B_N_) and instructions to produce only the to-be-remembered response from the second list and exclude that from the first list. Subjects were tested with a "response deadline" procedure, requiring them to respond immediately to the stimulus word on hearing a tone, which arrived either one or three seconds after the visual stimulus was presented. Hay and Jacoby found that subjects intruded the strong associate more often the shorter the deadline and the greater was its initially established strength relative to that of the weaker associate.

This outcome is consistent with the present theory which supposes that subjects need time to retrieve the weak second-list context tag that is required to suppress the stronger response to the stimulus KNEE-B_N_. Thus, when a fast response is demanded, the strong associate that fits the situation may be "blurted out" before the weak associate (attached to the second study context) can be retrieved to inhibit the strong associate. In this manner, the theory may explain cases of strong habits overriding more considered, "socially acceptable" responses.

The Diagnostic Context Model

Although the present theory implies Jacoby's equations for the stem completion task, it diverges from his analysis of "recognition" in two-list tasks. Let us consider the difference in more detail. In the typical experiment, subjects study two distinguishable lists of items, say, one presented visually and the other auditorily; the items may be temporally blocked by their two types or may be mixed together during presentation. Subjects then have a "recognition" test with Old and New items. That test occurs under either Inclusion instructions, to say "Yes" to items from either list, or Exclusion instructions, to say "Yes" only to items from one of the lists, and "No" otherwise. Jacoby suggests that false acceptance of the to-be-excluded old items indexes the automatic or familiarity component of recognition.

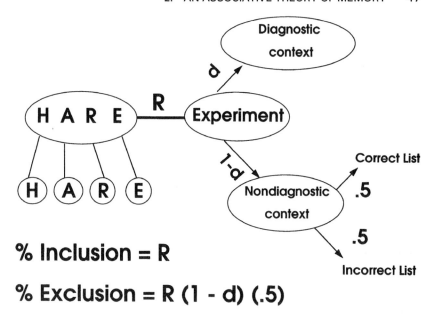

% Inclusion = R

% Exclusion = R (1 - d) (.5)

FIG. 2.9.   The model elaborated for learning of diagnostic contexts. With probability R the presented item becomes associated to the general experimental context, and with further probability d that context proves to be diagnostic of the item's specific list-membership. (Adapted by permission from "Measuring the bases of recognition memory: An investigation of the process dissociation framework" by N.W. Mulligan & E. Hirshman, 1997, *Journal of Experimental Psychology Learning, Memory, and Cognition, 23*, 280–304. Copyright by the American Psychological Association.)

I believe that this task is better viewed as involving source discrimination (see Fig. 2.9). As an item is studied, subjects form an association to the experimental context, let us say with probability R. Moreover, for given list conditions, that contextual information may be diagnostic of the item's exact list, let us say with probability d. Whether a given contextual association is diagnostic depends on the list conditions. For example, associating a word with the female voice of its speaker would be diagnostic if that speaker were unique to a given list, but would not be diagnostic if she presented both lists. As a second example, thinking of a semantic associate to a presented word could be diagnostic if the two list contexts differed in type of orienting task, but not if both asked for semantic processing.

When asked to judge whether items had been presented in the target list, Inclusion subjects will do so if the item has an association to any aspect of the general experimental context, which happens with probability R. On the other hand, Exclusion subjects will make an error of commission if the item is associated to the general context but not to a diagnostic feature of it, so they guess the wrong list. The probability of these joint events (shown in the lower branch of Fig. 2.9) is R (1–d) (.5). These are the equations of the "Diagnostic Context" model for such two-list discrimination tasks as proposed by Mulligan and Hirshman (1997). An important implication of the model is that Exclusion subjects will make more errors of commission the greater is R, their nondiagnostic memory for items in the to-be-excluded list, and more errors the more similar are the two sources to be discriminated. R can be increased by requiring semantic rather than phonetic processing of the individual words in the to-be-excluded list. Also, 1–d can be increased by making the two sources (lists) more similar or the two orienting tasks more similar, which should cause more errors of commission by Exclusion subjects. On the other hand, this increased interlist similarity should not affect R, which controls the Old/New recognition rate of Inclusion subjects.

Mulligan and Hirshman (1997) found both these effects. The problems these commission errors create for Jacoby's analysis of the two-list task are clear. His "process dissociation" equation for Exclusion errors is (1–R)A. Yet, Mulligan and Hirshman found that semantic encoding, which Jacoby usually conceives as a factor increasing recollection (R), increased rather than decreased Exclusion errors. They also found that interlist similarity (reflected in 1–d) increased Exclusion errors, although one is hard-pressed to see how that variable would increase an item's perceptual fluency (Jacoby's A factor). Even if we were to grant that interlist similarity somehow increased perceptual fluency (A), we could not explain why it did not elevate the Old recognition rate for Inclusion subjects, as that is supposed to reflect perceptual fluency.

The Diagnostic Context model can also be used to explain some results that Jacoby presented at the conference (Jacoby & Hay, this volume). In that experiment, subjects studied a given word one, two, or three times throughout a first list, then were presented with a second study list. Subjects were then instructed to recognise (say "Yes") only to items from the second list (and exclude those from the first list). Half the subjects were tested with a very short deadline interval (750 milliseconds) and half with an appreciably longer interval (to respond between 1250 and 2000 milliseconds). The results showed that with the fast deadline, subjects were more likely to make an error of commission (say "Yes" to a list-1 item) the more often it had been studied in list 1. In theory this arises because the deadline provided insufficient time to retrieve the distinctive ("list 1 or 2") context tag required to exclude the increasingly stronger, faster first-list response. In contrast, with the slower deadline, subjects showed the reverse trend, being better able to exclude the first-list response the more often they had studied it. This could arise in theory because more study trials provide more opportunities for subjects to associate a distinctive list-1 context tag to those response terms, and the longer deadline provides subjects sufficient time to retrieve this distinctive context, enabling them to exclude the first-list response to the test pattern. Thus, depending on the time pressure to respond to the test stimulus, the theory expects multiple study trials of a to-be-excluded item to either increase or decrease its intrusion in the exclusion procedure.

I conclude along with Mulligan and Hirshman (1997) that their Diagnostic Context model is more appropriate than Jacoby's "process dissociation" analysis of this two-list task. The diagnostic-context formulation is also consistent with other data that question the familiarity view of recognition memory, such as the way multiple tests of the same distractor slow down later recognition that it is not an Old target item (see e.g. Atkinson & Juola, 1974).

Remember and Know Judgements in Recognition

The theory in Figs. 2.8 and 2.9 asserts that recognition memory judgements arise from association between the concept corresponding to the test item and aspects of the context. The associated context may be sufficiently discriminating to enable the subject to remember when and where the item was presented, by what means, and how he or she reacted to it. In other cases, the context retrieved by the test stimulus may be far more diffuse and vague, simply suggesting that the item seems "familiar" in the experiment. We may think of this process in terms of the test item retrieving from memory more or less evidence for the hypothesis that the item had been presented in the experiment. Anderson and Bower (1972) showed how to effect this translation from an item's number of contextual associations to a more or less continuous variation in amount of evidence for its recognition. This continuous output from memory provides the basis for applying statistical decision theory to recognition memory. Test items that retrieve appreciable evidence of having been presented on the target list will be classified as Old, whereas other test items that retrieve less than a criterion amount of evidence for list membership will be classified as New.

Tulving (1985a) and Gardiner and Java (1993) have proposed a qualitative distinction between two kinds of recognition judgements: "Remember" judgements, which are accompanied by recollection of some specific details of the context, and "Know" judgements, which correspond to subjects' vaguer feelings of familiarity about a test stimulus without retrieval of more specific information about the encoding episode. Gardiner and Java have argued that these two types of recognition judgements exhibit different functional relationships to experimental variables. For example, intentional learning and various kinds of elaborative encoding increase "Remember" judgements but not "Know" judgements (Gardiner & Parkin, 1990).

By adopting a proposal from Hirshman and Masters (1997) and Donaldson (1996), the present approach can perhaps accommodate the findings of Gardiner and his associates. Let us begin by supposing that when the contextual evidence retrieved is clear and specific—that is, when the amount of evidence exceeds a high criterion—the subjects will have the subjective experience that leads to a

Remember 2 > Remember 1, Know 2 = Know 1

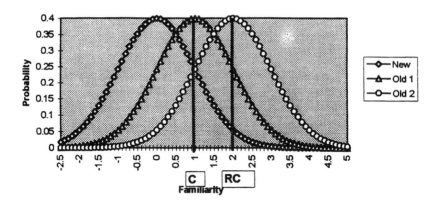

Remember 2 > Remember 1, Know 1 > Know 2

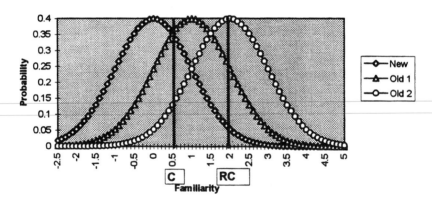

FIG. 2.10. A model for the Know–Remember paradigm. The Old 2 distribution of Familiarity (amount of evidence) has a higher average strength than the Old 1 distribution, and both exceed that of the nonpresented New ("distractor") items. The lower criterion (C) is used for Old/New recognition judgements, and the upper criterion (RC) for Recollection judgements. Items with strengths between the lower and upper criteria are judged as "Know" items. Top panel: Remember 2 exceed Remember 1 judgements, whereas Know 2 equal Know 1 judgements. Bottom panel: Remember 2 exceed Remember 1 judgements, whereas Know 1 exceed Know 2 judgements. (From "Modeling the conscious correlates of recognition memory: Reflections on the Remember–Know paradigm" by E. Hirshman & S. Master, 1997, *Memory and Cognition, 25,* 345–351. Copyright by the Psychonomic Society.)

"Remember" judgement. When the evidence is less, is vague and diffuse, the subjective experience will be more like a feeling of familiarity, leading subjects to render a "Know" judgement. We may think of such cases as exceeding a lower criterion for saying "Old," but not exceeding an upper criterion sufficient for making a "Remember" judgement (see Fig. 2.10).

One implication of this analysis is that estimates of Old–New memory discrimination (such as d') based on the upper ("Remember") criterion should be the same as those based on the lower ("Know" plus "Remember") criterion. This prediction, first noted by Donaldson (1996), was tested by his reviewing reported results from 80 conditions of 28 different experiments in the literature which permitted these estimates. Donaldson found that the Old–New discriminability estimates (d's) were approximately the same whether based on the Remember judgements alone or the sum of the Remember and Know judgements. That outcome provides strong support for the criterion-based interpretation of Remember versus Know recognition judgements.

The theory expects that increases in degree of learning will lead to higher levels of evidence ("familiarity" in Fig. 2.10) for an item's list membership. Example distributions of familiarity for New ("distractor") items and for weak ("Old1") and strong ("Old2") learning conditions are shown in Fig. 2.10, from a paper by Hirshman and Masters (1997). The strong versus weak memory distributions might correspond to semantic-versus-phonetic processing during encoding, generate-versus-read study conditions, intentional-versus-incidental learning, divided-versus-undivided attention during encoding, more-versus-less rehearsals, and more-versus-less retention (for a review, see Gardiner & Java, 1991).

Curiously, in each of these conditions, the proportion of Know judgements remained approximately constant. Such an outcome is consistent with the distributions shown in the top half of Fig. 2.10: Old2 items exceed the upper criterion (RC) more often than Old1 items, but the proportion of the two Old distributions falling within the Know region (between the upper and lower criteria) remains approximately constant. Clearly, the theory does not require unusual criteria in order to accommodate such results.

This theory can accommodate a number of other findings. The lower panel of Fig. 2.10 illustrates the case where better learning leads to more Remember but fewer Know judgements than does a poorer learning condition. Results of this kind have been frequently reported. For example, Rajaram (1993, Experiment 1) found that study items processed semantically by subjects later yielded more Remember recognition judgements but fewer Know judgements than were given to items processed phonetically. A similar pattern of more Remember but fewer Know recognition judgements was found in a second experiment by Rajaram (1993) when comparing recognition by subjects who studied pictures versus those who studied words at encoding. A third example (reported by Gardiner & Java, 1990) is that study of words produced more Remember than Know judgements, whereas study of nonwords produced more Know than Remember judgements. Such results are consonant with the distributions in the lower panel of Fig. 2.10 in which semantic compared to phonetic processing (or picture vs. word encoding, or words vs. nonwords) produces stronger contextual associations (such as Old2 compared to Old1 distributions in Fig. 2.10), and the criterion for Old recognition is lowered slightly.

An advantage of the criterion-based theory is that by altering the setting of the criteria, the model has a way to explain the influence of nonmemory or decision factors on recognition memory judgements. For example, Strack and Förster (1995) showed that informing subjects in advance that a higher percentage of the test items were Old caused them to lower their criterion for Old recognition, increasing both their false alarm rate and the proportion of Know judgements without affecting the proportion of Remember judgements. There was also a decrease in the average confidence (of being Old) assigned to the Know judgements. Such results would be expected by setting the lower criterion (C in Fig. 2.10) at a lower level the higher the proportion of Old to New items in the test series. This is also a more optimal decision criterion given knowledge of the composition of the test list. Presumably, similar criterion shifts could be induced by differential monetary pay-offs and penalties for Remember, Know, and New judgements given to Old versus New test items.

The serious disadvantage of the two-threshold model is its flexibility; it often has as many parameters as there are degrees of freedom in the scant data to be fit, so it is difficult to reject the model. I realise too that Gardiner (1988) and his colleagues have mounted a spirited defence of the utility of the Remember–Know distinction, arguing that it captures more than just high versus low confidence in memory judgements. Nonetheless, the ease with which Donaldson (1996) and Hirshman and Masters (1997) have explained a range of results with the two-threshold model suggests that more discriminating tests of the alternative hypotheses may be needed in investigations of Remember–Know judgements.

AN HYPOTHESIS REGARDING GLOBAL AMNESIA

Much of the interest in indirect versus direct memory tests arises from the fact that brain-injured patients with global amnesia are greatly impaired on direct memory tests but not much impaired on indirect tests. Global amnesia patients suffer from damage to several different areas of the brain, either diencephalic mid-brain structures or bilateral medial-temporal (hippocampal) structures. Global amnesia is typically diagnosed from the person's impairment on explicit memory tasks—a lowered ability to recall or recognise recently presented events and information. Yet patients may be only moderately impaired, if at all, on indirect memory tasks, in semantic-memory judgements, and in retrieving long-term memories of autobiographic events from before their brain injury. A controversy in this literature concerns the extent of amnesics' impairment in recognition-memory tests (e.g. Hirst et al., 1986), but the consensus view is that it is significant.

The hypothesis suggested by this reactivation theory is a very old one, proposed earlier by Rozin (1976) and Graf, Squire, and Mandler (1984), among others. It proposes that global amnesia results from a reduction in the person's ability to establish and consolidate into long-term memory novel, new associations of Type-2. These include associations between perceptually distinct items (e.g. word–word paired associates) and between an item and the context of its presentation. Although the brain injury of amnesics has weakened their ability to consolidate Type-2 associations, it has left intact the amnesics' ability to reactivate, retrieve, and momentarily strengthen old Type-1 associations. That is the basis in this theory for amnesics being able to show relatively intact semantic memory, perceptual priming, stem-completion priming, and conceptual priming (e.g. category exemplar generation). Although amnesics will show good priming in these cases, their lesser ability to form novel contextual associations means that they will often be unable consciously to remember having witnessed the priming episode itself. The hypothesis also explains the fact that amnesics are relatively unimpaired in retrieval of autobiographic episodes stored in long-term memory from before their brain injury.

One consequence of amnesics' deficit in contextual learning is their inability to utilise updating information from memory in order to control current responding. Such updating and editing problems arise whenever subjects must learn to replace an old learned response with a second, new response demanded by the same situation. The classic illustration of such problems is the A–B, A–C interference paradigm of paired-associate learning in which subjects must learn to give a new response, C, to an old stimulus, A. Indeed, one of the earlier observations of the amnesic syndrome was that patients were unusually susceptible to response competition (causing negative transfer and interference) in the A–B, A–C paradigm. In classic experiments by Warrington and Weiskrantz (1974, 1978), amnesics studied two related lists of words, where recall of each word was cued by its first three letters, as in STA(MP) and TAB(LE). Once a given stem-to-word association had been primed, however, amnesics then suffered inordinate interference in trying to learn to give a different response to those same stem cues, as in completing STA_ as STA(ND) and TAB_ as TAB(BY). The first-learned, A–B association continued to be intruded to compete with the new, to-be-remembered, A–C association. Rather similar results for amnesics were reported for priming of related word–word associations, such as STAMP–MAIL, then STAMP–LETTER (Mayes, Pickering, & Fairbairn, 1987; Winocur & Weiskrantz, 1976).

Exactly such results are expected by the hypothesis that amnesics can prime old associations but have difficulty consolidating new contextual associations. So, although they can prime and express pre-existing stem-to-word associations STA(MP) and word–word associations (STAMP–MAIL), they are unable to utilise contextual information (e.g. earlier versus later list) to modulate, control, and suppress the expression of the different primed associations.

The theory predicts that amnesics will be impaired in learning novel pairings of distinct materials such as word–word paired associates; consequently, amnesics will show impaired associative priming. Thus, having studied word pairs such as BELL–CRADLE, amnesics should show lesser pair-specific facilitation in completing the stem when given the intact test compound BELL–CRA_ _ _ than when given a test with a different left-hand word (e.g. CALL–CRA_). Shimamura and Squire (1989) found this result, as have others.

Some Limitations on the Amnesia Hypothesis

In contrast to the theory's expectations, however, the outcome in such associative priming experiments appears to depend on the exact manner in which the configuration of sensory elements is presented and the degree to which the test for priming reinstates that sensory configuration. Apparently, if the words are presented as a unified perceptual gestalt and the test involves either perceptual identification (Gabrieli, Keane, Zarella, & Poldrack, 1997), reading speed, or lexical decision (Goshen-Gottstein & Moscovitch, 1995) for the pair of words presented in the same configuration as before, then almost normal pair-specific facilitation is observed in amnesic patients. In his review of this literature, Squire (1992) reported that amnesics learn a strong binding of a word to the colour in which it is printed; after practice reading a word printed in a given colour, amnesics were significantly slowed in reading that word when its colour was changed. Similarly, Squire (1992) reported that anmesics show a nearly normal "false fame" effect, judging that a novel name (such as Simon Wiesenthal) they had studied earlier applied to a famous person. But in order to show such effects, amnesics must have stored and accessed the novel bindings of word-to-colour in the former case, or first-to-last name in the latter case; and that successful binding violates the hypothesis that novel pairings cannot be learned by amnesics. The false fame effect suggests, nonetheless, that amnesics cannot establish and use contextual associations to control whatever novel pairings they do learn. Consistent with this result, amnesics cannot inhibit heavily primed words from intruding into their performance in recognition Exclusion tests (Verfaellie & Treadwell, 1993).

Similarly, amnesics can learn and show repetition priming in perceptual identification for, novel geometric objects (Schacter, Cooper, Theran, & Rubens, 1991) and for strings of three to five consonants (Keane, Gabrieli, Noland, & McNealy, 1995). The dependence of such priming on the specificity of reinstating the exact configural pattern during testing as during encoding suggests that normals and amnesics are storing unitary but novel perceptual gestalts in memory. The result suggests that the primary sensory areas involved in such learning (e.g. occipital lobe, striate and prestriate cortex) may store unitary sensory patterns independent of facilitatory input from those brain areas (e.g. medial temporal area) that are usually damaged in global amnesia patients.

Relation to Memory Systems Theories

It is tempting to relate aspects of this reactivation theory to the various brain systems of memory suggested by others (e.g. Schacter & Tulving, 1994; Squire, 1992; Tulving & Schacter, 1990). There are some disagreements among memory-systems theorists regarding what constitutes a memory system, the number of different systems, their locations in the brain, how to characterise their relevant features, and how much the different memory systems contribute to performance on various memory tasks. The formulations also diverge between theorists who primarily focus on memory disorders in human patients versus those who focus on behavioural deficits caused by brain lesions in lower animals (for a survey of the differences, see the compilation edited by Schacter & Tulving, 1994). For illustrative purposes, I will relate the reactivation theory to the memory systems proposed by Tulving (1983, 1985b) and Tulving and Schacter (1990).

First, Tulving's (1985b) proposed "semantic memory" system comprises what in my theory are collections of nodes and Type-1 associations in long-term memory—old concepts, words (logogens), imagens, conceptual associations, and sensory-to-logogen (or imagen) associations that existed before the experiment.

Second, Tulving's (1985b) episodic memory system contains what in my system are those event memories that have retained a strong association to the temporal-spatial context of their encoding. Of course, these memories begin as a set of novel Type-2 associations, but with rehearsal and repetition, the contextual association becomes old (of Type-1) and can thus be primed.

Third, in Tulving's approach, amnesics have difficulty establishing new episodic memories. In my theory these reflect amnesics' impaired ability to form new associations, most especially the contextual associations that support episodic memories.

Fourth, my theory recognises the ability of amnesics as well as normals to learn novel, integrated perceptual configurations. Postulation of this distinct ability in my theory runs parallel to the word-form and object-form representational systems proposed by Tulving and Schacter (1990).

Different areas of the brain may be implicated in mediating different storage and retrieval processes within the reactivation model. For example, long-term semantic and episodic memories may be stored in the cerebral cortex, presumably in different areas according to whether they are predominantly verbal, visual, olfactory, auditory, and so on. The frontal lobes seem intimately involved in retrieving memories from semantic and episodic memory, especially those that may require strategic search processes. The frontal lobes also seem greatly involved in storage and retrieval of source and temporal recency information. The frontal lobes also seem critical for utilising contextual information to control and inhibit the expression of other memories, e.g. to update new memories and suppress old ones in interference paradigms. The medial temporal regions have been strongly implicated as necessary for establishing new Type-2 associations; bilateral damage to these areas produces the full amnesic syndrome. The brain systems for storing and retrieving word-form and object-form representations have been identified with the primary sensory projection areas for vision, audition, and so on. Finally, completeness requires mention of the brain systems for acquiring motor skills (e.g. sensory-motor cortex, basal ganglia, cerebellum), emotions (e.g. limbic system, amygdala), and eyeblink conditioned responses (e.g. cerebellum)—about which the present theory has nothing new to offer.

These identifications of constructs from the reactivation theory with memory systems of the brain are tentative and subject to change as new evidence arises. I think it is important, however, that we try to indicate how a psychological theory based on behavioural (and subjective) evidence might coordinate its constructs to those brain structures identified within the memory-systems viewpoint, as it seems to have captivated the attention of many memory researchers in the contemporary scene.

FINAL SUMMARY AND COMMENTS

To wrap up, let me briefly review what I have presented. I first outlined the logogen framework with its assumption that perceptions both strengthen old sensory feature-to-logogen associations and leave some residual activation on the logogen. I showed how this explains many forms of repetition priming, inter-ference effects, cross-modal, semantic, associative, and conceptual priming, and I illustrated one way to explain picture priming. I then proposed that explicit memory tasks require storage and retrieval of novel associations of the item to its context of presentation. I assumed these contextual associations were established independently of strengthening of the prior sensory associations. Such in-dependence explains a number of dissociations between direct and indirect memory tasks. I illustrated how that theory explained several results including those from Jacoby's opposition procedure. I then subscribed to the hypothesis that global amnesia was characterised by gross impairment of the person's ability to form or consolidate novel associations, especially those to an item's context of presentation. Finally, I offered a few speculations for coordinating constructs within this theory to the brain systems underlying different forms of memory.

In closing, let me state that this simple theory will doubtless not account for all the thousands of facts known about implicit and explicit memory and the brain systems subserving them. However, I feel that it is a good enough beginning to help cognitive psychologists organise and convey to our students a large portion of the literature on the topic. After all, the goal of science is not the accumulation of thousands of disconnected facts but rather the development of a simple and coherent understanding of most of the facts. For that purpose, I believe that the theory offered may serve as a useful beginning.

ACKNOWLEDGEMENTS

The author's research is supported by Grant MH-47575 from the National Institute of Mental Health. The writer is grateful to Larry Jacoby, and to Elliot Hirshman and Neil Mulligan for permission to cite their work. I am also grateful to Anthony Wagner and Endel Tulving for their comments on an earlier draft of this paper.

REFERENCES

Anderson, J.R. (1976). *Language, memory, and thought.* Hillsdale, NJ: Lawrence Erlbaum Associates Inc.

Anderson, J.R. (1983). *The architecture of cognition.* Cambridge, MA: Harvard University Press.

Anderson, J.R., & Bower, G.H. (1972). Recognition and retrieval processes in free recall. *Psychological Review, 79,* 97–123.

Anderson, J.R., & Bower, G.H. (1973). *Human associative memory.* Washington: V.H. Winston.

Anderson, J.R., & Bower, G.H. (1974). A proportional theory of recognition memory. *Memory and Cognition, 2,* 406–412.

Anderson, J.R., & Reder, L.M. (1979). An elaborative processing explanation of depth of processing. In L.S. Cermak & F.I.M. Craik (Eds.), *Levels of processing in human memory.* Hillsdale, NJ: Lawrence Erlbaum Associates Inc.

Atkinson, R.C., & Juola, J.F. (1974). Search and decision processes in recognition memory. In D.H. Krantz, R.C. Atkinson, R.D. Luce, & P. Suppes (Eds.), *Contemporary developments in mathematical psychology. Vol. 1: Learning, memory, and thinking* (pp.243–293). San Francisco: W.H. Freeman.

Barsalou, L.W., & Ross, B.H. (1986). The roles of automatic and strategic processing in sensitivity to superordinate and property frequency. *Journal of Experimental Psychology: Learning, Memory, and Cognition, 12,* 116–134.

Biederman, I. (1986). Recognition by components: A theory of visual pattern recognition. In G.H. Bower (Ed.), *The psychology of learning and motivation,* (Vol. 20, pp.1–54). San Diego, CA: Academic Press.

Biederman, I. (1987). Recognition by components: A theory of human image understanding. *Psychological Review, 94,* 115–147

Biederman, I., & Cooper, E.E. (1991). Priming contour-deleted images: Evidence for intermediate representations in visual object recognition. *Cognitive Psychology, 23,* 393–419.

Bower, G.H. (1984). *Prime-time in cognitive psychology.* Address delivered at the 1984 convention in Brussels of the Association of European Behavior Therapists. [Later published in 1986 in the conference proceedings under P. Eelen (Ed.), *Cognitive research and behavior therapy: Beyond the conditioning paradigm.* Amsterdam: North Holland Publishers].

Bower, G.H. (1996). Reactivating a reactivation theory of implicit memory. *Consciousness and Cognition, 5,* 27–72.

Chiu, C.-Y.P., & Schacter, D.L. (1995). Auditory priming for nonverbal information: Implicit and explicit memory for environmental sounds. *Consciousness and Cognition, 4,* 440–458.

Donaldson, W. (1996). The role of decision processes in remembering and knowing. *Memory and Cognition, 24,* 523–533.

Dorfman, J. (1994). Sublexical components in implicit memory for novel words. *Journal of Experimental Psychology: Learning, Memory, and Cognition, 20,* 1108–1125.

Gabrieli, J.D., Keane, M.M., Zarella, M., & Poldrack, R. A. (1997). Preservation of implicit memory for new associations in global amnesia. *Psychological Science, 8,* 326–329.

Gardiner, J.M. (1988). Functional aspects of recollective experience. *Memory and Cognition, 16,* 309–313.

Gardiner, J.M., & Java, R. (1990). Recollective experience in word and nonword recognition. *Memory and Cognition, 18,* 23–30.

Gardiner, J.M., & Java, R.I. (1991). Forgetting in recognition memory with and without recollective experience. *Memory and Cognition, 19,* 617–623.

Gardiner, J.M., & Java, R.I. (1993). Recognizing and remembering. In A.E. Collins, S.E. Gathercole, M.A. Conway, & P.E. Morris (Eds.), *Theories of memory.* (Ch. 6, pp.163–188). Hove, UK: Lawrence Erlbaum Associates Ltd.

Gardiner, J.M., & Parkin, A.J. (1990). Attention and recollective experience in recognition memory. *Memory and Cognition, 18,* 579–583.

Goshen-Gottstein, Y., & Moscovitch, M. (1995). Repetition priming for newly-formed associations are perceptually based: Evidence from shallow encoding and format specificity. *Journal of Experimental Psychology: Learning, Memory, and Cognition, 21,* 1249–1262.

Graf, P., & Mandler, G. (1984). Activation makes words more accessible but not necessarily more retrievable. *Journal of Verbal Learning and Verbal Behavior, 23,* 553–568.

Graf, P., & Schacter, D.L. (1985). Implicit and explicit memory for new associations in normal and amnesic subjects. *Journal of Experimental Psychology: Learning, Memory, and Cognition, 11,* 501–518.

Graf, P., Squire, L.R., & Mandler, G. (1984). The information that amnesic patients do not forget. *Journal of Experimental Psychology: Learning, Memory, and Cognition, 10,* 164–178.

Hay, J.F., & Jacoby, L.L. (1996). Separating habit and recollection: Memory slips, process dissociations, and probability match. *Journal of Experimental Psychology: Learning, Memory, and Cognition, 22,* 1323–1335.

Hirschman, E., & Masters, S. (1997). Modeling the conscious correlates of recognition memory: Reflection on the remember–know paradigm. *Memory and Cognition, 25,* 345–351.

Hirst, W., Johnson, M.K., Phelps, E.A., Risse, G., & Volpe, B.T. (1986). Recognition and recall in amnesics. *Journal of Experimental Psychology: Learning, Memory, and Cognition, 12,* 445–451.

Jacoby, L.L. (1991). A process dissociation framework: Separating automatic from intentional uses of memory. *Journal of Memory and Language, 30,* 513–541.

Jacoby, L.L., & Dallas, M. (1981). On the relationship between autobiographical memory and perceptual learning. *Journal of Experimental Psychology: General, 110,* 306–340.

Jacoby, L.L., & Kelley, C.M. (1991). Unconscious influences of memory: Dissociation and automaticity. In D. Milner & M. Rugg (Eds.), *The neuropsychology of consciousness.* (pp. 201–233). London: Academic Press.

Keane, M.M., Gabrieli, J.D., Noland, J.S., & McNealy, S.I. (1995). Normal perceptual priming of orthographically illegal words in amnesia. *Journal of the International Neuropsychological Society, 1,* 425–433.

Kirsner, K., & Speelman, C.P. (1993). Is lexical processing just an ACT? In A.F. Collins, S.E. Gathercole, M.A. Conway, & P.E. Morris (Eds.), *Theories of memory* (pp.303–326). Hove, UK: Lawrence Erlbaum Associates Ltd.

Kirsner, K., & Speelman, C.P. (1996). Skill acquisition and repetition priming: One principle, many processes? *Journal of Experimental Psychology: Learning, Memory, and Cognition, 22,* 563–575.

Logan, G.D. (1990). Toward an instance theory of automaticity. *Psychological Review, 49,* 492–527.

Mandler, G. (1980). Recognizing: The judgment of previous occurrence. *Psychological Review, 87,* 252–271.

Mandler, G., Graf, P., & Kraft, D. (1986). Activation and elaboration effects in recognition and word priming. *Quarterly Journal of Experimental Psychology, 38a,* 645–662.

Mayes, A.R., Pickering, A., & Fairbairn, A. (1987). Amnesic sensitivity to proactive interference: Its relationship to priming and the causes of amnesia. *Neuropsychologia, 25,* 211–220.

McCann, R.S., & Besner, D. (1987). Reading pseudohomophones: Implications for models of pronunciation assembly and the locus of word-frequency effects in naming. *Journal of Experimental Psychology: Human Perception and Performance, 13,* 693–706.

McClelland, J.L., & Rumelhart, D.E. (1981). An interactive activation model of context effects in letter perception; Pt 1. An account of basic findings. *Psychological Review, 88,* 375–407.

Morton, J. (1969). Interaction of information in word recognition. *Psychological Review, 76,* 165–178.

Morton, J. (1979). Facilitation in word recognition: Experiments causing change in the logogens model. In P.A. Kolers, M. Wrolstead, & H. Bouma (Eds.), *Processing of visible language.* (Vol. 1, pp.259–268) New York: Plenum Press.

Mulligan, N.W., & Hirschman, E. (1997). Measuring the bases of recognition memory: An investigation of the 'process dissociation' framework. *Journal of Experimental Psychology: Learning, Memory, and Cognition, 23,* 280–304.

Paivio, A. (1978). The relationship between verbal and perceptual codes. In E.C. Carterette, & M.P. Friedman (Eds.), *Handbook of perception: Vol. Ix, perceptual processing.* New York: Academic Press.

Paivio, A. (1986). *Mental representations: A dual coding approach.* New York: Oxford University Press.

Paller, K.A., & Mayes, A.R. (1994). New-association priming of word identification in normal and amnesic subjects. *Cortex, 30,* 53–73.

Poldrack, R.A., & Cohen, N.J. (in press). Repetition priming of new associations in reading time is inflexible: What is learned? *Psychonomic Bulletin and Review.*

Rajaram, S. (1993). Remembering and knowing: Two means of access to the personal past. *Memory and Cognition, 21,* 89–102.

Ratcliff, R., & McKoon, G. (1996). Bias effects in implicit memory tasks. *Journal of Experimental Psychology: General, 125,* 403–421.

Ratcliff, R., McKoon, G., & Verwoerd, M. (1989). A bias interpretation of facilitation in perceptual identification. *Journal of Experimental Psychology: Learning, Memory, and Cognition, 15,* 378–387.

Reingold, E.M. (1995). Facilitation and interference in indirect/implicit memory tests in the process dissociation paradigm: The letter insertion and the letter deletion tasks. *Consciousness and Cognition, 4,* 459–482.

Reingold, E.M. & Goshen-Gottstein, Y. (1996). Separating consciously controlled and automatic influences in memory for new associations. *Journal of Experimental Psychology: Learning, Memory, and Cognition, 22,* 397–406.

Roediger, H.L. III, & Blaxton, T.A. (1987). Effects of varying modality, surface features, and retention interval on priming in word fragment completion. *Memory and Cognition, 15,* 379–388.

Roediger, H.L. III, Weldon, M.S., Stadler, M.L., & Riegler, G.L. (1992). Direct comparison of two implicit memory tests: Word fragment and word stem completion. *Journal of Experimental Psychology: Learning, Memory, and Cognition, 18,* 1251–1269.

Rozin, P. (1976). The psychobiological approach to human memory. In M.R. Rosenzweig & E.L. Bennett (Eds.), *Neuromechanisms of learning and memory* (pp. 308–346). Cambridge, MA: MIT Press.

Rumelhart, D.E., & McClelland, J. (1986). *Parallel distributing processing. Vol. 1. Foundations.* Cambridge, MA: MIT Press.

Salasoo, A., Shiffrin, R.M., & Feustel, T.C (1985). Building permanent memory codes: Codification and repetition effects in word identification. *Journal of Experimental Psychology: General, 114*, 50–77.

Schacter, D.L., Cooper, L.A., Tharan, M., & Rubens, A.B. (1991). Preserved priming of novel objects in patients with memory disorders. *Journal of Cognitive Neuroscience, 3*, 118–131.

Schacter, D.L., & Tulving, E. (Eds.) (1994). *Memory systems.* Cambridge, MA: MIT Press.

Seidenberg, M.S., Petersen, A., MacDonald, M.C., & Plaut, D.C. (1996). Pseudohomophone effects and models of word recognition. *Journal of Experimental Psychology: Learning, Memory, and Cognition, 22*, 48–62.Squire, L.R. (1992). Memory and the hippocampus. *Psychological Review, 99*, 195–231.

Shimamura, A.P., & Squire, L.R. (1989). Impaired priming of new associations in amnesia. *Journal of Experimental Psychology: Learning, Memory, and Cognition, 15*, 721–728.

Smith, S.M., & Tindell, D.R. (1997). Memory blocks in word fragment completion caused by involuntary retrieval of orthographically related primes. *Journal of Experimental Psychology: Learning, Memory, and Cognition, 23*, 355–370.

Squire, L.R. (1992). Memory and the hippocampus. *Psychological Review, 99*, 195–231.

Strack, F., & Förster, J. (1995). Reporting recollective experiences: Direct access to memory systems? *Psychological Science, 6*, 352–358.

Stuart, G.P., & Jones, D.M. (1996). From auditory image to auditory percept: Facilitation through common processes? *Memory and Cognition, 24*, 296–304.

Tulving, E. (1983). *Elements of episodic memory.* Oxford: Clarendon Press.

Tulving, E. (1985a). Memory and consciousness. *Canadian Journal of Psychology, 26*, 1–12.

Tulving, E. (1985b). How many memory systems are there? *American Psychologist, 40*, 385–398.

Tulving, E., & Schacter, D.L. (1990). Priming and human memory systems. *Science, 247*, 301–306.

Tulving, E., Schacter, D.L., & Stark, H. (1982). Priming effects in word fragment completion are independent of recognition memory. *Journal of Experimental Psychology: Human Learning and Memory, 8*, 336–342.

Verfaellie, M., & Treadwell, J.R. (1993). Status of recognition memory in amnesia. *Neuropsychology, 7*, 5–13.

Vriezen, E.R., Moscovitch, M., & Bellos, S.A. (1995). Priming effects in semantic classification tasks. *Journal of Experimental Psychology: Learning, Memory, and Cognition, 21*, 933–946.

Wagner, A.D., Gabrieli, J.D.E., & Verfaellie, M. (1997). Dissociations between familiarity processes in explicit-recognition and implicit-perceptual memory. *Journal of Experimental Psychology: Learning, Memory, and Cognition, 23*, 305–323.

Warrington, E.K., & Weiskrantz, L. (1974). The effect of prior learning on subsequent retention in amnesic patients. *Neuropsychologia, 12*, 419–428.

Warrington, E.K., & Weiskrantz, L. (1978). Further analysis of the prior learning effect in amnesic patients. *Neuropsychologia, 16*, 169–179.

Winocur, G., & Weiskrantz, L. (1976). An investigation of paired-associate learning in amnesic patients. *Neuropsychologia, 14*, 97–110.

Wolters, G. (1996). *Interference in implicit and explicit memory performance.* Paper delivered at the *1996 International Conference on Memory*; Abano Terme, Italy. [Abstract published in conference proceedings.]

3 Encoding and Retrieval Processes: Similarities and Differences

Fergus I.M. Craik
University of Toronto and Rotman Research Institute, Canada

Moshe Naveh-Benjamin
Ben-Gurion University of the Negev, Israel

Nicole D. Anderson
University of Toronto, Canada

INTRODUCTION

In this chapter we describe some recent experiments on the effects of divided attention on encoding and retrieval processes in human memory. There were two main reasons for embarking on this series of studies. The first was that division of attention (DA) in young adults results in memory performance that is very similar quantitatively and qualitatively to that observed in elderly adults working under full attention (Craik, 1982, 1983; Rabinowitz, Craik, & Ackerman, 1982). This finding is in line with the suggestion that older adults have diminished attentional resources with which to carry out various mental activities, including memory encoding and retrieval (Craik & Byrd, 1982). In the same vein, other researchers have pointed to similarities between DA in young adults and the effects of Alzheimer's Disease on memory performance (Gabrieli et al., 1996). In this context, then, the effects of DA on encoding and retrieval processes are of interest in that they may provide clues to the impairments seen in normal and abnormal ageing, as well as in other functional impairments of memory.

The second reason for studying the effects of DA on memory was given by Craik, Govoni, Naveh-Benjamin, and Anderson (1996). In that paper we pointed out some similarities and differences between the processes of encoding and retrieval. Craik (1983) had previously suggested that encoding and retrieval processes may be similar or even identical; his idea was that memory encoding processes are essentially those carried out primarily for the purposes of perception and comprehension (Craik & Lockhart, 1972), and that retrieval processes represent the cognitive system's attempt to reinstate the same pattern of cognitive activity again at the time of recollection. This suggestion of a similarity between the two sets of processes is in line with the influential concepts of encoding specificity (Tulving & Thomson, 1973), remembering operations (Kolers, 1973), and transfer-appropriate processing (Morris, Bransford, & Franks, 1977; Roediger, Weldon, & Challis, 1989). All of these concepts embody the notion that effective retrieval processes must at least reflect the specific manner in which the event was originally encoded. Further support comes from the field of cognitive neuroscience where a number of researchers have shown that the same neural pathways involved in the initial perception and registration of information are again involved in the recovery of that information at the time of retrieval (Mishkin & Appenzeller, 1987; Moscovitch, Kapur, Köhler, & Houle, 1995; Nyberg et al., 1995; Squire, Cohen, & Nadel, 1984). It is also clear, however, that some brain processes are quite different in encoding and retrieval; Tulving and his colleagues have shown that whereas the left prefrontal regions are consistently involved in effective encoding operations, right prefrontal areas are involved in the retrieval of that same information (Nyberg, Cabeza, & Tulving, 1996; Tulving et al., 1994).

To the extent that encoding and retrieval are similar, it might be expected that further variables would have the same effect on both sets of processes. This may be true of some variables (e.g. the effects of ageing, fatigue, and sleep deprivation; Nilsson, Bäckman, & Karlsson, 1989) but it is clearly not true of others. For example, alcohol impairs encoding processes but has very little effect on retrieval (Birnbaum, Parker, Hartley, & Noble, 1978), and the same asymmetry has been reported in the case of benzodiazepines (Curran, 1991). When division of attention is considered, it is well established that DA at encoding impairs later recollection, and that the degree of impairment is a function of the difficulty of the secondary task (Anderson & Craik, 1974; Baddeley, Lewis, Eldridge, & Thomson, 1984; Murdock, 1965). In contrast to this disruptive effect on encoding, studies by Kellogg, Cocklin, and Bourne (1982) and by Baddeley et al. (1984) found essentially no effects of dividing attention at the time of retrieval. Baddeley and his colleagues therefore suggested that (surprisingly) retrieval processes were automatic and required minimal amounts of attentional resources. However, this suggestion does not fit well with earlier studies that found substantial secondary task costs in dual-task paradigms in which memory retrieval was the primary task (Johnston, Greenberg, Fisher, & Martin, 1970; Trumbo & Milone, 1971). In fact, Griffith (1976) and Johnston, Griffith, and Wagstaff (1972) found that retrieval consumes *more* processing capacity than does encoding, as measured by the reduction in secondary task performance.

This set of findings presents some interesting puzzles to researchers in human memory. In some ways encoding and retrieval processes appear similar, but in other ways they seem very different; can we come up with a coherent account that reconciles the similarities and differences? In the specific case of the effects of DA on memory, how does it come about that a secondary task has very little effect on retrieval performance, yet performance on the secondary task itself is substantially impaired? Is it a simple case of trade-off between the tasks, with greater priority always given to memory retrieval? If so, why is the same pattern not observed at memory encoding? In an attempt to answer at least some of these questions, we set out to explore the effect of DA on encoding and retrieval processes.

EFFECTS OF DA ON RECALL AND RECOGNITION

The first set of studies was carried out in collaboration with Richard Govoni. The experiments examined the effects of DA during either encoding or retrieval, and were planned partly to replicate the results reported by Baddeley et al. (1984), although they used a somewhat different methodology (Craik et al., 1996). In overview, memory performance was assessed by presenting lists of single words or word-pairs at encoding, and then requesting free recall, cued recall, or recognition at the time of retrieval. The encoding and retrieval phases were performed either under full attention conditions (with no secondary task present), or under divided attention conditions, in which case a second task was carried out simultaneously with either the encoding or the retrieval phase. In order to avoid interference effects of a simple sensory-motor type, the memory task was always presented auditorily with the participant responding vocally, whereas the secondary task was presented visually with the participant responding manually.

The same secondary task was used in all of these first experiments. It was a continuous reaction time (CRT) task in which participants viewed a horizontal row of four boxes presented visually on a computer monitor. An asterisk was present in one of the boxes, and the participant's task was to press the corresponding one of four keys lined up horizontally (in a spatially compatible fashion with the boxes) on the computer keyboard placed beneath the visual display. A correct key press caused the asterisk to jump immediately to one of the other three boxes at random; the subject's task was thus to continue pressing the series of appropriate keys for the duration of the trial (either 30 or 60 seconds). An incorrect press had no effect on the display, so the participant had to press another key, and errors were therefore recorded as especially long reaction times (RTs). The measure of performance was simply the mean RT across the total encoding or retrieval interval. This task was chosen because each response was followed immediately by the next stimulus; thus there was no "dead time" between events. To obtain a baseline measure, experimental participants performed the CRT task on its own, with the participant being instructed to work as rapidly as possible. We argue that this procedure essentially consumes all available attentional resources[1], and that the attentional costs of the simultaneously performed memory task are reflected in the amount of slowing found in the CRT task.

The memory tasks used were either free recall, cued recall, or recognition memory in the three experiments reported here. In all cases, the memory task was presented under full attention conditions, and also under dual-task (or DA) conditions. We ran three separate trials in the DA cases; in one, the participant was instructed to emphasise memory (but to continue performing the CRT task); in a second condition the participant was instructed to emphasise CRT performance (but to continue performing the memory task); and in a third condition, the participant was instructed to put equal emphasis on the two simultaneous tasks. These conditions are referred to as Memory, RT, and 50/50, respectively.

In the free recall experiment, lists of 15 unrelated common nouns were presented auditorily at a rate of four seconds per word. This 60-second encoding phase was then followed by a simple arithmetic task which the subject performed for 20 seconds; its purpose was to eliminate recency. Immediately following the arithmetic task, the participant recalled as many words as possible from the preceding list, in any order for 30 seconds. The recall responses were given orally and were tape-recorded for later transcription. The CRT task was performed alone for both 60 seconds (to match the duration of the encoding phase) and 30 seconds (to match the retrieval phase). The memory task was also performed alone (i.e. under single-task conditions) for two trials; in the DA conditions the 3×2 combinations of three emphasis instructions with DA at encoding or retrieval were performed twice each for a total of 12 dual-task trials. Further details of the method and design are given in Craik et al. (1996).

The results of the free recall experiment are shown in Fig. 3.1. Figure 3.1A shows memory performance under conditions of full attention, DA at encoding, and DA at retrieval. It is clear that DA at encoding reduces performance considerably—from almost 9 items under full attention to $4\frac{1}{2}$ items in the RT emphasis condition—and that emphasis has a systematic effect on recall. In contrast, DA at retrieval has a much smaller effect, and there is no systematic effect of emphasis. Although the drop from full attention to DA at retrieval was statistically significant in this case, the pattern of results is similar to the findings of Kellogg et al. (1982) and of Baddeley et al. (1984); a large effect of DA at encoding, but a much smaller effect at retrieval. Performance on the CRT task is shown in Fig. 3.1B. Obviously mean RTs slow from full attention to DA conditions, but they slow much more in the case of DA at retrieval than under DA at encoding; also, there is an equal effect of emphasis on the two DA conditions.

These results clearly demonstrate some major differences in the effects of DA on encoding and retrieval. In the case of encoding, the secondary task reduces memory performance substantially and (given the effects of emphasis) the amount of the reduction appears to be under conscious control. Concurrent RT

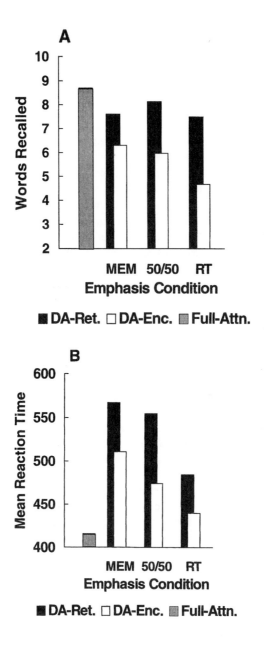

FIG. 3.1. (A) Mean numbers of words recalled under full attention (Full Attn.), divided attention at encoding (DA-Enc.), and divided attention at retrieval (DA-Ret.). In the divided attention conditions, participants emphasised either the memory task (MEM), both tasks equally (50/50), or the RT task (RT). (B) Reaction time data on the secondary task in these same conditions.

costs are moderately high and they trade off against memory performance; that is, the least slowing in the CRT task is associated with the greatest drop in memory performance. For retrieval, on the other hand, there is clearly no such trade-off between memory and RT; mean RTs decreased approximately 90ms per key press between memory and RT emphasis without any concomitant change in memory performance. It seems possible that, overall, encoding and retrieval do trade off against performance on the CRT task as retrieval is affected only slightly by DA, yet RT costs are greater. We return to this point after considering the further experiments in the series.

In the paired-associate version, each memory list consisted of 12 pairs of unrelated nouns presented auditorily at a six-second rate. After a 30-second arithmetic task, the first word of each pair was re-presented auditorily and in a different random order from that of presentation; a six-second rate was again used. The subject's task was to recall the second word associated with each first word. The memory task and the CRT task were again performed alone under full attention conditions, and also under dual-task conditions at either encoding or retrieval. The same three emphasis conditions were performed.

Figure 3.2 shows that the paired-associate results were broadly similar to the results obtained with free recall. At encoding, DA reduced memory performance substantially, and there was a systematic effect of emphasis (Fig. 3.2A). When attention was divided at retrieval, on the other hand, the drop in memory performance was much less, and performance was unaffected by the emphasis manipulation. Figure 3.2B shows the CRT results. The DA conditions were associated with increases in mean RT, the increases were greatest under memory emphasis, and (in contrast to free recall) there were no reliable differences in RT costs between DA at encoding and DA at retrieval. The possibility of a simple trade-off between memory and CRT performance therefore does not hold in this experiment. Otherwise the pattern of results is clearly very similar to the pattern observed with free recall.

In the recognition version, lists of 30 unrelated nouns were presented auditorily at a four-second rate. This encoding phase was followed by a 30-second arithmetic task, and then by the retrieval phase. In this case the memory test was presented in two blocks; each block consisted of a list of 25 words (15 targets mixed randomly with 10 distractors) presented auditorily at a four-second rate. The participant responded "yes" or "no" orally after each test word to indicate whether or not each word was a target. As before, both the memory task and the CRT task were performed alone and in combination during either encoding or retrieval. The results are shown in Fig 3.3.

Figure 3.3A shows that DA at encoding was again associated with a marked drop in memory, and that performance was sensitive to changes in emphasis. On the other hand, DA at retrieval had essentially no effect on recognition performance, and there was again no effect of emphasis. Figure 3.3B shows that RTs were higher in the DA conditions than in the full attention condition, and that

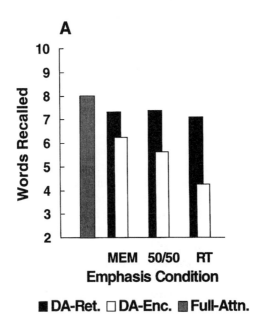

A

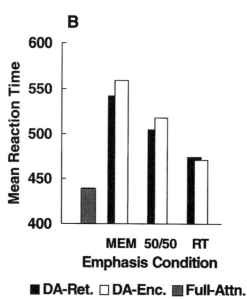

B

FIG. 3.2.   (A) Mean number of words recalled under full attention (Full Attn.), divided attention at encoding (DA-Enc.), and divided attention at retrieval (DA-Ret.). In the divided attention conditions, participants emphasised either the memory task (MEM), both tasks equally (50/50), or the RT task (RT). (B) Reaction time data on the secondary task in these same conditions.

RT costs rose from RT emphasis to memory emphasis for both DA at encoding and DA at retrieval. There was no significant difference in RT costs between DA at encoding and DA at retrieval, so the difference in memory performance between these two conditions cannot be attributed to a differential trade-off between the concurrent tasks.

In summary, these first three experiments have shown that (in contrast to our prior expectations, e.g. Craik, 1983) encoding and retrieval processes are affected rather differently by division of attention. The effect of DA during encoding is to reduce later memory performance considerably; this reduction is associated with a moderate rise in RT for the concurrent task, and the tasks appear to trade off against each other over emphasis conditions, in the sense that higher levels of memory performance are accompanied by greater amounts of slowing in the CRT task. This pattern is in line with previous results (e.g. Murdock, 1965). When attention is divided at retrieval, however, memory performance is affected only slightly, or not at all in the case of recognition, yet RT costs are as great (or greater in the case of free recall) as they are during encoding. One persistent but puzzling finding is that whereas changes in emphasis affect RT costs during retrieval, these changes have no effect on memory.

The implication of these results for theoretical views of encoding and retrieval processes will be discussed later, but for the moment two other findings from this initial series of experiments are mentioned briefly. The first observation concerns the pattern of RT costs at retrieval for the three experiments. Averaging over emphasis conditions, the costs were 123ms, 68ms, and 32ms per key press for free recall, cued recall (paired associate learning), and recognition, respectively. That is, performance on the CRT task was slowed less as the amount of retrieval support afforded by the cueing condition increased from no cues (free recall) to "copy cues" (recognition). The second observation also concerns RT costs at retrieval. In a further free recall study (Craik et al., 1996, Expt. 1) we measured mean RTs in each successive five-second interval during the 30-second retrieval phase. We also recorded the number of words recalled during each five-second interval, and so were able to aggregate intervals in which no words were recalled, one word was recalled, and so on up to four and more words. Our expectation was that RTs would rise as a function of number of words recalled, but that is not what the data showed. In that experiment the RT baseline was 420ms, and the average RTs when participants recalled 0, 1, 2, 3, and 4+ words were 514ms, 581ms, 618ms, 550ms, and 518ms, respectively. That is, the dual-task RTs were all reliably longer than RTs under single-task conditions, but there was no systematic effect on RT costs of the number of words recalled. It therefore seems unlikely that these RT costs are reflecting the actual processes of retrieving each word (i.e. ecphoric processes, in Tulving's 1983 terminology); instead we suggested that RT costs at retrieval may reflect the participant's readiness, set, or attempt to retrieve (i.e. retrieval mode in Tulving's 1983 terminology). We will

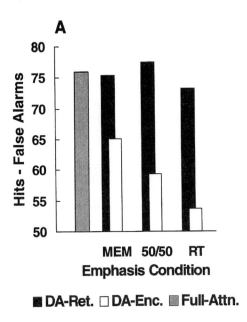

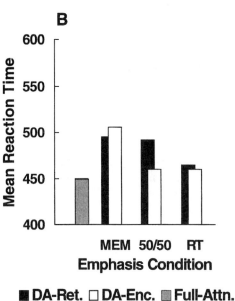

FIG. 3.3. (A) Mean percentages of words recognised (hits minus false alarms) under full attention (Full Attn.), divided attention at encoding (DA-Enc.), and divided attention at retrieval (DA-Ret.). In the divided attention conditions, participants emphasised either the memory task (MEM), both tasks equally (50/50), or the RT task (RT). (B) Reaction time data on the secondary task in these same conditions.

return to the retrieval mode idea later in the chapter, but it should be noted (combining the two observations mentioned in this paragraph) that if the present interpretation is correct, it costs more in attentional resources to be set for cued recall than for recognition, and more for free recall than for cued recall. That is, retrieval mode costs rise as environmental support declines. They also rise as more emphasis is put on the memory task as opposed to the CRT task itself (Figs 3.1–3.3), although as previously noted, this extra allocation of attentional resources does not appear to confer any benefit on memory performance.

FURTHER EXPERIMENTS ON DIVIDED ATTENTION

In this section we describe some further experiments whose purpose was to clarify aspects of the findings and conclusions from the initial series of studies. One result that we still found difficult to accept was the virtual absence of an effect of a secondary task on retrieval performance. To some extent the finding fits the neuropsychological ideas put forward by Moscovitch (1992, 1994; Moscovitch & Umilta, 1990), who suggested that episodic memory performance is mediated by two major areas of the brain—the medial temporal/hippocampal region and the frontal lobes. In Moscovitch's model, the medial temporal component functions in an automatic fashion to encode information presented to it, and retrieve information when presented with compatible cues. In contrast, the frontal component is deliberate and strategic, serving to elaborate information at the time of encoding, and to augment and sharpen retrieval cue information before applying it to the medial temporal/hippocampal complex. The finding of little or no effect of DA at retrieval is in line with Moscovitch's model if it is assumed that the retrieval information in our experiments was more or less sufficient to act on the medial temporal complex to produce the sought-for event without much involvement of the strategic (and presumably effortful) processes mediated by the frontal lobes. This assumption seems reasonable for cued recall and recognition, but is less plausible for free recall. It seemed likely, in any event, that in really difficult retrieval circumstances, strategic augmentation of cues would be necessary, and that DA at retrieval would then be associated with a substantial drop in memory performance given that the secondary task would impair the efficient functioning of the frontal component.

This hypothesis was tested in an experiment devised and run by Jim Perretta in our Toronto lab. He noted that older people (whose memory performance resembles that of younger adults working under conditions of DA at encoding) have particular difficulty with names, and so designed an experiment in which young adults were taught to associate names to faces. The participants were shown 16 pictures of unknown people, clipped from magazines, and were asked to learn each person's name plus two facts about them. For example "*Jessica Borden* likes to play *chess* and to grow *roses*". Both the names and the facts were made up by the experimenter. Each picture, plus the name and two facts were shown for six seconds during the learning phase; in the retrieval phase the pictures were shown alone, in a different order from that of presentation, and the participant's task was to write down the name and the salient words describing the two facts (the italicised words in the previous example). The subject was given up to 20 seconds to retrieve each name and its associated facts. The learning and retrieval phases were conducted either under full attention conditions, or under dual-task conditions (at *either* encoding or retrieval). In this case, as the material was presented visually and the participant responded in writing, the secondary task consisted of a very long series of single digits presented auditorily; the subject's task was to monitor the series for target runs of three successive odd digits (e.g. 317, 791, 535), and to write down each target run when it occurred (Craik, 1982). The sequence of learning and retrieval phases was then repeated, as pilot work had shown that performance was quite low after one trial.

The results are shown in Table 3.1. For both names and facts, DA at encoding is again associated with a marked reduction in performance, whereas DA at retrieval has a relatively small detrimental effect on performance. Analyses of variance revealed that for names, the effect of DA at encoding was highly reliable, but the effect of DA at retrieval was not. In the case of facts, the effect of DA at encoding was again highly reliable, and the effect of DA at retrieval was again nonsignificant. These results are thus in close agreement to those for free recall shown in Fig. 3.1. Apparently even very difficult newly learned material is relatively immune to the effects of divided attention at the time of retrieval. Performance on the secondary task did drop slightly from the DA at encoding conditions (78% target detection) to the DA at retrieval conditions (75%), but this difference was nonsignificant by *t*-test. Thus the differences in recall between DA at encoding and DA at retrieval cannot be attributed to differentially greater attention to the secondary task during encoding.

At this point our reading of the differences between encoding and retrieval was that encoding is a controlled process; subjects can choose to allocate various

TABLE 3.1
Names and Facts

	Names		*Facts*	
	Trial 1	*Trial 2*	*Trial 1*	*Trial 2*
Full Attn.	0.13	0.44	0.48	0.89
DA - Ret.	0.11	0.43	0.42	0.86
DA - Enc.	0.03	0.15	0.21	0.64

Proportions of correct names and facts recalled when attention was full, divided at retrieval (DA-Ret.) or divided at encoding (DA-Enc.).

amounts of attention to encoding processes, with consequent benefits to later memory performance, and reciprocal costs to secondary task performance. In contrast, retrieval processes appear to be more obligatory—they run off relatively automatically—although with substantial secondary task costs which we attribute to the processes underlying the "retrieval mode". An alternative account is possible, however. Several people pointed out to us that another difference between encoding and retrieval is that whereas the presentation of stimuli at encoding is under the experimenter's control, the retrieval of information is under the subject's control. That is, the subject can decide when to deploy retrieval operations, and may well do this at times to maximise retrieval performance; this flexibility is much less at encoding, given that encoding operations must be carried out predominantly at the time of stimulus presentation. This argument is less persuasive for cued recall and recognition than it is for free recall, as retrieval cues are also presented by the experimenter in the first two cases, but the alternative account was clearly worth investigating.

Accordingly we set up the following experiment, which was planned and run in collaboration with Galit Ishaik in Toronto. Lists of 10 unrelated noun pairs were presented visually in a paired-associate paradigm; after performing a 30-second arithmetic task, the subject was presented with the first words in each pair (visually, and in a new random order), and attempted to recall orally each relevant paired word. The secondary task was again a CRT task, but in this case the stimuli were three distinct tones (high, medium, and low) and the subject responded to each tone by pressing the designated key; a correct response caused the next tone to sound, analogously to the visual CRT task used by Craik et al. (1996). As in previous experiments the paired-associate memory task was performed either under full attention throughout, with the secondary task at encoding only, or with the secondary task at retrieval only. To address the issue of experimenter control vs. subject control, Ishaik presented word pairs at encoding and stimulus words at retrieval at either a fixed rate of four seconds per stimulus, or at a rate determined by the subject. The fixed four-second rate exemplified experimenter control at encoding and retrieval, and the flexible rate exemplified subject control. In the latter case, subjects controlled the appearance of the next pair or stimulus word by saying "next"; the experimenter then pressed a key to display the next event. A maximum of 10 seconds was allowed between stimulus events.

The logic of the experiment was that if the previously observed differences between DA at encoding and DA at retrieval were actually attributable to differential control, then the reverse pattern should be observed when encoding is under subject control and retrieval is under experimenter control. That is, now encoding should be affected only slightly by the presence of the secondary task, whereas retrieval should be greatly affected. An alternative prediction might be that when both encoding and retrieval are under subject control, they should show the same pattern of little effect of DA on memory, but a big negative effect on the secondary task. In outline, then, the experimental design was $3 \times 2 \times 2$; full attention, DA at encoding, DA at retrieval $\times$ experimenter/subject control at encoding $\times$ experimenter/subject control at retrieval.

The results for the paired-associate task are shown in Fig. 3.4. The most obvious feature of the results is that, as before, memory performance declined sharply with DA at encoding under all conditions, but was very little affected by DA at retrieval. Subject control at encoding improved performance generally, but this effect was as apparent for full attention as for the other two conditions. When there was subject control at encoding, it made no difference whether retrieval was under subject or experimenter control. With experimenter control at encoding, performance was somewhat better when subjects controlled retrieval, but this was again a main effect, as apparent under full attention as under the DA conditions. In general, the lack of interactions between the three attention conditions and the locus of control (experimenter vs. subject) may be interpreted as evidence that differential control is not a major factor in the pattern of results obtained. Rather, it seems that the differences between encoding and retrieval processes are more fundamental in nature.

The next experiment was designed and run by Simon Tonev in Toronto. His original idea was that if retrieval is truly automatic as suggested by Baddeley et al. (1984), then a dual-task study in which both tasks are memory retrieval tasks should show no decrement in either task. We know from previous studies that secondary task costs can be particularly high when attention is divided at retrieval, so an alternative outcome was that one retrieval task would be unaffected by DA conditions, but that the other would suffer. Tonev's idea had the further advantages that both tasks could be verbal memory tasks, and that both primary and secondary task performance were therefore on the same measurement scale. This feature enables us to assess possible trade-offs more precisely—final performance levels would reflect whichever task the subject emphasised. The design also allowed us to generalise beyond cases in which the secondary task was a perceptual-motor one (as in Ishaik's experiment and the experiments by Craik et al., 1996); conceivably different results might be obtained when the two tasks were similar.

The experiment used lists of 12 unrelated noun pairs in a paired-associate paradigm. In all cases both the word pairs at encoding and single first words at retrieval were presented visually at a six-second rate. In the baseline full-attention condition, subjects simply learned one list and then recalled it after a 30-second arithmetic task had intervened. All other cases involved two lists in the critical phase of each condition, either two lists to be encoded together, two lists to be retrieved together, or one list being learned while the other was retrieved; the six-second rate per word (or per pair) was maintained throughout. When a list was being retrieved in the critical phase, it was learned previously under full attention conditions; similarly, when a list was learned during the critical phase, it was retrieved later under full attention conditions.

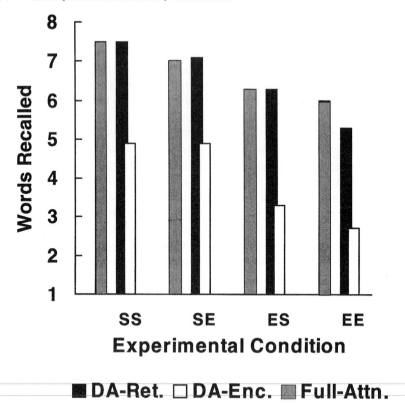

FIG. 3.4   Mean numbers of words recalled as a function of attention condition and subject or experimenter control. Full-Attn. = full attention; DA-Enc. = divided attention at encoding only; DA-Ret. = divided attention at retrieval only; SS, SE, ES, and EE refer to subject (S) or experimenter (E) control at encoding [first letter] or retrieval [second letter] respectively.

The main results are shown in Fig. 3.5. The figure shows the probability of retrieving words correctly as a function of full attention, divided attention at encoding, or divided attention at retrieval. The two DA conditions are further split down as a function of the operations being performed on the secondary task—either learning or retrieval. The figure shows that when attention was divided at encoding (white bars), performance levels dropped markedly from the full attention level (grey bar); further, that the drop in performance was somewhat greater when the secondary task was retrieval rather than encoding. When attention was divided at retrieval (black bars), performance was affected much less, although the drop was more pronounced when the secondary task was also retrieval. There was no interaction between the location of the DA manipulation (at encoding or retrieval) and the nature of the secondary task (encoding or retrieval). An analysis of variance revealed main effects only, showing first that performance was more disrupted by DA at encoding than at retrieval, and second that retrieval tasks are more resource-consuming than encoding tasks, given that they reduce primary task performance to a greater degree. The main conclusion from this study is that the same differences between encoding and retrieval were obtained as were found in previous studies, despite rather substantial changes in the nature of the secondary task.

The final behavioural experiment to be described was designed and carried out by one of us (M N-B) at Ben-Gurion University of the Negev. It was again a free recall study, but in this case the secondary task was a variant of the visual tracking task previously used by Johnston and his collaborators (e.g. Johnston et al., 1970, 1972). In this task a visual target moves unpredictably around the computer screen, and the subject's task is to track the target as closely as possible by moving a visual cursor by means of the computer mouse. The program computed the distance between the cursor and the target every 10ms; this very fine-grained temporal analysis thus allowed us to follow fluctuations in the

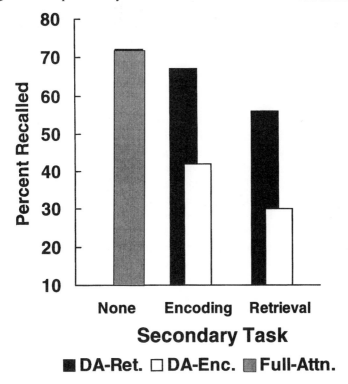

FIG. 3.5.   Percentages of correct recall as a function of condition (Full-Attn. = full attention; DA-Ret. = divided attention at retrieval; Enc. = divided attention at encoding) and type of secondary task when present (Encoding or Retrieval).

attention paid to the tracking task on a moment-by-moment basis. The logic is that as attentional resources are required by encoding or retrieval processes, these resources are diverted from the tracking task; the resource requirements of various aspects of the memory task are therefore reflected and measured by the distance between cursor and target at any particular moment.

To simplify the analysis and the description of results, three measures of secondary task costs were computed. First, the tracking task was performed on its own, and this yielded a baseline measure of tracking performance. Specifically, the task was performed for 30 seconds, and the baseline measure for each subject was the average performance over the full 30-second period. The second and third measures were taken in the dual-task conditions. During encoding, two 500ms samples of tracking deviation were taken immediately before and after the presentation of each word to be learned. Analogously, two similar samples were taken immediately before and after each word was recalled in the retrieval phase. These deviations are assumed to reflect the attentional costs of encoding and retrieval respectively. The final measure was taken *between* encoding events, or between retrieval events; that is, one-second samples were averaged from the mid-points of the four-second gaps between the words presented to be learned during encoding, and from the pauses between recalled words during the retrieval phase. These "between" measures are taken to reflect the costs of being *set* to encode or to retrieve—being in the "encoding mode" or "retrieval mode"—separated from the costs associated with actually encoding the word or retrieving the word.

Having obtained these three average deviations—baseline, during encoding/retrieval events, and between encoding/retrieval events—the final step is to argue that the difference [Between events minus baseline] reflects the costs of encoding mode and retrieval mode respectively, and the difference [During events minus Between events] reflects the extra costs associated with actually encoding or retrieving each word. The timing of these measurements and the values obtained are shown in Fig. 3.6. The results can be described easily; the encoding mode has a moderate cost, and this cost is increased as each word is presented to be learned. At retrieval, on the other hand, the cost of retrieval mode is substantial, but there is virtually no further increase in costs associated with the actual retrieval of each word. The overall finding that retrieval costs are greater than encoding costs is in line with the free recall results reported by Craik et al. (1996), and the further finding that retrieval costs are very largely attributable to retrieval mode, rather than to the costs associated with actual retrieval of each word ("ecphory" in Tulving's terms), is nicely in line with the previous observation that RT costs are unaffected by the number of words retrieved in each five-second recall interval. The findings from this somewhat different paradigm thus bolster and complement the earlier results and conclusions. Despite our original suppositions, it looks more and more as if the differences between encoding and retrieval processes outweigh their similarities! Before summing up the

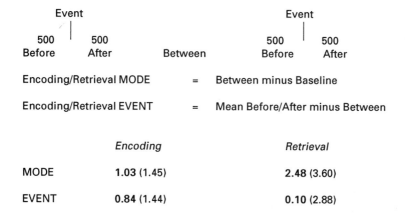

FIG. 3.6   Sequence of events in the tracking study (see text). The values shown are average deviations in mm (standard deviations in parentheses).

arguments for and against our initial position, we will describe some recent evidence from a very different source—positron emission tomography (PET) studies.

PET STUDIES OF ENCODING AND RETRIEVAL

One major problem with attempts to differentiate encoding and retrieval processes on purely behavioural grounds is that we observe only the final product of the memory test under consideration, as opposed to direct observation of the component processes themselves. Whereas we can be fairly sure that a behavioural manipulation at retrieval will have its effects on retrieval processes only (assuming that encoding was held constant), we cannot be so sure about a manipulation at encoding; the effects may be attributable to an effect on encoding processes, on subsequent retrieval processes, or on both sets of processes. This difficulty has recently been overcome by the use of neuroimaging procedures. The rapidly evolving field of cognitive neuroscience has encouraged the application of positron emission tomography (PET), functional magnetic resonance imaging (fMRI), and event-related potentials (ERP) to the study of various aspects of human memory. In particular, these techniques enable researchers to examine the brain correlates of encoding and retrieval processes separately.

In this section we describe some studies of encoding and retrieval using PET imaging. From the perspective set out at the beginning of this chapter—that encoding and retrieval processes are very similar—we might expect to see similar patterns of brain activation. However, as with the behavioural studies described earlier, the work to date has shown that the two sets of processes are more distinguished by their differences than by their similarities. In one study, Kapur et al. (1994) explored the effects of processing words in either a shallow fashion or a deep fashion on patterns of neural activity during the encoding phase. During each 60-second scan, 40 unrelated nouns were presented at a 1.5-second rate on a computer screen; the subject made either a shallow decision (whether or not the word contained the letter "a") or a deeper decision (whether the word represented a living or nonliving object) by pressing one of two buttons on a hand-held computer mouse. In two scans all 40 words were processed in the shallow fashion, and in a further two scans all words were processed in the deeper fashion.

In a subsequent recognition test (following the PET scans) hit rates were 0.57 and 0.75 for the shallow and deep words respectively; thus the standard levels of processing effect was observed. The crucial data from the brain scans came from the subtraction of the shallow pattern of activation from the deep pattern of activation. According to the logic of the PET method, the residual activation reflects a relative increase in regional cerebral blood flow and therefore the extra processing carried out by the brain to make the living/nonliving judgement. In this case the subtraction yielded one contiguous region in the left inferior prefrontal cortex involving Brodmann's areas 45, 46, 47, and 10. Activation of this same region had previously been observed by Petersen et al. (1988) in a word-processing experiment in which activations associated with a word repetition task (FOOD–"food") were subtracted from activations associated with a verb generation task (FOOD –"eat"). These and other studies make it likely that this area of the left prefrontal cortex is concerned with the processing of meaning; not simply *word* meaning, given that the same region was activated during learning of faces (Grady et al., 1995) and spatial locations (Owen, Milner, Petrides, & Evans, 1996).

From our initial expectation that retrieval processes recapitulate encoding processes it should follow that retrieval of episodic information should show the same pattern of activation in the left prefrontal lobe. However, it is now very clearly established that episodic retrieval is associated with activation in *right* frontal regions (Nyberg et al., 1996; Tulving et al., 1994). This pattern of findings— episodic memory encoding on the left and episodic memory retrieval on the right—is referred to as hemispheric encoding/retrieval asymmetry (the HERA model) and is widely accepted in the field (Fletcher, Frith, & Rugg, 1997).

What is the function of this right frontal activity at retrieval? In another study carried out by the Toronto PET group (Kapur et al., 1995), scans were carried out under three conditions. In the first task, subjects were shown a series of concrete nouns on a computer screen at a 1.5-second rate, and they judged whether each word represented a living or nonliving thing; the subjects conveyed their decision by pressing the appropriate mouse button. After two such scans, subjects were then told that the subsequent scans were recognition memory tasks in which a further series of concrete nouns would be shown; in these recognition tasks, the targets were words repeated from the initial living/nonliving scans and the distractors were new words of a similar type. Subjects made their old/new decision by pressing one of two mouse buttons. Unknown to subjects, in one recognition condition 34 of the 40 words shown during the 60-second scan window were targets, whereas in a second condition only 6 of the 40 words were targets. The idea behind this manipulation was that in the high target condition the experimental participants would be both trying to retrieve information from memory and successfully recognising a high proportion of the words presented (hit rate was 0.80). In contrast, the low target condition would be associated with an equivalent attempt to retrieve, but in this case retrieval success would be much lower, given that only six words were targets and the hit rate was 0.75. In Tulving's (1983) terms, activations in both types of recognition scan should reflect the operation of a retrieval mode, whereas successful retrieval or ecphory should be reflected primarily in the high target condition.

In outline, the results showed that both recognition conditions were associated with equivalent activations in the right prefrontal cortex, and that the high target condition showed additional bilateral activations in the medial parietal cortex in the region of the precuneus. This pattern of results was interpreted as showing that the right prefrontal activations signalled retrieval attempt or retrieval mode, and that the posterior activations in the high target situation were associated with ecphoric processes or actual recognition of the word stimuli. Later work by Michael Rugg and his colleagues has shown that the right prefrontal region is also activated following successful retrieval (Rugg et al., 1996; Wilding & Rugg, 1996). It thus appears that the right prefrontal cortex may be involved both in setting the cognitive system into a retrieval mode, and in carrying out a post-retrieval check of retrieved information before committing the person to an overt response (Shallice et al., 1994).

Do these findings using neuroimaging techniques signal the demise of the notion that retrieval processes recapitulate encoding processes? Not necessarily, in our view. Logically it seems necessary that the brain correlates of encoding and retrieval must overlap to *some* degree, given that both sets of processes pertain to the same initial event. Arguably, the findings just described are telling us that the *control* processes associated with encoding and retrieval are quite different; it still seems likely, however, that the cortical areas concerned with an event's representation are activated when the event is encoded, and again when the event is retrieved. Some evidence supporting this view has been reported by Nyberg et al. (1995). In their study, auditorily presented words were encoded either by voice (decide whether the word was spoken by a male or female speaker) or by meaning (decide whether the word represented a living or non-living object). Retrieval was performed in the PET scanner; words were presented visually and subjects decided whether each word was or was not a previously presented target word. Words encoded by voice and by meaning were tested in separate scans. The results showed that both types of recognition involved activation of the right prefrontal cortex, but that further specific activations were different in the case of voice-encoded words (right frontal and temporal regions) and meaning-encoded words (left temporal regions). These specific activations have been observed in previous studies of the encoding of auditory pitch and of single words, respectively, and so the authors conclude that the activations seen at retrieval may be related to the type of processing performed during encoding (presumably involving the same brain regions). Nyberg et al. (1995, p.252) also conclude that "By suggesting a strong interdependency of encoding and retrieval, the results are consistent with the encoding specificity principle."

DISCUSSION

Some results from this research programme are reasonably clear, whereas other aspects remain puzzling. In the first category, dividing attention during encoding has a substantial negative effect on later memory performance, but division of attention during retrieval has little or no effect. Instructions to emphasise either memory performance or the concurrent RT task have a complementary effect at encoding (in the sense that memory performance improves when it is emphasised, but performance slows on the RT task), but an independent effect at retrieval (in the sense that RT can be speeded up with no corresponding deleterious effect on memory). It thus seems that memory and RT processes are under conscious control at the time of encoding and that they trade off against each other, but that this relationship does not hold at retrieval. Baddeley et al. (1984) suggested that retrieval processes may be automatic, but this position is difficult to maintain in light of the substantial concurrent task costs observed at retrieval in the present studies. It may be the case that retrieval is less amenable to control than encoding, but retrieval processes appear to require at least as much in the way of attentional resources as do encoding processes.

One unexpected result from Experiment 1 in Craik et al. (1996) was the finding that RT costs were unaffected by the number of words retrieved in any five-second retrieval interval; in fact, these costs were substantial even when no words were retrieved. Our suggestion is therefore that the observed slowing reflects the attentional cost of maintaining the system in retrieval mode, and this speculation fits with the conclusion of Kapur et al. (1995) that the right prefrontal activations observed in PET studies of retrieval largely reflect the attempt to retrieve, rather than the ecphoric processes of retrieval itself. Given that RT costs decline systematically from free recall through cued recall to recognition, it is also necessary to conclude that retrieval mode cannot be a uniform set to interpret incoming stimuli in terms of past events, but must also reflect the complexity of the operations held in readiness to be performed on these stimuli, with more costly (and presumably more complex) operations in the case of free recall than in the case of recognition memory. An alternative possibility is that retrieval mode involves active search processes as well as a more passive state of readiness, and that these search processes demand more attentional resources in free recall than in recognition. One puzzle in this connection is the further finding that emphasis instructions affect RT costs at retrieval, but have no systematic effect on memory performance. Clearly there is no direct trading relationship between performance on the RT task and retrieval performance, but this remains a puzzle to be solved through further experiments.

The notion that retrieval mode differs as a function of the type of memory test expected can be linked to several other theoretical ideas. First, Craik (1983) and others have made the point that mental operations reflect some mixture of self-initiated processes and processes driven by the external environment; further, that greater amounts of environmental support result in a reduced need for self-initiated processing. On the assumption that recognition memory involves more environmental support than does free recall, the present pattern of RT costs at retrieval can be interpreted as showing paradigm-specific retrieval modes which differ in their involvement of self-initiated processing operations, carried out primarily in the right frontal lobe. Second, the possibility that the retrieval apparatus can be set to interpret incoming information in qualitatively different ways mirrors the suggestion from the levels of processing framework (Craik & Lockhart, 1972) that encoding processes take a variety of qualitatively different forms, with profound consequences for later memory performance (Craik & Tulving, 1975). The suggestion from that earlier work was that intention to learn is much less crucial than the type of processing carried out; later memory improves to the extent that the event is interpreted in an elaborate and meaningful fashion. Possibly, then, the functions of the left prefrontal area are not primarily "encoding" as such, but rather the interpretation of incoming events in terms of accumulated schematic knowledge. It is known, for example, that retrieval from semantic memory is associated with activation of left prefrontal regions (Nyberg et al., 1996). Correspondingly, one of the functions of the right frontal lobe may not be "episodic retrieval" as such, but rather the interpretation of incoming events in terms of earlier specific, self-related episodes.

If the right frontal activation observed in PET studies of retrieval signals retrieval mode, and if retrieval mode varies in complexity as a function of the memory paradigm used, it would be expected that paradigms showing greater amounts of retrieval cost at a behavioural level (e.g. free recall as compared with recognition) would also show greater amounts of activation under PET. This expectation was disconfirmed, however, in a PET study designed to compare recall and recognition directly (Cabeza et al., 1997); the study showed essentially the same pattern of right frontal activation in both cases. One possible explanation is that Cabeza and his colleagues deliberately equated the difficulty of the recognition and recall tasks; so it may be that levels of PET activation and the concurrent task costs associated with a particular retrieval paradigm reflect the amount of self-initiated activity required, and hence the degree of effort involved. Again, further experiments are required to provide answers to these questions.

Is it possible that the observed asymmetry between the effects of DA on encoding and retrieval stems from subjects giving retrieval higher priority in the dual-task situation? The consequences of paying more or less attention to encoding operations are not felt until a later time, as opposed to the immediate feedback of success or failure at retrieval. Also, it has been shown that experimental participants are not very sensitive to the effects of different types of encoding operations on later memory performance (Shaw & Craik, 1989), so subjects in a dual-task situation may not allocate as much attention to encoding operations as they might. Our view is that the asymmetry reflects fundamental differences between encoding and retrieval, rather than a simple difference in attentional allocation policy. In the cases of paired-associate learning and recognition memory the concurrent task costs are the same at encoding and retrieval, yet the effects of DA are much greater on encoding. Also, in the experiment in which the secondary activity was a further encoding or retrieval task (see Fig. 3.5), performance was substantially higher in the case where both tasks were retrieval (0.55) than when both tasks were encoding (0.41). This result suggests that encoding is more vulnerable to the effects of a second task than is retrieval, regardless of whether the concurrent task is very different (as in the RT task used by Craik et al., 1996) or very similar (as in the secondary tasks in Tonev's experiment).

One final theoretical point concerns the relations between the concepts of "attentional resources" on the one hand and "control" on the other. We have taken the position that dual-task situations involve a withdrawal of resources from the primary task, thereby leading to a reduction in performance. However, an alternative account suggests that division of attention, normal ageing, frontal lobe dysfunction, sleep deprivation, and fatigue have their effects through *loss of control* of specialised cognitive functions, rather than through a reduction in the resources needed to fuel cognitive operations. In turn, this loss of control means that the cognitive system will not adapt sensitively to changing conditions but must fall back on undifferentiated routine procedures of a more automatic type. This is the view essentially advocated by Hasher and Zacks (1979) and developed more recently by Jacoby and his colleagues (Jacoby, 1991; Jacoby, Toth, & Yonelinas, 1993; Jennings & Jacoby, 1993) in the context of cognitive psychology and by Moscovitch and Umilta (1990) in the context of neuropsychology. Alternatively, it is possible that the concepts of attentional resources (e.g. Craik & Byrd, 1982), self-initiated processing (Craik, 1983), and strategic conscious control (Hasher & Zacks, 1979; Jacoby, 1991; Moscovitch & Umilta, 1990) have much in common; they may simply be different labels for the same underlying idea, or may emphasise different aspects of the same set of processes.

SUMMARY AND CONCLUSIONS

The experiments described in the present chapter have shown that division of attention affects encoding processes much more than retrieval processes. This asymmetry holds even when retrieval is very difficult, as shown by Perretta's experiment on the recall of names, and it does not appear to reflect a difference between experimenter control and subject control at encoding and retrieval respectively, as shown in Ishaik's experiment. The asymmetry is found with a wide range of concurrent tasks, and does not seem to be a function of memory retrieval receiving a higher priority than the secondary task (Tonev's experiment). The results of the experiment using the visual tracking task give further support to the conclusion that retrieval costs largely reflect the maintenance of a retrieval task set, or retrieval mode, whereas encoding costs are more reflective of event-related processing operations. These various findings were related speculatively to recent work in neuropsychology suggesting differential roles for the left and right prefrontal lobes in encoding and retrieval (Tulving et al., 1994), and to suggestions concerning the complementary functions of the frontal lobes and medial hippocampal areas in memory (Moscovitch & Umilta, 1990).

How are all these differences between encoding and retrieval to be reconciled with the incontrovertible evidence from earlier behavioural studies that memory performance is a function of the *similarity* between encoding and retrieval? The work of Kolers (1973) on repetition of operations, the ideas of encoding specificity (Tulving & Thomson, 1973) and transfer-appropriate processing (Morris et al., 1977; Roediger et al., 1989) with their many empirical illustrations, all point to similarities rather than differences between the two sets of processes. One possibility is that the actual representations of encoded events must be reactivated at the time of retrieval, and that *these* processing operations (presumably occurring largely in posterior areas of the cerebral cortex) must be similar at encoding and retrieval if recollection is to take place. But the control operations (mediated largely by the frontal lobes) involved in encoding and retrieval may be substantially different.

However the debate is resolved, it seems clear that evidence from neuro-psychology and from cognitive neuroscience can now be brought to bear usefully on ideas and models in more traditional areas of cognitive psychology. Any final model of encoding processes, retrieval processes, and their interactions will have to show how the neurological substrate, the behavioural expression, and the subjective experience relate to one another to give an overall picture of learning and remembering.

NOTE

[1]We are aware of the arguments for task-specific resource pools (e.g. Allport, Antonis, & Reynolds, 1972; Navon & Gopher, 1979), but did not wish to enter the controversy. We argue that the meaningful patterns of dual-task costs on the CRT measure justify our assumptions, at least in terms of *relative* RT costs across the various task conditions.

ACKNOWLEDGEMENTS

The work reported in this chapter was supported by grants from the Natural Sciences and Engineering Research Council of Canada to the first author, and from the Canada–Israel Foundation for Academic Exchanges to the second author.

REFERENCES

Allport, D.A., Antonis, B., & Reynolds, P.L. (1972). On the division of attention: A disproof of the single channel hypothesis. *Quarterly Journal of Experimental Psychology, 24,* 225–235.

Anderson, C.M.B., & Craik, F.I.M. (1974). The effect of a concurrent task on recall from primary memory. *Journal of Verbal Learning and Verbal Behavior, 13,* 107–113.

Baddeley, A.D., Lewis, V., Eldridge, M., & Thomson, N. (1984). Attention and retrieval from long-term memory. *Journal of Experimental Psychology: General, 13,* 518–540.

Birnbaum, I.M., Parker, E.S., Hartley, J.T., & Noble, E.P. (1978). Alcohol and memory: Retrieval processes. *Journal of Verbal Learning and Verbal Behavior, 17,* 325–335.

Cabeza, R., Kapur, S., Craik, F.I.M., McIntosh, A.R., Houle, S., & Tulving, E. (1997). Functional neuroanatomy of recall and recognition: A PET study of episodic memory. *Journal of Cognitive Neuroscience, 9,* 254–256.

Craik, F.I.M. (1982). Selective changes in encoding as a function of reduced processing capacity. In F. Klix, J. Hoffmann, & E. van der Meer (Eds.), *Cognitive research in psychology* (pp.152–161). Berlin: FRG.

Craik, F.I.M. (1983). On the transfer of information from temporary to permanent memory. *Philosophical Transactions of the Royal Society of London, Series B302,* 341–359.

Craik, F.I.M., & Byrd, M. (1982). Aging and cognitive deficits: The role of attentional resources. In F.I.M. Craik & S.E. Trehub (Eds.), *Aging and cognitive processes* (pp.191–211). New York: Plenum Press.

Craik, F.I.M., Govoni, R., Naveh-Benjamin, M., & Anderson, N.D. (1996). The effects of divided attention on encoding and retrieval processes in human memory. *Journal of Experimental Psychology: General, 125,* 159–180.

Craik, F.I.M., & Lockhart, R.S. (1972). Levels of processing: A framework for memory research. *Journal of Verbal Learning and Verbal Behavior, 11,* 671–684.

Craik, F.I.M., & Tulving, E. (1975). Depth of processing and the retention of words in episodic memory. *Journal of Experimental Psychology: General, 104,* 268–294.

Curran, H.V. (1991). Benzodiazepines, memory and mood: A review. *Psychopharmacology, 105,* 1–8.

Fletcher, P.C., Frith, C.D., & Rugg M.D. (1997). The functional neuroanatomy of episodic memory. *Trends in Neuroscience, 20,* 213–218.

Gabrieli, J.D.E., Stone, M., Vaidya, C.J., Askari, N., Zabinski, M.F., & Rabin, L. (1996, November). *Neuropsychological and behavioral evidence for the role of attention in implicit memory.* Paper presented at the 37th annual meeting of the Psychonomic Society, Chicago, IL.

Grady, C.L., McIntosh, A.R., Horwitz, B., Maisog, J.M., Ungerleider, L.G., Mentis, M.J., Pietrini, P., Schapiro, M.B., & Haxby, J.V. (1995). Age-related reductions in human recognition memory due to impaired encoding. *Science, 269,* 218–221.

Griffith, D. (1976). The attentional demands of mnemonic control processes. *Memory and Cognition, 4*, 103–108.

Hasher, L., & Zacks, R.T. (1979). Automatic and effortful processes in memory. *Journal of Experimental Psychology: General, 108*, 356–388.

Jacoby, L.L. (1991). A process dissociation framework: Separating automatic from intentional uses of memory. *Journal of Memory and Language, 30*, 513–541.

Jacoby, L.L., Toth, J.P., & Yonelinas, A.P. (1993). Separating conscious and unconscious influences of memory: Measuring recollection. *Journal of Experimental Psychology: General, 122*, 139–154.

Jennings, J., & Jacoby, L.L. (1993). Automatic versus intentional uses of memory: Aging, attention and control. *Psychology and Aging, 8*, 283–293.

Johnston, W.A., Greenberg, S.N., Fisher, R.P., & Martin, D.W. (1970). Divided attention: A vehicle for monitoring memory processes. *Journal of Experimental Psychology, 83*, 164–171.

Johnston, W.A., Griffith, D., & Wagstaff, R.R. (1972). Speed, accuracy, and ease of recall. *Journal of Verbal Learning and Verbal Behavior, 11*, 512–520.

Kapur, S., Craik, F.I.M., Jones, C., Brown, G.M., Houle, S., & Tulving, E. (1995). Functional role of the prefrontal cortex in retrieval of memories: A PET study. *Neuroreport, 6*, 1880–1884.

Kapur, S., Craik, F.I.M., Tulving, E., Wilson, A.A., Houle, S., & Brown, G.M. (1994). Neuroanatomical correlates of encoding in episodic memory: Levels of processing effect. *Proceedings of the National Academy of Science of USA, 91*, 2008–2011.

Kellogg, R.T., Cocklin, T., & Bourne, L.E. Jr. (1982). Conscious attentional demands of encoding and retrieval from long-term memory. *American Journal of Psychology, 95*, 183–198.

Kolers, P.A. (1973). Remembering operations. *Memory and Cognition, 1*, 347–355.

Mishkin, M., & Appenzeller, T. (1987). The anatomy of memory. *Scientific American, 256*, 80–89.

Morris, C.D., Bransford, J.D., & Franks, J.J. (1977). Levels of processing versus transfer appropriate processing. *Journal of Verbal Learning and Verbal Behavior, 16*, 519–533.

Moscovitch, M. (1992). Memory and working-with-memory: A component process model based on modules and central systems. *Journal of Cognitive Neuroscience, 4*, 257–267.

Moscovitch, M. (1994). Cognitive resources and dual-task interference effects at retrieval in normal people: The role of the frontal lobes and medial temporal cortex. *Neuropsychology, 8*, 524–534.

Moscovitch, M., Kapur, S., Köhler, S., & Houle, S. (1995). Distinct neural correlates of visual long-term memory for spatial location and object identity: A positron emission tomography (PET) study in humans. *Proceedings of the National Academy of Sciences of USA, 92*, 3721–3725.

Moscovitch, M., & Umilta, C. (1990). Modularity and neuropsychology: Implications for the organization of attention and memory in normal and brain-damaged people. In M.E. Schwartz (Ed.), *Modular processes in dementia* (pp.1–59). Cambridge, MA: MIT/Bradford Press.

Murdock, B.B. Jr. (1965). Effects of a subsidiary task on short-term memory. *British Journal of Psychology, 56*, 413–419.

Navon, D., & Gopher, D. (1979). On the economy of the human-processing system. *Psychological Review, 86*, 214–255.

Nilsson, L.G., Bäckman L., & Karlsson, T. (1989). Priming and cued recall in elderly, alcohol-intoxicated and sleep-deprived subjects: A case of functionally similar memory deficits. *Psychological Medicine, 19*, 423–433.

Nyberg, L., Cabeza, R., & Tulving, E. (1996). PET studies of encoding and retrieval: The HERA model. *Psychonomic Bulletin and Review, 3*, 135–148.

Nyberg, L., Tulving, E., Habib, R., Nilsson, L.-G., Kapur, S., Houle, S., Cabeza, R.E.L., & McIntosh, A.R.L. (1995). Functional brain maps of retrieval mode and recovery of episodic information. *Cognitive Neuroscience and Neuropsychology, 7*, 249–252.

Owen, A.M., Milner, B., Petrides, M., & Evans, A.C. (1996). A specific role for the right parahippocampal gyrus in the retrieval of object-location: A positron emission tomography study. *Journal of Cognitive Neuroscience, 8,* 588–602.

Petersen, S.E., Fox, P.T., Posner, M.I., Mintun, M., & Raichle, M.E. (1988). Positron emission tomographic studies of the cortical anatomy of single-word processing. *Nature, 331,* 585–589.

Rabinowitz, J.C., Craik, F.I.M., & Ackerman, B.P. (1982). A processing resource account of age differences in recall. *Canadian Journal of Psychology, 36,* 325–344.

Roediger, H.L. III, Weldon, M.S., & Challis, B.H. (1989). Explaining dissociations between implicit and explicit measures of retention: A processing account. In H.L. Roediger III & F.I. M. Craik (Eds.), *Varieties of memory and consciousness: Essays in honour of Endel Tulving* (pp.3–41). Hillsdale, NJ: Lawrence Erlbaum Associates Inc.

Rugg, M.D., Fletcher, P.C., Frith, C.D., Frackowiak, R.S.J., & Dolan, R.J. (1996). Differential activation of the prefrontal cortex in successful and unsuccessful memory retrieval. *Brain, 119,* 2073–2083.

Shallice, T., Fletcher, P., Frith, C.D., Grasby, P., Frackowiak, R.S.J., & Dolan, R.J. (1994). Brain regions associated with acquisition and retrieval of verbal episodic memory. *Nature, 368,* 633–635.

Shaw, R.J., & Craik, F.I.M. (1989). Age differences in predictions and performance on a cued recall task. *Psychology and Aging, 4,* 131–135.

Squire, L.R., Cohen, N.J., & Nadel, L. (1984). The medial temporal region and memory consolidation: A new hypothesis. In E. Weingartner & E. Parker (Eds.), *Memory consolidation* (pp.185–210). Hillsdale, NJ: Lawrence Erlbaum Associates Inc.

Trumbo, D., & Milone, F. (1971). Primary task performance as a function of encoding, retention, and recall in a secondary task. *Journal of Experimental Psychology, 91,* 273–279.

Tulving, E. (1983). *Elements of episodic memory.* New York: Oxford University Press.

Tulving, E., Kapur, S., Craik, F.I.M., Moscovitch, M., & Houle, S. (1994). Hemispheric encoding/retrieval asymmetry in episodic memory: Positron emission findings. *Proceedings of the National Academy of Science of USA, 91,* 2016–2020.

Tulving, E., & Thomson, D.M. (1973). Encoding specificity and retrieval processes in episodic memory. *Psychological Review, 80,* 352–373.

Wilding, E.L., & Rugg, M.D. (1996). An event-related potential study of recognition memory with and without retrieval of source. *Brain, 119,* 889–906.

4 Memory and Imagery: A Visual Trace is Not a Mental Image

Cesare Cornoldi and Rossana De Beni
University of Padova, Italy

Fiorella Giusberti
University of Bologna, Italy

Manfredo Massironi
University of Verona, Italy

People's intuitive idea of what a mental image is refers to any form of mind representation that maintains properties of sensory experiences in the absence of those experiences.

Furthermore, naïf beliefs are based on the idea that mental images are directly derived from corresponding experiences, for example visuo-spatial mental images are the by-products of visual experiences (Cornoldi, 1995; Cornoldi et al., 1991b, 1995a). The following implicit equations are widespread:

(a) visual images = visual memories
(b) visual memories = f (visual experiences)

where 'f' is a function that substantially varies only quantitatively, but not qualitatively. This chapter will not consider equation (b) in detail, being focused on a critical analysis of the implications of equation (a). This last equation, although belonging to naïf beliefs about mental imagery, has found nurture and support in a mechanical interpretation of different theories suggesting analogies between perception and mental imagery. For example, Paivio's (1971) dual-code theory has assumed that similar imagery processes are involved in the generation of mental images and in the memorisation of pictures (see also Marks, 1972); this happened at the same moment as Shepard (e.g. Shepard & Metzler, 1971) argued in favour of strict analogies between perception and mental images (see also Finke, 1989). More recently, neuropsychological evidence has been used to show that an imagery deficit can be related to visual memory problems (e.g. Farah,

1985) and that visual perception, visual memory, and visual mental imagery can even share the same neurological mechanisms (Kosslyn, 1994). The typical use of these theoretical approaches has led to the conclusion that a mental imagery theory requires the assumption of a near-perfect analogy between perception, memory, and imagery. As anticipated, the present chapter argues against a too simplistic assumption of an analogy between visual memory and visual mental imagery, on the basis of an analysis of the differences in the underlying processes and of a distinction between different types of visual memories and of visual mental images. Our focus will be on the visual modality, although our view concerns all types of sensory modalities.

Actually, theories that are known for analogy assumptions also offer articulated views of the mental image generation process, which have more complex implications. For example, Kosslyn's (1980, 1994) theory excludes the possibility that image generation is the simple result of the retrieval from long-term memory of a corresponding already formatted representation. On the contrary, he hypothesises that the process starts with the retrieval from a possibly amodal associative memory system of a pattern code. In Kosslyn's (1994) view, the image generation process is more complex when multipart images must be generated. Stored perceptual units must be integrated to form the image. To do this, we operate sequentially, accessing the foundation part, which is the portion of the shape that is indexed by the spatial relation associated with a to-be-imaged part or property. Once the part or the property is properly positioned, the generative attentional mechanism (attention window) encodes a new pattern. At this point the attention window is adjusted and the appropriate representation is activated to project feedback into the visual buffer. Increases in details and time processing determine an increase in the image vividness.

Therefore the image generation process is often sequential, starting from a global image (skeleton image in Kosslyn, 1980), which is stronger because it has been activated more often (Kosslyn, 1994, p.290). Subsequently, the global image could be enriched with details which make it closer to a visual experience. This position is in agreement with our observation (Cornoldi, De Beni, & Pra Baldi, 1989a, see also De Beni & Pazzaglia, 1995) that people can generate either very general, low-resolution images, or rich specific images: general images are more often generated in standard conditions, take less time to be generated, are rated as less vivid, and are less memorable.

The position we have briefly illustrated here can explain why we can have stable representations of objects we have seen many times from different perspectives, leaving out those specific perspectives, and why a generated mental image can be different from each of these preceding experiences. Furthermore, from our point of view, the organisation of knowledge in people's minds suggests that more integrated information is involved in the process of generating an image. The task of generating an image is necessarily involved in a particular context of knowledge activation and task demands, which influence the sources of information used in the generation process. Not only a specific pattern code, but also the related pathways and other implicated nodes are activated at the same time, producing a representation that uses a mixture of different information.

VISUAL IMAGES AND SENSORY INFORMATION

All these considerations argue in favour of a critical role of long-term memory properties (also different from visual sensory memory properties) in image generation and representation, and in favour of a distinction between images simply based on visual spatial short-term memory and images largely based on long-term memory.

In our view, we cannot exclude that long-term memory can maintain the sensory properties of a stimulus to some extent (Norman, Rumelhart, & Group, 1975, similarly argued that in an associative network an object node could be related to a node conveying imaginal information). Cases of involuntary memories primed, also after very long periods of time, by re-exposure to the same sensations experienced in other moments, in Proustian experiences, or in the everyday recognition of a face (Bahrick, Bahrick, & Wittlinger, 1975), suggest that the memory pattern code also involves memory for specific sensory information. The possibility that this sensory information persists or at least can be used after a long period of time seems to depend on its original repeated exposure, on its encoding in conditions of high activation, and on particular retrieval contexts. In general, visual memories, if these favourable conditions are not present, seem subjected to decay functions which produce a rather rapid loss of specific sensory information, maintaining more schematic information (Mandler & Ritchey, 1977). This result suggests that visual memories initially maintain elements encoded during the perceptual exposure but that they are progressively subjected to processes of transformation and integration in long-term memory which determine an increasing loss of specific sensory details.

According to the popular dual system view of memory, a memory decay function includes a strong discontinuity element represented by the passage from short- to long-term memory. Therefore the probability of maintenance of specific perceptual details should strongly decrease when the limits of short-term memory are clearly exceeded. In fact, Hitch, Brandimonte and their co-authors (e.g. Hitch, Brandimonte, & Walker, 1995) found that the passage from short- to long-term retention intervals reduces the probability that a visual trace maintains sensory features (like contrast sensitivity) which are critical in perception but lose their role in long-term memory.

In looking for evidence of a difference between a recent visual piece of information (which we called "visual trace") and an image generated on the basis of long-term memory information (which we called "generated image"), we considered cases where this difference could be made more evident, i.e. on the one hand, multi-object images generated from long-term memory on the basis of sequential verbal instructions; on the other hand, visual traces resulting from very recent visual exposures. As the visual traces are largely influenced by the immediately preceding visual experiences, the study of differences between generated images and visual traces raises the more general point concerning differences between visual perception and visual mental imagery.

Reisberg (1997) also reviews data and suggestions in favour of a distinction between perceptual pictures and mental images. For example, mental images can be three-dimensional in a more direct way than pictures. Furthermore, mental images can be essentially spatial, based on movement and perhaps more abstract, with modest reference to visual features, whereas perceptual pictures by definition rely on vision. In particular, Reisberg reviews research showing that perception (i.e. the phenomenal object) can be subjected to illusory perceptions, reversals, reinterpretations of the physical object, which are related to the perceptual exposure but which cannot happen when the perceptual exposure of an object is withdrawn and the object is maintained in memory based on a particular interpretation. This point was made evident in a study by Chambers and Reisberg (1985) who very briefly showed their subjects a drawing of an ambiguous figure (such as the Necker cube or a drawing that could be interpreted either as a duck or as a rabbit). The subjects were then asked to form a mental image based on that drawing and asked if they could reinterpret their image. Across several experiments, no subject succeeded in reinterpreting the images. For example, subjects who had interpreted the figure as a duck were not able to reinterpret it as rabbit.

Reisberg's results could be considered from different perspectives. On the one hand, they show that typically visual memories of an object preserve the phenomenal rather than the physical object. On the other hand, they seem to suggest that properties of a recent visual memory are highly conceptual, as we have suggested for generated mental images. However, data obtained using the Chambers and Reisberg (1985) paradigm are more complicated and are subject to a series of different interpretations which were considered in a book contrasting and debating the different positions (Cornoldi et al., 1995a). In fact, it was also found that the results were different if slight modifications in the procedure were introduced. In an experiment by Chambers and Reisberg, subjects were given a blank piece of paper, immediately after their failure to reinterpret their images, and asked to draw the figure. Looking at their own drawings, subjects were able to reinterpret the configuration in the appropriate way, suggesting that a visual memory is different (includes different information) from a mental image. These results are open to the objection that subjects were not simply using their memory of the figure, but could also use pencil and paper to study new possibilities and combinations of the parts of the preceding figure. However, this objection does not apply to the methodology followed by Brandimonte and co-authors who, by preventing verbal interpretation of the stimulus with an articulatory suppression request, found that subjects were able to reinterpret the figure from their memory.

Altogether, these results seem to suggest that visual memories can maintain visual features that are lost in a mental image.

VISUO-SPATIAL IMAGES AND VISUO-SPATIAL MEMORIES: EVIDENCE FROM THE BLIND

Preliminary evidence in favour of a distinction between visuo-spatial memories and visuo-spatial mental images was collected by us through the study of mental images generated by totally congenitally blind people. Despite the fact that increasing evidence was showing that in visual imagery tasks the blind behave, in many respects, in the same way as sighted people (e.g. Carpenter & Eisenberg, 1978; Cornoldi, Calore, & Pra Baldi, 1979), and that these results cannot be explained by assuming that both groups of subjects are using a verbal or a more abstract code (see also Cornoldi et al., 1989b, 1991a), a popular view argued that blind people, as they do not have any visual experience, cannot have visual images (see Zimler & Keenan, 1983). This position has now been corrected, but a common argument (e.g. Reisberg, 1997, p.409) assumes that:

> it seems unlikely that blind subjects are using visual imagery to perform these tasks. Therefore, these subjects must have some other means of thinking about spatial layout and spatial relations. This 'spatial imagery' might be represented in the mind in terms of a series of imagined movements, so that it is 'body imagery' or 'motion imagery' rather than visual imagery. Alternatively, perhaps spatial imagery is not tied to any sensory modality, but is part of our broader cognition about spatial arrangements and lay-out.

It must be noted that the last hypothesis could also be applied to the case of visual properties of objects, as the blind can have extended knowledge about them (size, shape, and even colour), both from verbal information, and by the other sensory modalities. Furthermore, if both spatial and visuo-pictorial aspects of mental images are largely based on other sources of long-term information as well as on the visual one, there are no reasons for expecting, as Reisberg does, that the blind would be rich in spatial images and poor in visuo-pictorial images. In fact, we have found results in the opposite direction, showing that blind people can be poorer in a task more directly involving the spatial imagery modality (manipulation of images of three-dimensional patterns) than in tasks involving to a larger extent the pictorial modality (manipulation of images of two-dimensional patterns, recognition of shapes). Our argument is not that blind people are better at generating and using pictorial images than at generating and using spatial images, but that both kinds of images do not require, as a necessary prerequisite, direct visual experience. However, visual experience is a fundamental source of information and support, and both kinds of mental images suffer limitations in the blind due to the absence of that experience: these limitations are more evident when the task is difficult and the subject is required to generate or manipulate a very complex image (see Cornoldi et al., 1991a; De Beni & Cornoldi, 1988a,b).

ANALOGIES AND ASYMMETRIES BETWEEN IMAGERY AND PERCEPTION

Despite this evidence, research on visual imagery has repeatedly attempted to show the analogies between imagery and perception, thus making it possible to illustrate, on the one hand, the specific analogical properties of images distinguishable from the properties of more abstract propositional representations and, on the other, the characteristics of visual images (see Finke, 1985; Kosslyn, 1980). However, when the "ontological preoccupation" of showing the distinguishability between images and propositions became weaker, and at the same time research also began to explore more deeply the most obscure areas of this domain, evidence was progressively collected showing that, in some respects, visual perception and visual imagery work in different ways. For example, Intons-Peterson and McDaniel (1990), in reviewing the literature, found a series of asymmetries between perception and imagery, e.g. in distance and magnitude estimations, relative contrast, structural factors, mental rotation, and influence of knowledge.

Another area that could be taken into consideration when looking for similarities and asymmetries between imagery and perception is the first phases of visual information processing. A classic study showing similarities on this aspect was carried out by Perky (1910), who found that trying to observe weak, not perfectly perceivable pictures on a screen affected the images subjects were creating at the same time. Similarly, Segal (1972) found that weak perceptual stimuli were assimilated into the subjects' images. Kosslyn (1994) observed that, given such results, it is not surprising that sometimes people confuse their images for percepts and vice versa. In fact, there is evidence that people sometimes cannot carry out a correct "reality monitoring", i.e. remember whether they had actually seen something or merely imagined that they were seeing it (e.g. Intraub & Hoffman, 1992). Along a different line of research, Brooks has shown, in a series of studies (e.g. Brooks, 1968), that an imagery task is more greatly disturbed by the simple visual activities of reading or producing a visual response than by the parallel activities of listening or giving a verbal response. These data were replicated and extended to the case of people using imaginal mnemonics in learning from texts (De Beni et al., in press).

Two lines of research more directly focused on the first phases of visual information processing are addressed by studies on the McCollough effect and studies on pre-attentional feature analysis. Finke (1989) observed that evidence showing the similarities in after-effect in perception and imagery is so strong that it calls into question whether mental imagery really does involve the direct stimulation of bar detectors and feature analysers which are involved in perception. However, there is some ambiguity in the imagery data on the McCollough effect (McCollough, 1965). On the perceptual level, the effect shows that after a prolonged exposure to vertical and horizontal lines of two different colours, followed by a new pattern with white lines having both vertical and horizontal orientations, the different orientations produce the perception of the complementary colours of the preceding exposures. Some research succeeded in replicating the effect in imagery (Finke & Schmidt, 1977; Marks, 1983), while other research extended the effect to imagery tasks, beyond the constraints that can be found in perception, e.g. in the communication between information affecting both eyes (Kaufman, May, & Kunen, 1981) and also independently from the orientation of the lines in the first exposure (Rhodes & O'Leary, 1985), two cases that cannot be found at the perceptual level. These results seem to suggest that a phenomenon that has its locus, at the perceptual level, in the peripheral sensory systems (low level), has its locus in more central systems at the imagery level (high level).

Another line of research that can support this point of view concerns the first phases of feature analysis (Julesz, 1975; Treisman, 1986), which seems to involve only a limited number of features or characteristics, like colour, contrast, inclination, roundness, contours, and size. Depending on the relationships between these features, one or more of them can pop out during the first phase of visual information processing which produces, on the basis of simple properties, a segregation of some elements of the visual field. Only in a subsequent processing phase will there be the partly attentional constructive process which allows pattern identification. The distinction between these two phases may be critical for the comparison between visual perception and visual imagery. The first perceptual phase, in contrast to the subsequent one, has characteristics not easily found in imagery because it is automatic, very rapid, parallel to and independent from the subject's control. In a series of studies (Giusberti et al., 1992a; Rocchi, Cornoldi, & Massironi, 1992) we found that visual imagery and visual perception do not share the processes and the effects related to this first phase. The methodology of these studies required subjects to perceive or generate the image of a pattern consisting of arrays of letters where one letter was different in a particular feature, such as colour, inclination, movement (Giusberti et al., 1992a) or size, roundness, and the presence of a trait (Rocchi et al., 1992). Subjects were invited to rate the vividness of the critical letter in relation to the distractors. While the specific characteristics increased the vividness of the stimulus in the perceptual condition, no effect was found in the imagery condition.

Further, it was shown that the difference between perception and imagery is not absolute but depends on the nature of the underlying processes. In fact, when a perceptual activity is preceded by an attentional constructive process, or when an imagery representation is based on a perceptual actively, the phenomenological experience tends to reverse (Giusberti et al., 1992a).

VISUAL TRACES AND GENERATED IMAGES

This line of research implies a main differentiation in the imagery domain between "loaded" images based on perceptual exposure (described here as "visual traces" VT) and generated images (GI). This differentiation should be more evident in short- and intermediate-term memory tasks, rather than in long- and very long-term memory tasks, where a visual trace can be subjected to transformations that lose its original properties. This difference may seem intuitive and obvious, but its implications have never been studied and even the distinction itself is not well specified in the literature.

TABLE 4.1
Aspects that could Distinguish Between a Visual Trace and a Generated Image

	Visual Trace	Generated Image
Access	directly received	generated
Attention	very low (often pre-attentive)	high
Represented object	phenomenic object	constructed object
Perception analogy	almost complete	partial
Main characteristics	sensorial-phenomenic properties	selected perceptual-conceptual properties
Role of LTM	marginal	substantial
Process penetrability	almost none	substantial
Modality of loss	same as sensorial information	same as elaborated information
Interference	visual similarity	representations requiring similar processes, different processes requiring attention
Capacity limitations	limits of storage	limits of storage and operator
Memory variation related to age development	minimal	substantial

A general case can be made in trying to differentiate between the two representations (Giusberti et al., 1992b). Table 4.1 shows some differences between the two kinds of representation which are, more or less, the direct implication of the difference in the underlying processes typically producing the two representations. In fact, a visual trace is the result of perceptual processes, often largely affected by primitive sensory analysis. On the contrary, a generated image is the result of conceptual processes, retrieving and organising long-term information into an image buffer. In other words, we assume that a visual trace and a generated image involve different encoding processes which affect the format and the functional characteristics of subsequent representations. This distinction could be useful not only to examine the imagery literature, but also to detect new lines of research about images properties. Table 4.1 does not aim to present data that is already known: on the contrary, it must be considered a tentative hypothesis, waiting to be verified, regarding the difference between the processes and representations involved in a VT and a GI respectively.

Let us examine these differences in order to better explain the difference between visual trace and generated image. As far as access is concerned, the VT is directly received from perception, whereas the GI is generated from long-term memory: for this reason in the first case the role of long-term memory is marginal, and in the second one it is, on the contrary, substantial. We need some semantic and conceptual information to generate an image: if we are asked, for example, to imagine an animal like a tiger we must know that it is feline, it has four paws, and it is striped. With this kind of information we can easily create the image (GI). The process is very different if someone shows us a picture of his new house and, after a short time, asks us to remember it. In this case we are able to create the image (VT) from the perceptual-phenomenic information received by looking at the picture, the role of long-term memory being substantially marginal. From these features follows another difference concerning VT and GI main characteristics: sensorial and phenomenic properties define the visual trace, whereas conceptual ones characterise the generated image. In fact, in the first case we use mostly information we have received in a sensorial way—that is, visual perception—and in the second one we use, above all, our knowledge about the imagined object. It must be underlined, however, that we use one kind of information instead of the other prevalently but not exclusively: actually some sensorial properties can also define the generated image, and some conceptual ones could be used to create a visual trace.

Other characteristics differentiate the VT from the GI: attention resources are involved to a greater extent in the generation of an image than in loading a VT. The represented object in the VT is a phenomenic object because it is the result of a visual-perceptual process; the GI is a constructed object—that is, a mental representation we create by our knowledge about that object, the semantic and conceptual information we own about it. Another important difference concerns the relationship between imagery and perception in the case where imagery produces a VT or a GI. As far as VT is concerned, in contrast to GI, it is possible to affirm an almost complete analogy between imagery and perception. The last 10 years' literature shows an experimental confirmation of this difference: most studies on functional equivalence between imagery and perception refer to images that, following our distinction, are to be considered VT. Scanning and rotation studies, the most important contribution to demonstrating the equivalence between imagery and perception, use regular figures that, once shown, have to be imagined, analysed, and transformed by subjects. Whereas in this case we have an almost complete functional analogy between imagery and perception, in the case where the subject must generate an image from LTM, the analogy is only partial because of the greater weight of conceptual elements involved in this performance.

Furthermore, the VT is hardly affected by other information coming from different cognitive processes: actually it is a kind of perceptual by-product and is much less conceptually elaborated than the GI. Perhaps we could say that the VT is above all the result of low-level processes compared with the GI, which is, on the contrary, the result of high-level processes: for this reason the latter seems richer in elements coming from different cognitive processes. Therefore "penetrability" of the two kind of images should be different: to construct an image using data from LTM implies the use of shared, personal, and even autobiographical knowledge and this is not the case for the VT. According to these assumptions it is sensible to suppose also that the modalities of maintenance and loss are different for the VT and the GI. The VT should be maintained and lost like sensorial information, whereas it is likely that GI maintenance and loss are similar to those of elaborated conceptual information. As far as the possibility of interference is concerned, it is mainly the similarity between visual characteristics that could affect the VT more than the GI, whereas other variables should be critical to produce interference in the GI: for example, highly attention-demanding activities, or similarity of the generation processes involved.

Capacity limitations are also different: in one case (VT) they are caused by limits of storage, whereas in the other (GI), limits of active processes, involved in manipulation of stored representation, could intervene in addition to limits of storage. Finally, it is worth noting developmental differences: in our opinion, the visual trace is less affected than the generated image by developmental variations. Therefore, in young children cognitive developmental processes should privilege the VT more than the GI, in consequence of VT's greater automaticity. In contrast, both the relation with categorisation and semantic processes and a greater involvement of attentive resources make the GI more sensitive to cognitive development effects: that is, subject to formal and content transformations characteristic of developmental process and for this reason influenced by age.

STUDIES ON THE DISTINCTION BETWEEN
A VT AND A GI

In this section we will focus on a recent study devoted to exploring some predictions of the differentiation between a visual trace and a generated image by looking for evidence in memory tests concerning characteristics of configurations. As the analysis of characteristics seems to involve specific perceptual processes that are not present in imagery, we focused on memory for characteristics present in sets of simple figures. For example, a figure can be defined by its shape, size, and colour, three basic characteristics, which are strictly interconnected, but which can be separately manipulated. According to the boundary conditions, one characteristic should be made particularly salient in the perceptual field and consequently made more memorable when the visual trace is considered. For example Treisman and Souther (1985) and Treisman (1986) claimed that there are few visual characteristics—such as colour, size, slope, contrast—that are extracted in the first pre-attentive stages of perception and are particularly salient in perceptual results. In a previous study (Giusberti et al., 1992a) we found that this kind of salience does not emerge in the same way in imagery. For this reason we hypothesised that those characteristics could be more memorable in a VT condition than in a GI condition whereas, in other respects, a GI could even be advantaged. If a generated visual image is not affected by the same processes, the principles highlighting some characteristics in a visual trace should not be evident in the image. Our task tested memory for different characteristics based on accuracy of reproduction of correct positioning of an image in drawings made by the subject. We assumed that if a characteristic was lost, or reproduced but in an incorrect position, its memory was weaker than if it was correctly reproduced; in this way memory for one characteristic is assumed to be a measure for its saliency in both conditions.

In the study, two experiments using stimuli varying in shape, size, and colour tested the hypothesis that the characteristics that are more memorable for a visual trace are not necessarily the same as for generated images. A third experiment examined the implications of a distinction between generated images and visual traces. It was assumed that a generated image is more greatly influenced by conceptual information and that a visual trace is more influenced by stimulus sensory properties. A fourth experiment examined how formal properties of the stimulus can vary the memorability of its characteristics. Finally a fifth experiment tested the assumption that development differentially affects visual traces and generated images.

Memory for Characteristics in VT and GI

The first experiment aimed at seeing how a visual trace or a generated image maintained different stimulus characteristics, like shape, size, and colour. Thirty-two subjects were invited either to observe and then remember a series of varying geometrical figures or to generate and then remember an image of them. In order to focus the subjects' attention on the pictorial properties of the stimuli, they were also invited to give vividness ratings for them (and their effective use of imagery was controlled through informal interview). Our hypothesis was that the visual trace (VT) and the generated image (GI) would reveal some differences in the three characteristics we considered. In particular we expected that the characteristics emerging in the first phase of the analysis of sensory information, such as colour, could be advantaged in the VT condition, whereas a characteristic critical for conceptual information, shape, could be advantaged in the GI condition. Further, the presence of a third group of 16 subjects, invited to process verbally rather than use visual imagery in a condition in which stimuli were only described, offered the opportunity of verifying whether the group required to use visual imagery (GI group) under verbal instructions was actually using different processes from the verbal group. If the performance was not the same—that is, lower for the group that did not use mental imagery, then the processes should be functionally different.

The material was made up of six series of 12 stimuli each, balancing complexity and characteristics. Each stimulus was composed of three geometrical figures arranged along a vertical line. Each figure was characterised by a particular shape (triangle, square, circle), colour (blue, red, yellow), and size (small, medium, large). For the visual trace (VT) group, each stimulus, drawn on a sheet of paper, was presented for five seconds.

For the generated image (GI) group, the experimenter invited the subject to image a verbally described picture, mentioning its shape, its size, its colour, and the position of a small circle. At the end of the verbal description of all the three figures of each stimulus, the subject had five seconds to image the overall picture and was then invited to rate its vividness. The procedure from then on was identical to that of the VT group. For the VR group the subjects were first invited to verbally rehearse the description of the figure and, when a stimulus had been presented completely, to rate on a 100-point scale how difficult the task appeared. In order to check for a possible use of imagery, after drawing each figure the subject received a specific request on this subject. In this experiment and in all the other experiments of this study the subjects were always tested individually.

The mean numbers of characteristics remembered by each group are presented in Fig. 4.1. It is immediately evident that the VR group had a lower performance than the other two groups. Therefore we can assume that the GI subjects were effectively using a different process.

An omnibus ANOVA revealed a significant main effect of groups, and a significant interaction between groups and characteristics. Looking at Fig. 4.1 we can see that the characteristics were differently affected by the three conditions with a reverse order in recall. The GI group performed significantly better than the other two groups in memory for shape in the correct position, whereas both the GI and VT groups performed better than the third group for memory of size

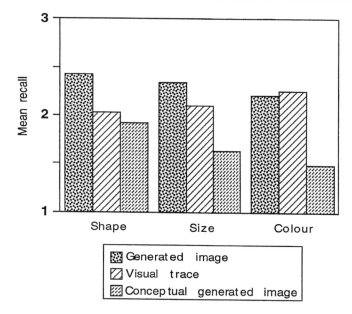

FIG. 4.1. Mean numbers of characteristics that were recalled by a group instructed to generate images, by a visual trace group, and by a group instructed to rehearse the verbal descriptions of the stimuli.

and colour. Shape was significantly better recalled in the GI condition than in the other conditions, suggesting that imagery can privilege shape. This result could be explained with reference to the memory advantages of using two codes (verbal and imaginal) rather than one, but this could not explain why the GI superiority involved the shape but not the other characterisics, and why single visual code produced better memory than a single verbal code.

Furthermore, a different focus on the data could examine difference in characteristics assuming that GI and VT conditions produce a similar overall recall. The GI superiority could be due to the fact that the exposure producing the visual trace was too short to allow consideration of all the characteristics. If, in the comparison between the GI and VT groups, we partial out the overall difference between the groups, we can see that colour can be more relevant than size and shape in the VT, but not in the GI condition. This outcome is coherent with the assumption that a visual trace is affected by visual exposure where colour is a particularly salient characteristic which can then be better maintained. With the particular procedure we adopted, the absence of a reference frame could have reduced the importance of the size characteristic in the VT condition. On the contrary, the saliency of colour for the VT confirmed that colour is particularly critical in early processing of visual stimuli (Treisman, 1986).

A second experiment used the same set of stimuli tested in Experiment 1. However, the test was made more simple in some aspects. Sixteen subjects underwent a VT condition and another sixteen a GI condition.

We found a significant interaction between groups and characteristics (see Fig. 4.2) showing that the VT and the GI conditions produced different effects in memory of the various characteristics. Colour was remembered significantly better in the VT condition than in the GI condition whereas size was better remembered in the GI than in the VT condition. Furthermore, in the VT condition, colour was remembered significantly better than size and shape; on the contrary, in the GI condition size was remembered better than colour.

Altogether the results of the two experiments show that a VT and a GI can be differentiated. The main result is that, within the context of this experiment, a visual trace selectively maintains different characteristics from a geometrical figure and colour is particularly advantaged. This effect is not present for a generated image, where colour is tendentially the most disadvantaged characteristic. This outcome is coherent with our general prediction that visual traces and generated images have different memory implications, and also with our more specific prediction that, in the case of the material used in this experiment, the colour of a visual trace is particularly memorable. The fact that size was particularly well remembered in the GI but not in the VT condition could be due to the role of a reference frame, critical for a VT, but not necessary for a GI.

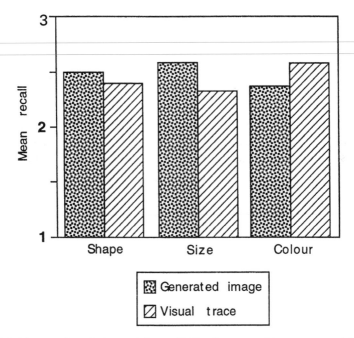

FIG. 4.2. Mean numbers of characteristics recalled by the generated image group and the visual trace group (Experiment 2).

Memory for Characteristics in VT and GI

The results of the first two experiments had suggested that a distinction between VT and GI can be useful. However, the two experiments did not explore the various implications of the distinctions between VT and GI. Three further experiments were devoted to examining some of these implications. In particular we considered the implications related to the difference we had found in memory for colour in the VT and in the GI conditions. In fact, we assumed that a colour superiority in the VT could be eliminated through appropriate manipulations coherent with our theoretical general framework. In one respect, colour should be less critically emergent in a VT if the other stimuli were of similar colour, in the sense of the same hue but different in saturation. On the other hand, colour should be salient and more memorable within a generated image if it were generated in connection with the retrieval of relevant long-term information.

In the third experiment, in order to increase the saliency of the imaged colour, we included a third group (CGI = conceptual generated image) where we added semantic information related to the colour during the instructions given for the image generation task. For example, a green triangle was described as a triangle of grass.

Subjects were 36 university students divided in three groups of 12: a visual trace (VT) group, a generated image (GI) group, and a conceptual generated image (CGI) group.

Part of the material (different colours) was similar to that used in the preceding experiment, based on three figures changing shape, size, colour (RED, YELLOW, and BLUE). A second pool of materials (similar colours) was prepared following the same criteria with the only difference that the three colours used (294 BLUE, 298 AZZURRO [light blue], 290 CELESTE [very light blue], from the Pantone Catalogue by Letraset) were similar in hue but different in saturation. In the Italian language, unlike English, there are three different colour definitions for the three different blue saturations that we used. For the conceptual generated image (CGI) group we also prepared six tables, each of them presenting a large squared surface coloured in one of the six different colours used in the experiment.

For the VT and the GI group the procedure was the same as in the preceding experiment. Subjects of the CGI group were invited to imagine the object colour of the geometrical figure through the name of a previously associated object, e.g. "Image a triangle, large, of grass, with a circle at the bottom" etc.

Data are presented separately for similar (Fig. 4.3) and different colours (Fig. 4.4) and show that, in general, the CGI drew advantage from the reference of colour to an object: this advantage was evident not only for the memory for colours, which was disadvantaged in the preceding experiments in the generated image condition, but also for the other characteristics.

For different colours, the CGI group had a performance significantly higher than both the other groups, and the VT group had a performance higher than the

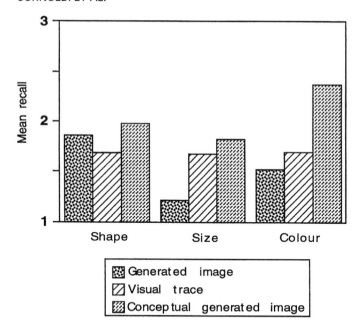

FIG. 4.3. Mean numbers of characteristics recalled by the generated image group, by the visual trace group, and by the conceptual generated image group (stimuli of similar colours).

GI group. When the colours were similar, the CGI group had a performance significantly higher than the other two groups. However, in this case the GI and VT groups did not differ significantly.

The introduction of the semantic reference for colours during the image generation task had the effect of making colour more memorable, but also advantaging the other characteristics. This result is not surprising if we consider the fact that a large square of grass becomes a large square lawn and the semantic reference can also be extended to the other characteristics. Compared to the other experiments, the image generation procedure for all the characteristics was disadvantaged with respect to the visual trace procedure. This result could be due to the fact that variations implying six different colours rather than only three could have particularly overloaded the working memory system involved during the generation of the image. Similarity in colour seemed to especially depress the performance of the visual trace group, as if the colour was no more salient when presented together with similar colours.

The results obtained in the three experiments were related to the specificities of the stimuli we had chosen. In particular, colour could be advantaged against shape, after a visual exposure, because, in the standard procedure, we used three radically different colours and large coloured surfaces (and in Experiment 3 we also had a higher range of variations between six colours). On the contrary, shape

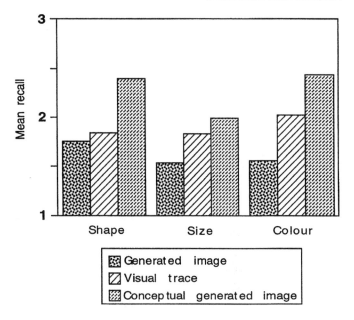

FIG. 4.4. Mean numbers of characteristics recalled by the generated image group, by the visual trace group, and by the conceptual generated image group (stimuli of different colours).

could be disadvantaged by the fact that the shapes were not particularly distinctive because they belonged to the same subsample of the universe of shapes—they were all very simple geometrical forms, a disadvantage that was, however, compensated in the GI condition by the ease with which the name of the shape can be processed and so can help to retrieve the corresponding shape. Also the size characteristic could be influenced by the particular kind of shapes: in fact, geometrical figures can be affected by size more at a representational imaginal level than at a perceptual level where they are often considered for their shape regularity and constancy.

In other words, the relationships in a figure between different characteristics such as shape, size, and colour could be varied according to the boundary conditions, such as, for example, the particular considered shapes. Therefore, in order to explore the generality of the assumption that a visual trace and a generated image are differently affected by characteristics and the implications of different stimuli we ran a further experiment where the preceding shapes were substituted by three other shapes ($, %, ≠) with different peculiarities. These shapes were chosen because they were different in many respects from the preceding ones. In fact, they belonged to partially different samples of shapes, were presumably less overlearned, and presented a smaller quantity of internal area to be filled by a colour, possibly making the colour characteristic less evident in the perceptual condition. In order to make the figures' dimensions more easily detectable we drew a size frame around each of them: namely an outline square with sides of 6.5cm. In this way subjects could also have the same reference schema. In fact, under these conditions not only colour, but also size was a salient perceptual stimulus characteristics. Furthermore, we made the procedure of the VT group more similar to that of the other group, by sequentially presenting the three figures forming one stimulus.

Thirty-two young adults were randomly assigned to a visual trace (VT) and to a generated image (GI) group.

Figure 4.5 presents the mean numbers of characteristics remembered for each stimulus by the two groups. We found a significant difference between groups, and a significant interaction between groups and characteristics. In contrast to the preceding experiments the slight modifications introduced in this experiment were also able to produce a visual trace advantage over the generated image condition. Simple effect analysis revealed that this difference was significant for size, and for colour, but not for the shape, confirming that different contexts have specific effects on GI and VT. In particular, under some conditions, size can also be a characteristic privileged in the VT condition.

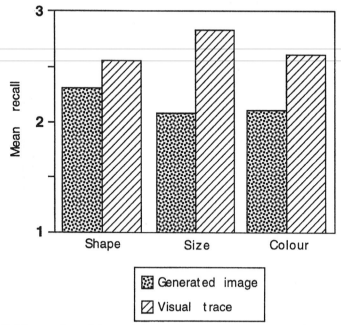

FIG. 4.5. Mean numbers of characteristics recalled by the generated image group and the visual trace group (Experiment 4).

VT and GI: Passive and Active Working Memory Components

Finally, a fifth experiment, using the same methodology as our first experiment, tested another prediction of our frameworks. It has been hypothesised (Cornoldi et al., 1995b) that developmental differences more directly affect active highly demanding visuo-spatial working memory components than passive storage visuo-spatial working memory components. As the visual trace is directly stored in the passive component it should not be particularly related to development. On the contrary, the image generation task largely depends on active components related to age and thus should be affected by an age variation.

Subjects were 96 children belonging to three different age-groups of 32. The three groups were: third-graders (mean age approximately 8 years and 6 months), fifth-graders (mean age approximately 10 years and 6 months), seventh-graders (mean age approximately 12 years and 6 months). Each age-group was then divided into two groups according to the experimental condition (following the procedure of the first experiment): visual trace (VT) and generated image (GI).

The mean numbers of characteristics correctly remembered by the three groups in the two conditions (Fig. 4.6) were computed. We found significant

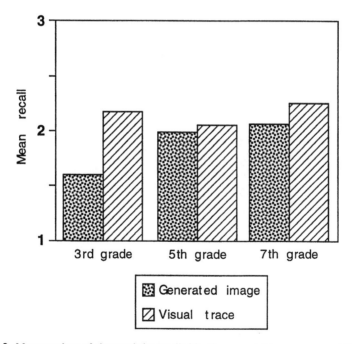

FIG. 4.6. Mean numbers of characteristics recalled by the generated image group and the visual trace group of different ages (Experiment 5) (mean values for each category).

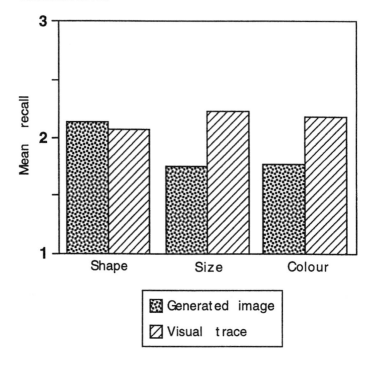

FIG. 4.7. Mean numbers of different characteristics recalled by the generated image group and the visual trace group (Experiment 5).

main effects of age, condition (VT vs GI), and characteristics. Furthermore, both interactions of condition with age and characteristics were significant. The mean numbers of characteristics remembered for each figure by the three groups are presented in Fig. 4.6, showing that performance increased with age and that the visual trace condition produced a higher performance; however, this difference was significant only in the younger children's group.

The mean numbers of characteristics remembered in each condition are presented in Fig. 4.7, showing that the VT groups were better than the GI groups both in memory for colour and size.

CONCLUSIONS

On the basis of the experiments in the study comparing visual traces and generated images presented here, we are able to confirm that as far as the considered characteristics are concerned, they are elaborated in a different way during the two kinds of task: their recall is different according to whether they are attributed to a VT or to a GI. The characteristics and their weight difference in the recall of two different kinds of representation images is not a permanent or stable element and, for this reason, it is defined by particular boundary conditions. Our results show that the different characteristics' weight varies according to the context within which the VT and the GI are utilised. In the first two experiments perceptual display elicited a better recall of colour while the opposite trend was true for the other two characteristics. In the third experiment the advantage of colour was lost as, in contrast to the first experiment, similarly coloured figures were included in the same stimulus: this effect could be due to the sensorial properties of the visual trace, so that different hues "remain" while similar colours lose saliency and therefore depress the performance of the visual trace group. In the same way the visual image disadvantage in the recall of colour could be due to the remote possibility that subjects had to refer to their semantic knowledge about colours: if they can describe them by reference to known objects, in other words if they can use a categorical elaboration of the colour, the disadvantage is lost. These results suggest that different cognitive mechanisms underlying a visual trace and a generated image are related to the processes that led to the formation of the representation: in one case inherent in sensorial stimulation, in the other based on long-term memory information.

The last experiment added further evidence concerning the distinction between a VT and a GI. It was assumed that the system involved in the use of visual traces is a more simple system, more well developed in younger children than the system used for generating images. In fact, the same task that produced a GI advantage in adults reversed the effect in children and this was particularly evident for the youngest group. The VT advantage in children was evident for colour, confirming the visual salience of this characteristic, but was also extended to size, another characteristic that under some conditions appears more critical after a visual exposure than after the imagery generation process. On the contrary, the overall pattern of results of the study suggests that shape is a central characteristic of a generated image. However, it must be noted that the constraints of the image generation task (where the shape must be indicated before the other characteristics) do not allow evaluation of an eventual effect of presentation order on the recall of shape.

To summarise, our results confirm the hypothesis that mental imagery is a complex process, originating from long-term memory knowledge, which cannot be treated as a simple analogical by-product of visual perception. In particular, a visual trace is different from a generated image: some of the characteristics we have considered were better recalled in the VT group, whereas others were better recalled in the GI group. Nevertheless it is as important to note that these characteristics are not firmly charged to one kind of image or the other: it is impossible to identify some of them that are definitively typical in the VT or in the GI, independently of the context. On the contrary, the peculiarity of these two different kinds of mental representations depends on a balance of circumstances that produces the advantage, in recall, for one characteristic or the other. This balance of circumstances, far from being casual, is strictly linked to our basic theoretical hypothesis that assumes the existence of reconstructive multisource processes in image generation and then proposes different definitions for the VT and the GI.

REFERENCES

Bahrick, H., Bahrick, P.O., & Wittlinger, R.P. (1975). Fifty years of memory for names and faces: A cross-sectional approach. *Journal of Experimental Psychology: General, 104*, 54–75.

Brooks, L.R. (1968). Spatial and verbal components of the act of recall. *Canadian Journal of Psychology, 22*, 349–368.

Carpenter, P., & Eisenberg, P. (1978). Mental rotation and the frame of reference in blind and sighted individuals. *Perception and Psychophysics, 23*, 117–124.

Chambers, D., & Reisberg, D. (1985). Can mental images be ambiguous? *Journal of Experimental Psychology: Human Perception and Performance, 11*, 317–328.

Cornoldi, C. (1995). Imagery and meta-imagery in the VVIQ. *Journal of Mental Imagery, 19*, 131–136.

Cornoldi, C., Calore, D., & Pra Baldi, A. (1979). Imagery ratings and free recall on blind and normal subjects. *Perceptual and Motor Skills, 48*, 627–639.

Cornoldi, C., Cortesi, A., & Preti, D. (1991a). Individual differences in the capacity limitations of visuospatial short-term memory: Research on sighted and totally congenitally blind people, *Memory and Cognition, 19*, 459–468.

Cornoldi, C., De Beni, R., Giusberti, F., Marucci, F., Massironi, M., & Mazzoni, G. (1991b). The study of vividness of images. In R.H. Logie & M. Denis (Eds), *Mental images in human cognition* (pp. 305–312). Amsterdam: Elsevier.

Cornoldi, C., De Beni, R., & Pra Baldi, A. (1989a). Generation and retrieval of general, specific and autobiographical images representing concrete nouns. *Acta Psychologica, 72*, 25–39.

Cornoldi, C., De Beni, R., Roncari, S., & Romano, S. (1989b). The effects of imagery instructions on total congenital blind recall. *European Journal of Cognitive Psychology, 1*, 321–331.

Cornoldi, C., Logie, R., Brandimonte, M.A., Kauffman, G., & Reisberg, D. (1995a). *Stretching the imagination*. New York: Oxford University Press.

Cornoldi, C., Tressoldi, P.E., & Dalla Vecchia, F. (1995b). Visuo-spatial working memory in low visual spatial abilities children. *Journal of Child Psychology and Child Psychiatry and Allied Disciplines, 36*, 1053–1064.

De Beni, R., & Cornoldi, C. (1988a). Imagery limitations of total congenital blind imagery. *Journal of Experimental Psychology, 14(4)*, 650–655.

De Beni, R., & Cornoldi, C. (1988b). Weaknesses of imagery without visual experience: The case of the total congenital blind using imaginal mnemonics. In M. Denis, J. Engelkamp, & J.T.E. Richardson (Eds.), *Cognitive and neuropsychological approaches to mental imagery* (pp. 393–401). Amsterdam: M. Nijhoff.

De Beni R., Moè A., & Cornoldi, C. (in press). The loci method with prose and selective interference theory. *Journal of Psychology*.

De Beni, R., & Pazzaglia, F. (1995). Memory for different kinds of mental images: Role of contextual and autobiographic variables. *Neuropsychologia, 33(11)*, 1359–1371.

Farah, M.J. (1985). Psychophysical evidence for a shared representational medium for mental images and percepts. *Journal of Experimental Psychology: General, 114*, 91–103.

Finke, R.A. (1985). Theories relating mental imagery to perception. *Psychological Bulletin, 98*, 236–259.

Finke, R.A. (1989). *Principles of mental imagery*. Cambridge, MA: MIT Press.

Finke, R.A., & Schmidt, M.J. (1977). Orientation-specific colour after-effects following imagination. *Journal of Experimental Psychology: Human Perception and Performance, 3,* 599–606.

Giusberti, F., Cornoldi, C., De Beni, R., & Massironi, M. (1992a). Differences in vividness ratings of perceived and imagined patterns. *British Journal of Psychology, 83,* 533–547.

Giusberti, F., Cornoldi, C., De Beni, R., & Massironi, M. (1992b). *A visual memory trace is not a visual image.* Paper presented at the FEWIC, Fourth European Workshop on Imagery and Cognition, Universidad de la Laguna, Tenerife, December.

Hitch, G., Brandimonte, M.A., & Walker, P. (1995). Two types of representation in visual memory: Evidence from the effects of stimulus contrast of image combination. *Memory and Cognition, 23,* 147–154.

Intons-Peterson, M.J., & McDaniel, M.A. (1990). Symmetries and asymmetries between imagery and perception. In C. Cornoldi & M.A. McDaniel (Eds.) *Imagery and cognition.* New York: Springer Verlag.

Intraub, H., & Hoffman, J.E. (1992). Reading and visual memory. Remembering scenes that were never seen. *American Journal of Psychology, 105,* 101–114.

Julesz, B. (1975). Experiments in the visual perception of texture. *Scientific American, 232,* 34–43.

Kaufman, J.H., May, J.G., & Kunen, S. (1981). Interocular transfer of orientation-contingent color aftereffects with external and internal adaptation. *Perception and Psychophysics, 30,* 547–551.

Kosslyn, S.M. (1980). *Image and mind.* Cambridge, MA: Harvard University Press.

Kosslyn, S.M. (1994). *Image and brain.* Cambridge, MA: Bradford.

Mandler, G.M., & Ritchey, G.H. (1977). Long-term memory for pictures. *Journal of Experimental Psychology: Human Learning and Memory, 3,* 386–396.

Marks, D.F. (1972). Individual differences in the vividness of visual imagery and their effect on function. In P.W. Sheehan (Ed.), *The function and nature of imagery* (pp.83–108). New York: Academic Press.

Marks, D.F. (1983). Mental imagery and consciousness: A theoretical review. In A. Sheikh (Ed.), *Imagery, current theory, research and application.* New York: Wiley.

McCollough, C. (1965). Colour adaptation of edge-detectors in the human visual system. *Science, 149,* 1115–1116.

Mosconi, G.E., & D'Urso, V. (Eds.) (1973). Il farsi e il disfarsi del problema. In *La soluzione di problemi.*

Norman, D., Rumelhart, D.E., & Group, T.L.R. (1975). *Explorations in cognition.* San Francisco: Freeman.

Novick, R.L. (1988). Analogical transfer, problem similarity, and expertise. *Journal of Experimental Psychology: Learning, Memory and Cognition, 14,* 510–520.

Paivio, A. (1971). *Imagery and verbal processes.* New York: Holt, Reinhart & Winston.

Perky, C.M. (1910). An experimental study of imagination. *American Journal of Psychology, 21,* 422–452.

Politzer, G. (1990). Raisonnements formels et raisonnements en situation. In J.F. Richard, C. Bonnet, & R. Ghiglione (Eds.), *Traité de psychologie cognitive.* Montrouge: Dunod.

Reed, S.K. (1988). *Cognition: Theory and applications.* Pacific Grove, CA: Brooks/Cole Publishing Company.

Reisberg, D. (1997). *Cognition. Exploring the science of the mind.* New York: Norton & Company.

Rhodes, G., & O'Leary, A. (1985). Imagery effects on early visual processing. *Perception and Psychophysics, 37,* 382–388.

Rocchi, P., Cornoldi, C., & Massironi, M. (1992). Differenze tra matrici di lettere percepite e immaginate. In L. Vecchio (Ed.), *Le immagini mentali.* Firenze: La Nuova Italia.

Segal, S.J. (1972). Assimilation of a stimulus in the construction of an image: The Perky effect revisited. In P.W. Sheehan (Ed.), *The function and nature of imagery.* New York: Academic Press.

Shepard, R.N., & Metzler, J. (1971). Mental rotation of three-dimensional objects. *Science, 171,* 701–703.

Treisman, A. (1986). Properties, parts and objects. In K. Boff, L. Kaufmann, & J. Thomas, (Eds.), *Handbook of perception and performance, Vol.2.* New York: Wiley & Sons.

Treisman, A., & Souther, J. (1985). Search asymmetry: A diagnostic for preattentive processing of separable features. *Journal of Experimental Psychology: General, 114,* 310.

Wertheimer, M. (1965). *Il pensiero produttivo* (trans.) [Productive thinking]. Florence: Giunti-Barbera. (Original work published in 1945).

Zimler, J., & Keenan, J.M. (1983). Imagery in the congenitally blind: How visual are visual images? *Journal of Experimental Psychology: Learning, Memory and Cognition, 9,* 269–282.

5 Age-related Deficits in Memory: Theory and Application

Larry L. Jacoby and Janine F. Hay
McMaster University, Ontario, Canada

Over the last few years there has been a proliferation of demonstrations that memory can affect performance in the absence of awareness of the past. Even amnesiacs who, by definition, cannot remember an earlier presentation of a word when given a test of recognition memory or recall (direct tests), show evidence of memory by using a word more often as a completion for a word stem or word fragment (indirect tests) than they would had the word not been presented earlier (for a review, see Moscovitch, Vriezen, & Gottstein, 1993). Dissociations between performance on these two types of test are also shown by people with normal memory functioning (e.g. Roediger & McDermott, 1993).

Findings of dissociations are important for applied purposes as well as for theorising about memory. Much of our recent research has been aimed at investigating age-related deficits in memory. We believe the distinction between automatic and consciously controlled influences of memory is important for understanding memory dissociations and is critical to the assessment and treatment of memory deficits. Failure to distinguish between these different bases of responding can create interpretation difficulties because there is evidence that elderly adults possess preserved automatic influences of memory in the presence of significant recollection deficits (see Jacoby, Jennings, & Hay, 1996). Our goals have been to devise better methods for diagnosing such deficits along with treatment programmes to remedy or diminish age-related differences.

Automatic processing has been described as a fast, unaware process that is under the control of stimuli rather than intention (e.g. Hasher & Zacks, 1979; Posner & Snyder, 1975; Schneider & Shiffrin, 1977) whereas consciously controlled memory is aware and intentional (Jacoby, 1991; Klatzky, 1984; Logan, 1989). Indirect tests might be more reliant on automatic forms of processing than are direct tests of memory. However, equating tasks with underlying processes as done by the direct/indirect test distinction can be problematic because consciously controlled, intentional processes (recollection) might contaminate performance on indirect tests (Reingold & Merikle, 1990; Toth, Reingold, & Jacoby, 1994) and, less obviously, automatic influences (familiarity) might contaminate performance on direct tests (Jacoby, Toth, & Yonelinas, 1993). More important, the indirect/direct test distinction does not provide a means of measuring the separate contributions of automatic and consciously controlled processing when the two types of processing both contribute to performance.

There is a growing consensus that it is important to separate the contributions of processes within a task; however, there is still disagreement about how this should be done. As will be described later, our process-dissociation procedure is based on the assumption that automatic and consciously controlled processes serve as *independent* bases for responding. In contrast, Gardiner and his colleagues (Gardiner, 1988; Gardiner & Java, 1991; Gardiner & Parkin, 1990) have used a Remember/Know procedure to reveal differences in the phenomenology that accompanies memory use, and have been critical of our independence assumption, as others have been (e.g. Curran & Hintzman, 1995; Joordens & Merikle, 1993). Later, we address the question of independence of processes along with the relation between the Remember/Know and process-dissociation procedures. We emphasise similarities between results from the two procedures because convergence in results is mutually supportive of the validity of the procedures.

There is good reason to search for support. Both the Remember/Know and process-dissociation procedures have been controversial and some critics have questioned the utility of postulating a dual-process model of memory. We begin by describing experiments that placed automatic and consciously controlled processing in opposition so as to reveal deficits in recollection in combination with preserved automatic influences of memory. The "opposition" procedures used in those experiments provide results that show the necessity of distinguishing between different uses of memory and highlight the importance of doing so for purposes of diagnosis and treatment of memory disorders.

PROCESSES IN OPPOSITION: IRONIC EFFECTS OF MEMORY

Our "false fame" experiments (Jacoby, Kelley, Brown, & Jasechko, 1989; Jacoby, Woloshyn, & Kelley, 1989) illustrate the use of opposition procedures to infer recollection deficits through the errors that people commit. In these experiments, automatic influences of memory (familiarity) were placed in opposition to recollection. Participants read a list of nonfamous names followed by a fame-judgement test consisting of old nonfamous names mixed with new famous and new nonfamous names. At test, participants were instructed to identify famous names and were told if they could remember a name from the earlier presentation list, then they could be certain that the name was nonfamous. However, the prior presentation of nonfamous names increased their familiarity, making it more likely that the nonfamous names would later be mistakenly identified as being famous. If participants could recollect reading the name earlier in the experimental setting, then any automatic influence of familiarity would be opposed, allowing them to be certain that the name was nonfamous.

A goal of our false fame experiments was to find manipulations that reduce the probability of recollection and, thereby, leave automatic influences of memory unopposed. For example, results revealed a "false fame" effect after nonfamous names were read under conditions of divided attention by showing that old nonfamous names were *more* likely to be mistakenly called famous than were new nonfamous names. In contrast, when participants gave full attention to the reading of nonfamous names, the results were the opposite—old nonfamous names were *less* likely to be called famous than were new nonfamous names. After full attention to reading nonfamous names, participants were able to escape misleading effects of automatic influences of memory by recollecting the earlier reading of the names. However, when recollection was reduced by dividing attention at study or test, or by extending the retention interval, then the false fame effect was observed.

Because of a deficit in their ability to recollect, those suffering a memory impairment might show a false fame effect even after full attention to reading names. Indeed, elderly adults do show a pronounced false fame effect (Bartlett, Strater, & Fulton, 1991; Dywan & Jacoby, 1990; Jennings & Jacoby, 1993), as do amnesiacs (Cermak, Verfaellie, Butler, & Jacoby, 1993; Squire & McKee, 1992) and patients who have sustained a closed-head injury (Dywan, Segalowitz, Henderson, & Jacoby, 1993). We have made use of such misleading effects of automatic influences of memory to diagnose age-related deficits in recollection.

We refer to the false fame effect and to other misleading effects of repetition as "ironic effects" to highlight their similarity to the ironic effects described by Wegner (1994). Wegner has shown that attempts to avoid mental states can have the ironic effect of increasing the probability of their occurrence. In all these cases, the result is a strengthened automatic influence which can produce an outcome opposite to that which is desired if left unopposed by cognitive control.

Two Effects of Repetition

A friend whose mother is suffering symptoms of Alzheimer's disease tells the story of taking her mother to visit a nursing home, preliminary to her mother moving there. During an orientation meeting at the nursing home, the rules and regulations were explained, one of which regarded the dining room. The dining room was described as similar to a fine restaurant, except that tipping was not required. The absence of tipping was a central theme in the orientation lecture, mentioned frequently to emphasise the quality of care along with the advantages of having paid in advance. At the end of the meeting, the friend's mother was asked whether she had any questions. She replied that she only had one question: "Should I tip?"

Similar to that unwanted effect of repetition, repeated asking of questions is one of the most striking and frustrating symptoms of Alzheimer's disease (AD). Earlier asking of a question seems to "strengthen" and increase the probability of later asking the same question for the AD patient, whereas those with normally functioning memory would not repeat the question because of the ability to recollect asking it earlier, as well as the ability to recollect the answer. Repetition may well have two effects, serving both to increase the strength of questioning, an automatic influence, and to increase the probability of recollecting the earlier asking. Because of a deficit in recollection, the AD patient is left only with the increase in strength and so repeatedly asks the same question. The result is similar to the false fame effect in showing automatic influences of memory that are unopposed by recollection.

An opposition procedure was used to examine age-related differences in memory and to show that repetition does have two effects (Jacoby, submitted). Elderly participants were community-dwelling and aged 60 years and older, whereas young participants were volunteers from an Introductory Psychology course. Young and elderly adults read a list of words, with each word being read either one, two, or three times. Next, they listened to a list of words that they were told to remember for a later test. At test, participants were instructed to identify words that they had *heard* and were warned that the test list would also include words that they had read. They were further told that the earlier-read words were to be excluded because none of those words was in the list of words that they heard. Repeatedly reading a word was expected to increase its familiarity and consequently, participants might misattribute the word's familiarity to its having been heard. However, recollection of having read the word should oppose its familiarity, allowing the word to be correctly excluded, similar to the logic used in the fame experiments.

Due to their deficits in recollection, the performance of elderly participants revealed the strengthening effect of repetition. For elderly participants, repeatedly reading a word *increased* the probability of mistakenly accepting that word as one that had been heard (Table 5.1). The strengthening effect of repetition, unopposed by recollection, is the same as that responsible for AD patients' repeated asking of questions. Younger participants, in contrast, were better able to use recollection to oppose familiarity. For younger participants, repeatedly reading a word made it more likely that they would later recollect that the word had been read, allowing them to be certain it had not been heard. For them, repeated reading of a word *decreased* the probability of mistakenly accepting the word as one that had been heard.

However, under some conditions, young participants produced a pattern of results that was the same as that produced by the elderly participants. When forced to respond rapidly, young participants showed that repeatedly reading a word made it more likely that the word would later be mistakenly accepted as having been heard (Table 5.1). In the rapid responding condition, a test word was exposed for 750ms and participants were required to respond during that interval. In contrast, for the condition that required slower responding, a word was exposed for 1250ms before participants were allowed to respond and then they too were required to respond within a 750ms interval. Just as in the fame experiments, we found that dividing attention while presenting the words to be read also led to a lower probability of later recollection, and produced the pattern for young participants whereby repeatedly reading a word made it more likely that the word was later misclassified as earlier-heard.

The effect of shortening the response deadline for younger participants suggests that the problem for elderly participants may have been that they simply did not have enough time to engage in recollection. The use of recollection is generally slower and more effortful than the use of familiarity to make decisions. As suggested by general slowing hypotheses (e.g Salthouse, 1994), elderly participants might require more processing time than younger participants. However, allowing elderly participants a greater amount of time to respond was not sufficient to eliminate the ironic effect of repetition. Elderly participants given extra time were told to respond "as soon as possible" rather than being required to respond within the 750ms response interval. Even when allowed

TABLE 5.1
Probability of Accepting Items as Heard

| | False Alarms | | | | Hits |
| | Repetitions | | | | |
Condition	1×	2×	3×	New	Heard
Young–Long (1250/750)	.32	.28	.20	.18	.56
Young–Short (750)	.24	.35	.38	.16	.37
Elderly–Long (1250/750)	.27	.34	.38	.13	.35
Elderly–Extra long (1250/ASAP)	.35	.42	.44	.14	.52

more time, repeated reading of a word still increased the probability of its being mistakenly categorised as a heard word. From these results, we suggest the ironic repetition effect found for the elderly reflects an age-related deficit in recollection rather than a general slowing of processes.

The retention test in these experiments incorporated a standard test of recognition memory by including words that were earlier-heard to which participants should respond "yes". Also included in the test list were new words to which participants should respond "no". Performance on new test words can be used to detect any difference between young and elderly participants in the criterion used for responding "yes". Increasing the amount of time allowed for responding resulted in elderly participants correctly accepting words that were earlier-heard with a probability that was nearly the same as that for younger participants who were required to respond at a somewhat faster rate. The probability of false recognition of new words was slightly less for elderly than for younger participants. Thus, as measured by this standard test of recognition memory, performance of the elderly participants who were given extra time to respond did not differ from that of the younger participants.

The opposition procedure, implemented by having participants respond "no" to earlier-read words if they could recollect having read them, was a more sensitive measure of age-related differences in memory than was the standard test of recognition memory just described. Tests of recognition memory sometimes show nonsignificant age differences in performance (e.g. Craik & McDowd, 1987; Dywan & Jacoby, 1990; Rabinowitz, 1984). In our study, allowing elderly participants more time to respond eliminated age differences on the standard test of recognition; however, the elderly still made many more errors on words that were earlier-read than did younger participants. Why was the opposition procedure a more sensitive measure of memory deficits? In the opposition paradigm, familiarity leads to errors. In contrast, familiarity is a basis for correct responding on standard tests of recognition memory, producing effects that are the same as those produced by recollection (e.g. Jacoby & Dallas, 1981; Mandler, 1980). Consequently, for recognition-memory performance, correct responding due to familiarity may mask a deficit in recollection (e.g. Jacoby et al., 1993). By placing automatic and consciously controlled processes in opposition, errors in performance allow us to examine age-related declines in recollection that cannot be offset by relying on familiarity.

Jennings and Jacoby (1997) investigated age-related declines in memory by using an opposition procedure meant to mimic the repeated telling of a story. Repeatedly telling a story to the same audience can be a sign of automatic influences of memory that are not successfully opposed by recollection. Unwanted repetition provides clear evidence of a failure in recollection and so can be used to measure severity of memory deficits. For example, one would be much more concerned if an elderly relative repeated a story immediately after telling it than if he or she repeated it a week later. Results of experiments by

Jennings and Jacoby showed that elderly participants were likely to make an error akin to the repeated telling of a story after a much shorter delay than were younger participants. As in the experiment just described, the opposition procedure used by Jennings and Jacoby provided a more sensitive measure of age-related decline in memory than did a standard test of recognition memory. Such findings again highlight the utility of an opposition procedure as an effective diagnostic tool.

Two Effects of Context: Environmental Support

Reinstating study context can also produce an ironic effect of memory. Note that in the "tipping" example, the question about tipping was asked in the same context and of the same person who had earlier said that tipping was not allowed. The error is striking because one might expect the context and person to provide very powerful cues for recollection. However, reinstating context has two effects just as does repetition: it produces automatic influences of memory and it enhances recollection.

In an experiment similar to the one described earlier, words were read at study paired with context words. Re-presenting the context words at test increased the probability of the word mistakenly being accepted as having been heard compared to when the context word was not presented. This result emerged for both elderly participants and young participants forced to respond rapidly. When given more time to respond, young participants showed an opposite effect of reinstating context: the context word increased the likelihood that they could recollect the earlier-read words, and therefore allowed them to reject read words as heard words. Manipulating full versus divided attention during study along with reinstatement of associative context produces a similar pattern of results in cued-recall performance. Reinstating associative context *decreases* the probability of excluding read words after divided attention during study but has the opposite effect after full attention during study (Jacoby, 1994, 1996).

The finding of two effects of reinstating context is important for the possibility of using environmental support to remediate age-related differences in memory. Craik (1983, 1986) proposed an environmental support hypothesis to account for variations across situations in the magnitude of age-related differences in memory performance. He suggested that age-related differences are partially due to deficiencies in self-initiated processing that can be compensated for by increasing environmental support at the time of test. Reinstating associative context is an example of providing environmental support. The prediction is that age-related differences in memory performance should decrease as the amount of environmental support is increased. Craik and Jennings (1992) reviewed the relevant literature and concluded that the results of some experiments agree with the environmental support hypothesis, whereas results of other studies conflict with the hypothesis by showing that age-related differences are constant across different levels of environmental support or even larger when the amount of environmental support is increased. Such mixed results are understandable if providing environmental support has separate effects on recollection and automatic influences of memory. The aged may suffer a deficit in self-initiated processing and, consequently, show smaller effects of environmental support (e.g. associative context) on recollection. That deficit in recollection leaves the elderly open to ironic effects of memory produced by the automatic influences of increasing environmental support.

Age differences in repetition errors observed using opposition procedures are closely related to deficits in source or context memory (for reviews, see Johnson, Lindsay, & Hashtroudi, 1993; Spencer & Raz, 1995). However, opposition paradigms differ in an important way from the form of tests traditionally used to measure memory for source. Standard tests of source memory explicitly instruct participants to report the source of information, rather than examine the monitoring of source as part of some ongoing task as done by opposition paradigms. To appreciate the difference, consider the discrepancy between the task of avoiding repeatedly telling a story while engaging in conversation and the task of listing all the people to whom one has told the story. This difference and its importance is illustrated by results from a fame study by Multhaup (1995).

Multhaup did not find a "false fame" effect with older adults when participants were explicitly asked to specify whether a test name was one they had read earlier, one that was actually famous, or one that was new. Increasing the structure or support of a task by directly asking participants about source benefits older adults' performance by allowing them to avoid errors produced by automatic influences of memory. However, increased structure also limits the role of self-initiated processing. An inability to monitor in unstructured situations may be a critical aspect of memory problems experienced by older adults. Suggestions that age-related differences in memory performance reflect a decline in frontal-lobe functioning (e.g. Parkin, in press; West, 1996) are consistent with this possibility.

Remembering, Knowing, and Excluding

The experiments just described used opposition procedures to show errors produced by automatic influences of memory unaccompanied by recollection. Familiarity without recollection is also central to the Remember/Know procedure. That procedure, introduced by Tulving (1985), asks participants to report on the subjective experience of memory. As an example, after judging a word on a test of recognition memory as being "old", participants are required to report whether they "remember" or only "know" that the word was studied earlier. A "remember" response is to be made only when participants are able to recollect the details of the study presentation of a word, such as its appearance or associations that came to mind during its presentation. Participants are to say "know" if the word is so familiar that they are certain the word was studied but they are unable to recollect any details of its prior presentation.

Gardiner and his associates (e.g. Gardiner, 1988; Gardiner & Java, 1991; Gardiner & Parkin, 1990) as well as others (e.g. Conway & Dewhurst, 1995; Rajaram, 1993) have shown that a number of variables produce dissociations between "remember" and "know" responses. Our opposition experiments described earlier demonstrated that elderly participants suffer a deficit in recollection, as do young participants responding under a deadline or under conditions of divided attention. Because "remember" responses necessitate recollecting specific information about an item, it is not surprising that parallel effects on the probability of a "remember" response have been found. That is, it has been demonstrated that elderly participants are less likely to "remember" a word they called old in a test of recognition memory or gave as a correct response in a test of cued recall than are younger participants (Mäntylä, 1993; Parkin & Walter, 1992). The correspondence in definitions and results using these different procedures encourages the identification of "remember" responses with recollection.

Although "remember" responses may closely map onto recollection, there are problems for identifying familiarity with the probability of a "know" response. Such problems arise because manipulations that would be expected to influence familiarity have been shown to leave "know" responses invariant. For example, repetition and factors such as similarity are usually treated as fundamental to familiarity yet Gardiner, Kaminska, Dixon, and Java (1996) found repetition of Polish melodies increased both "remember" and "know" responses, but repetition of obscure classical melodies increased only "remember" responses, leaving "know" responses unchanged. It seems counter-intuitive that the familiarity of obscure classical melodies is not influenced by repetition, especially when Polish melodies are affected by the same manipulation. These findings suggest that it may be very problematic to equate "know" responses with familiarity. We will now describe a refinement of the Remember/Know procedure in which we make very different assumptions about the nature of the underlying relationship between recollection and familiarity.

We examined the effects of repetition in an experiment using a procedure similar to that described in conjunction with the "tipping" example. Words were presented one, two, or three times for study and then intermixed with new words for a test of recognition memory. Participants were required to respond "remember" or "know" to recognised items. Results (see Table 5.2) showed that the probability of a "remember" response increased with number of repetitions but "know" responses were unchanged. The pattern of results is the same as found by Gardiner et al. (1996) for obscure classical melodies.

One could claim that common words are similar to obscure classical melodies in that neither becomes more familiar with repetition. However, interpretation of the results depends on the assumption adopted regarding the relationship

TABLE 5.2
Probability of Responding "Remember",
"Know", and Estimates of Familiarity
across Repetitions

Response	Repetitions		
	1×	2×	3×
"Remember"	.40	.52	.59
"Know"	.35	.36	.35
Familiarity	.58	.74	.83

Estimates of familiarity, based on an independence assumption,
were computed as: "Know"/(1–"Remember")

between recollection and familiarity. If the two bases for responding are assumed to be independent, familiarity should be computed as the probability of a "know" response conditionalised on the opportunity for such a response. Specifically, familiarity should be calculated as the probability of a "know" response divided by 1 minus the probability of a "remember" response [familiarity = "know"/(1– "remember")]. As shown in the bottom row of Table 5.2, familiarity computed in this way increases with the number of repetitions, as does recollection, indexed by the probability of a "remember" response. In contrast, Gardiner and other investigators analyse the straight proportion of "know" responses as a measure of familiarity. That calculation implicitly assumes an exclusivity relation between the process that gives rise to instances of "remember' and the process that gives rise to instances of "know". If a variable powerfully increases the likelihood of "remembering", there is little opportunity for a person to express familiarity in the absence of remembering. Consequently, the probability of "knowing" is highly constrained by the probability of "remembering".

The conclusion that both familiarity and recollection increase with repetition is consistent with results of experiments that used the opposition procedure. In contrast, identifying familiarity with the probability of a "know" response, as done using the exclusivity assumption, would not allow one to explain the ironic effects described earlier. Yonelinas and Jacoby (1995) described other cases in which apparent anomalies are resolved by combining the Remember/Know procedure with the assumption that recollection and familiarity serve as independent bases for responding. For example, increasing visual similarity between a study and a test item increases familiarity as computed using the independence assumption but not when the straight proportion of "know" responses is analysed.

Donaldson and his colleagues (Donaldson, 1996; Donaldson, MacKenzie, & Underhill, 1996) have noted that dissociations between "remember" and "know" responses do not require that two processes be involved. They use signal-detection theory to show that apparent dissociations might simply reflect differences in criteria for responding applied to a single memory process—participants might use a higher criterion for "remember" responses than for "know" responses. In contrast, findings from the use of opposition procedures provide stronger evidence for dual processes. For example, repeatedly reading a word either increases or decreases the probability of the word later being mistakenly accepted as earlier-heard, depending on factors such as the age of participants and the required speed of responding. Results such as these are easily understood by distinguishing between recollection and familiarity, but it is not obvious how they can be explained by postulating a single process even if multiple criteria are allowed.

THE PROCESS-DISSOCIATION PROCEDURE

Results from experiments using opposition procedures are sufficient to show the necessity of adopting a dual-process model, and to reveal age-related deficits in recollection. However, the results do not allow one to measure the severity of such deficits. To produce what we call an exclusion error (i.e. accepting an earlier-read word as heard), automatic influences must be sufficiently strong to produce a response *and* recollection must fail. Suppose that elderly participants suffer diminished automatic influences of memory as well as a deficit in recollection. If this is the case, then the difference in exclusion performance between young and elderly would be diminished. Errors in exclusion performance would *underestimate* the difference in recollection because although elderly participants would more often be unable to recollect, they would also be less likely than young adults to make a familiarity-based error when recollection failed. To distinguish between these possibilities one needs some means of separating the contributions of automatic and consciously controlled uses of memory. We now describe the process-dissociation procedure which was designed to accomplish that goal and then discuss its relation to the Remember/Know procedure.

The process-dissociation procedure (Jacoby, 1991) defines conscious control as the difference in performance between conditions where one is trying to, versus trying not to, do something. In the exclusion procedure outlined earlier, one can try not to call a name famous when one can remember that it was presented in a list of nonfamous names. We can also arrange an inclusion test condition, where one tries to call a name famous when one can consciously recollect that it was on the study list (by telling participants that all the names were famous), or when it simply seems famous. If we assume that conscious recollection and the familiarity that can be misattributed to fame are independent, then calling an old item "famous" in the inclusion condition is either due to conscious recollection or familiarity, or both: Prob(famous) Inclusion =

Recollection + Familiarity, minus the overlap of the two processes, RF, or R + (1–R)F.

In the exclusion condition, an old name will be called famous if it fails to be recollected (1–R), but it nonetheless has gained sufficient familiarity (F) from prior study to pass the criterion the participant sets for the fame decision: Prob(famous) Exclusion = (1–R)F.

To obtain estimates of recollection, or R, one subtracts the probability of calling a name famous in the exclusion condition from the probability of calling a name famous in the inclusion condition. Once an estimate of R is obtained, the equations can be used to solve for an estimate of F.

If it is true that two processes make independent contributions to a particular task, then one should be able to find manipulations that affect one estimate derived with the process-dissociation procedure without affecting the other estimate. In the fame task as well as other procedures, elderly adults show decrements in the conscious component but the automatic component remains unchanged (Jennings & Jacoby, 1993, 1997).

The process-dissociation procedure has been used in a variety of memory paradigms to separate out processes that afford conscious control from those that do not. Such paradigms have included stem cued recall, word cued recall, and recognition (for a review, see Jacoby, Yonelinas, & Jennings, 1997.) In each of those cases, divided versus full attention at study disrupted the processing necessary for conscious recollection, but had no effect on the remaining component, the automatic influence. The minimal processing of reading the name or word aloud in these memory paradigms appears to be enough to produce an unconscious or automatic influence of memory. Similarly, a short deadline for retrieval reduces conscious recollection but does not affect the automatic memory component (Yonelinas & Jacoby, 1994). Other manipulations produce an opposite pattern of results. Training can have the effect of increasing automatic influences of memory in the form of habit while leaving recollection relatively invariant (Hay & Jacoby, 1996).

Experiments reported by Jacoby et al. (1993) illustrate use of the process-dissociation procedure to examine recall cued with word stems. Participants studied words under conditions of full or divided attention and then were tested with word stems. For an *inclusion test,* participants were told to use the stem as a cue to recall an old word or, if they could not do so, to complete the stem with the first word that came to mind. An inclusion test is similar to a standard test of cued recall with instructions to guess when recollection fails. Participants could complete a stem with an old word either because they recollected the old word, with a probability of R, or because the old word came automatically to mind, with a probability of A. If these two bases for responding are independent, then performance equals R + A – RA. For an *exclusion test*, participants were instructed to use the stem as a cue to recall an old word, but then they were told *not* to use recalled words to complete stems. That is, participants were instructed to exclude old words and complete stems only with new words. Following these instructions, participants would mistakenly complete a stem with an old word only if the word came automatically to mind without recollection of its prior presentation: $A(1-R) = A-RA$. As in the fame example, the difference between inclusion and exclusion tests provides a measure of recollection that can then be used to compute an estimate of automatic influences. Computing estimates this way, Jacoby et al. (1993, Experiment lb) found that dividing attention significantly reduced estimates of recollection (.25 vs .00) but left automatic influences essentially invariant (.47 vs .46).

In addition to the independence assumption, the estimation procedure rests on the assumption that R is equal for the inclusion and exclusion tests and furthermore, it is assumed that A is equal for the two types of test. To assess automatic influences of memory, Jacoby et al. compared A (.46) to completion rates for stems corresponding to new words (.35) and found a significant difference. Base rates did not differ significantly across the inclusion and exclusion tests nor across the manipulation of full vs divided attention. These results provide support for the assumption that A was equivalent across types of test and conditions created by manipulating full vs divided attention at study.

Base-rate performance reflects guessing based on pre-experimental knowledge, which is a third basis for correct performance on a test of recall cued with word stems. Our estimation procedure (e.g. Jacoby et al., 1993) treats A as reflecting the sum of automatic influences of memory and guessing based on pre-experimental knowledge. Others have proposed alternative procedures that they favour for taking guessing into account (Roediger & McDermott, 1994). Buchner, Erdfelder, and Vaterrodt-Plünnecke (1995) proposed a multinomial model that treats guessing as independent of automatic influences of memory. Their model uses performance on new items to estimate the probability of correct responding on the basis of guessing. We have compared results produced by various procedures, and have described the advantages of using a model based on signal-detection theory for examining automatic influences of memory in recognition performance (Yonelinas & Jacoby, 1996; Yonelinas, Regehr, & Jacoby, 1995).

Controversy Surrounding Assumptions: Boundary Conditions

The most controversial assumption underlying the process-dissociation procedure is the assumption that recollection and automatic influences of memory serve as independent bases for responding. Our findings of process dissociations provide support for the independence assumption. However, some attempts to conceptually replicate our results have failed. Most prominent has been work by Curran and Hintzman (1995). We briefly describe their work and then consider boundary conditions for the independence assumption.

Curran and Hintzman (1995) examined recall performance cued with word stems, and found results that they interpret as invalidating the independence assumption underlying the process-dissociation procedure. They manipulated study duration and found what they term a "paradoxical dissociation" between R and A. More specifically, they showed that lengthening study time produced an increase in R but a decrease in A. The dissociation is paradoxical because experiments using stem completion as an indirect test of memory have shown that manipulating study time leaves stem-completion performance unchanged (e.g. Greene, 1986). Similarly, increasing study time would be expected to increase R and leave A relatively invariant—the same form of process dissociation produced by manipulating full vs divided attention during study.

Significant correlations between R and A were found by Curran and Hintzman and were interpreted as direct evidence against independence. Due to a violation of the independence assumption, A was said to be underestimated by an amount that increased with the magnitude of R, explaining the paradoxical dissociation produced by manipulating study time. However, as discussed in later papers (Curran & Hintzman, 1997; Hintzman & Curran, 1997; Jacoby, Begg, & Toth, 1997; Jacoby & Shrout, 1997), interpretation of correlations involves a number of complexities. We believe the correlations between R and A found by Curran and Hintzman do not speak to the independence assumption underlying the process-dissociation procedure.

One reason for the general reluctance to accept the independence assumption is because it seems likely that participants sometimes use a generate/recognise strategy to accomplish recall cued with word stems. Using that strategy, participants would first generate a completion for a stem and then output the generated word only if a recognition-memory check revealed that the generated completion word was earlier-studied (Jacoby & Hollingshead, 1990). The generation strategy might rely on an automatic process of memory, and the recognition check might rely on a mixture of recollection and familiarity. If such a strategy was employed, then the independence equations would not capture the processes involved, as Jacoby et al. (1993) noted. Indeed, we argue that the test instructions in Curran and Hintzman's (1995) experiments encouraged participants to engage in a generate/recognise strategy rather than rely on direct retrieval.

The possibility that participants sometimes use a generate/recognise strategy raises the general issue of participants' understanding of exclusion instructions. Critics of the process-dissociation procedure (e.g. Graf & Komatsu, 1994) have argued that participants fail to understand instructions for exclusion tests. A high probability of failure to exclude old words on an exclusion test might be interpreted as a failure to understand instructions, and it is results of this sort that have received most attention. However, the total absence of exclusion errors can also reflect a failure to understand instructions. The goal of our instructions is to satisfy assumptions underlying the process-dissociation procedure, and doing so requires that participants exclude old words *only on the basis of recollection.* If participants exclude words based on familiarity, or by using a generate/ recognise strategy, assumptions underlying our equations are violated and estimates are invalid. We see these as important caveats for how to set up experiments using the process-dissociation procedure, rather than as a basis for rejecting the use of process dissociation as a tool. Studies that aim to estimate the processes people use in the generate/recognise strategy will require different techniques.

Next we show how paradoxical dissociations can be produced in experiments using a Remember/Know procedure. We then return to the inclusion/exclusion procedure and describe an experiment that shows a corresponding paradoxical dissociation produced by instructing participants to use a generate/recognise strategy.

Process Dissociation and Remember/Know

To link the process-dissociation procedure to the Remember/ Know procedure, one must move from phenomenological reports of "remember" and "know" to effects on control of responding. For "remember" responses to serve as a valid measure of recollection, participants must be aware of recollecting old words that come to mind as completions for word stems. Such awareness is also required to use recollection as a means to avoid mistakenly producing old words on an exclusion test. The inclusion/exclusion procedure differs from the Remember/ Know procedure in that it requires participants to use awareness as a basis for conscious control of responding, rather than simply to report on awareness.

When examining the effects of repetition using the Remember/Know procedure combined with the independence assumption (which we have named "IRK"), results appear to be consistent with those found using opposition procedures. An experiment done to examine the effects of dividing attention during study illustrates the relation between the process-dissociation and Remember/Know procedures, and also illustrates how use of a generate/ recognise strategy can produce paradoxical dissociations. In that experiment, as for an inclusion test, participants were told to use stems as a cue for recall of an earlier-studied word or, if they could not do so, to complete stems with the first word that came to mind. After completing each stem, participants were to classify their completion word as one that they "remember" having studied, one that they "know" was earlier-studied, or one that was "new" (not earlier-studied).

Results (Table 5.3) showed that dividing attention during study reduced the probability of "remembering" and also slightly reduced the probability of a "know" response. The probability of remembering serves as a measure of recollection. Further, participants should classify an old word as "know" or "new" only if the word came automatically to mind but was not recollected as earlier-studied: A (1–R). That combination is the same as for mistakenly producing an old word on an exclusion test. Consequently, the independence

TABLE 5.3
Mean Probability of Completion with Study
Word with "Remember"/"Know"/"New"
Responses across Full/Divided Attention and
New Items

Response	Study Condition		
	Full Attention	*Divided Attention*	*New*
"Remember"	.25	.09	.02
"Know"	.23	.20	.11
"New"	.24	.36	.33
Pr(completion)	.72	.65	.46

assumption can be used to estimate A as: $[P(Know) + P(New)]/[1–P(Remember)]$.

Use of the IRK procedure to obtain estimates produced results (top row, Table 5.4) that were the same as found by Jacoby et al. (1993, Experiment 1) using inclusion/exclusion tests along with direct-retrieval instructions. Dividing attention during study reduced recollection but left automatic influences of memory unchanged.

However, suppose that instead of relying on direct retrieval, participants used a generate/recognise strategy. That strategy would result in participants excluding words that came to mind automatically and were recognised, as well as words that were recollected. Recognition without recollection describes words judged as "know" in the IRK procedure. When using a generate/recognise strategy for an exclusion test, failure to exclude will result only when old words are mistakenly judged as "new".

To mimic effects of a generate/recognise strategy, words that participants "know" were earlier-studied can be grouped with old words judged as "remember" rather than with those judged as "new". Therefore, estimating A using a generate/recognise strategy becomes: $P(New)/[1–(P[Remember] + P[Know])]$. Estimates computed in this way (bottom row, Table 5.4) show a paradoxical dissociation of the form found by Curran and Hintzman (1995)—dividing attention decreases R but increases A. Although the effects on A were fairly modest in this case, we have obtained more striking "paradoxical" dissociations in other experiments (Jacoby, in press).

Using the Remember/Know results to simulate performance on inclusion and exclusion tests shows that reliance on a generate/recognise strategy would produce base-rate differences. New words that gave rise to either a false

TABLE 5.4
Estimates of Recollection and Automatic
Influences Across Conditions of Full and
Divided Attention, Using IRK and Generate/
Recognise Assumptions

| | Estimates | | | |
| | Recollection | | Automatic Influences | |
Assumption	Full Attn	Div Attn	Full Attn	Div Attn
IRK	.25	.09	.61	.61
G/R	.48	.29	.44	.48

"remember" or a false "know" response would be withheld as completions on an exclusion test but would be used for completions on an inclusion test. Because of the relatively high probability of false knowing, the result would be to produce a lower base rate for the exclusion than for the inclusion test. As discussed later, such base-rate differences should alert experimenters that a generate/recognise strategy is likely being employed and therefore signal a violation of independence as assumed by the process-dissociation procedure.

The IRK procedure is a refinement of a procedure that Curran and Hintzman (1995, Experiments 2 & 3) used to produce a paradoxical dissociation by manipulating study time. For their "recollect and exclude" procedure, participants were required to try to write down two completions for each stem, a recalled word in one column and a new word in another column. The probability of recalling a studied word served as a measure of recollection that was used to estimate automatic influences of memory. A weakness of the "recollect and exclude" procedure is that it does not discriminate between words that participants "remember" and those that they "know" were studied earlier. It seems likely that participants at least sometimes "recalled" words that would have been called "know" had they been given the option. Their doing so would result in an overestimate of recollection along with a paradoxical dissociation, just as did the generate/recognise version of our IRK procedure.

Similarly, not requiring participants to make the Remember/Know distinction is likely responsible for Richardson-Klavehn and Gardiner's (1996) finding of a paradoxical dissociation produced by manipulating level of processing. They investigated effects in stem cued recall using a procedure that is very similar to Curran and Hintzman's (1995) "recollect and exclude" procedure. Deeper processing increased the probability that words used as a completion were recognised as old, but produced a decrease in A estimated using the independence assumption. Again, this paradoxical dissociation likely occurred because the procedure used did not discriminate between remembering and knowing but, rather, grouped the two together as in the aforementioned generate/ recognise version of the IRK procedure. In contrast, Toth et al. (1994) used inclusion and exclusion tests with direct-retrieval instructions and found that manipulating levels influenced R but left A unchanged.

Effects of Instructions on Inclusion/Exclusion

Results that are the same as those shown for the generate/recognise variant of the IRK procedure can be produced using generate/recognise instructions with inclusion and exclusion tests. Jacoby (in press) varied instructions for tests and examined the effects of dividing attention. For a direct-retrieval condition, instructions were the same as used in our earlier experiments. Participants were told to use stems as cues for recalling earlier-studied words. Recalled words were to be used as completions for inclusion tests but to be withheld on exclusion tests. In contrast, for the generate/recognise condition, instructions for inclusion tests were the same as for an indirect test of memory—participants were told to complete stems with the first word that came to mind. For exclusion tests in that condition, participants were instructed to generate a completion and then to do a recognition-memory check. If a generated word seemed at all familiar from study, it was not to be used as a completion.

Results for the direct-retrieval condition (Table 5.5) showed that full attention, as compared with divided attention, to the study presentation of words made it more likely that the words could later be recollected and included or excluded, whichever was required by the test. However, for the generate/ recognise condition, the advantage of full attention for performance on the inclusion test was slightly diminished. This result was expected because instructions for that condition did not ask participants to intentionally use memory. More impressive was the difference in exclusion performance. Participants in the generate/ recognise condition were much more successful at

TABLE 5.5
Probability of Stem Completion in Inclusion/Exclusion
Conditions across Full/Divided Attention at Study Using
Direct-Retrieval and Generate/Recognise Instructions

	Inclusion			Exclusion		
Instructions	Full	Divided	New	Full	Divided	New
D/R	.70	.62	.45	.40	.48	.43
G/R	.63	.59	.45	.16	.29	.29

excluding earlier-studied words than were those in the direct-retrieval condition, as would be expected if the former used familiarity as well as recollection as a basis for exclusion.

Estimates of R and A computed for the direct-retrieval condition (Table 5.6) showed a process dissociation that was the same as found by Jacoby et al. (1993, Experiment 1). Dividing attention during study reduced the probability of recollection but left automatic influences of memory unchanged. In contrast, the probability of recollection was estimated as being much higher in the generate/recognise condition than in the direct-retrieval condition. Further, results for the generate/recognise condition showed a paradoxical dissociation. Dividing attention reduced recollection but *increased* estimated automatic influences of memory.

The cause of the paradoxical dissociation observed in the generate/recognise condition is likely the same as in our Remember/ Know experiment. Generate/recognise instructions lead participants to exclude words they only "know" are old. This strategy inflates the probability of recollection and results in an underestimation of automatic influences.

Base rates (Table 5.5) signal the differences between the two strategies. For the direct-retrieval condition, base-rate performance did not differ for the inclusion and exclusion tests (.45 vs .43, respectively). For the generate/recognise condition, in contrast, the base rate was lower for the exclusion test than for the inclusion test (.29 vs .45, respectively). This lower base rate likely occurred because some new words were falsely recognised as old, and consequently were not used as completions for the exclusion test.

Reading a word makes it more likely that the word will later come readily to mind as a completion for a word stem. When participants use a generate/recognise strategy or are asked to make Remember/Know judgements, the increase in the likelihood of a word coming to mind can be correctly attributed to

TABLE 5.6
Estimates of Recollection and Automatic Influences
Across Full/Divided Attention at Study for Direct-
Retrieval and Generate/Recognise Instructions

| | *Estimates* | | | |
| | *Recollection* | | *Automatic Influences* | |
Assumption	*Full Attn*	*Div Attn*	*Full Attn*	*Div Attn*
D/R	.29	.14	.54	.55
G/R	.46	.30	.30	.40

its source and experienced as familiarity or "knowing". However, the same fluent generation of the word can be ignored or misattributed to differences among items and so not experienced as memory when direct-retrieval instructions are given (cf. Jacoby, Kelley, & Dywan, 1989). Fluency of completing a stem is ambiguous in that it does not specify its source. Because of its ambiguity, reliance on fluency as a basis for recognition or "knowing" results in the exclusion of fluently generated new words as well as old words, creating a difference in base rate between inclusion and exclusion tests. Exclusion on the basis of "knowing" or familiarity violates the assumption of independence along with the assumption that R is equal for inclusion and exclusion tests, and thereby invalidates the equations used to gain estimates. The process-dissociation equations model performance when people use the stems as cues for retrieval. They were not written to model the generate/recognise strategy.

Other experiments reported by Jacoby (in press) paralleled those described earlier but manipulated study time rather than full vs divided attention during study. Results were the same as those found for the effects of dividing attention. Grouping "know" and "new" responses together to obtain estimates of A using the IRK procedure showed that increasing study time produced an increase in recollection but left automatic influences unchanged. A corresponding dissociation was found when direct-retrieval instructions were used for inclusion and exclusion tests. In contrast, generate/recognise instructions produced a paradoxical dissociation as did the generate/recognise version of the IRK procedure. Base rates for inclusion and exclusion tests did not differ in the direct-retrieval condition but in the generate/recognise condition, base rate was lower for the exclusion than for the inclusion test. The paradoxical dissociation and base-rate differences parallel those reported by Curran and Hintzman (1995).

Jacoby et. al. (1997) showed other similarities between results from the process-dissociation procedure and results from the IRK procedure. Such convergence between the procedures is encouraging. However, because the process-dissociation procedure measures R as that which affords control over responding and the Remember/ Know procedure measures phenomenological experience, we expect that the two need not always coincide.

SUMMARY AND CONCLUSIONS

Many anomalies of memory and, in particular, of ageing and memory can be resolved by distinguishing between the consciously controlled process of recollection and the relatively automatic process of familiarity. However, the conceptual distinction must be accompanied by new tools to measure those processes. We have developed paradigms that place familiarity and recollection in opposition to reveal that recollection is reduced in ageing, and also in the young who encode material under conditions of divided attention, or who must respond under a short deadline. One consequence of impaired recollection is that the elderly are susceptible to ironic effects such as repeatedly asking the same question.

However, some ambiguity remains in results obtained with the opposition procedure because, for example, ageing could lead to deficits in both recollection and familiarity. We developed the process-dissociation procedure and the accompanying independence equations that describe performance to estimate familiarity and recollection when participants are attempting direct retrieval. These estimates confirm that familiarity is intact in the elderly, and that familiarity increases with repetitions. Reinstatement of study context affects both recollection and familiarity.

The process-dissociation procedure is a tool that can only be used when certain conditions are met. The equations only apply to situations in which people are attempting to use cues to retrieve, and therefore, care must be taken that participants do not shift to a completely different strategy, such as the generate/recognise strategy. One can use particular patterns of different base rates in the inclusion versus exclusion conditions to detect whether participants have adopted a generate/recognise strategy.

The Remember/Know procedure gives important insights into the phenomenology of memory, but additional assumptions are required to use those reports to study the underlying processes of recollection and familiarity. We argue that the underlying processes are independent, and so the process of familiarity can co-occur with the process of recollection, even though the phenomenology of "Remember" will dominate. Using the IRK calculations to estimate familiarity leads to striking parallels with results from the process-dissociation procedure. However, the process-dissociation procedure emphasises the use of recollection for controlled responding (differentially including vs excluding items), whereas the Remember/Know distinction emphasises phenomenology, and so parallel results will not always be found.

For purposes of theory, it is important to establish boundary conditions for the assumptions underlying the process-dissociation procedure and to consider alternative accounts of results. The same can be said for the Remember/Know procedure. However, for applied purposes, it is important to emphasise commonalities of approaches towards the goal of developing better techniques for diagnosis and treatment of memory disorders.

REFERENCES

Bartlett, J.C., Strater, L., & Fulton, A. (1991). False recency and false fame of faces in young adulthood and old age. *Memory and Cognition*, *19*, 177–188.

Buchner, A., Erdfelder, E., & Vaterrodt-Plünnecke, B. (1995). Toward unbiased measurement of conscious and unconscious memory processes within the process dissociation framework. *Journal of Experimental Psychology: General*, *124*, 137–160.

Cermak, L.S., Verfaellie, M., Butler, T., & Jacoby, L.L. (1993). Attributions of familiarity in amnesia: Evidence from a fame judgment task. *Neuropsychology*, *7*, 510–518.

Conway, M.A., & Dewhurst, S.A. (1995). The self and recollective experience. *Applied Cognitive Psychology, 9,* 1–19.

Craik, F.I.M. (1983). On the transfer of information from temporary to permanent memory. *Philosophical Transactions of the Royal Society, B302,* 341–359.

Craik, F.I.M. (1986). A functional account of age differences in memory. In F. Klix & H. Hapendorf (Eds.), *Human memory and cognitive capabilities, mechanisms and performances* (pp.409–422). Amsterdam: Elsevier.

Craik, F.I.M., & Jennings, J.M. (1992). Human memory. In F.I.M. Craik & T.A. Salthouse (Eds.), *The handbook of aging and cognition* (pp.51–110). Hillsdale, NJ: Lawrence Erlbaum Associates Inc.

Craik, F.I.M., & McDowd, J.M. (1987). Age differences in recall and recognition. *Journal of Experimental Psychology: Learning, Memory, and Cognition, 13,* 474–479.

Curran, T., & Hintzman, D.L. (1995). Violations of the independence assumption in process dissociation. *Journal of Experimental Psychology: Learning, Memory, and Cognition, 21,* 531–547.

Curran, T., & Hintzman, D.L. (1997). Consequences and causes of correlations in process dissociation. *Journal of Experimental Psychology: Learning, Memory and Cognition, 23,* 496–504.

Donaldson, W.L. (1996). The role of decision processing in remembering and knowing. *Memory and Cognition. 24,* 523–533.

Donaldson, W., MacKenzie, T.M., & Underhill, C.F. (1996). A comparison of recollective memory and source monitoring. *Psychonomic Bulletin & Review, 3,* 486–490.

Dywan, J., & Jacoby, L.L. (1990). Effects of aging on source monitoring: Differences in susceptibility to false fame. *Psychology and Aging, 5,* 379–387.

Dywan, J., Segalowitz, S.J., Henderson, D., & Jacoby, L.L. (1993). Memory for source after traumatic brain injury. *Brain and Cognition, 21,* 20–43.

Gardiner, J.M. (1988). Functional aspects of recollective experience. *Memory and Cognition, 16,* 309–313.

Gardiner, J.M. & Java, R.I. (1991). Forgetting in recognition memory with and without recollective experience. *Memory and Cognition. 19,* 617–623.

Gardiner, J.M., Kaminska, Z., Dixon, M., & Java, R.I. (1996). Repetition of previously novel melodies sometimes increases both remember and know responses in recognition memory. *Psychonomic Bulletin & Review, 3(3),* 366–371.

Gardiner, J.M., & Parkin, A.J. (1990). Attention and recollective experience in recognition memory. *Memory and Cognition, 18,* 579–583.

Graf, P., & Komatsu, S. (1994). Process dissociation procedure: Handle with caution! *European Journal of Cognitive Psychology, 6,* 113–129.

Greene, R.L. (1986). Word stems as cues in recall and completion tasks. *Quarterly Journal of Experimental Psychology: Human Experimental Psychology, 38(A),* 663–673.

Hasher, L., & Zacks, R.T. (1979). Automatic and effortful processes in memory. *Journal of Experimental Psychology: General, 108,* 356–388.

Hay, J.F., & Jacoby, L.L. (1996). Separating habit and recollection: Memory slips, process dissociations and probability matching. *Journal of Experimental Psychology: Learning, Memory and Cognition, 22,* 1323–1335.

Hintzman, D.L., & Curran, T. (1997). More than one way to violate independence: Reply to Jacoby and Shrout. *Journal of Experimental Psychology: Learning, Memory, and Cognition, 23,* 511–513.

Jacoby, L.L. (1991). A process dissociation framework: Separating automatic from intentional uses of memory. *Journal of Memory and Language, 30,* 513–541.

Jacoby, L.L. (1994). Measuring recollection: Strategic versus automatic influences of associative context. In C. Umiltà & M. Moscovitch (Eds.), *Attention and performance XV* (pp. 661–679). Cambridge, MA: Bradford.

Jacoby, L.L. (1996). Dissociating automatic and consciously controlled effects of study/test compatibility. *Journal of Memory and Language, 35,* 32–52.

Jacoby, L.L. (in press). Invariance in automatic influences of memory: Toward a user's guide for the process-dissociation procedure. *Journal of Experimental Psychology: Learning, Memory, and Cognition.*

Jacoby, L.L. (submitted). *Ironic effects of repetition: Measuring age-related differences in memory.*

Jacoby, L.L., Begg, I.M., & Toth, J.P. (1997). In defense of functional independence: Violations of assumptions underlying the process-dissociation procedure? *Journal of Experimental Psychology: Learning, Memory and Cognition, 23,* 484–495.

Jacoby, L.L., & Dallas, M. (1981). On the relationship between autobiographical memory and perceptual learning. *Journal of Experimental Psychology: General, 3,* 306–340.

Jacoby, L.L., & Hollingshead, A. (1990). Toward a generate/ recognize model of performance on direct and indirect tests of memory. *Journal of Memory and Language, 29,* 433–454.

Jacoby, L.L., Jennings, J.M., & Hay, J.F. (1996). Dissociating automatic and consciously controlled processes: Implications for diagnosis and rehabilitation of memory deficits. In D.J. Herrmann, C.L. McEvoy, C. Hertzog, P. Hertel, & M.K. Johnson (Eds.), *Basic and applied memory research: Theory in context* (Vol.1, pp.161–193). Mahwah, NJ: Lawrence Erlbaum Associates Inc.

Jacoby, L.L., Kelley, C.M., Brown, J., & Jasechko, J. (1989). Becoming famous overnight: Limits on the ability to avoid unconscious influences of the past. *Journal of Personality and Social Psychology, 56,* 326–338.

Jacoby, L.L., Kelley, C.M., & Dywan, J. (1989). Memory attributions. In H.L. Roediger & F.I.M. Craik (Eds.), *Varieties of memory and consciousness: Essays in honour of Endel Tulving* (pp.391–422). Hillsdale, NJ: Lawrence Erlbaum Associates Inc.

Jacoby, L.L., & Shrout, P.E. (1997). Toward a psychometric analysis of violations of the independence assumption in process dissociation. *Journal of Experimental Psychology: Learning, Memory and Cognition, 23,* 505–510.

Jacoby, L.L., Toth, J.P., & Yonelinas, A.P. (1993). Separating conscious and unconscious influences of memory: Measuring recollection. *Journal of Experimental Psychology: General, 122,* 139–154.

Jacoby, L.L., Woloshyn, V., & Kelley, C.M. (1989). Becoming famous without being recognized: Unconscious influences of memory produced by dividing attention. *Journal of Experimental Psychology: General, 118,* 115–125.

Jacoby, L.L., Yonelinas, A.P., & Jennings, J. (1997). The relation between conscious and unconscious (automatic) influences. A declaration of independence. In J.D. Cohen & J.W. Schooler (Eds.), *Scientific approaches to consciousness* (pp.13–47). Mahwah, NJ: Lawrence Erlbaum Associates Inc.

Jennings, J.M., & Jacoby, L.L. (1993). Automatic versus intentional uses of memory: Aging, attention, and control. *Psychology and Aging, 8,* 283–293.

Jennings, J.M., & Jacoby, L.L. (1997) An opposition procedure for detecting age-related deficits in recollection: Telling effects of repetition. *Psychology and Aging, 12,* 352–361.

Johnson, M.K., Lindsay, D.S., & Hashtroudi, S. (1993). Source monitoring. *Psychological Bulletin, 114,* 3–28.

Joordens, S., & Merikle, P.M. (1993). Independence or redundancy? Two models of conscious and unconscious influences. *Journal of Experimental Psychology: General, 122,* 462–467.

Klatzky, R.L. (1984). *Memory and awareness.* New York: Freeman & Company.

Logan, G.D. (1989). Automaticity and cognitive control. In J.E. Uleman & J.A. Bargh (Eds.), *Unintended thought* (pp.52–74). New York: Guilford Press.

Mandler, G. (1980). Recognizing: The judgment of previous occurrence. *Psychological Review, 87,* 252–271.

Mäntylä, T. (1993). Knowing but not remembering: Adult age differences in recollective experience. *Memory and Cognition, 21*, 379–388.

Moscovitch, M., Vriezen, E.R., & Gottstein, J. (1993). Implicit tests of memory in patients with focal lesions or degenerative brain disorders. In H. Spinnler & F. Boller (Eds.), *Handbook of neuropsychology* (Vol.8, pp.133–173). Amsterdam: Elsevier.

Multhaup, K.S. (1995). Aging, source, and decision criteria: When false fame errors do and do not occur. *Psychology and Aging, 10*, 492–497.

Parkin, A.J. (in press). Normal age-related memory loss and its relation to frontal lobe dysfunction. In P. Rabbitt (Ed.), *Methodology of frontal and executive functions.*

Parkin, A.J., & Walter, B.M. (1992). Recollective experience, normal aging, and frontal dysfunction. *Psychology and Aging, 7*, 290–298.

Posner, M.I. & Snyder, C.R.R. (1975). Attention and cognitive control. In R.L. Solso (Ed.), *Information processing in cognition: The Loyola Symposium* (pp.55–85). Hillsdale, NJ: Lawrence Erlbaum Associates Inc.

Rabinowitz, J.C. (1984). Aging and recognition failure. *Journal of Gerontology, 39*, 65–71.

Rajaram, S. (1993). Remembering and knowing: Two means of access to the personal past. *Memory and Cognition, 21*, 89–102.

Reingold, E.M., & Merikle, P.M. (1990). On the inter-relatedness of theory and measurement in the study of unconscious processes. *Mind and Language, 5*, 9–28.

Richardson-Klavehn, A., & Gardiner, J.M. (1996). Cross-modality priming in stem completion reflects conscious memory, but not voluntary memory. *Psychonomic Bulletin & Review, 3(2)*, 238–244.

Roediger, H.L., & McDermott, K.B. (1993). Implicit memory in normal human subjects. In H. Spinnler & F. Boller (Eds.), *Handbook of neuropsychology* (Vol.8, pp.63–131). Amsterdam: Elsevier.

Roediger, H.L., & McDermott, K.B. (1994). The problem of differing false-alarm rates for the process dissociation procedure: Comment on Verfaellie and Treadwell (1993). *Neuropsychology, 8*, 284–288.

Salthouse, T. (1994). The nature of the influence of speed on adult age differences in cognition. *Developmental Psychology, 30*, 240–259.

Schneider, W., & Shiffrin, R.M. (1977). Controlled and automatic human information processing: I. Detection, search and attention. *Psychological Review, 84*, 1–66.

Spencer, W.D., & Raz, N. (1995). Differential effects of aging in memory for content and context: A meta-analysis. *Psychology and Aging. 10*, 527–539.

Squire, L.R., & McKee, R. (1992). Influence of prior events on cognitive judgments in amnesia. *Journal of Experimental Psychology: Learning, Memory and Cognition, 18,* 106–115.

Toth, J.P., Reingold, E.M., & Jacoby, L.L. (1994). Towards a redefinition of implicit memory: Process dissociations following elaborative processing and self-generation. *Journal of Experimental Psychology: Learning, Memory and Cognition, 20*, 290–303.

Tulving, E. (1985). Memory and consciousness. *Canadian Psychologist, 26*, 1–12.

Wegner, D.M. (1994). Ironic processes of mental control. *Psychological Review, 101*, 34–52.

West, R.L. (1996). An application of prefrontal cortex function theory to cognitive aging. *Psychological Bulletin, 120(2)*, 272–292.

Yonelinas, A.P., & Jacoby, L.L. (1994). Dissociations of processes in recognition memory: Effects of interference and response speed. *Canadian Journal of Experimental Psychology, 48*, 516–534.

Yonelinas, A.P., & Jacoby, L.L. (1995). The relation between remembering and knowing as bases for recognition: Effects of size congruency. *Journal of Memory and Language, 34*, 622–643.

Yonelinas, A.P., & Jacoby, L.L. (1996). Response bias and the process dissociation procedure. *Journal of Experimental Psychology: General, 125(4)*, 422–439.

Yonelinas, A.P., Regehr, G., & Jacoby, L.L. (1995). Incorporating response bias in a dual-process theory of memory. *Journal of Memory and Language, 34*, 821–835.

6 Imaginary Memories

Elizabeth F. Loftus
University of Washington, USA

Suggestion and imagination have the power to influence our recollections of the past. This we have known quite some time, as is well articulated in a stunning book, *The harmony of illusions*, by anthropologist Allan Young (1995). Over a century ago, the well-known director of the Salpetriere infirmary, Jean-Martin Charcot, reported on a case in which he placed a patient into a hypnotic state and then told her she had been attacked, and had received an injury to her hip. Charcot described the attack in detail, and told his patient that she would experience severe pain later on. When awakened from the trance the woman recalled the blow to her hip, and suffered the pain that had been suggested to her (Charcot, 1889, cited in Young, 1995, p.19). Apparently the patient was completely unaware of the actual source of her newly created memories and symptoms.

Charcot was also well aware that intervention by him was not necessary for the development of pseudomemories. The patients could accomplish this by themselves—a kind of autosuggestion. One patient called Le Log was diagnosed with hystero-traumatic paralysis. The patient, who steadfastly believed that he had been run over by a van, complained of a heaviness, and of feeling as though his legs were gone. Charcot traced these symptoms to autosuggestion on the part of the patient. The patient even had dreams of the wheels of the van passing over his body, despite the fact that this had never happened. In Charcot's words (Young, 1995, p.27) "this conviction, which has even appeared to him in his dreams, is absolutely erroneous". It did not escape Charcot's notice that the paralysis occurred not moments after the accident, but only after an interval of many days during which "unconscious mental elaboration" had a chance to take

135

place (Charcot, 1889, p.387, cited in Young, 1995, p.27). From these kinds of observations, Charcot developed his striking metaphor: Suggested ideas are real parasites in thought (Young, 1995, pp.27, 35).

Young's history also delves into the ideas of W.H.R. Rivers, a psychiatrist at the Craiglockhart Military Hospital, near Edinburgh. Rivers well appreciated the important role that suggestion played in the production and cure of disease in both Western and non-Western medicine. During the first two decades of the twentieth century, when Rivers was publishing, two forms of suggestion were noted: (1) heterosuggestion, wherein an idea is implanted by someone else, and (2) autosuggestion, in which the individual is his or her own source of suggestion. But these ideas were hardly new to nineteenth- and twentieth-century scholars. Centuries before, the term "imagination" was tossed about by Renaissance physicians and philosophers in ways that included the idea of suggestion. As early as the sixteenth century, imagination/suggestion was thought to be a cause of physical and emotional disease, and by the eighteenth century, we saw titles such as "On the power of human imagination" that anticipated the thinking of Charcot and Rivers (Young, 1995, p.46). By the early twentieth century, suggestion was commonly used with psychiatric patients, sometimes in connection with hypnosis, sometimes with electrotherapy, and sometimes with plain, simple education.

ON THE POWER OF HUMAN IMAGINATION

What happens when you imagine things that have not happened? In an unsigned essay in *The Economist* (1996, p.82), a writer answers: "When you think about things that do not exist (unicorns, lottery winnings, dead friends), the real connects, in a sense, with the unreal." Although this is eloquently put, one can still ask, more concretely, what exactly are the consequences of imagining a counterfactual past? To explore this, I and my collaborators conducted a study which found that one single simple act of imagining a childhood event increased a person's subjective confidence that the event happened to them in the past—a phenomenon we called "Imagination Inflation" (Garry, Manning, Loftus, & Sherman, 1996). In this study, subjects were asked about a long list of possible childhood events (e.g. broke a window with your hand), and they told us the likelihood that these events had happened to them as a child. Two weeks later, subjects were instructed to imagine that some of these events had actually happened to them. Finally, they responded for a second time about the likelihood of that long list of possible childhood events.

Consider one of the critical items. "Imagine that it's after school and you are playing in the house. You hear a strange noise outside, so you run to the window to see what made the noise. As you are running, your feet catch on something and you trip and fall." While imagining themselves in this position, subjects answer some questions such as: "What did you trip on?" They further imagine: "As you're falling you reach out to catch yourself and your hand goes through the window. As the window breaks you get cut and there's some blood." While imagining themselves in this predicament, they answer further questions such as: "What are you likely to do next? How did you feel?"

After imagining several items, subjects once again told us about their childhood by filling out the same form they had filled out two weeks previously. We could then compare the changes in their assessment of their childhood. We were particularly interested in what happened to experiences that subjects explicitly said were unlikely to have happened in the first place. (By unlikely, I mean that on a scale from 1 = definitely did not happen to 8 = definitely did happen, they initially checked 1 through 4.) Would their second score change in a positive direction after imagination, indicating that they now felt it was more likely that the event had happened to them in childhood? We found that a one-minute act of counterfactual imagination led to positive changes in a significant minority of subjects. To give one example, after engaging in the act of imagination about breaking a window with their hand, 24% of subjects increased their subjective confidence that something like this actually happened to them. For those who had not imagined the event, only 12% showed a corresponding increase.

The other seven critical items used in this study similarly showed increased subjective confidence after imagination. Collapsed across all critical items and all subjects, we found that 34% of items moved in a positive direction (increased subjective confidence) after Imagination, compared to only 25% after No-Imagination.

These findings show that even a single act of imagining a known counter-factual event can increase the subjective likelihood that the event would be remembered as having happened in the past. As for why imagining an event led to more positive changes, we considered a number of explanations. Of course it is always possible that some subjects might be reminded of a true experience by the act of imagination, but for various reasons we concluded that this possibility, while occasionally true, did not account for the bulk of our findings. One of those reasons is this: if the imagination exercise had brought to mind a real memory, would not subjects express this by increasing their Life Events Inventory (LEI) score to an "8" indicating that this event definitely did happen? Garry et al. found that very few subjects made such "big jumps" in their LEI scores.

Another possible explanation for Imagination Inflation is that the act of imagination simply makes the event seem more familiar at the time the second assessment of childhood is made. That familiarity is mistakenly related to childhood, rather than to the act of imagination. The Inflation phenomenon can also be thought of in terms of a source monitoring error. In fact, there may be more than a single mental route to the kinds of inflation we have observed. And inflation from "very unlikely" to "somewhat unlikely" might involve different mental processes than inflation from "unlikely" to "likely".

After completing the initial study, we began to ask other questions about Imagination Inflation. For example, under what conditions are people more susceptible to Inflation? What types of people are more susceptible to Inflation?

Who Inflates?

One measure that appears to be related to the construction of false memories more generally is a measure of the extent to which a person has dissociative experiences, or lapses in attention and memory. One simple method for measuring this aspect of an individual is the Dissociative Experiences Scale (Bernstein & Putnam, 1986) which is a 28-item "test" that can be completed and scored in 15 minutes (Ross, 1994), yielding a score for an individual ranging from 0 to 100. Test items present a description of an experience to subjects and ask them for the percentage of time this kind of experience happens to them. Some items deal with amnesia and dissociation (e.g. Some people have the experience of being accused of lying when they do not think that they have lied). Other items concern absorption and imaginative involvement (e.g. Some people find that sometimes they are listening to someone talk and they suddenly realise that they did not hear part or all of what was said). Others items tap into experiences of depersonalisation and derealisation (e.g. Some people have the experience of feeling that other people, objects, and the world around them are not real). Hyman and Billings (in press) found that people who provided false memories of childhood events (e.g. knocking over a punchbowl at a family wedding) scored higher on the DES than people who did not provide false memories.

In collaboration with clinical psychologist John Paddock and his colleagues, we have examined imagination inflation in a study in which we also obtained DES scores from subjects. The study used a procedure similar to our original one (Garry et al., 1996). Subjects first filled out a LEI containing eight critical items. Later they imagined experiencing four scenarios, while other subjects imagined a different four. Finally they filled out the LEI again. The results were clear: a one-minute act of counterfactual imagination led to more positive changes in subjective confidence that an event occurred relative to no imagination. Collapsed across all critical items and all subjects, and confining the analysis to those cases in which subjects initially said the event was unlikely to have happened, we found that 38% of the items moved in a positive direction after Imagination, compared to only 21% after No-Imagination. In other words, we found evidence for Imagination, Inflation and, importantly, the DES predicted Inflation. A number of specific items on the DES were especially predictive: the top item was "Some people sometimes find that they cannot remember whether they have done something or have just thought about doing that thing...". Also strongly related was another absorption item: "Some people find that in certain situations they are able to do things with amazing ease and spontaneity that would usually be difficult for them ...".

The finding that self-reported dissociative symptoms are related to memory distortion induced by imagination has important implications. After discovering a positive association between the DES and false memory construction, Hyman and Billings (in press) hypothesised that people with dissociative tendencies may be more accustomed to integrating external information with their self-concept and may use less stringent standards of reality monitoring. Practical consequences may result. Many patients who enter therapy have higher DES scores than the general population. So, for example, nonclinical samples of adults have produced mean DES scores in the range of 4 to 8 (Carlson & Putnam, 1993), while those with certain mental health diagnoses have much higher scores (11 to 21 for schizophrenics, 19 to 20 for borderline personality disorder, 41 to 57 for multiple personality disorder). Thus, the patients who might be led through imagination-induced memory extraction exercises in therapy, which is a technique that some therapists use (Poole, Lindsay, Memon, & Bull, 1995), may be the very individuals who are most susceptible to imagination-induced distortion.

Imagining Oneself vs Imagining Another

In the Imagination studies just described, the subjects were induced to imagine themselves as the main character in the scenario. Is it necessary to imagine oneself or would inflation also occur if the subjects were induced to imagine someone else in the scene? In collaboration with Chuck Manning and Maryanne Garry, we explored this question. Predictions about the outcome of such a manipulation are not all that straightforward. On the one hand, you might think that there would be more source confusions when you imagine yourself, say, breaking a window with your hand, than when you imagine another person breaking the window with her or his hand. After all, the LEI is asking you about your own autobiography, not someone else's. More inflation with the self in the image than another person in the image would be expected. On the other hand, there is a long and rich literature on the mnemonic aspects of the self (Symons & Johnson, 1997). Relating information to the self often yields superior memory for that information, sometimes called the self-reference effect (SRE). Thus, imagining the self might lead to better memory that the scene, say about breaking a window, was imagined—not experienced. Less inflation with self than other imagination might result.

In our self versus other imagination study, subjects filled out an LEI, imagined several experiences, and then filled out the LEI again. However, some subjects were instructed to imagine themselves in the scene and others to imagine another individual. Again, a one-minute act of imagination led to more positive changes in subjective confidence that an event had occurred to the subject in childhood, relative to No-Imagination. Imagining the self in the scene produced greatest inflation.

The Timing of Imagination

How long does the Imagination exercise have a memory-altering effect? In collaboration with Marcos Nunes-Ueno and Chuck Manning, we explored this question. One possibility is that imagination has its strongest influence when it immediately precedes the second LEI, as the image would be the strongest, compared to imagination in the distant past. After all, the image would begin by being relatively clear but would be expected to fade over time—a simple forgetting phenomenon. Inflation might be strongest immediately. On the other hand when imagination immediately precedes the second LEI and the image is strong, it might be relatively easy for subjects to attribute any familiarity they feel about the LEI item to the image, and not to their earlier childhood. Inflation might be less strong immediately after Imagination than after some time has passed. Our study exploring these issues involved three time intervals: In one condition subjects had the imagining session immediately prior to the final LEI test. In another condition, subjects had the imagining session one week prior to the final LEI test. In the third condition, subjects had the imagining session two weeks prior to the final LEI test. We found a nonmonotonic relationship between timing and inflation. The greatest inflation effect occurred when the imagination session and the final test were separated by one week. This makes sense if we think about the inflation mechanism in the following way.

Immediately after imagining that you broke a window with your hand you may find it relatively easy to respond to the LEI item concerning this scene, as you did before. Any enhanced familiarity you may experience over the item can be understood to be due to the recent image. On the other hand when a bit of time has passed (a week in this case), you may not remember as well that you imagined breaking a window, and you may be more likely to relate feelings of familiarity for the item to your childhood rather than to the imagination exercise. Finally, when more time passes, the impact of the single image may completely fade. In an extreme case, one probably would not expect a single image of breaking a window in an experimental setting to influence childhood memories assessed over a year later. Imagination might conceivably have rather long-ranging effects if the subject were to repeatedly rehearse the image, or the imagination experience were to change other aspects of the subject's information processing. But in the absence of such happenings, one might not expect such a long-range result for such a simple manipulation.

OTHER WAYS OF EXAMINING IMAGINATION

Imagination and Planting False Childhood Memories

A different way of inducing people to believe they had experiences that they did not have involves enlisting relatives to help persuade family members about a counterfactual past. For example, in one study, individuals were asked to recall events that were supplied by their mother, father, older sibling, other close relative (Loftus & Pickrell, 1995). Three of the events were true, and one was a research-crafted false event about getting lost in a shopping mall, department store, or other public place. After being told that their family member recalled the particular episode of getting lost, about a quarter of the subjects created false childhood memories about it. In other studies using a similar methodology, people have been led to "remember" that when they were younger they had to go to a hospital for some particular health-related problem (Devitt, Honts, & Loftus, 1996; Hyman, Husband, & Billings, 1995), that they got their finger caught in a mousetrap and had to go to the hospital to get it removed (Ceci, Huffman, Smith, & Loftus, 1994), that they fell off a tricycle and had to get stitches in their leg (Ceci, Loftus, Leichtman, & Bruck, 1994), and that they spilled punch all over the parents of the bride at a wedding reception (Hyman et al., 1995).

Hyman and Pentland (1996) explored whether "mental imagery" (by which they meant creating images from imagination) would enhance the likelihood that a false childhood memory could be planted. In this research subjects were asked about true childhood experiences and about a false event that was suggestively mentioned (spilling punch on the bride's parents during a wedding reception). In this research, whenever subjects failed to recall a suggested event, they were asked to form a mental image of the event and to describe that image. They were told that this would help them to remember the event. This went on for two sessions, and after each session subjects were encouraged to continue trying to remember any unremembered events. During a third and final session, subjects answered questions about their memories. A major finding was that the imagery manipulation influenced false recall. By the third session, about 12% of control subjects had developed clear or partial false memories, but 37% of imagery subjects did so. Interestingly the imagery manipulation also slightly increased the likelihood of remembering a true experience.

Why does imagining lead to greater acceptance of the false suggestion? Hyman and Pentland point out that the imagination instructions lead subjects to do two things: form an image and also to talk about that image. Their current methodology does not enable them to disentangle the influence of these two processes. They offer one interesting speculation: perhaps the imagery instructions are especially good at providing a demanding social context, with added pressure to remember, which facilitates memory creation by encouraging individuals to engage in memory construction while simultaneously discouraging careful reality monitoring strategies.

Imagining Recent Actions

Imagination can also make people believe that they have done things in the recent past that they did not in fact do. This was shown in a pair of studies that involved multiple sessions (Goff, 1996; Goff & Roediger, 1996). During the initial "encoding session", subjects listened to a list of action statements as they were read aloud. For each statement subjects were instructed to do the stated action, to imagine doing it, or simply to listen to the statement but do nothing else. The actions were simple ones such as these: knock on the table, lift the stapler, break the toothpick, cross your fingers, roll your eyes. During a second "imagination session", subjects had to imagine various actions. Finally during a "test session", they had to answer questions about what they actually did during the initial session. The investigators found that, after imagination, subjects sometimes claimed that they had actually performed an action on the first occasion when they had not. The more times they imagined an unperformed action, the more often they made this mistake. So, for example, in one study, after five imaginings, subjects claimed they had performed a nonperformed action 13% of the time.

Imagining led not only to higher false alarm rates, but also to higher hit rates. The investigators offer a number of possible explanations for these findings. Perhaps imagining an action many times makes the statement itself seem very familiar, and subjects may think it was familiar because it occurred during the first session even if they do not actually remember performing that action. This explanation could explain why both hits and false alarms rise after multiple imaginings. Of course familiarity is not the total answer here. Goff and Roediger also found that if the imagination session was very close to the test session, subjects were not very likely to claim that imagined experiences were previously performed. Presumably if subjects were trying to make a source-monitoring judgement (did I do it or did I just imagine doing it?), they would have an easier time knowing that they imagined it if the imaginations had very recently been performed. They could readily attribute any experienced familiarity to the recent imagination rather than to a real experience from weeks earlier.

Diary Studies

Diary studies provide a unique method for examining false autobiographical recollection. In a series of studies by Barclay and his collaborators (e.g. Barclay & DeCooke, 1988; Barclay & Wellman, 1986), diarists recorded their everyday experiences sometimes for months at a stretch. Later, the diarists were tested with original diary entries, or with distractors that had been created by the experimenters. In some cases the distractors were real entries with altered detail, in other cases they were completely new items constructed to be plausible by examining the collection of entries made by a particular diarist. Although true recognition of real entries were much higher than false recognition of altered entries, still the diarists often recalled as true events that were false. In one study about half of the altered memories were judged to be real, and over a fifth of the wholly false entries were judged to be real.

In the Barclay research, diarists misremembered their past when responding to altered entries supplied by the experimenter. The mistakes appear to be occurring at the time the diarist is tested. What might happen if the diarists themselves were to imagine a counterfactual past, prior to the time of testing? A paradigm for investigating this issue was included in a diary study conducted, in large part, for the purpose of creating a corpus of false memories (Conway, Collins, Gathercole, & Anderson, 1996). The method departed from Barclay's in that the diarists themselves provided the false reports long before they were tested. It worked like this: Two diarists wrote down events and thoughts from their lives over a period of five months. As they recorded these true experiences, they also recorded false events that had not occurred but could plausibly have occurred on the day of the recording. The false events, therefore, were only imagined. Some seven months after completion of the diaries, the two individuals were tested. For items that were judged as true, the subjects indicated whether they consciously remembered the event, or, if not, whether the item simply evoked feelings of familiarity, or whether there was no sense of familiarity but simply a guess.

Conway et al. (1996) found that the diarists occasionally reported their earlier imaginations as if they were real experiences. A total of 55 imagined experiences were later reported as real. The false memories were less likely than the true ones to be accompanied by conscious feelings of recollection, but over 40% of the false memories were of this type. A forced-choice test, in which diarists had to choose between a true and false memory and say which was which, produced lower false memory rates. Conway et al. note that the present method may overestimate the accuracy of everyday memories, as the diary method is one that gives preferential rehearsal to certain true memories. Unrehearsed and randomly selected everyday events may be recalled less accurately. Setting aside the matter of how the diary results might generalise to the larger population of memories, these results were sufficiently impressive to warrant the conclusion (Conway et al., 1996, p.93): "False memories can be a common occurrence." The value of this research lies in part in its rather clever method for showing that people will sometimes erroneously accept as true, and even occasionally recollectively experience, descriptions of their past that are in fact completely false.

FINAL REMARKS

Taken together these findings show a new power to imagination—it can sometimes make people believe that they have had experiences that they didn't have. These findings fill in our understanding of the rather flimsy curtain that separates imagination and memory.

We have much to learn about how imagination influences past recollection. The way that imagination influences past memory might be different when one is imagining while trying to remember the past versus when one is imagining while not particularly trying to remember. Perhaps it is the case that generating an image while one is trying to recall the past helps to convince people that they are actually remembering a previously experienced event. Generating an image may also facilitate those processes responsible for bringing about the phenomenal experience of remembering, and that phenomenal experience may serve to convince people that what they are doing is genuinely remembering. Put another way, generating an image while in the act of remembering something may trigger a cascade of processes that together produce the evidence for a person that what is in the mind at that moment is a real memory. Now this line of thought makes sense when we are thinking about the impact of imagination during the act of remembering, but something else must be taking place in cases where imagination and autobiographical recall are separated in time. In any event, this distinction may be an important one for deepening our understanding of why images do have this powerful role in memory.

A relatively unresearched issue about imagination is whether its power could be deliberately put to some good use. Could you induce people to imagine past experiences that might distort their memory, but might benefit them in some way? If they imagined happy childhood experiences and came to believe they had occurred, would that translate into better current mental functioning? Milton Erickson, one of the foremost practitioners of hypnotherapy, appeared to be onto this idea a half century ago (Erickson & Rossi, 1989).

Could imagination be harnessed to improve physical well-being? Consider the problem faced by a perplexing group of insomniacs who have trouble estimating, knowing, or remembering their sleep (Klinkenborg, 1997). They complain of insomnia, but when they are brought into a laboratory setting and actual sleep is measured, these individuals have been known to sleep well and deeply, and upon awakening remark "See? I told you I wouldn't sleep" (Klinkenborg, 1997, p.31). Klinkenborg speculates perhaps the illusion that we have slept well and deeply might in fact produce a more rested and content individual. Perhaps imagination exercises could produce just the needed illusion. Whether such illusions would work in this way, both for those who actually did sleep well but think they did not, and for those who actually did not sleep well but could still be persuaded that they did, remain a provocative question for future researchers in their exploration of imagination and its memory-engineering potential. Imagineering might conceivably become a field unto itself.

ACKNOWLEDGEMENTS

I thank Dan Wright and Martin Conway for thoughtful comments on this chapter.

REFERENCES

Barclay, C.R., & DeCooke, P.A. (1988). Ordinary everyday memories: Some of the things of which selves are made. In U. Neisser & E. Winograd (Eds.), *Remembering reconsidered* (pp. 91–125). New York: Cambridge University Press.

Barclay, C.R., & Wellman, H.M. (1986). Accuracies and inaccuracies in autobiographical memories. *Journal of Memory and Language, 25,* 93–103.

Bernstein, E.M., & Putnam, F.W. (1986). Development, reliability, and validity of a dissociation scale. *Journal of Nervous and Mental Disease, 174,* 727–735.

Carlson, E.B., & Putnam, F.W. (1993). An update on the dissociative experiences scale. *Dissociation, 6,* 16–25.

Ceci, S.J., Huffman, M.L., Smith, E., & Loftus, E.F. (1994). Repeatedly thinking about non-events. *Consciousness and Cognition, 3,* 388–407.

Ceci, S.J., Loftus, E.F., Leichtman, M.D., & Bruck, M. (1994). The possible role of source misattributions in the creation of false beliefs among preschoolers. *International Journal of Clinical and Experimental Hypnosis, 42,* 304–320.

Conway, M.A., Collins, A.F., Gathercole, S.E., & Anderson, S.J. (1996). Recollections of true and false autobiographical memories. *Journal of Experimental Psychology: General, 125,* 69–95.

Devitt, M.K., Honts, C.R., & Loftus, E.F. (1996, April). *The effects of misinformation on memory for complete events.* Southwestern Psychological Association Annual Meeting, Houston.

Economist, The. (1996, July 20). Science does it with feeling, 81–83.

Erickson, M.H., & Rossi, E.L. (1989). *The February man.* New York: Brunner/Mazel.

Garry, M., Manning, C., Loftus, E.F., & Sherman, S.J. (1996) Imagination inflation. *Psychonomic Bulletin and Review, 3,* 208–214.

Goff, L.M., (1996). *Imagination inflation: The effects of number of imaginings on recognition and source monitoring.* Unpublished Master's thesis, Rice University.

Goff, L.M., & Roediger, H.L. (1996, November). *Imagination inflation: Multiple imaginings can lead to false recollection of one's actions.* Paper presented at the Annual Meeting of the Psychonomic Society, Chicago.

Hyman, I.E., & Billings, F.J. (in press) Individual differences and the creation of false childhood memories. *Memory.*

Hyman, I.E., Husband T.H., & Billings, F.J. (1995). False memories of childhood experiences. *Applied Cognitive Psychology, 9,* 181–197.

Hyman, I.E., & Pentland, J. (1996). The role of mental imagery in the creation of false childhood memories. *Journal of Memory and Language, 35,* 101–117.

Klinkenborg, V. (1997, Jan 5) Awakening to sleep. *The New York Times Magazine,* 26–31, 41, 48, 51, 55.

Loftus, E.F., & Pickrell, J.L. (1995). The formation of false memories. *Psychiatric Annals, 25,* 720–724.

Poole, D.A., Lindsay, D.S., Memon, A., Bull, R. (1995). Psychotherapy and the recovery of memories of childhood sexual abuse: US and British practitioners' opinions, practices and experiences. *Journal of Consulting and Clinical Psychology, 63,* 426–437.

Ross, C.A. (1994). *The Osiris complex: Case-studies in multiple personality disorder.* Toronto: University of Toronto Press.

Symons, C.S., & Johnson, B.T. (1997). The self-reference effect in memory. A meta-analysis. *Psychological Bulletin, 12,* 371–394.

Young, A. (1995). *The harmony of illusions.* Princeton, NJ: Princeton University Press.

7

The Rise and Fall of Semantic Memory

Jean M. Mandler
University of California, USA

INTRODUCTION

I have been studying concept formation in infancy, and so have been learning about the origins of semantic memory. The developmental findings suggest some interesting parallels with the loss of meaning that occurs in cases of semantic dementia and related neuropsychological disorders. In particular, a comparison of the data on acquisition and breakdown of the semantic system suggests something like "first in, last out". So in this chapter I first lay out the early developmental sequence in so far as we know it, and then make some comparisons with its breakdown. It is important to emphasise, however, that the developmental data are still sketchy because this kind of work in the preverbal period is very recent. Furthermore, the changes that take place with the onset of language are apt to be profound. Still, the comparison of the earliest preverbal concepts with the disappearance of concepts in dementia may be of interest to researchers in both fields.

It is also important to be clear about the kind of concepts under discussion. I am concerned with the meanings that form the declarative knowledge base (sometimes called explicit knowledge). These are the ideas we use for making inferences, planning, and other kinds of thought, as well as to communicate with other people. These are the kinds of concepts studied in semantic dementia; the various tests used to determine semantic breakdown assess declarative knowledge, such as the ability to recognise an object, name it, describe its uses or category membership, and so forth. I am not concerned in this chapter with implicit knowledge about objects of the kind that has most often been studied in infancy. For example, a great deal of research has been carried out on the "object concept" in infancy, but that term is misleading *vis-à-vis* the development of the conceptual or semantic system. The object concept has to do with the ontological nature of objects themselves, such as that objects are solid and permanent, not with the meanings of particular objects. I am interested here in how concepts of animals, vehicles, plants, furniture, and so forth come to be formed. I am also interested in how more specific concepts of dogs, trucks, palm trees, and beds arise. It is the origin of these concepts in infancy about which we still know relatively little.

ACQUISITION

Many researchers concentrate exclusively on the intricacies of the adult semantic system, and tend to have a fairly casual theory of its origins. It is commonly assumed that infants first form basic-level categories on the basis of similarity in physical appearance. These categories are said to provide a foundation on which to build up a repertoire of concepts of dogs and cats, chairs and tables, cars and trucks, and so on. It is assumed that at first infants don't know anything about these objects, but they can see that they are the same kind of thing because they look alike. Gradually with experience, associations (eating, walking, barking, and so forth) accrue that begin to give these categories meaning. Eventually they reach the status of concepts (Eimas, 1994). There are many reasons, however, to think that this view is too simple (Mandler & McDonough, 1996a). Among others, it has difficulty accounting for the early acquisition of the kinds of global categories such as animals and vehicles described in the present chapter.

Right from the beginning there appear to be two separate strands to concept formation about objects. One strand has to do with the meaning of an object—what the infant thinks it is. For example, what does a 1-year-old think a dog is—a thing with legs and a mouth, or a thing that makes a barking sound, or a kind of animal? The other strand has to do with identification of the object—the information the infant uses to identify a particular object as exemplifying a certain meaning (whatever that meaning might be). For example, what enables an infant to decide that something is a dog? I will be saying the most about early meaning, as that is central to understanding semantic development, but how exemplars are identified as members of a class is obviously important as well.

Let's start with the classical picture. An infant sees one dog and another dog and another dog and thinks they are all the same kind of thing because they all look alike (e.g. Mervis & Rosch, 1981). This view is partly true and partly false. It is true that from early infancy babies are capable of forming perceptual categories of objects such as dogs and cats. Quinn and Eimas and their colleagues have shown that as young as 3 months, infants quickly form perceptual categories of dogs, cats, horses, zebras, and lions just from a few exposures to pictures of them, and do not confuse them with each other (Eimas & Quinn, 1994; Quinn, Eimas, & Rosenkrantz, 1993). Assuming that infants can do something similar in their normal, daily experience, then that is the true part. The false part is that they consider each of these perceptual categories to be different kinds. As far as anyone knows these early perceptual categories are merely perceptual schemas and have no conceptual content whatsoever. They are, if you will, dog-patterns and cat-patterns, and so forth. The notion of kind is a more conceptual form of representation. To say that two objects are different kinds is to say something about their defining or essential characteristics, which of course perceptual appearance does not provide. We do not think that two chairs are different kinds of things just because one is blue and has three legs and the other is red and has four legs.

What I think infants do when they differentiate the world into different kinds of things, is to rely on an assumption very much like what Medin and Ortony (1989) called "psychological essentialism". Indeed, I believe this is part of our human conceptual make-up, to divide the world into different kinds. By this I don't mean that infants decide that animals have essences, but rather that infants have a propensity to divide the world into domains that each differ in a few fundamental ways. These differences are fundamental in the sense that they are based on perceptual characteristics distinctively associated with different domains, in particular, kinds of movement and other aspects of the events in which the objects take part. It is events that capture infants' attention, and, in the theory I have proposed, it is attentive analysis that forms the first concepts (Mandler, 1988, 1992). For example, I have suggested that the earliest concept of animal for infants is something like the following: An animal is the kind of thing that can start itself, that acts on other objects, and does so contingently and sometimes from a distance. If a thing behaves in these ways, they treat it as an animal; if a thing doesn't they treat it as a nonanimal. It is in this sense that the concept of animal has a core meaning, or a set of necessary and sufficient conditions. As adults, we may argue about this core, but babies don't—they merely categorise self-moving interactors as different from things that are acted upon, because these interactions are the salient aspects of events that they have attentively analysed. Thus, the claim that infants form concepts based on selected features that are defining is not meant to imply metacognitive activity. Rather the claim is that in addition to forming perceptual categories (which so far as we know do not require attention-directed processing) babies also form categories that are more selective in nature and less influenced by overall perceptual similarity. It is these selective categories that I call concepts; that is, the categories that form the basis of the semantic system.

The onset of the conceptual system begins early in infancy, so nonverbal measures are needed. In Laraine McDonough's and my laboratory we work with three. There is only one measure that we have found suitable for use under 9 months of age, and that is a familiarisation/preferential-examining measure that uses realistic little models of animals, vehicles, plants, and furniture (Mandler & McDonough, 1993). As soon as infants are old enough to manipulate objects, you give them little models of, say, animals, and let them handle them one a time. Then you can give them a new animal or a vehicle and see which they examine longer. We call this test object-examination. It is a version of the habituation/ dishabituation test (or to be precise, its near neighbour, familiarisation/ preferential-looking) that has been widely used to assess cognitive development in infancy. In the standard version, looking-time at pictures is measured. However, our test depends on examining objects rather than inspecting pictures. Before describing the data I should say a few words about differences between picture-looking and object-examining in infancy.

One might not think that using objects instead of pictures would make an important difference in a habituation/dishabituation (or familiarisation/ preferential-looking) measure. In principle, a habituation/dishabituation test, whether using pictures or objects, can depend on either perceptual or conceptual differences in the stimuli. That is, the infant can look longer at a new stimulus either because it is conceptually different or perceptually different from the ones that have preceded it, which means that the test is potentially ambiguous as to the underlying processes that mediate performance. It is interesting, therefore, that this kind of test elicits different responses from infants when objects rather than pictures are used. The data with objects suggest that infants are responding to conceptual differences more than to perceptual ones. By conceptual I mean the distinction described earlier: the infants appear to respond selectively in their categorisation rather than on the basis of overall perceptual similarity. As one illustration, when 7-month-olds interact with objects they do not respond to the perceptual differences that they do when looking at pictures. When infants look at pictures they categorise dogs and cats very easily, but they do not treat them differently on our object-handling test. This is not due to a lack of sensitivity of the object test, because 9-month-olds categorise our little models of birds as different from aeroplanes, in spite of their great perceptual similarity (see Fig. 7.2), and from about 7 months onward infants categorise animals as different from vehicles (Mandler & McDonough, 1993). In contrast, no one studying young infants has yet found this kind of superordinate categorisation of the entire animal domain (i.e. including birds and fish) when pictures are used (Mandler, 1997). It may be that categorisation cannot take place by perceptual processing alone if the range of perceptual variation is very great.

We have suggested that one reason for these differences is that different processes are being measured in the two tests (Mandler & McDonough, 1993). The conceptual system that guides attentive processing during object examination may not be fully engaged when young infants look at pictures. Typically in picture-looking experiments, young infants are seated in their mother's lap in a darkened room, given a bottle to keep them content, and they suck away while staring at the patterns presented to them. They are clearly processing the patterns but they may do so shallowly, processing the perceptual information in a relatively unselective way. Sustained attention occurs only some of the time that infants are looking at the pictures (Richards & Casey, 1992), so total fixation time is not very informative as to the types of cognitive activity taking place. In the object-examination experiments, on the other hand, we measure examining, not just looking. Ruff and her colleagues (Ruff, 1986; Ruff & Saltarelli, 1993) have shown that when objects are manipulated, examining measures a more active attentive process than does looking. During examining, infants do not merely shift their attention in an automatic way to a new stimulus appearing before them, but focus intently on an object, often picking it up, and turning it over and around. It may also be the case that in spite of our models being detailed and realistic in appearance, the picture stimuli used in the studies of Quinn, Eimas, and colleagues provide more detailed perceptual information and so may emphasise perceptual details. Without more research we cannot tell which of these differences is the most important. The crucial point, however, is that despite the similarity between one habituation/dishabituation test and another, they do not produce the same data from young infants. We began to concentrate on object tests of one sort and another after we first compared the two kinds of tasks directly (Mandler, Fivush, & Reznick, 1987); data were easier to obtain, subject loss was markedly reduced, and clearer results were found when objects rather than pictures were used. This is not to say that picture-looking tests are not useful; they certainly are for many purposes. But we should be alerted to the possibility that infants are not necessarily responding in a conceptual manner when they dishabituate in picture-looking tasks.

The most striking aspect of the data from the object-examination test is the ease with which infants categorise whole domains, such as animals, vehicles, plants, and so forth. Our earliest work on this topic studied 7- to 11-month-olds and concentrated on animals and vehicles (Mandler & McDonough, 1993). Figure 7.1 shows a sample of the exemplars we used. It can be seen that for both categories there are wide within-category variations in shape of the exemplars. Thus, this degree of perceptual variation provides no impediment to categorisation on this test. At the same time, infants also have no difficulty categorising birds and aeroplanes as different, in spite of the great between-category similarity of the exemplars (see Fig. 7.2). It may be noted that the exemplars are plastic-coated, which removes tactual texture differences as well. In contrast to these successes, infants in this age range do not differentiate fish from dogs (see Fig. 7.3) in spite of the within-class similarity and between-class dissimilarity that this contrast provides. Hence, it is difficult to describe these data in terms of either within-class or between-class perceptual differences, but easy to describe in terms of responsivity to a conceptual difference between the domains of animals and vehicles.

Our recent work has looked at other categories as well. By 9 months infants categorise animals as different from furniture. They also categorise vehicles as

FIG. 7.1. A contrast between animals and vehicles.

FIG. 7.2 A contrast between birds and aeroplanes.

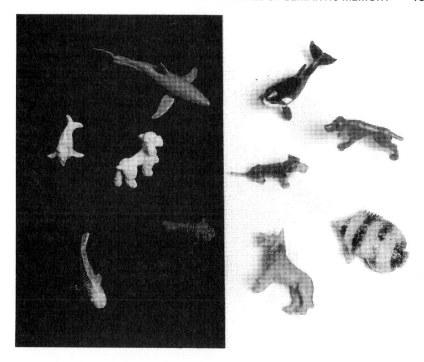

FIG. 3.   A contrast between dogs and fish.

different from furniture. There is mixed evidence as to whether 9- to 11-month olds differentiate furniture from kitchen utensils (7-month-olds were not tested), but we have no clearly significant results. We have also done some assessment of plants, although not before 11 months because younger subjects try to eat the plant stimuli (which suggests some categorisation, perhaps!). Eleven-month-olds categorise plants as different from both animals and vehicles. So there is an animal–artifact (or natural–artifact) distinction from very early on. But it is more than that, because at least some distinctions are being made within the artifact range, such as categorising vehicles as different from furniture. In addition, the distinction between animals and plants implies that the categorisation taking place is not just based on differences in fractal and nonfractal texture. These results, which as of this writing are completed but (except for animals and vehicles) not yet written up for publication, are summarised in the first three rows of Table 7.1.

We can now turn to *within*-domain categorisation. Within the animal domain, 7- to 11-month-olds make very few distinctions on this task. For example, until 11 months they make almost no distinctions among land creatures or between land creatures and sea creatures. The only early differentiation we have found is

TABLE 7.1
Some Categorical Contrasts and the Age at
which Demonstrated

Age	Animate		Inanimate
7 months	Animals	vs	Vehicles
9 months	Animals	vs	Furniture
			Vehicles vs Furniture
11 months	Plants	vs	Vehicles
	Plants vs animals		
14 months			Kitchen vs Bathroom things
17 months			Vehicles vs Household items
24 months			Furniture vs Utensils
> 24 months			Tools vs Musical instruments

between dogs and birds (i.e. a life-form distinction between land- and air-creatures). This distinction can be observed at 7 months. Recently we have begun to investigate the extent to which familiarity affects the course of differentiating the animal domain. We contrasted dogs and cats, the two animals with which infants in our culture are most apt to have direct experience. Recall that at 3 months, infants are perfectly capable of categorising pictures of dogs and cats (Quinn et al., 1993). At 7 months they show no signs of differential response to our little models, but by 9 months categorisation has begun and by 11 months clear-cut categorisation is found. However, 9- and 11-month-olds still do not treat dogs and rabbits as different, suggesting, not surprisingly, that familiarity with dogs and cats is what speeds the process of their differentiation.[1]

Familiarity may also have something to do with the fact that we see more differentiation in the vehicle domain than in the animal domain on the object-examination test. From 7 to 11 months infants treat cars as different from both motorcycles and aeroplanes. We suspect that this is due to the culture of southern California, in which infants spend a good deal of their formative years on the road inside cars. However, it is not just familiarity nor an early developing sensitivity to artifacts in general that determines the vehicle results, because we find no differentiation within the furniture domain, with which, of course, infants also have a great deal of experience. In spite of familiarity, infants show no categorisation of chairs, tables, or beds between 7 and 11 months. They can obviously see the difference between a chair and a table or a chair and a bed, but they do not treat these objects as belonging to separate kinds.

The object-examination task works well with this age group, but as I mentioned earlier it does suffer from the fact that it can be solved on the basis of visual novelty preference alone. This limitation may be relatively unimportant for the assessment of domain-level concepts such as vehicles or animals, because there is so much perceptual variation among exemplars that a perceptual solution is unlikely. However, for assessing *within*-domain knowledge it clearly does matter, because differentiating two categories can take place on the basis of purely perceptual processing without any conceptual implications. A life-form distinction between dogs and birds, for example, could be easily accomplished on the basis of high within-category similarity and low between-category similarity.

With somewhat older infants we can use the sequential-touching task, which more easily escapes this criticism. This test is the closest test to categorical sorting that can be used with children below age 2. Eight objects are put in front of the child, four from one category and four from another. In this test infants have a choice of many different objects to touch and/or manipulate. Although until about age 2 children don't spontaneously sort the categories into groups, we can measure the order in which they touch them and whether this involves sequences of runs from one category or the other significantly more often than expected by chance. Pat Bauer, Laraine McDonough, and I have used this task with 18- to 30-month-old children. We found domain-level categorisation of animals and vehicles throughout this age range. In another experiment we tested 2-year-olds and found categorisation of plants vs animals, and kitchen items vs furniture (Mandler, Bauer, & McDonough, 1991). In still another study 14- and 20-month-olds demonstrated categories of kitchen things and bathroom things (Mandler et al., 1987). These contextual categories are interesting because their exemplars have no perceptual similarity and must be based entirely on associative processes. The only domain-level failure of categorisation we found in these experiments was a contrast between tools and musical instruments (Mandler et al., 1991). Two-year-old children showed they knew the uses of these objects, (for example they might "fix" a piano with a screwdriver), but they didn't show any appreciation of tools or musical instruments as classes.

In addition, and perhaps especially interesting for those who study semantic dementia, Bauer and I found a category of manipulable household items that our subjects differentiated from vehicles (unpublished data). We discovered this category when we tried to assess responding on the sequential-touching test when there was only one taxonomic category available. We contrasted vehicles with what we called a junk category, namely sets of items we considered to be unrelated. The items in the sets we used (e.g. a lamp, hairbrush, teacup, and wristwatch, or a chair, guitar, spoon, and shoe) seemed to us to come from different semantic categories. However, these sets were inadvertently similar to those used by Warrington and McCarthy (1987) in their study of the fractionation of semantic memory along categorical lines. To our surprise, our 17- and 20-month-old subjects showed clear categorisation of this category of indoor manipulable things or household items when it was contrasted with vehicles. They were equally likely to categorise when the indoor category was contrasted with cars or with a superordinate set of vehicles.[2] This kind of category is another that must be based on associative processes, like the kitchen and bathroom categories discussed earlier. The results of all these tests in the second year are also shown in Table 7.1. It should be noted that the ages shown in the table represent the earliest successes at the ages we tested in a given experiment, but because in some experiments we did not test younger subjects, the data do not necessarily reflect the age at which the distinction is first acquired.

As far as differentiation *within* these domains is concerned, we found that 18-month-olds made a tripartite division of the animal domain into land-, air-, and sea-creatures, and the vehicle domain into land- and air-vehicles (boats were not tested). This result from the sequential-touching task was the same as for our younger subjects on the object-examining test, except that now dogs were differentiated from fish. Although there was a clear tripartite division of the animal domain, there was still no differentiation within mammals.[3] Not until 2 years of age were dogs differentiated from rabbits, and horses were not treated as different from dogs until 2½. In addition, there was no differentiation of cars, trucks, and motorcycles until 2 years; thus, performance on vehicles was poorer on the sequential-touching test than in our younger subjects on the object-examination test. This is one of the few discrepancies among the various measures we have used.[4] In addition to the lack of differentiation in the animal and vehicle domains, we also found no differentiation within the plant, furniture, or utensil domains. Two-year-olds were not responsive to trees and cacti as different kinds, nor to tables and chairs, or spoons and forks. Not surprisingly, given that they did not categorise musical instruments as a domain, they also did not categorise stringed instruments as different from horns (Mandler et al., 1991).

In summary, on the basis of the two object-manipulation techniques, we find from as early as 7 months of age, that children conceptualise animals and vehicles as different kinds of things. By 9 months they have begun to form a concept of furniture, and at least by 11 months they have begun to form a global concept of plants as well. Vehicles as a class appear to become differentiated more rapidly than do animals and plants, as we find some evidence for differentiation of cars and motorcycles in the first year. In addition, in the second year a distinction is made between indoor or household items and vehicles. By two years the household domain is subdivided at least into utensils and furniture, and somewhat earlier into the event-related or location-based categories of kitchen and bathroom things. However, even at 2 years of age, there is essentially no differentiation of the furniture or utensil domains, and relatively little differentiation among land animals. We also found no evidence of categorisation of tools or musical instruments at 2 years of age. It should be noted that not only are some of these accomplishments likely to be earlier than our data indicate (because not all ages were tested), there are also likely be other conceptual categories that are formed during this period. These are the only ones investigated to date. Hence, the absence of information about categories such as foods, clothing, buildings, and so forth, should not be taken as negative evidence. Other techniques may also be invented that will uncover earlier sensitivity to various distinctions than we have found. However, McDonough and I have developed a third technique that produces results similar to those already described. This technique, which uses imitation to assess the inductive generalisations that infants have made, is another way to test conceptual category boundaries.

Like adults, infants can make only a relatively limited number of observations of events in the world. From those observations they must make generalisations. The traditional theory about the origins of this kind of inductive process is that in the earliest stages it takes place on the basis of perceptual similarity (e.g. Quine, 1977). As discussed earlier, infants are supposed to form categories such as dogs or horses on the basis of innate perceptual schematising. So the infant observes a dog eat, or perhaps several dogs eat, and on the basis of perceptual similarity generalises eating to all dogs. The inductive inference stops there, according to this theory, because it is constrained by perceptual similarity, not by a notion of kind. To be sure, the infant also observes people eat, and maybe cats eat, and in this view eventually does make the more abstract and difficult inductive leap of inferring that all animals eat, but this is considered to be a late accomplishment. Notice that this traditional account does not explain how infants know to stop at the boundary of the animal domain. That is, there is no stop rule other than decreasing similarity. As no concept of animal appears in this account, once infants generalise across dogs and cats, they might as well infer that lots of nonanimal things eat too.

We have been using imitation to measure the limits on the inductive generalisations that infants make. These limits provide a good estimate of conceptual boundaries, because they tell us how broadly or narrowly infants think that various categorical properties apply. Imitation is our way of asking infants such questions as: What kinds of things sleep or drink? What kinds of things are started with keys or give people rides? In this technique we model a property such as drinking or keying. For example, we might give a little model of a dog a drink from a cup. Then, we give the infant the cup but instead of the dog we offer another kind of animal along with a vehicle. Or we might offer the infant another dog and a cat. In either case, we measure which object infants choose for their imitations. Do they generalise at all, only to the other dog, to any animal, or to a vehicle as well? Thus, this technique can be used to check whether our hypothesis of broad early concepts or the more traditional hypothesis of narrow perceptually based concepts (Mervis & Rosch, 1981) is correct.

To date we have tested the animal and vehicle domains and have useful data from 11-month-olds (Mandler & McDonough, submitted) and 14-month-olds (Mandler & McDonough, 1996). Data from 9-month-olds look similar, but 9 months is about the lower limit on the ability to imitate events, and only a small portion of 9-month-olds engage with our tests. What we find is that infants generalise widely from the observations they have made, but tend to stay within the appropriate domain. That is, the domain boundaries provide the stop rule for their inferences. When we model an action with an animal and then give the infants another animal and a vehicle, the infants are happy to use any exemplar of the animal domain for their imitations, no matter how perceptually different the exemplar may be. So, if we model a dog sleeping in a bed, and we give the infants the bed along with a rabbit and a truck, they put the rabbit to bed, not the truck. If instead we give them a bird (which of course looks less like the dog than does the rabbit) along with an aeroplane, they are equally willing to put the bird in the bed, but ignore the aeroplane. The same kind of results are found for unfamiliar animals (such as an aardvark) as for familiar ones. The same domain-wide generalisation is also found for vehicles; infants put a key to any vehicle and use any vehicle to give a ride, but do not key animals or use the animals to give rides. An example of these data taken from Mandler and McDonough (1996) is shown in Fig. 7.4; the percentage of actions performed that were appropriate and inappropriate to a domain are displayed, both those that occurred spontaneously in a baseline period and those that occurred during generalisation.

Thus, infants have generalised that all animals drink and sleep (fish, as well as mammals), and that all vehicles give people rides and are opened with keys (planes and forklifts as well as cars). In these experiments there was no evidence of a similarity generalisation gradient; the generalisation was uniform across all the exemplars we used. These data tell us that infants expand their limited observations to the limits of the domain, whether appropriate or not from the adult point of view.

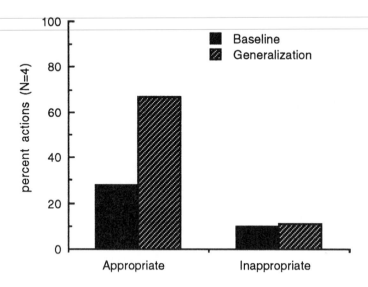

FIG. 7.4. Percentage of actions performed on appropriate and inappropriate objects (reprinted from *Cognition*, 1996, *59*, Mandler & McDonough, Drinking and driving don't mix: Inductive generalization in infancy, p.321, with permission of Elsevier Science–NL).

We are sure that the infants are using their existing conceptual knowledge rather than merely playing the experimenter's game, because when we model an incorrect property, such as giving a car a drink, infants are reluctant to imitate us (Mandler & McDonough, 1996). Furthermore, infants' responses are different when they imitate domain-general properties (Mandler & McDonough, 1997). For example, when we model going into a building, infants are willing to imitate this action with both animals and vehicles, regardless of which domain we used for the modelling. This behaviour is very different from the way they limit their imitations of domain-specific properties, such as drinking or keying, to a single domain. So they are not just playing a game of "follow the experimenter", but are using the little models as representations of the real world, to be treated accordingly.

In addition to these tests of the breadth of the concepts of animals and vehicles that infants have formed, we have also used imitation to see whether they have formed subcategories in these domains (Mandler & McDonough, 1997). The technique is especially useful in this regard because one can compare the first and second choices of the exemplars that the infants use for their imitations. The first choice tells us the infants' preferred interpretation of what they have just watched being modelled. But they have the option of using the other exemplar as a second choice, and if they consider it also to be an appropriate object on which to display the action, they often go on to demonstrate the action again with the other object. So we used the same general technique in the new experiments (e.g. modelling drinking with a dog) but for test exemplars we contrasted another exemplar from the same basic-level category (another dog) with an exemplar outside the category but from the same domain (e.g. a cat or a bird). When the contrast is dog vs cat, if infants choose the dog first we assume they interpreted the modelled event as a dog drinking from a cup. If they then go on to make the cat drink from the cup, they are indicating appreciation of the fact that dogs and cats belong to the same category in the sense that the property is appropriate for both exemplars. On the other hand, if they choose the cat first we assume they interpreted the modelled event not as a dog drinking from a cup but as an animal (or perhaps a land animal) drinking from a cup.

We found that 14-month-olds showed no preferential treatment of exemplars within the mammal class, being just as likely to choose a cat or a rabbit for their first imitations when our modelling was with a dog. This kind of result suggests that they interpreted the events as happening to an animal rather than to a particular animal kind. However, they did make a distinction within the larger animal domain, namely the life-form distinction between dogs and birds. When given a choice of generalising an observed action of a dog to another dog or to a bird, they preferred to stay within the dog category for their first choice. This kind of result suggests that they interpreted the events as happening to a land animal. At the same time, they frequently went on to demonstrate the same property on the bird as their second choice, indicating the same domain-wide associations seen in our previous work. These data are consistent with our previous categorisation data (Mandler & McDonough, 1993), showing that even younger infants categorise birds as animals, but nevertheless differentiate them from dogs when given a contrast between dogs and birds. For land animals, however, most of our work indicates no differentiation up to 18 months. (The exception is the differentiation of dogs and cats at 11 months on the object-examination test, which was not confirmed in the inductive generalisation tests just described).

Overall the vehicle tests gave similar results, but the infants were more selective than they were in the animal domain. They showed greater reliance on basic-level categories when they imitated our modelling of cars, although they frequently went on to make second choices of other road vehicles. For example, if they watched a motorcycle being keyed, they were more likely to choose another motorcycle rather than a car for their first imitation, suggesting that they had interpreted the event as a motorcycle being keyed. However, they would then frequently key the car as well, indicating their appreciation of the appropriateness of the keying action to both subcategories of vehicles. On the other hand, for the "life-form" contrast of cars and planes, the infants tended not to use the aeroplane when a car had been modelled, even as a second choice. This result occurred in spite of the fact that in our prior work (Mandler & McDonough, 1996a), when given the choice of using a rabbit or an aeroplane to imitate actions appropriate to a car, infants were quite willing to use the plane. We are not quite sure why this result occurred, although in general the greater selectivity shown in the vehicle domain fits well with our other categorisation work described earlier, in which the vehicle domain is differentiated earlier than the animal domain.

The kinds of inductive generalisation shown in these studies, especially in the vehicle domain, seems similar to that shown by toddlers, older children, and adults (Carey, 1985; Gelman & O'Reilley, 1988). Older subjects often make inductions at the domain level, but in general show greater willingness to form inductions, or express more certainty about them, when smaller classes are used. Infants also make inductive generalisations at the domain level, but in the animal domain they have fewer subclasses to act as constraints on the inductive process. Therefore, their generalisations about land animals did not show any basic-level effects. The infants showed greater selectivity when a life-form contrast was used (dogs vs birds). They preferred to generalise observed behaviour to other members of the same life-form, although they were also willing to generalise across the life-form boundary secondarily. In the vehicle domain, on the other hand, their stronger preference for staying within the smaller class when generalising seems in some sense comparable to the kinds of "certainty" effects found in older subjects. Infants might be willing to key an aeroplane if no other vehicle is around to use, but less willing to do so when an exemplar that better fits the model is available.

Overall, our results indicate that the traditional view that the earliest inductive inferences occur solely on the basis of physical similarity and therefore take place at the basic level will have to he modified. It does not appear to be the case that infants first generalise at the basic level and then go on to generalise more abstractly across these conclusions to the domain level. On the contrary, as far as the domains of animals and vehicles are concerned, infants generalise very broadly at first. The data also suggest that they learn to narrow down their inferences to the basic level as they gain more experience, and that this differentiation takes place in the vehicle domain earlier than in the animal domain for the population we have studied.

IMPLICATIONS FOR THE ORGANISATION OF SEMANTIC MEMORY

I interpret all these data to mean that property association and generalisation are controlled by the concepts that infants have already formed. In the initial stages the boundaries of these concepts tend to be quite broad. The world has been divided into a few global domains of different kinds of things. The meaning of these broad classes, such as animals or vehicles, does not arise from commonality of physical features. Babies do learn these features; indeed, they must learn them to identify an object as a member of a particular category. But in terms of what the meaning of an object is, infants observe the events in which animals and vehicles take part, and then base their interpretation of what kind of thing something is on a very general analysis of the movements and spatial relations that characterise the event. I have speculated that what infants analyse from animate events is that animals are things that move themselves and interact contingently with other things, whereas vehicles move in a different way and do not act on other things in the same fashion (Mandler, 1992). The most important aspect of this meaning creation is that it appears to be the meaning of the class as a whole that determines what gets associated with what, not just the individual objects or features of objects actually experienced.

Even though infants must be using various physical features to tell animals such as dogs and cats apart, they do not rely on them as concept delimiters. They do not restrict the associations they make to dogs to that category. The fact that infants are as apt to choose a cat as a dog to demonstrate an association modelled on a dog is one illustration of this principle. As another example, one of the aeroplanes we use has a Flying Tiger face, but our subjects do not feed it. The association is not just between mouths and feeding but between *animals* and feeding. And I have already mentioned that our 14-month-old subjects use a key on a forklift which has no door and no visible ignition, and also on an aeroplane, associations that of course they have never observed. Their personal experience of keys with vehicles has been confined exclusively to cars. So it cannot be a feature such as a door or an ignition that constitutes the meaning of "vehicle" for the young infant. Whatever that meaning is, it is what is fixing the limits on generalisation, not the range of the physical properties themselves. The infant has only observed keying with cars but has generalised it to all vehicles.

So what are physical features good for? Clearly they are necessary for recognising our little models. I assume that from a fairly early age infants pick out the individual features of mouths and legs, wheels and windows. Such features are necessary to recognise one of our new exemplars as a member of a class. Our models are not engaging in the kind of events that give their real-world counterparts meaning. However, eyes and mouths have become associated with animate things moving, and wheels and windows have become associated with inanimate things moving, and so these features can be used to identify objects that are not engaging in their customary activities. In the typical real-world case infants see a familiar object with various features engaging in animate activities. In our task the infants see only the features and must infer the animate meaning.

I have been using the expression "physical features" in order to differentiate properties such as having a specific shape or a part such as a mouth from properties such as "self-moving" or "interacts from a distance". The latter properties are what I have called essential or defining characteristics. Until recently we have had more speculation than hard data on what these properties are for most infant concepts (e.g. Mandler, 1992), but recently we have begun to learn something about the relevant properties for the animal domain: as suggested earlier, they all involve the kinds of movements and actions that animate objects engage in. For example, 2-month-olds show negative reactions to people who don't react contingently to them (Legerstee, 1992). Six-month-olds prefer to look at people interacting in a contingent fashion with other people than at people carrying out the same contingent interactions with inanimate objects (Molina, Spelke, &, King, 1996). Seven-month-olds are not surprised when people move by themselves but do not expect inanimate objects to do so (Spelke, Philips, & Woodward, 1995). Nine-month-olds show a negative emotional response to a mechanical robot engaging in self-motion (Poulin-Dubois, Lepage, & Ferland, 1996). Negative affect in particular suggests that something essential is being violated rather than an optional property.

We have the most data on infants' understanding of animals, but similar criteria should apply to inanimate objects. It is often assumed that the essential or defining characteristics of artifacts are their functions. This assumption may be true for adults, but it is unlikely to be true for infants. Infants see objects being manipulated by people, but they begin forming concepts about them before they understand what these manipulations are for. They see pans put on stoves, watches looked at, and telephones lifted to the ear, but presumably none of these events carries functional significance in the first instance. A few functions may be obvious early on, as in food as something to be eaten. In most cases, however, the specific function that differentiates one artifact from another must be obscure.

Indeed, pilot data in our laboratory suggest that 14-month-olds consider both a pan and a cup as appropriate objects from which to drink, and both bathtubs and cribs as appropriate places to sleep. Thus, even at 14 months, infants may conceive of many functions only at an abstract level, such as containment and support. Taxonomies of artifact categories have not received anything like the attention that has been given to taxonomies of animals and plants. But just as various behavioural and biological functions characterise animals as a domain, so artifacts such as tools and furniture also have higher-order commonalities in their functions, such as containing or being contained, and it may be these relatively abstract aspects of utensils and furniture that infants first analyse.

It is surprising how many categories are difficult even for adults to define in terms of anything but very general functions. Furniture is a notorious example. And the domain of household items is likely to remain primitively defined as things that people handle or as things found indoors rather than by their widely varying functions. In any case, the property of "being acted on" is the primitive precursor of the more sophisticated notion of function. As young as 3 months of age, infants appreciate the causal role of hands in moving objects about (Baillargeon, Kotovsky, & Needham, 1995; Leslie, 1984). Even when functions of artifacts begin to be better understood they may still be conceived too generally to distinguish one artifact category from another. Thus, the first division of the world into kinds is apt to be organised around different kinds of motion and the differences between acting vs being acted upon that accompany those kinds of motions. Note, however, that this kind of conceptualisation comes from observation, not from the infant's own motor activity.

This division of object properties into physical features and "meaning-bearing" properties has a number of implications for the organisation of semantic memory. First, the physical features that are used for perceptual identification are not as important to the structuring of the conceptual system as is often assumed. In the first instance the conceptual system is constructed on the basis of the meaning of objects. What I have called essential or meaning-bearing features are rather abstract and characterise large domains rather than being limited to smaller, basic-level categories. For example, rhythmic and somewhat unpredictable motion, self-starting motion, and interaction with objects from a distance characterise the behaviour of animals of all shapes, sizes, and textures. Mechanical motion, being made to start, and lack of responsivity to other objects from a distance characterise the behaviour of vehicles of all kinds as well as other inanimate objects. In addition, a whole set of disparate household objects are moved around solely by people's hands.

The result of the breadth of these early types of meaning is that the first conceptual divisions of the world tend to be at the superordinate level. (In our laboratory we call such categories global or domain-level, because a category that doesn't have any subdivisions cannot properly be called a superordinate.) They are rather abstractly defined and do not depend on overall physical appearance or on physical feature lists. As discussed earlier, I have theorised that the source of these conceptual categories is a process of perceptual analysis (Mandler, 1988, 1992). In this process infants attentively analyse perceptual displays and extract spatial relational information of a relatively abstract nature, as in the different trajectories that animate and inanimate objects take. Thus, conceptual divisions such as animate or inanimate objects do not have to be built in, but can be formed by abstracting commonalities from the different types of movement and interactions that objects display. In the first instance, a division of the world into kinds must depend on some such analysis, because for some months infants are still too young to manipulate objects themselves and are unlikely to understand most functions merely from seeing others do so.

These broad conceptual divisions form the underpinning of all more specific categories. For example, the domain of animals first becomes subdivided into life forms (mammals, birds, and fish), and these broad divisions themselves gradually become subdivided into basic-level categories such as dogs and cows. (Of course, for some people birds and fish hardly become subdivided at all, but that's another story.) For at least some domains this subdivision takes place relatively slowly. Our data say that many basic-level distinctions are not clearly made until 2 years of age or even older. It seems likely that language often plays a major role in their formation. Before the end of the first year, infants are attending to labels and apparently use them to direct their attention to perceptual distinctions they might not otherwise attend to. They are not very good at it during the second year; overextension of basic-level labels is common, not only in production but also in comprehension (Behrend, 1988; Kuczaj, 1982). And throughout this period there is often confusion as to the limits on various properties that adults associate with specific basic-level kinds.

Nevertheless, language often stimulates the child to do the analysis that will identify relevant basic-level features, and a lot of the information that will become associated with basic-level categories is language-based. This is a very different situation from the earlier division of the world into animate and inanimate, or self-moving vs caused-to-move. For example, take the dividing up of mammals into cows and rabbits. In my culture, infants have few if any contacts with either of these. They learn that cows moo and rabbits eat carrots from adults reading picture books to them, not from the kind of observation of events that taught them the meaning of animal in the first place. In short, the division between cows and rabbits is not only secondary, in the sense that at first each of these is just an animal; these concepts are also learned in a different way.

In terms of the organisation of semantic memory, the division of the world into animals, vehicles, plants, furniture, and so forth so early in life means that all the subcategories of these domains are learned and organised in the first instance as members of superordinate (global) categories. Superordinate concepts are not gradually constructed out of basic-level perceptual categories, but exactly the opposite: superordinate (global) categories form the underpinning for the formation of lower-level concepts. It is hardly surprising, then, that superordinate categories should be more resilient and longer-lasting than the more detailed subdivisions carved out of them. "First in, last out" may be due to the fact that more detailed concepts were constructed out of superordinate ones and their most fundamental meaning stems from their superordinate class membership.

BREAKDOWN

The literature on semantic dementia suggests that the breakdown of semantic memory goes from the loss of specific details to more general categories in quite an orderly fashion. Hodges, Graham, and Patterson (1995) have provided one of the most systematic studies of the pattern of breakdown. Their patient, JL, showed a progressive loss of the features that enable discrimination between specific category instances, such as dogs vs horses or cars vs buses. At first, slightly more general knowledge was spared. JL sometimes indicated that an object was a flying animal, or a tool, or something to sit on. The last distinction to go was the animate–inanimate distinction. So the pattern was first to lose basic-level class identification, then broader divisions within the domains of animals, plants, vehicles and other artifacts, and finally to lose the animate–inanimate distinction itself.

Patients have also been reported who selectively lose animate or inanimate concepts. Typically, only subsets of these two great domains are impaired, but the subsets themselves tend to follow major categorical divisions. Consider a patient studied by Warrington and McCarthy (1987), [YOT] who was impaired on tests of artifacts. Further tests showed that the impairment in object knowledge was greater for manipulable household objects than for large outdoor objects (vehicles and buildings). When the domain of household objects was examined in still greater detail, by dividing it into office supplies, interior house parts (such as doors), clothes, utensils, and furniture, she could tell these subdomains apart; for example, she might confuse a pencil with an envelope, but would not confuse it with a fork. So she retained the major subdivisions of furniture, utensils, clothes, and so forth, but she did confuse items *within* these subdomains of the larger domain of household items.

Other patients fail the chimera test (Riddoch & Humphreys, 1987), in which parts of animals or tools are combined to make chimeric objects. For example a head of a horse on a tiger is considered acceptable, as is a set of scissor blades on a screwdriver handle. Findings such as these also indicate a genuine loss of basic-level category details, leaving the broader domains themselves relatively intact. The size of the impaired and intact domains varies from patient to patient, but in all of them it is the details that are lost first, typically followed by loss at the higher levels of organisation.

Such data implicate a hierarchical organisation of semantic memory. Of course, this has been a common interpretation of the findings in this area of neuropsychological research at least since Warrington (1975) proposed it. Nevertheless, it has more recently been suggested that the loss of detail and the sparing of superordinate knowledge reflects the fact that superordinate knowledge can be sustained even in a degraded semantic net, because such a net is better able to support general than specific distinctions. In this view, the semantic system need not be organised hierarchically. Hodges et al. (1995, p. 464) describe this point of view in the following way:

> If one's knowledge about an elephant consists of a network of semantic features, then, even when a substantial number of these have been lost or blurred, it is possible that the remaining information would permit the classification of an elephant as an animal (rather than a man-made object), because almost any "animal" feature distinguishes it from a nonliving thing.

This approach to the organisation of knowledge denies the presence of hierarchies *per se* (although "general" and "specific" information do seem to serve a similar function). Instead, spared superordinate judgements of animal-ness or birdiness stem from the use of the remaining features in a gradually disintegrating undifferentiated network of features. In this view, you do not need to put categorical information into the system to get categorical impairment; in that sense superordinate knowledge is emergent rather than foundational. Farah and McClelland (1991), who take this point of view, suggest that the organising principle for semantic memory might be visual vs functional information instead (see also Warrington & Shallice, 1984). They suggest that living things are distinguished primarily by their perceptual appearance and nonliving things primarily by their functional attributes. They further suggest that this might be a more reasonable division of the semantic system than a distinction between animate and inanimate, as different brain areas are dedicated to representing information from sensory and motor channels.

One can certainly devise a model in which no hierarchical information is put into the system directly, yet breakdown occurs along categorical lines. Farah and McClelland (1991) showed that weighting visual and functional information differentially was sufficient to model the semantic memory deficits that have been found. However, even if this approach can account for the data on break-down, it may have more difficulty in accounting for acquisition. Superordinate class membership is woven into the way that the conceptual system is formed, and its foundations begin before much motor manipulation of objects has yet taken place. In the first instance, vehicles are objects that move in different ways from animals and get acted upon instead of acting. But the concept of being acted upon is *not* a motor pattern. It is not even functional in the usual way that term is used. So it is not clear how a division of conceptual knowledge into visual vs functional can substitute for categorical understanding. It is also unclear how such an approach would handle the pattern of early inductive inference I have described.

It may be that patterns of breakdown cannot by themselves answer the question of the organisation of semantic memory, not only because the hierarchical position and the degraded feature position tend to make similar predictions, but because breakdown along visual vs functional lines could occur even in a hierarchically organised system. This is where the developmental data can be useful. The argument I have made is that every time an infant or young child learns a new distinction within a conceptual realm, as part of the very learning process the object is understood as a member of a superordinate class. In so far as the meaning system is concerned, the infant looking at dogs and cats does not at first conceptualise them as two different kinds, but only as two different-looking self-movers. When they do become conceptually distinct it is as two animals that vary in their names or the sounds they make, and so forth, but their animal membership is never in question. Furthermore, our data imply that the association of features to objects occurs via the superordinate and is not an associative pairing of, for example, mouths and eating or even dogs and eating. The pairing is between animals and eating. Therefore, the superordinate domain is not emergent but is crucial for the formation of specific concepts in the first place.

NOTES

[1]We do not yet have information about how infants understand the relation between people and other animals. As animals are relatively rare in the experience of many of our young subjects, it seems likely that most of their conception of animate creatures is derived from experience with people. If this is correct, they have generalised their experiences of people to other animals, as shown in our imitation studies of drinking and sleeping discussed later.

[2]Somewhat surprisingly, they did not categorise the indoor items when they were contrasted with animals. The data suggested that the combination of animals and varied objects encouraged thematic play (e.g. putting a dog in a basket, making a turtle eat from a plate, or trying to put a shirt on a seal). Any such tendency in a sequential touching task would be likely to prevent categorical runs from reaching significance.

[3]We did not test dogs vs cats in these experiments, but instead contrasted dogs with rabbits and horses.

[4]The sequential-touching task, which is a primitive form of sorting, is a more demanding test than object-examination. Indeed, it is too difficult for infants younger than about 15 months. When two categories of geometric forms that have no conceptual meaning but are identical in colour and/or shape are used, sequential-touching can be used with infants as young as 9 months (Starkey, 1981). Models of real-world objects, however, are much more varied and can often be considered alike only in terms of conceptual commonality. This apparently is what makes it a more difficult task (see Gopnik & Meltzoff, 1992).

ACKNOWLEDGEMENTS

The research reported in this chapter was supported in part by National Science Foundation Research Grants BNS89-19035 and DBS92-21867.

REFERENCES

Baillargeon, R., Kotovsky, L., & Needham, A. (1995). The acquisition of physical knowledge in infancy. In D. Sperber, D. Premack, & A.J. Premack (Eds.), *Causal cognition.* Oxford: Clarendon Press.

Behrend, D.A. (1988). Overextensions in early language comprehension: Evidence from a signal detection approach. *Journal of Child Language, 15,* 63–75.

Carey, S. (1985). *Conceptual change in childhood.* Cambridge, MA: MIT Press.

Eimas, P.D. (1994). Categorization in early infancy and the continuity of development. *Cognition, 50,* 83–93.

Eimas, P.D., & Quinn, P.C. (1994). Studies on the formation of perceptually based basic-level categories in young infants. *Child Development, 65,* 903–917.

Farah, M., & McClelland, J.L. (1991). A computational model of semantic memory impairment: Modality specificity and emergent category specificity. *Journal of Experimental Psychology: General, 120,* 339–357.

Gelman, S.A., & O'Reilley, A.W. (1988). Children's inductive inferences within superordinate categories: The role of language and category structure. *Child Development, 59,* 876–888.

Gopnik, A., & Meltzoff, A.N. (1992). Categorization and naming: Basic-level sorting in 18-month-olds and its relation to language. *Child Development, 63,* 1091–1103.

Hodges, J.R., Graham, N.L., & Patterson, K. (1995). Charting the progression of semantic dementia: Implications for the organisation of semantic memory. *Memory, 3,* 463–495.

Kuczaj, S.A. (1982). Young children's overextensions of object words in comprehension and/or production: Support for a prototype theory of early object word meaning. *First Language, 3,* 93–105.

Legerstee, M. (1992). A review of the animate-inanimate distinction in infancy: Implications for models of social and cognitive knowing. *Early Development and Parenting, 1,* 59–67.

Leslie, A.M. (1984). Infant perception of a manual pick-up event. *British Journal of Developmental Psychology, 2,* 18–32.

Mandler, J.M. (1988). How to build a baby: On the development of an accessible representational system. *Cognitive Development, 3,* 113–136.

Mandler, J.M. (1992). How to build a baby: II. Conceptual primitives. *Psychological Review, 99,* 587–604.

Mandler, J.M. (1997). Development of categorization: Perceptual and conceptual categories. In G. Bremner, A. Slater, & G. Butterworth (Eds.), *Infant development: Recent advances.* Hove, UK: Lawrence Erlbaum Associates Ltd.

Mandler, J.M., Bauer, P.J., & McDonough, L. (1991). Separating the sheep from the goats: Differentiating global categories. *Cognitive Psychology, 23,* 263–298.

Mandler, J.M., Fivush, R., & Reznick, J.S. (1987). The development of contextual categories. *Cognitive Development, 2,* 339–354.

Mandler, J.M., & McDonough, L. (1993). Concept formation in infancy. *Cognitive Development, 8,* 291–318.

Mandler, J.M. & McDonough, L. (1996). Drinking and driving don't mix: Inductive generalization in infancy. *Cognition, 59,* 307–335.

Mandler, J.M., & McDonough, L. (1997). Category boundaries and inductive inference in infancy. Unpublished manuscript.

Mandler, J.M., & McDonough, L. (submitted). Inductive generalization in 9- and 11-month-olds.

Medin, D.L., & Ortony, A. (1989). Psychological essentialism. In S. Vosniadou & A. Ortony (Eds), *Similarity and analogical reasoning.* New York: Cambridge University Press.

Mervis, C.B., & Rosch, E. (1981). Categorization of natural objects. *Annual Review of Psychology, 32,* 89–115.

Molina, M., Spelke, E.S., & King, D. (1996). *The animate–inanimate distinction in infancy: Sensitivity to distinctions between social interactions and object manipulations.* Poster presented at the Tenth International Conference on Infant Studies, Providence, RI, April.

Patterson, K., & Hodges, J.R. (1995). Disorders of semantic memory. In A.D. Baddeley, B.A. Wilson, & F.N. Watts (Eds.), *Handbook of memory disorders.* London: John Wiley & Sons.

Poulin-Dubois, D., Lepage, A., & Ferland, D. (1996). Infants' concept of animacy. *Cognitive Development, 11,* 19–36.

Quine, W.V. (1977). Natural kinds. In S.P. Schwartz (Ed.), *Naming, necessity, and natura kinds.* Ithaca, NY: Cornell University Press.

Quinn, P.C., Eimas, P.D., & Rosenkrantz, S.L. (1993). Evidence for representations of perceptually similar natural categories by 3-month-old and 4-month-old infants. *Perception, 22,* 463–475.

Richards, J.E., & Casey, B.J. (1992). Development of sustained visual attention in the human infant. In B.A. Campbell, H. Hayne, & R. Richardson (Eds.), *Attention and information processing in infants and adults.* Hillsdale, NJ: Lawrence Erlbaum Associates Inc.

Riddoch, M.J., & Humphreys, G.W. (1987). Visual object processing in optic aphasia: A case of semantic access agnosia. *Cognitive Neuroscience, 4,* 131–185.

Ruff, H. (1986). Components of attention during infants' manipulative exploration. *Child Development, 57,* 105–114.

Ruff, H.A., & Saltarelli, L.M. (1993). Exploratory play with objects: Basic cognitive processes and individual differences. In M.H. Bornstein & A.W. O'Reilly (Eds.), *The role of play in the development of thought* (pp.5–16). San Francisco: Jossey-Bass.

Spelke, E.S., Philips, A., & Woodward, A.L. (1995). Infants' knowledge of object motion and human action. In D. Sperber, D. Premack, & A.J. Premack (Eds.), *Causal cognition.* Oxford: Clarendon Press.

Starkey, D. (1981). The origins of concept formation: Object sorting and object preference in early infancy. *Child Development, 52,* 489–497.

Warrington, E.K. (1975). Selective impairment of semantic memory. *Quarterly Journal of Experimental Psychology, 27,* 635–657.

Warrington, E.K., & McCarthy, R.A. (1987). Categories of knowledge: Further fractionations and an attempted integration. *Brain, 110,* 1273–1296.

Warrington, E.K., & Shallice, T. (1984). Category specific semantic impairments. *Brain, 107,* 829–854.

8 Stories, Selves, and Schemata: A Review of Ecological Findings

Ulric Neisser
Cornell University, NY, USA

This chapter is essentially a progress report. About 18 years have elapsed since my first presentation to an international memory conference: it was the 1978 Cardiff meeting on *Practical Aspects of Memory* (Neisser, 1978). My talk on that occasion was sharply critical of mainstream research. But a critique that is appropriate at one point may not apply at another; circumstances alter cases. The whole study of memory was different then, perhaps more different than you think. Be careful: Michael Ross (1989) has shown that major memory distortions can result from the assumption that the past was pretty much like the present. This might be such a case.

In 1978 we knew very little about most of the forms of memory that people use in daily life. There had, of course, been a bit of research on story memory: Bartlett (1932) had shown that people often get stories wrong, and Jean Mandler had begun to explore the concept of "story schema" in a series of systematic experiments (Mandler & Johnson, 1977). In what I consider to be a related line of research, Chase and Simon (1973) had started to study memory for chess positions. There was also a small smattering of research on memory for early life experiences, and Freud (1916/1963) had introduced the notion of "childhood amnesia". That was essentially all we had in the two research areas with which this paper is concerned:

- expert memory for oral texts and domain-specific displays;
- childhood amnesia, autobiographical memory, and the self.

My purpose is to review recent empirical findings in these areas, together with the theoretical concepts that have been developed to explain them. Those concepts will turn out to be remarkably similar across the two domains, with one salient exception.

DISTORTION AND ACCURACY IN ORAL RECALL

As everyone knows, Frederick Bartlett (1932) introduced the notion of *schema* to explain the results of his Cambridge story-memory experiments. He used two different experimental methods, both of which began by having someone read a brief one-page story and then write it out from memory. In the method of "repeated recall", the same person recalled the same story over and over again, often after delays of months or years. This procedure often produced gross distortions: the structure and substance of the remembered stories changed markedly from one recall to the next. Bartlett suggested that people come to such experiments with a pre-existing notion of what a story should be like: a *schema* for stories. Since that time, many researchers have confirmed that texts that fit the subject's schema are indeed better remembered than texts that do not. Nevertheless, the gross errors of commission made by Bartlett's Cantabrigian informants have proved difficult to replicate. There are few reports of such distortions in the modern literature, and my own attempts to produce them have been unsuccessful. Perhaps our subjects are more cautious today, setting higher confidence criteria for themselves than did their counterparts in the 1930s.

On the other hand, even Bartlett may have found it difficult to produce major distortions on a regular basis. Perhaps for that reason, or perhaps just because it was awkward to wait out such long delays, he soon devised a second technique. The so-called "method of serial recall" requires a number of subjects: A reads the story and tells it to B, who tells it to C, who tells it to D and so on. Gross distortions of the original text may appear after only a few steps in the chain. These results, unlike those with the single-subject method, are easy to replicate: the method of serial recall makes an excellent and often hilarious class demonstration.

Today Bartlett's distortions are old hat, but there have been important new findings in serial recall. It turns out that major distortions are by no means inevitable in this paradigm; on the contrary, some materials seem completely immune to them. I will consider two quick examples. The first focuses on the simple counting-out rhymes that children often chant as they decide who is to be "it" in a game of tag:

Eenie, meenie, miney, mo;
Catch a tiger by the toe;
If he hollers, let him go; Eenie, meenie, miney, mo.

Folklorists, who have been collecting these rhymes for a very long time, report that they persist with word-for-word precision from one generation of children to the next. How is this possible, given that they are transmitted exclusively via serial oral recall?

My second example is based on the oral transmission of epic poetry. This was the genre of Homer, and it remained vital and coherent in his corner of the world for more than two millenia. As recently as the 1930s, long oral epics were still being sung in the mountains of what was then called Yugoslavia. Skilled but entirely illiterate singers sang them in local coffee houses, all evening long and night after night. Every accomplished singer knew many different epics, each consisting of thousands of "lines", that had been preserved through centuries of oral transmission. How did these materials escape the fate of Bartlett's orally transmitted stories?

Multiple Constraints

These questions are not entirely new. We have known about the achievements of the Yugoslav singers for some time; there is even a chapter about them in my 1982 book *Memory observed*. What *is* new is that the questions have now been answered. David Rubin's book *Memory in oral traditions* (1995) presents evidence for a convincing hypothesis: such materials survive primarily because they are subject to multiple constraints. In counting-out rhymes like *Eenie meenie*, for example, a whole set of poetic devices is working at once. The most obvious of these are rhyme, alliteration, and metre; there are also subtler ones like front-to-back vowel progression. (The "ee, eye, oh" progression of *meenie, miney, mo* also appears in *Fee, fie, fo, fum.*) Almost every word in these rhymes is multiply constrained: it must rhyme with X, alliterate with Y, have such-and-such a metric pattern. This means that very few changes in *Eenie meenie* are possible, and indeed very few have occurred. Those that do happen (*tiger* was introduced rather recently), take predictable forms and appear at only a few predictable points in the text.

A different array of constraints operates in oral poetry. The Balkan epics include very little alliteration or rhyme, but every word in a given song must fit both the metre and the meaning. Constraints of this type readily permit minor variations from one performance to the next, while maintaining the song itself essentially unchanged. The singer tailors the poem to the metre line by line as he sings, drawing on a repertoire of familiar expressions to make each line come out just right. That is why a small number of standard epithets for each character appear over and over in the *Odyssey:* "noble" Odysseus, "brilliant" Odysseus, "long-suffering" Odysseus, sometimes even "long-suffering brilliant" Odysseus. Which one the singer uses in a given performance of the poem depends on what best fits the metrical pattern as well as his impulse of the moment. Loose yet firm, these constraints can preserve the essential core of an epic poem through centuries of oral transmission.

The power of poetic constraints is surprising. To see how rapidly a wide range of alternatives can be narrowed to a single choice, consider one of Rubin's examples. If I ask you to think of a colour word, you have many options: there are lots of colours. If I ask you to think of a word that rhymes with "bed", there are also quite a few possibilities. But if you now try to think of a *colour word* that rhymes with *bed* you will find exactly one: the single intersection of the set of colour words and the set of "-ed" words! Just such a situation often prevails in poetry and song.

To be effective, the constraints of a given genre must be somehow mentally represented—as "schemata"—in those who use it. The oral poets must have had schemata enabling them to produce their songs in appropriately constrained ways; children apparently have counting-out-rhyme schemata. For the most part these schemata are not sources of error, as in Bartlett's experiments; instead they are sources of accuracy. Remembering is still a process of construction, but one so tightly constrained that it produces the same result every time.

EXPERT MEMORY

The positive contributions that schemata make to memory are also obvious in a different area. As all cognitive psychologists know, experts are far better than novices at remembering material from their fields of expertise. This point, first established in Chase and Simon's (1973) classic study of chess memory, applies across a wide range of domains. This should not surprise us: experts have elaborate schemata, and schemata facilitate memory. I have always regarded the study of chess and similar skills as part of the naturalistic study of cognition (Neisser, 1976 p.7).

Most of Chase and Simon's empirical findings have stood the test of time. (This is less true of their original theoretical interpretation. The notion that chess memory depends on chunks in STM soon ran into serious problems; cf. Charness, 1976; Frey & Adesman, 1976.) Recently, however, Simon's group has reported an intriguing further result. Most accounts of chess memory have assumed that the expert advantage disappears in random positions, but this is not quite right. In a survey of published work, Gobet and Simon (1996) found better recall of random positions by experts than by novices in almost every study— albeit by smaller margins than in positions drawn from real games. Their explanation, with which I agree, is that a few familiar configurations usually appear by chance even in random arrangements of pieces. The experts' use of those configurations is probably what gives them their edge.

The result reported by Gobet and Simon may be regarded as a particular illustration of a general principle: expert schemata can often find toe-holds even in material for which they are not designed. Something similar apparently happened in Hunt and Love's (1972) famous study of the mnemonist VP. VP's memory for lists of nonsense syllables turned out to be virtually perfect, but for an unforeseen reason. His reading knowledge of several languages gave him a remarkable advantage: VP could link almost any trigram he saw to some word in some language he already knew. For him, the syllables were not nonsense at all.

Story Experts

Before leaving the topic of expertise, it is worth noting that one can be expert in story recall itself. This was the unexpected conclusion of Fred Dube's (1982) memory research in Botswana. Dube had set out to study the effects of literacy, not of story expertise. Would the memories of unschooled and nonliterate Tswanas, living in traditional bush villages, be better or worse than those of their educated counterparts in the capital city? As a control, Dube also tested American junior high school students in upstate New York. For all three groups, the material to be remembered was a set of four folk tales, two of African and two of European origin, which had been translated into the appropriate languages. The subjects heard the stories once via tape recorder and then repeated them from memory three times: once immediately, once again after a week, and then one more time a month later.

In the upshot, literacy made no difference at all. The recalls of the Tswana school children were neither better nor worse than those of their illiterate counterparts in the bush villages. In contrast, however, the memories of both African groups were far better than those of the American controls! For both types of stories (African and European), the recall of the top children in New York State was about on a par with that of the lowest scorers in Botswana. In hindsight, this finding is not hard to explain. Like many other Africans, the Tswana have a story-telling culture. Adults tell stories to children and to each other; older children tell stories to their younger sibs. It is fair to say that the Tswana are story experts, and that their expertise is broad enough to encompass even material from another culture. American children, who nowadays rarely tell stories or hear them told, are mere novices by contrast.

Note that the schemata of experts primarily support generic rather than episodic memory. The same children who remember *Eenie meenie* word-for-word need not—and perhaps could not—recall any single occasion when they actually heard it chanted! The constraints that make the literal rhyme so easy to remember are purely generic: they carry no information at all about episodes. By the same token, the Yugoslav tale-singers need not have been remembering particular past performances as they sang: what they recalled was just the timeless song itself. This principle also applies to chess memories in the Chase and Simon paradigm. Although that task itself focuses on episodic memory (the participants must reconstruct the particular chess position that was just presented), the schemata that give experts their advantage are presumably about chess in general rather than about any specific game. This is not the whole story (many players do remember particular games they have played or seen), but it is probably the most important factor.

To summarise so far: memory for both poems and chess positions depends on certain cognitive structures—so-called "schemata"—that exploit the constraints and regularities of the genre. It is because the schemata of experts are rich and elaborate that they have good domain-specific memories. Schemata can also distort recall, but such distortions are relatively rare. These theoretical notions were only embryonic in 1978; today they are strongly supported by data. Now, with this much cognitive structure in place, let us turn to the more difficult topic of autobiographical memory.

CHILDHOOD AMNESIA

Everyone's memory for life events begins with a void, a nothingness so profound that Dan Albright (1994) describes it as "Alzheimer's other disease". Why should this be so? It was Freud (1916/1963) who first called our attention to this phenomenon and christened it "childhood amnesia". He thought it resulted from repression; adults simply cannot bear to be reminded of the oedipal emotions of their childhood. This is a very odd theory; for one thing, it assumes that forgetting requires explanation while remembering does not. The first step towards a more adequate view was taken by Ernest Schachtel (1947), who offered an essentially Bartlettian interpretation of Freud's phenomenon. In his view, the fresh and innocent experiences of childhood are simply incompatible with the stereotyped schemata of adult life. Schachtel accepted Freud's idea that the amnesia covers a specific period of childhood, but in his view that period was defined chiefly by custom. There is a certain age at which society demands that we "put away childish things", and childish memories tend to go with them. Once the very different schemata of adulthood are in place, people can no longer access the memories that they established as children.

As early as the 1960s (Neisser, 1962), I wondered whether Schachtel's hypothesis might be testable in some other, perhaps non-Western culture. In societies where the end of childhood was differently defined, might we find an earlier or a later offset of childhood amnesia? This was little more than a rhetorical question at the time, but today it has been answered. As we shall see, cultural factors do indeed influence the onset of early memories. But before considering those data, we must take a closer look at the "amnesia" itself and its limits.

The first thing to notice is that the missing memories are *episodic*, not semantic or procedural. Adults have little or no trouble remembering the languages, the skills, or the social customs that they acquired in infancy: early childhood is the best time to learn such things. Each of us became an expert in the skills of everyday life when we were young, and we still have those abilities. Nevertheless, that early expertise was not accompanied by the creation of accessible episodic memories like those that adults so readily establish. Something more is evidently required before that can happen.

A methodological point is relevant here. In most studies of childhood amnesia, individuals are simply asked to recall their "earliest memory" and estimate how old they were at the time. This method has its advantages, but also its problems. Some of those problems are essentially empirical: the memory age estimates are far from certain and the memories themselves may be mistaken or confabulated. It seems to me, however, that an even greater difficulty appears at the theoretical level. To speak of an "earliest memory" in this way is to suggest that there is a single moment at which the amnesia lifts and memory begins, a moment roughly indexed by that memory. To avoid such difficulties in our own research, Jody Usher and I (1993) used a method that begins with events rather than with memories. We first establish that a given adult experienced a particular event at a known age in early childhood, and only then determine whether and how well it is remembered. In this vein we asked 222 Emory College students about four specific types of life events that had happened to them at ages from 1 to 5. We found that there is no one critical age at which amnesia lifts and memories begin. Rather, the chances of an event being remembered—and how much of it is remembered—depend on the nature of the event itself. If a very salient experience like getting a new baby brother or sister (or perhaps like spending the night in a hospital) happens to a 2-year-old, the chances are better than 50–50 that it will be remembered into adulthood. Less salient experiences are less likely to remain in memory, unless they happen at a later age.

The Development of Memory

These findings do not fit Freud's all-or-none notion of childhood amnesia. Autobiographical episodic memory doesn't suddenly "kick in" at age X, having been utterly absent before; rather, it *develops*. To understand that development, we must turn to the direct study of young children's memory. We know that adults recall very little of what happened to them at age 2 but how much do 2-year-olds themselves remember? What about 3- or 4-year-olds? As we shall see, there is one sense in which young children can be said to remember surprisingly much; in another sense, they recall little or nothing. Given specific cues, they produce clear evidence of recall; judged by the ability to produce coherent narrative, they are dismal failures.

Because these findings are fairly well known, I will review them only briefly. There definitely is memory in the first year of life: an infant who finds that kicking its leg makes a mobile move in interesting ways will keep on kicking (Rovee-Collier, 1989). Then, given appropriate cues and reminders, it will kick again on a later occasion. In recent research, Patricia Bauer (1996) and her collaborators have found that 1-year-olds can reproduce specific action sequences after substantial periods of time. In these studies the experimenter first demonstrates a sequence to a 13-month-old infant; for example, she unfolds a hinged track to form a ramp and then puts a toy car at the top so that it rolls down. Eight months later, the infant (now 21 months old) reproduces the same sequence from memory as soon as it is given the props. Note, however, that such memories are not necessarily episodic. The infants may have acquired a specific expertise rather than a specific memory; instead of recalling the occasion on which a skill was demonstrated, they may just have learned how to perform it.

At the verbal level, Katherine Nelson and her associates showed some years ago that young children find generic recall easier than episodic memory; i.e. they are better at telling you "what we do in playschool" than "what happened today in playschool" (Nelson, 1986). Nevertheless, episodic recall does make a fairly early appearance. Two-year-olds are quite capable of giving correct answers to simple questions like "Remember your trip to Disneyland? What did you see there?" (Fivush, Gray, & Fromhoff, 1987). But at this age the answers are brief ("Mickey Mouse!"), and must be elicited by specific questions. Even 3-year-olds rarely elaborate their memories or give them narrative form. Young children seem to acquire episodic memory before they acquire narrative: they can remember life events, but lack the schemata that would enable them to recall those events in a systematic way. Talking about the past is a *skill*, something one must learn how to do. Like other skills it develops with age, social support, and practice.

Once we think of remembering as a developing skill, we no longer need Freud's notion of a motivated "amnesia". There is no negative force that somehow *prevents* appropriate encoding; young children just don't have the schemata that would make later episodic remembering possible. Those schemata are still not fully understood, but they probably include some representation of one's own continuity through time. The beginnings of the life narrative may be what marks the beginning of the end of childhood amnesia.

Narrative skills are learned in the course of social experience. For young children, this means that they are learned in conversation with parents. Several investigators (e.g. Hudson, 1990) have tracked the development of those conversations. Two-year-olds do little more than answer occasional questions, but older children begin to make more substantive contributions to the dialogue. By the age of 4, most children probably know that they have had a past and can expect a future. They also know how to present selected portions of that life narrative to interested listeners, and hence to themselves. This is the age at which children start to think systematically and chronologically about their lives, thus finally establishing a time-organised cognitive structure to which they can later refer.

The Mullen Predictions

This story has an even more recent twist. A few years ago Mary Mullen, a researcher then at Harvard and now at Williams College, took the Nelson/Fivush theory seriously enough to make predictions from it. If systematic recall of life events goes back only as far as the beginnings of the self-narrative, and if young children's narrative skills develop primarily through dialogue with their parents, then the age at which childhood amnesia lifts should vary with the opportunity to engage in such dialogue. In other words, children whose parents talk to them about the past more often should grow up to be adults with better and earlier memories of childhood.

What variables might affect the frequency of parent–child conversations about the past? Mullen explored several possibilities:

- *Sibling position:* in general, children's birth order is negatively correlated with how much time they get to spend with their parents. First-borns, in particular, may get more quality talking time than later-borns.
- *Gender:* some data suggest that, on average, parents spend more time talking about the past with girls than with boys.
- *Culture:* How much parents talk with their children about shared experiences may vary from one culture to the next.

To test these hypotheses, Mullen (1994) gave Harvard students a questionnaire that asked key demographic questions—sibling position, sex, ethnic identity—and also asked them to recall and date their earliest childhood memory. Although the gender hypothesis was not strongly supported, there were two very significant results. The first was a correlation between birth order and reported age-at-first-memory: namely, later-born children had later "earliest memories". Second, Asian and Asian-American students reported substantially later "earliest memories" than Caucasians.

These results were so intriguing that Jody Usher and I tried to replicate them at Emory University. Our samples did not allow us to test the ethnic effect, but we did look seriously at sibling position. In general, we were unsuccessful: in our 682 subjects, there was no significant correlation between birth order and reported age at "earliest memory". We are not discouraged, however; this discrepancy may just reflect some quirky population difference. (The mean reported age of our informants' "earliest memories" was substantially higher than that of Mullen's Harvard subjects.) I still regard Mullen's findings as a major step forward. It is good to know that modern theories of childhood amnesia can make testable predictions.

Perhaps the most striking and best supported of those predictions concerns the effects of culture. Here Mullen herself has already enlarged on her first result, this time making a direct comparison between Koreans in Korea and Caucasians in the United States (Mullen & Yi, 1995). Korea, like many other East Asian societies, has a culture that is far more group-oriented and less individualistic than that of the United States. On the average Korean mothers may put less stress on their children's unique life experiences than American mothers do, and hence engage in less mother–child talk about the past. If the Fivush–Mullen hypothesis is correct, Korean children should typically acquire narrative skills somewhat later in life than American children. As a result the continuous memories of Korean adults should begin somewhat later as well, and it seems that they do. I am delighted with this result, which confirms that the reported age of "earliest memories" may indeed vary from one culture to the next. They do so because recalling life experience is a form of expertise that some cultural customs encourage more strongly—and develop at an earlier age—than others.

THE REMEMBERED SELF

Taken as a whole, this analysis of early memory seems to fit with my earlier discussion of songs and stories and chess positions. Experts with elaborated schemata remember more than novices do; older children with elaborated schemata remember more than younger ones, and establish memories that will be more accessible in later life. In my view, those memories are linked together by a particular narrative schema called the *remembered self*—a complex of self-referential beliefs and memories that represents who we are, how we think we have lived, and what we think we have done.

When the argument is put this way, it hardly seems new. In these post-modern times, the importance of self-narratives has already been widely recognised. Some authors go so far as to assert that the self *is* a narrative, perhaps even that it is a fiction (Dennett, 1991). But that can't be right—it is like saying that baseball games are nothing but box scores, or museums nothing but catalogues. I have argued elsewhere (Neisser, 1989, 1994) that the self-narrative is only one among five distinct sources of self-knowledge. The others include the ecological and interpersonal selves (which are given in perception), the conceptual self (a set of beliefs about one's own characteristics), and the private self of inner experience. I cannot elaborate that argument here, but hope that it seems at least plausible: the self-narrative is an important but not an all-important aspect of the self.

The Not-so-totalitarian Ego

If one's remembered life story does function as a memory schema, what are its major characteristics? What constraints does it reflect? Several different approaches to this question deserve our attention. The first is Anthony Greenwald's (1980) vision of the *totalitarian ego*: memory is always and only about the self, and its chief function is to ensure that the self comes out looking as good as possible. This hypothesis predicts that self-enhancing experiences will be remembered while negative experiences will tend to be forgotten or repressed. But although that sometimes does happen, it is hardly a universal principle. Depressives tend to recall negative rather than positive experiences, for example, especially when they are feeling low (Clark & Teasdale, 1982). Another interesting counter-example appears in Willem Wagenaar's classic diary study of memory (1986). For four years Wagenaar recorded one personally experienced event each day, together with his own reactions to it. In a later test (Wagenaar, 1994), his memory was best not for positive but for *negative* personal events, such as occasions on which he thought he had behaved badly.

A more plausible version of the totalitarian hypothesis might ignore positive and negative affect, simply claiming that memory is always focused on the self. But this is not true either; at least, Ira Hyman and I (1992) did not find such a trend in a recent study where it might easily have appeared. Our data base was a seminar that I taught at Emory some years ago, in which every weekly session was tape-recorded. A few weeks after the seminar was over, Hyman conducted one-on-one memory interviews with all the students. One goal of the study was to see whether the students' recall of things I had said (as their instructor) would be biased by their attitudes towards me personally. The results of that analysis have been briefly described elsewhere (Neisser, 1988), so I will not review them here. A second goal, more relevant here, was to compare the students' recall of their own actions—of reports they had presented, comments they had made, etc.— with their recall of other students' actions. Except in one domain, the data showed no tendency for individuals to remember themselves more fully or more favourably than other people. In general, the focus of recall corresponded to the actual focus of the event that was being remembered. When the topic was an occasion on which X had presented a paper or otherwise been the centre of attention, X did indeed remember a great deal about him- or herself. But when the topic was Y's presentation, X typically recalled a great deal about Y and relatively little about the self. The amount recalled varied sharply with the overall salience of the event in question, but hardly at all with whether the narrator had been the central figure of that event.

These results show that memory in this setting was essentially adaptive rather than autistic. It is worth noting, however, that recall of self *did* exceed recall of others for one particular class of responses, a class that we called "cognitive attributions". The students often said things like "I was surprised that...", or "it was real obvious to me..."; they rarely said things like *"he* was surprised at...", or "it was real obvious to *him"*. But this fact—that people remember their own cognitive attributions better than those of others—has a simple explanation. Although it is currently popular to downgrade introspection as a source of information about the self, the fact remains that we have better *access* to our own thoughts and feelings than those of other people. (At least, this is true in the controlled and talky atmosphere of a seminar. It may be less true in other, more emotional situations.) Apart from this cognitive factor, the hypothetical tendency for memory to focus on or flatter the ego was conspicuous by its absence. Such distortions do happen (e.g. Bahrick, Hall, & Berger, 1996), but they are by no means universal or inevitable.

Implicit Theories

Another useful perspective on how the self gets remembered—and misremembered—is that of Michael Ross (1989). He notes that people typically have fairly strong assumptions—"implicit theories"—about what is likely to be the case in certain situations. Among the most common of these implicit theories is that, generally speaking, the past was probably much like the present. People don't change all that much: if you voted Democratic this year you probably voted Democratic last year too, and for that matter 10 years ago (if you were old enough to vote). This principle also applies to the self: if *I* voted Democratic this year, *I* probably voted Democratic 10 years ago too. So if someone asks how I voted in 1986, one good strategy would be to recall how I voted *this* year and give that as my response. Most of the time this strategy will produce the right answer. To show that people actually use it, however, Ross had to find situations in which the answer it produces is wrong.

One such situation appeared in a study of pain memory by Eric Eich and his collaborators (Eich et al., 1985). At the beginning of the study, chronic headache sufferers were asked to keep pain diaries, making hourly ratings of pain intensity every day. On arrival at the clinic they then made two more judgements: they first rated their pain at that moment and then recalled the intensities of pain they had experienced since their last visit. Comparison of those recalls with the daily diaries showed that patients who happened to be experiencing strong pain at *the time of report* tended to overestimate their past pain levels, while those experiencing little pain at the time of report underestimated those levels. These patients evidently used an implicit theory to estimate their previous pain intensities, namely the theory that one's headaches are pretty much the same from day to day. What had seemed to be direct retrieval of a past experience was actually inference from a schema.

Different implicit theories can drive memory in different directions. Consider, for example, the assumption (held by most people, I suppose) that medical treatment generally produces improvement. In a different pain-memory study, Linton and Melin (1982) asked chronic pain patients who were about to get therapy to make baseline ratings of the intensity of their pain. They then underwent a treatment programme. When the programme was over, each patient tried to recall what his or her pre-treatment pain levels had been. This time those levels were *over*estimated: 11 of 12 subjects remembered their baseline pain as higher than it had been in fact. Here the implicit theory was that treatment has positive effects: if it hurts this much now, after all that therapy, the original pain must have been even worse!

One other example of a memory driven by implicit theories may also be worth mentioning. Some years ago (Neisser, 1981) I carried out a retrospective analysis of the testimony of John Dean, who had been a key witness in the Watergate hearings that brought down Richard Nixon's presidency. Dean's sworn accounts of his discussions with the President were so rich and detailed that the press nicknamed him "the human tape recorder". But because Nixon had secretly taped many of those same conversations, it later became possible to compare their actual content with what Dean had said about them. That comparison produced an interesting discrepancy between two levels of analysis. At the generic level Dean was generally right: there had indeed been a cover-up and Nixon had indeed been aware of it. The transcripts made this so obvious that everyone involved in the cover-up (except Nixon himself, who received a pardon) eventually went to jail for obstruction of justice. In his accounts of individual conversations, however, Dean was often wrong. In particular, Nixon never made many of the specific remarks attributed to him. Considered as episodic memories, then, Dean's accounts were very poor. Considered as representations of repeated episodes, however—a type of recall that I call "repisodic memory"—they were very good. In Ross's terminology, Dean had apparently formed an implicit theory of what was really going on at the White House. Like the subjects in the pain experiments, he then used that theory to generate what seemed to be direct episodic recall.

Implausible Implicit Theories

Impressive as Ross's demonstrations are, they do not begin to exhaust the implicit theories that people hold about the world. Here are some other common beliefs: no one can be in two places at once; people do not fly unaided through the air; some mode of transportation is required to travel long distances; each of us was born at a specific time and place and then grew up to become who we are today. These simple realistic assumptions often help to flesh out the self-narrative. I do not actually remember travelling from Ithaca to Cardiff in 1978, for example, but I am pretty sure I crossed the ocean by plane.

In calling these assumptions "realistic", it is only fair to admit that they are not universally shared. Some people report out-of-body experiences in which they seem to be in two places at once and have no need of mundane forms of transportation. Some people even believe in reincarnation, a notion that more or less knocks the usual assumptions about birth and development into a cocked hat. If schemata like these are used to support what seems to be memory, people may "recall" some very odd events indeed. What are we to make of such recalls? In many cases—including spirit flight and reincarnation—I feel confident that they are fabrications. (Admittedly, I do so on the basis of *my* implicit theories.) In other cases, however, the situation may be more complicated.

One case in point is the recent surge of accusations of childhood sexual abuse, accusations often made by adults who claim that they recovered their own memory of that abuse only recently. In one way or another—through the media, through friends, through psychotherapy—these individuals have come to adopt what amounts to a new set of assumptions about the world: that sexual abuse of children by parents is fairly common, that even apparently loving parents can be guilty of this behaviour, that such abusive events are often repressed at the time and remembered only in adulthood, and that those repressed memories can cause various kinds of psychological distress. Given implicit theories like these, one can misremember one's childhood just as easily as the subjects of Linton and Melin (1982) misremembered their pain levels. Just this evidently happens often. On the other hand, it may not be what always happens. Perhaps there are also cases in which such schemata help people recall things that actually happened to them, just as other schemata help people remember other kinds of things. Given what we know about memory, it behoves us to keep an open mind about particular cases.

THE EPISODIC PROBLEM

In less than a generation, the ecological study of memory has come a long way. The mnemonic achievements of the oral poets are no longer mysterious; neither are the domain-specific memory skills that come with expertise. In both cases, the individuals in question have internalised and incorporated the constraints of their genre. We also have a new hypothesis to explain why the events of early childhood are so difficult to remember: young children have not yet developed adequate skills of narrative memory. When those skills appear, they soon establish—and depend on—a particular cognitive structure called the "remembered self". But despite all this progress, one major problem seems to remain unsolved. It is a problem that puzzled Bartlett and remains a puzzle today: how do people isolate and preserve the *episodes* of episodic memory?

The cognitive structures that enable us to recall life experience differ from the schemata of poets and experts in one critical respect. In addition to averaging across broad general patterns of constraint (as in "implicit theories"), they also pick out and organise very specific episodes from the past. How is this possible? If there is no file of mental snapshots (and I believe there is not), how do rememberers ever find their way back to specific past events and recognise their specificity? Until we answer that question, we are still papering over a fairly large crack in the foundations of cognitive psychology. Bartlett's own repeated answer was that "the organism discovers how to turn round upon its own schemata"—a phrase he used repeatedly (1932, pp. 208, 211, 213). Unfortunately, I don't know what it means. Perhaps Bartlett didn't know either; he did say that it had something to do with consciousness. The problem of episodicity remains one of the major challenges facing the ecological study of memory—a challenge that I hope someone will soon rise to meet.

NOTE

An earlier version of this paper was presented at the Second International Congress on Memory, in Padova, Italy (July 1996).

REFERENCES

Albright, D. (1994). Literary and psychological models of the self. In U. Neisser & R. Fivush (Eds.), *The remembering self*. New York: Cambridge University Press.

Bahrick, H.P., Hall, L.K., & Berger, S.A. (1996). Accuracy and distortion in memory for high school grades. *Psychological Science, 7*, 265–271.

Bartlett, F.C. (1932). *Remembering*. Cambridge: Cambridge University Press.

Bauer, P.J. (1996) What do infants recall of their lives? Memory for specific events by one- to two-year-olds. *American Psychologist, 51*, 29–41.

Charness, N. (1976). Memory for chess positions: Resistance to interference. *Journal of Experimental Psychology: Human Learning and Memory, 2*, 641–653.

Chase, W.G., & Simon, H.A. (1973). The mind's eye in chess. In W.G. Chase (Ed.), *Visual information processing*. New York: Academic Press.

Clark, D.M., & Teasdale, J.D. (1982). Diurnal variation in clinical depression and accessibility of memories of positive and negative experiences. *Journal of Abnormal Psychology, 91*, 87–95.

Dennett, D.C. (1991). *Consciousness explained*. Boston: Little Brown.

Dube, E.F. (1982). Literacy, cultural familiarity, and "intelligence" as determinants of story recall. In U. Neisser (Ed.), *Memory observed: Remembering in natural contexts*. New York: Freeman.

Eich, E., Reeves, J.L. Jaeger, B., & Graff-Redford, S.B. (1985). Memory for pain: Relation between past and present pain intensity. *Pain, 23*, 375–380.

Fivush, R., Gray, J.T., & Fromhoff, F.A. (1987). Two-year-olds talk about the past. *Cognitive Development, 2*, 393–410.

Freud, S. (1963). Introductory lectures on psychoanalysis. In J. Strachey (Ed. & Trans.), *The standard edition of the complete psychological works of Sigmund Freud* (Vol.15, pp. 199–201). London: Hogarth Press. Original work published 1916.

Frey, P.W., & Adesman, P. (1976). Recall memory for visually presented chess positions. *Memory and Cognition, 4*, 541–547.

Gobet, F., & Simon, H.A. (1996). Recall of rapidly presented random chess positions is a function of skill. *Psychonomic Bulletin and Review, 3*, 159–163.

Greenwald, A.G. (1980). The totalitarian ego: Fabrication and revision of personal history. *American Psychologist, 35*, 603–618.

Hudson, J.A. (1990). The emergence of autobiographical memory in mother–child conversation. In R. Fivush & J.A. Hudson (Eds.) *Knowing and remembering in young children*. New York: Cambridge University Press.

Hunt, E., & Love, T. (1972). How good can memory be? In A.W. Melton & E. Martin (Eds.), *Coding processes in human memory*. Washington, DC: Winston-Wiley.

Hyman, I.E.R. Jr. (1984). Conversational remembering: Story recall with a peer versus for an experimenter. *Applied Cognitive Psychology, 8*, 49–66.

Hyman, I.E. Jr., & Neisser, U. (1992). The role of the self in recollections of a seminar. *Journal of Narrative and Life History, 2*, 81–103.

Linton, S.J., & Melin, L. (1982). The accuracy of remembering chronic pain. *Pain, 13*, 281–285.

Mandler, J.M., & Johnson, N.S. (1977). Remembrance of things parsed: Story structure and recall. *Cognitive Psychology, 9*, 111–151.

Mullen, M.K. (1994). Earliest recollections of childhood: A demographic analysis. *Cognition, 52*, 55–79.

Mullen, M.K., & Yi, S. (1995). The cultural context of talk about the past: Implications for the development of autobiographical memory. *Cognitive Development, 10,* 407–419.

Neisser, U. (1962). Cultural and cognitive discontinuity. In T.E. Gladwin & W. Sturtevant (Eds.), *Anthropology and human behaviour.* Washington, DC: Anthropological Society of Washington.

Neisser, U. (1976). *Cognition and reality.* New York: Freeman.

Neisser, U. (1978). Memory: What are the important questions? In M.M. Gruneberg, P.E. Morris, & R.N. Sykes (Eds.), *Practical aspects of memory.* London: Academic Press.

Neisser, U. (1981). John Dean's memory: A case study. *Cognition, 9,* 1–22.

Neisser, U. (Ed.) (1982). *Memory observed: Remembering in natural contexts.* New York: Freeman.

Neisser, U. (1988). Time present and time past. In M.M. Gruneberg, P.E. Morris, & R.N Sykes (Eds.) *Practical aspects of memory: Current research and issues.* London: Wiley.

Neisser, U. (1989). Five kinds of self-knowledge. *Philosophical Psychology, 1,* 35–39.

Neisser, U. (1994). Self-narratives: True and false. In U. Neisser & R. Fivush (Eds.), *The remembering self.* New York: Cambridge University Press.

Nelson, K. (1986). *Event knowledge: Structure and function in development.* Hillsdale, NJ: Lawrence Erlbaum Associates Inc.

Ross, M. (1989). Relation of implicit theories to the construction of personal histories. *Psychological Review, 96,* 341–357.

Rovee-Collier, C. (1989). The joy of kicking: Memories, motives, and mobiles. In P.R. Solomon, G.R. Goethals, C.M. Kelley, & B.R. Stephens (Eds.), *Memory: Inter-disciplinary approaches.* New York: Springer-Verlag.

Rubin, D.C. (1995). *Memory in oral traditions: The cognitive psychology of epic ballads, and counting-out rhymes.* New York: Oxford University Press.

Schachtel, E.G. (1947). On memory and childhood amnesia. *Psychiatry, 10,* 1–26.

Usher, J.A., & Neisser, U. (1993). Childhood amnesia and the beginnings of memory for four early life events. *Journal of Experimental Psychology: General, 122,* 155–165.

Wagenaar, W.A. (1986). My memory: A study of autobiographical memory over six years. *Cognitive Psychology, 18,* 225–252.

Wagenaar, W.A. (1994). Is memory self-serving? In U. Neisser & R. Fivush (Eds.), *The remembering self.* New York: Cambridge University Press.

9 The Role of Associative Processes in Creating False Memories

Henry L. Roediger, III, Kathleen B. McDermott, and
Kerry J. Robinson
Washington University in St. Louis, USA

INTRODUCTION: A SURVEY OF ASSOCIATIONISM

Associationism is the doctrine, popular in both ancient and modern times, that mental processes and phenomena can be explained by reference to hypothetical bonds, called associations, that link basic mental representations (Whitlow, 1992). The idea that memory and thinking have their basis in associations dates at least to the time of Aristotle (384–322 BC). Aristotle (1966, p.328) hypothesised that "acts of recollection, as they occur in experience, are due to the fact that one movement [that is, one thought] has by nature another that succeeds it in regular order." However, associationism as a doctrine did not really emerge until the 1600s, with the rise of the British associationists. Thomas Hobbes (1588–1679) wrote of the "trayne of thoughts" (1651) that was associative in character. John Locke (1632–1704) introduced the phrase "the association of ideas" in his *Essay concerning human understanding* (1690), and David Hartley even attempted to provide a physiological explanation for associations in 1749. The British associationist tradition culminated in James Mill's thoroughgoing associative theory in his *Analysis of the phenomena of the human mind* (1869).

Not long after the publication of Mill's book, Ebbinghaus (1885/1913) reported the first empirical studies of human memory. His basic assumption was that memory was associative in nature, and he used serial lists of nonsense syllables as his basic tool of study because such lists were learned (he thought) by associating each syllable to the next one and its successors. Associations could be either direct (one item to the next) or remote (between two items that are

187

separated by one or more items). Through ingenious experiments, Ebbinghaus provided evidence (in patterns of transfer) for the concept of remote associations. The powerful influence of Ebbinghaus's experimental results, superimposed on the backdrop of the British associationists' penetrating philosophical analyses, defined the study of human memory as the study of the formation and retention of associations. Mary Calkins (1863–1930) developed the paired-associates learning technique to study the formation and retention of associations more directly (Calkins, 1894). The interference theory of forgetting, which dominated the study of human learning and memory for many years, was fundamentally associative in nature; the techniques of serial and paired-associate learning were used to study effects of proactive and retroactive interference (e.g. Melton & Irwin, 1940; Postman & Underwood, 1973; Underwood, 1957).

The behaviouristic approaches to learning in animals were also largely associative in character. E.L. Thorndike (1874–1949) assumed that rewards "stamped in" (1903) the connection between stimulus and response. I.P. Pavlov (1849–1936) provided a physiological/associative analysis (1928) of how an originally neutral stimulus could, through its pairing with a stimulus that caused an automatic physiological reaction, acquire the ability to produce a similar reaction. The ascendancy of behaviourism in American psychology in the first half of the twentieth century gave associationistic analyses great force. Many of the hotly debated theories used the concept of association as a core assumption (e.g. Guthrie, 1935).

In the 1950s and 1960s the cognitive revolution began, and for a time it seemed that associationism might be supplanted by other concepts. Psycholinguists argued that associative theories could not explain the complex phenomena of language, in general, and language learning, in particular (e.g. Bever, Fodor, & Garrett, 1968). Moreover, some psychologists studying human memory believed that newer techniques, such as free recall, would resist associative analyses (e.g. Slamecka, 1968; Tulving, 1966, 1968). Despite its vague nature, the concept of schema, popularised by Bartlett (1932), seemed a worthy replacement to some (e.g. Neisser, 1967, Ch. 10). Others preferred Miller's (1956) description of higher-order units in memory (e.g. Tulving, 1964). However, associative theories were not to be denied. Anderson and Bower (1973) provided a tour de force in their book, *Human associative memory*, showing how associative analyses could be applied to many different memory phenomena. Other models of memory, such Raaijmakers and Shiffrin's (1980) Search of Associative Memory (SAM) model, also built on the assumption that memory is fundamentally associative in character. The rise of connectionism (Rumelhart & McClelland, 1986), with the avowedly associative character of its formulations, also revealed the power of associative analyses.

As this brief survey of some 2300 years of thought reveals, the concept of association has a pre-eminent status in explaining phenomena of learning and memory. Associations are generally viewed, in all these theories, as a powerful force that benefits memory. Strength of associations determines accuracy of memory. Theoreticians dating from Aristotle speculated on the laws of association, on what factors caused strong associative bonds (similarity of elements, contiguity of elements, contrast among elements, and so on). Powerful associations have uniformly been considered good for learning, retention, and retrieval.

In this chapter we raise the spectre that there is a downside to powerful associations. In particular, we explore the idea that strong associations can lead to false memories. Can powerful associations mislead, as well as lead, memory? Until recently, researchers and theorists working in the domain of associationism have rarely asked this question. We can date interest in the phenomenon to the publication of papers in the late 1950s and early 1960s, but we also note that (at least until after 1965), the issue received very little attention. Some 23 centuries of thought about the nature of associations apparently had not led scholars to realise that powerful associations can be a source of errors, until the introduction of relatively recent experimental results.

Indeed, experimental psychologists studying memory have not, until recently, been much interested in studying errors at all. For example, in the period of 1850–1900, several hundred papers were published on errors of perception in the form of perceptual illusions (Coren & Girgus, 1978), whereas virtually no papers were published on errors of memory (memory illusions). Experimental psychologists have rarely been interested in drawing strong theoretical conclusions from error analyses, although a few exceptions do exist in the literature (e.g. Conrad, 1964; Melton & Irwin, 1940). More generally, psychologists have often considered errors only to reflect processes of "guessing" that might inflate correct responding. Researchers studying recognition and cued recall were frequently concerned with the corrections that should be applied to nominally accurate responses because a portion of responses judged correct are thought to arise by chance from guessing. As a result, in many studies of cued recall (e.g. Roediger, 1973; Tulving & Pearlstone, 1966 among numerous others), errors were not treated as an interesting measure in their own right but only as revealing a process that created interpretive problems for measuring correct responses. In recognition memory the guessing problems and corrections have been deemed even more severe, and entire models of recognition memory have arisen from the theory of signal detection and its utility in correcting for rates of guessing (e.g. Lockhart & Murdock, 1970). In sum, errors were rarely considered to be of interest in memory, unlike in perception research, where their systematic study has stood for well over a hundred years as a crucible for theory construction and testing.

Roediger (1996, p.76) defined memory illusions as "cases in which a rememberer's report of a past event seriously deviates from the event's actual occurrence." Either the memory for details of the event can be distorted, or (in the most dramatic case) people can remember events that never happened at all. As we will review later, associative processes can make people believe that an event (the occurrence of a word in a list) actually happened, if the nonoccurring event was merely associated to other events in a sequence. These processes therefore reveal a powerful memory illusion.

As far as we can tell, several papers published in the late 1950s to mid-1960s were the first to raise the possibility that associative processes could lead to erroneous memories. However, the impact of these papers was rather variable. Only one paper, Underwood's (1965) "False recognition produced by implicit verbal responses", created much interest at the time. Briefly, if a subject saw a word such as *smooth* in a long list on which he or she was making recognition judgements for each item, the later appearance of *rough* was more likely to elicit a false alarm, relative to the case in which the originally exposed word was an unrelated control (such as *weak*). (We provide a more thorough review of this research later.) Underwood's (1965) research was replicated and extended, with perhaps a dozen or so papers on the topic appearing in the following decade.

Two other papers appeared before Underwood's (1965) but did not attract as much attention. Bilodeau, Fox, and Blick (1963) used a cued recall paradigm in which they tried to predict errors in cued recall by analysing the normative strength of association between the cue and a nonpresented (but associated) word. This research is also reviewed in detail later, but the basic question they framed was whether a word strongly associated to a cue word would be intruded in recall even if the word had not appeared in the study list. The answer was *yes*, and the type of normative association between the two words could be used to predict the pattern of errors.

The third paper addressing associative influences on errors had appeared even earlier. Deese (1959b) presented subjects with lists of 12 words, all of which were associated to one nonpresented word. For a few of the lists, Deese (1959b) observed that on an immediate free recall test, subjects often falsely recalled the critical word that had not been presented—the associate word around which the list had been constructed. Therefore, Deese (1959b) showed how false recall could occur in a free recall paradigm, albeit in only a few lists. Although Deese's (1959b) report was known to a few researchers, it did not spur much further research at the time, unlike Underwood's (1965) paper. We speculate on the reasons for this state of affairs later. However, the study of false recall caused by associative factors did not assume much importance in the 1950s through 1970s. For example, in Deese's (1965) book, *The structure of associations in language and thought*, he did not mention the findings of his previous paper on intrusions and did not deal with the idea that associative processes could lead to error, despite his extensive treatment in the book of many other topics about associationism in experimental psychology. Similarly, Anderson and Bower's compendious *Human associative memory* (1973) did not include the issue of errors produced by associative processes in its 511 pages, citing neither Deese (1959b; although Deese, 1959a, was cited), Bilodeau et al. (1963), nor

Underwood (1965). The issue of how associative processes might cause errors was not of much interest at the time.

The aim of the present chapter is to review what is known about the role of associative processes in causing false recognition and false recall. We delimit our subject matter to include only experiments using lists of associated words. Of course, the issues of false recall and false recognition have been studied extensively within a prose memory tradition dating back to Bartlett (1932). This approach received renewed interest in the 1970s and continues today. We make occasional contact with that literature, but its complete review is beyond the scope of this chapter (see Alba & Hasher, 1983). Similarly, other bodies of research—such as that using Loftus's (1993) misinformation paradigm—have explored related issues. Again, we draw on this related work when it is germane but primarily review the literature on associative processes in remembering in straightforward laboratory paradigms using word lists.

We organise our chapter in the following manner. First, we consider Underwood's (1965) false recognition paradigm and the numerous related experiments that followed it. We turn next to the cued recall paradigm introduced by Bilodeau et al. (1963). After a review of these literatures, we turn to Deese's (1959b) report and discuss how the paradigm was developed into the modern version introduced by Roediger and McDermott (1995). We then review the literature that has developed on false recall (and false recognition) since their report. Although Deese's (1959b) experiment predates Bilodeau et al.'s (1963), which in turn antedates Underwood's (1965), the development of these literatures generally proceeded in the opposite chronological order, so we order our review accordingly: false recognition, false cued recall, and finally errors produced in free recall. However, because Roediger and McDermott (1995) adapted the free recall paradigm to measure both false recognition and false free recall, we also consider other measures in this last section. Finally, at the end of the chapter, we briefly consider some of the theories that have been used to explain phenomena of false recall and false recognition and note some strengths and weaknesses of each approach.

FALSE RECOGNITION PRODUCED BY ASSOCIATIVE PROCESSES

With the conceptualisation of the implicit associative response (IAR) by Underwood in 1965, the power of natural language associations between words became the subject of increasing research interest. According to Underwood, the perception of a word may result not only in the activation of the *representative response* (the meaning of the word itself), but also in the unintentional activation of a word that is associatively related to the presented word, the *implicit associative response*. For example, when the word *give* is encountered, the meaning of that word is activated as well as the meaning of that word's strongest associate; in this case, *take*. Underwood contended that the IAR was not simply a hypothetical construct but indeed an actual event: the unintentional arousal of a nonpresented word in conscious awareness.

Accordingly, these implicitly occurring associates began to be recognised as a source of interference and error on recognition memory tests, appearing as predictable false alarms to nonstudied items. Underwood (1965) argued that if a certain associate is activated when a study word is encountered, an individual may be likely to confuse the words in memory and believe that the associate had been presented. Evidence of implicit associate activation on a later memory test—in other words, high probabilities of false alarm to words like *take* in the previous example—could be interpreted as strong support for the IAR theory.

With this idea in mind, Underwood (1965) constructed a 200-word continuous recognition test, designed to measure rates of false alarms produced by IAR activation. In this paradigm, subjects heard a list of words while they indicated whether or not each word had appeared previously in the list. Four types of words occurred in Underwood's test list (although to the subjects the list was simply a long series of words): stimulus words, critical or experimental words, control words, and filler words. The stimulus words were those like *give;* they were intended to produce a specific IAR when encountered. Critical words were those believed to be the subject of the IAR, for example, *take*. Control words were similar to critical words, except that they were not expected to be subject to any IAR activation from the list: They were included to provide a baserate measure of false alarms to unrelated words. Filler words were believed to be neutral and were included and repeated multiple times to increase the feeling of repetition within the list. The data of interest were the subjects' responses to the critical lures: words that had never been previously presented but that had been preceded in the list by stimulus words expected to elicit them as an IAR. The rate of false alarms to these words was compared to that of the control words, which were not expected to have been implicitly triggered by previously studied items.

Underwood (1965) was also interested in manipulating the nature of the relationship between the stimulus and the critical words, and examining the effect that this might have on false alarm rates to the critical words. Accordingly, he tested four types of stimulus words with respect to their putative IAR (see Table 9.1): antonyms of the critical words, sets of multiple associates converging on the critical words, superordinate words (such that the preceding stimulus words were instances of a category and the critical word was the category name), and sensory impressions (the set of stimulus words all demonstrated a particular characteristic and the critical word was the name of that characteristic, e.g. *barrel, doughnut, dome, globe*, and *spool* might elicit *round*).

It should be noted that in all cases except for the antonyms, multiple stimulus words were expected to elicit a single IAR. For example, in the converging associates case, *animal, cat,* and *bark* were all expected to elicit *dog* as an IAR; in the superordinate condition, *maple, oak, elm,* and *birch* were meant to converge

TABLE 9.1
Stimuli and Selected Results from Underwood (1965)

Stimulus Words	Experimental Word	Prob.	False Alarm
False Alarm Baserate:		.13	
Antonyms Presented Once			
bottom	top		.09
give	take		.11
day	night		.24
man	woman		.05
MEAN		.12	
Antonyms Presented Three Times			
rough	smooth		.28
false	true		.12
hard	soft		.37
slow	fast		.49
MEAN		.31	
Converging Associates			
butter, crumb	bread		.21
bed, dream	sleep		.23
sugar, bitter, candy	sweet		.24
animal, cat, bark	dog		.20
dark, heavy, lamp, match	light		.42
warm, chill, freeze, frigid, hot, ice	cold		.39
MEAN		.28	
Superordinates			
maple, oak, elm, birch	tree		.19
cotton, wool, silk, rayon	cloth		.18
robin, sparrow, bluejay, canary	bird		.38
MEAN		.25	
Sensory Impressions			
barrel, doughnut, dome, globe, spool	round		.07
atom, cabin, germ, gnat, village	small		.14
bandage, chalk, milk, rice, snow	white		.03
MEAN		.08	

on the critical word *tree*. In the case of the antonyms, some stimulus words were presented once, whereas other antonyms (corresponding to different experimental words) were presented three times before the experimental word.

Underwood (1965) reported that the frequency of false alarms to the critical items was highly variable and depended in part on the specific relation between the studied stimulus and the nonstudied critical words. The primary data are summarised in Table 9.1. Few false alarms were observed in the sensory impression condition, leading Underwood to conclude that sensory impression words rarely occur as IARs. He further found that false alarms tended to occur more readily when an antonym to the critical item had been previously presented on three occasions relative to when it had only been presented once, although, as may be noted from Table 9.1, specific words were confounded across conditions. Underwood also reported that four or five different but converging stimulus associates produced higher rates of false alarm to a common critical item than did the presentation of only two or three converging associates. Based on these patterns, Underwood suggested that the *frequency* of an IAR's occurrence, or the number of times it was elicited in the preceding study list, is a strong variable in predicting the likelihood of false alarm errors to the critical items. Again, however, it should be noted that materials were confounded across the conditions, and examination of Underwood's (1965) data reveals strong inter-item differences. For instance, the single-presentation antonym *day* clearly produced more false recognition responses than did the three-presentation antonym *false*. Despite the irregularities, Underwood's (1965) method and theoretical conclusions provoked a great deal of interest and closer examination of the phenomenon.

Anisfeld and Knapp (1968) further examined the nature of the relationship between the eliciting stimulus and the critical word. Using a paradigm similar to that of Underwood (1965), they studied the relative abilities of associates and synonyms of the critical word to produce false alarms to that word on the recognition test. Unlike Underwood (1965), Anisfeld and Knapp (1968, Experiment 1) included both the critical word that was an associate (e.g. *white)* to the stimulus word and the critical word that was a synonym (e.g. *dark)* to the same stimulus word (in this case, *black)* in the same test list.

Anisfeld and Knapp (1968) expected that synonyms should produce high rates of false alarms not because they elicited the critical word as an IAR but because they exhibited a considerable amount of meaning-overlap with the critical words. As explained by Anisfeld and Knapp (1968, p.172):

> The constant use of paraphrasing in everyday life communication suggests that in coding for memory under normal conditions speakers retain primarily the semantic content of the message. Since synonyms have a large area of meaning in common, they would seem natural candidates for confusion ...

This outlook has a clear similarity to explanations of false recognition in the prose literature (e.g. Bransford & Franks, 1971). The data from Anisfeld and Knapp's (1968) study and other similar experiments are shown in Table 9.2. As predicted, Anisfeld and Knapp reported significant false recognition for both the associate critical items and the synonymous critical items.[1]

In a second experiment, Anisfeld and Knapp (1968) examined more closely the associative relationship between the eliciting stimulus words and the critical false alarms. They compared three types of associate stimulus words: those that tended to elicit the critical item on a free association task (e.g. stimulus: *bitter;* critical word: *sweet),* those that tended to be themselves elicited by the critical item on a free association task (e.g. stimulus: *sweet*; critical word: *bitter)* and

TABLE 9.2
False Alarm Rates in a Continuous Recognition Task

Reference	Unrelated Baserate	Antonyms	Synonyms	Associates Producing Critical Word	Associates Produced by Critical Word	Both-ways Associates	Converging Associates (2–5 words)
Underwood, 1965	.13@	.12 .32*#					.27*
Anisfeld & Knapp, 1968							
Experiment 1	.03#@		.06*#	.09*#			
Experiment 2	.04&@			.07*&			
Fillenbaum, 1969		.17*&	.17*&	.12&	.03&		
Grossman & Eagle, 1970							
Experiment 2	.07&@	.12&	.11*&	.14*&		.07*&	
Hall & Kozloff, 1970	.03			.07*			
Hall & Kozloff, 1973	.06			.08#			
Paul, 1979	.17		.20*				.11*

*Found by the authors to differ significantly from the baseline.
& Preceding (stimulus) word presented 2 times.
# Preceding (stimulus) word presented 3 times.
@ Baseline is a weighted mean of control conditions involving unrelated words.

those that were bidirectional associates or shared both types of relationship (e.g. *white–black*).

Their motivation in comparing the two types of associates was to determine if the observed false alarms were the result of some encoding of the critical item during study or if they were due to a "reminder" of the studied item occurring during the later test presentation of the critical item. In the former case, false alarms would occur if the preceding item tended to *produce* the critical item, resulting in it being encoded during study along with the list items. The latter situation would occur if the preceding item tended to be *produced by* the critical item, inducing a feeling of familiarity when the critical item was encountered for test. In other words, does the phenomenon of false recognition arise more from encoding or from retrieval processes? If false alarms were observed when associates producing the critical item served as the stimulus items, it would suggest that the critical items were encoded during study of the preceding words. On the other hand, if false alarms were observed only when associates produced by the critical item were used on the test, then some mechanism occurring during testing of the critical item would be implicated. In the latter case, Anisfeld and Knapp (1968) argued, the occurrence of the false alarms could simply be a result of testing for them, as, in this case, the nonpresented items should not have been previously encoded.

Anisfeld and Knapp (1968) reported that both associates that produced the critical item during encoding and bidirectional associates (words that both produced and were produced by the critical item) resulted in a higher probability of false alarms to the critical item (.07), whereas associates specifically produced by the critical item did not (.03). Thus, they concluded that some variety of "initial coding" of the critical item during presentation of the preceding item probably does occur.

In discussing the implications of these data, Anisfeld and Knapp (1968, p.178) made no mention of Underwood's (1965) IAR hypothesis. Instead, they offered a feature-complex hypothesis to explain the findings:

> In order to account for these errors it must be assumed that the word is not the ultimate unit of coding. If it were, associates and synonyms should not produce more errors than control words. Rather, our finding ... supports the conception of words as complexes of features.

According to this scheme, the presentation of a word results in the activation of a pattern of features which vary in their salience and significance. Over time, the activation decays, and eventually any item(s) sharing a sufficient number of features with the studied item would be recognised as familiar. Such a conceptualisation would explain the tendency for critical items to be falsely recognised, and as such is an alternative to the IAR hypothesis. Underwood (1969) adopted a similar stance, arguing that memory traces comprised bundles of attributes.

One important difference between the IAR and the feature complex concep-tualisations is that the IAR hypothesis predicts that only one specific word will occur as an IAR during encoding, and that only it would be prone to false recog-nition. According to the feature pattern hypothesis, however, any word that shares a sufficient quantity of features with the studied word could be falsely recognised. Similarly, the feature overlap hypothesis suggests that synonyms—which share many features—should be falsely recognised at very high rates. However, as the data outlined in Table 9.2 show, synonyms do not show particularly high rates of false recognition; in Anisfeld and Knapp's study (1968, Experiment 1), false recognition of associates was actually somewhat higher than that for synonyms.

Fillenbaum (1969) did report evidence for this degraded feature complex hypothesis. Using a continuous recognition paradigm, he compared the ability of synonyms, antonyms, and control words (other associates) to elicit false alarms when they preceded the critical item on the recognition test. Importantly, the control words in this case were matched with the synonyms and antonyms for associative strength to the critical item. Fillenbaum found that both synonyms and antonyms elicited significantly more false alarms than the associate control words. Assuming that synonyms and antonyms have more features in common with the critical item than do the other associates, and because the synonyms and antonyms were matched with the control words on associative strength, he argued that the false alarms observed in this paradigm were the result of degraded feature complexes rather than simply associative relationships between the stimulus and critical items. However, the increase was relatively modest at 5% (see Table 9.2), and one might expect synonyms (*frigid–cold*) to share more features than antonyms (*hot–cold*), but the outcome does not support this prediction. As Fillenbaum (1969) did not include unrelated control items, it is impossible to determine the impact of the purely associative relationship on false alarms in this study. Nonetheless, Fillenbaum conceded that some part of the effect was probably due to associative relationships between the words, although he interpreted this effect as being mediated by features common to the stimulus and critical items rather than due to the occurrence of an IAR or some other strictly associative mechanism.

Independently of Fillenbaum (1969), Grossman and Eagle (1970) also examined the effect of the prior study of synonyms, antonyms, and other words matched for associative strength on the false recognition of a critical word. Using both a continuous recognition paradigm and a recognition task wherein the study and test components were separated by a five-minute interval, they found that the study of both synonyms (.11) and other associates (.14) led to significant levels of false recognition relative to unrelated control words, but that the study of antonyms (.12) did not.[2] They interpreted these results as support for the feature complex hypothesis, arguing that synonyms and other associates have more features in common with a critical item than do antonyms (see Table 9.2). These conclusions clearly contrast with those of Fillenbaum (1969) and Anisfeld and Knapp (1968).

Grossman and Eagle (1970) also attempted to correlate the probability of false recognition of a critical item with the association strength between it and its preceding stimulus item. They found no relationships that even approached significance (but see Deese, 1959b, which they did not cite). On the basis of these data, Grossman and Eagle argued against Underwood's (1965) IAR hypothesis, which they interpreted as predicting a strong positive relationship between associative strength and the probability of false recognition. Instead, they contended that false recognition occurs when the new (critical) word shares a sufficient quantity of features with the encoded representation of a previously studied stimulus.

The situation was complicated further by Cramer and Eagle's (1972) report of no false recognition for synonyms or antonyms in a similar paradigm. (Separate data for synonyms and antonyms are not available in their report, but the combined rate of false alarms for both types was .12; the false alarm baserate was also .12.) Additionally, Cramer and Eagle found that critical items that resembled the stimulus items phonemically produced very high rates of false recognition (.21). Methodological differences between this study and the others discussed here may be implicated in producing both the unusually high unrelated baserate and the high rate of false alarms for phonemically similar items; specifically, Cramer and Eagle (1972) used a speeded recognition procedure in which subjects were pressured to respond as rapidly as possible. Thus, Cramer and Eagle (1972) argued that perceptual or phonemic, rather than associative, properties were at work in producing the false alarms observed in this paradigm. Similar findings were reported by Gillund and Shiffrin (1984). Again using the continuous recognition paradigm, Gillund and Shiffrin found that error rates to phonemically and graphemically related items exceeded those of synonyms at both slow and rapid response rates. When subjects were required to respond very quickly (within 900ms), both phonemic and graphemic errors increased substantially (approximately a .09 increase), whereas false alarm rates to synonyms increased only modestly (about .02). However, this interaction between type of response and rate of presentation during the test did not reach significance.

Despite the popularity of the feature complex hypothesis, the importance of whole-word associations continued to be recognised. Hall and Kozloff (1970) attempted to expand on the findings of Underwood (1965), who reported that false recognition increased when a preceding associated item (an antonym) was studied three times rather than just once. In fact, an examination of Table 9.2 reveals that false recognition of related words is very small with only one presentation of the stimulus. Hall and Kozloff (1970) directly manipulated the number of preceding presentations and found that the probability of false recognition peaked with three presentations (.10) and dropped off at a systematic rate when the preceding item had been presented five (.07) or seven (.05) times, as shown in Fig. 9.1. Hall and Kozloff (1970) attributed this somewhat surprising pattern to the ability of the critical item to "remind" the subject of the stimulus word, especially when the stimulus word had been studied several times.

According to Hall and Kozloff (1970), subjects base their recognition responses on a criterion of perceived situational frequency for each item, such that items that have a perceived situational frequency exceeding some subjective level are judged old, and those that do not are judged new. In this model, perceived situational frequency counts are increased not only by the perception of the word itself, but also by its occurrence as an IAR to an associated item. Hall and Kozloff (1970, p.278) thus proposed that, due to IARs, some nonstudied (critical) words may register frequency counts above the criterion:

We propose that such prior occurrence of experimental [critical] words is a necessary but insufficient condition for their false recognition, because in most such cases the subject is able to avoid the incorrect judgment 'old' through a second comparison. It seems reasonable to assume that IARs occur during recognition just as they do earlier and that the word most likely to occur as an IAR is the ... stimulus word which previously elicited the experimental word as an IAR.

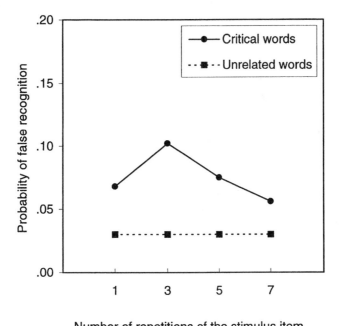

FIG. 9.1.   Probability of false recognition of the critical item as a function of the number of previous occurrences of the stimulus word. Adapted from Hall and Kozloff (1970).

In other words, when the critical item is presented for recognition, it is in focal attention as a stimulus word, and could then potentially elicit an IAR of the previously studied original stimulus word, which would remind the subject that it was the stimulus word that had occurred in the list. Hall and Kozloff (1970) went on to suggest that the more times the stimulus word is presented during study, the more likely it is to occur itself as an IAR during recognition. Thus, despite the fact that the critical item may enjoy a relatively high perceived situational frequency as a result of all the presentations of the preceding associate, this level should be much smaller than the situational frequency of the presented associate itself. The direct comparison is presumed to be made during the recognition test when the original stimulus word is brought into awareness by the presentation of the critical item. As a result, the probability of false recognition of a critical item should decrease when the preceding associate has been presented many times. This argument is in line with the earlier findings of Anisfeld and Knapp (1968, Experiment 2), who found that rates of false recognition are very low when the critical item has the tendency to produce the preceding associate as an IAR (see Table 9.2, column 6: Associates Produced by the Critical Word).

Along the same lines, Hall and Kozloff (1970) further argued that the use of a set of converging associates, rather than the multiple presentations of a single associate, would result in high perceived situational frequency counts for the critical item without a correspondingly high activation of any one studied stimulus word. In a second paper, Hall and Kozloff (1973) found support for this hypothesis. Using a continuous recognition paradigm, subjects saw either three or six presentations of a single associate (e.g. stimuli: *lamp, lamp, lamp*; critical item: *light*), or one or two repetitions of a set of three converging associates to the critical item (e.g. stimuli: *lamp, heavy, dark*, critical item: *light*). As predicted, Hall and Kozloff (1973) found that the probability of false recognition was higher when the set of three converging associates had been studied (.11 for one presentation of the set or .13 for two presentations of the set) than when a single associate had been repeated several times in the preceding list (probability of .08 for three and for six repetitions of the stimulus word; baserate for unrelated words = .06). Hall and Kozloff (1970, 1973) interpreted their results as support for both the IAR hypothesis and a perceived situational frequency criterion model of recognition decisions.

MacLeod and Nelson (1976) provided evidence at odds with both the IAR and the feature overlap explanations of false recognition. In a continuous recognition paradigm, they manipulated the lag (or the number of intervening words) between the preceding associate and the critical item. As shown in Fig. 9.2, MacLeod and Nelson reported that the probability of false recognition was near zero at no delay, peaked at a lag of 5 items, and then gradually decreased when the lag increased to 10 and 15 items. (For more recent evidence making a similar point, see Brainerd, Reyna, & Kneer, 1995.) MacLeod and Nelson (1976) argued that the nonmonotonic function observed in these data served as evidence against any single-step theories of false recognition, such as the occurrence of an IAR during study or the overlap of features between items. Instead, MacLeod and Nelson (1976) proposed two potential models that could account for the data, one describing the gradual diffusion and decay of feature representations over time, and the other based on differential forgetting rates for specific types of features over time. Several years later, Paul (1979) also examined rates of false recognition as a function of the lag between the stimulus and the critical item. Unlike MacLeod and Nelson (1976), Paul obtained to find a consistent effect of lag on false alarm rates. Paul (1979) concluded that probabilities of false recognition appear to be unaffected by variation in lags of 2 to 120 intervening items.

Vogt and Kimble (1973) addressed the fact that false recognition rates were so low. They proposed that the reason these rates rarely reached 20% was that the associative language structure probably varied highly from subject to subject. In other words, the most common normative associate to a word may not be the strongest associate to that word for a given subject, resulting in a dilution of the false recognition effect when it was based on purely normative relationships. According to the IAR theory, a more powerful way to elicit the false alarm should be to use, as the critical item, the individual person's preferred strongest associate to the stimulus word.

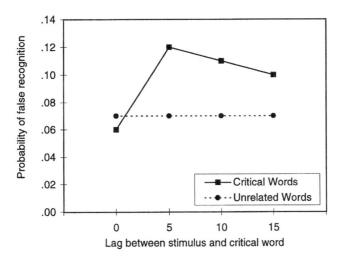

FIG. 9.2.   Probability of false recognition of the critical item as a function of the number of intervening items (lag) between the stimulus and the critical words. Adapted from MacLeod and Nelson (1976).

To test this hypothesis, Vogt and Kimble (1973) developed a two-part experiment designed to tap individual subjects' idiosyncratic associative hierarchies. In the first part, subjects rank-ordered five possible associates to a set of stimulus words provided by the experimenter. Two months later, the participants returned and each completed a specialised continuous recognition test in either the auditory or the visual modality. The 450-item test list always included the same set of stimulus items, but the specific critical items varied from subject to subject, based on their previous responses to the stimulus items. For each participant, 16 critical items were included that had been ranked first, 16 were included that had been ranked third, and 16 were included that had been ranked fifth. As may be seen in Fig. 9.3, items that were first-order personal associates generated high levels of false alarms (approaching .40); third- and fifth-order associates produced progressively lower levels. Auditory presentation of the test list appeared to increase the number of false alarms relative to visual presentation. Vogt and Kimble (1973) were appropriately troubled by the finding of higher levels of false alarms to control words than to fifth-order associates, but noted that the discrepancy was probably due to the unusual nature and the low frequency of occurrence of many of the fifth-order words. Based on these data, Vogt and Kimble (1973) concluded that close personal associates were highly effective at eliciting false recognition responses, and that relative distances within individual associative hierarchies could be used to predict rates of false recognition.

Several conclusions may be drawn from this section on false recognition. First, the false recognition phenomenon that Underwood (1965) discovered was replicated and extended by many others in the decade or so following the publication of his paper. Second, with a single presentation of the stimulus word, the false recognition effect to a related (but not presented) critical word was often quite small, with an enhanced false alarm rate of only a few per cent. Third, presenting several related words increased the false recognition phenomenon, but in the early experiments researchers used 3–5 associates at the maximum. Fourth, presenting the same stimulus word repeatedly to arouse false recognition produced a paradoxical effect: Two presentations increased later false recognition of the related word, but greater numbers of presentations actually produced a decrease in false recognition (Hall & Kozloff, 1973). Fifth, studies seeking to ask whether synonyms and antonyms produced false recognition rates beyond that of either other associates or unrelated items have produced mixed and inconsistent results. This issue probably bears re-examination. Sixth, two ideas were used to explain the phenomenon of false recognition in the early research: the notion that IARs occurring during encoding created false recognition later, as proposed by Underwood (1965), and the idea that false recognition was due to overlapping sets of features between test items and encoded items as proposed by Anisfeld and Knapp (1968). Much of the early

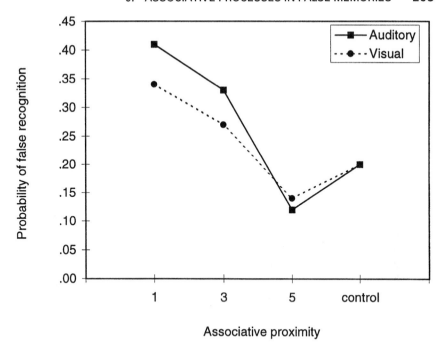

FIG. 9.3. Probability of false recognition of the critical item as a function of the subjective associative ranking of the critical item in the subject's idiosyncratic associative hierarchy. Adapted from Vogt and Kimble (1973).

research could be described in terms of both frameworks, and definitive evidence to decide the issue conclusively was not provided at the time (and still is not available).

FALSE CUED RECALL

Research on the critical topic of how retrieval cues provide access to forgotten memories is usually dated from the pioneering work of Tulving and Pearlstone (1966), who compared free recall of categorised word lists to recall under conditions when category names were provided as retrieval cues. They showed that when numerous categories were included in the list, subjects remembered many more items under conditions of cued recall than under free recall; this finding formed the basis for their distinction between availability of information in memory (what is stored) and its accessibility (what can be retrieved under a particular set of test conditions). The fact that cued recall exceeded free recall indicated that subjects did not exhaust their knowledge under free recall conditions. But a problem arises: Suppose, when subjects receive the category name retrieval cues, they simply begin guessing by providing responses that belong to the category. In this way, guessing could inflate category cued recall and therefore overestimate the power of retrieval cues. Tulving and Pearlstone (1966) were fully aware of this possibility and provided safeguards to rule it out. However, another possibility, which they did not consider, is that powerful retrieval cues could lead to false recall. That is, when subjects see the category name *bird* and write down a word that did not occur on the list (e.g. *robin*), they might not be guessing but rather "remembering" a word that did not actually occur on the list. Powerful retrieval cues may elicit false memories as well as veridical ones. This idea still has not been explored in any depth, but some work that appeared before Tulving and Pearlstone's (1966) experiments suggests that retrieval cues can elicit false recall.

Bilodeau et al. (1963) used normative association data to predict error patterns in a cued recall paradigm. However, in this experiment (and in most of the other experiments reviewed in this section on cued recall), the researchers did not use instructions that emphasised conscious recollection. Rather, subjects were told: "A short while ago you studied some words on page ___. The words below may help you remember those words. Write down the words that appeared on page ___. You must fill in every line. If you cannot remember, write in the first word that the printed word makes you think of" (Bilodeau et al., 1963, p.424). These instructions obviously encouraged free association as well as recollection and would now be considered inclusion instructions within the framework of Jacoby's (1991) process dissociation procedure. We report findings from these studies as suggestive of processes that might occur in explicit cued recall, but obviously the experiments would need to be repeated with more appropriate instructions, which emphasise remembering, before any firm conclusions can be drawn.

On the basis of the relative associative strengths of a set of words, Bilodeau et al. (1963) classified target (or cue) words into three types. R1-dominant target words have a single strong associate, such as *light* (*dark*, frequency = .57). For these words, the second most common associate has a much lower frequency of occurrence, e.g. *light* (*bulb,* frequency = .06). Bilodeau et al. predicted that words such as *light*, used as cues, would produce large numbers of errors if the correct response were something other than their primary associate. As the Bilodeau et al. paradigm involved using the second most common associates as the correct responses, they expected that these R1-dominant words would produce the highest levels of false cued recall, in the form of intrusions of the primary associate.

The second type of target words, R2-dominant words, had two primary associates that were almost equal in strength (e.g. for *ocean, water* was the most common associate, frequency = .31, but was followed closely by *sea*, frequency = .30). Bilodeau et al. (1963) expected this group of words to produce the most accurate cued recall with the fewest numbers of intrusions. The final class of words were R3-n-dominant words; these targets had many equally strong associates. For words in this third class, the two most common associates occurred at relatively low frequencies, e.g. for *cheese*, the associates with highest frequencies were *cracker* (frequency = .11), and *milk* (frequency = .10), as compared to the sum of the frequencies for all remaining associates of *cheese* (*cake + mouse*, etc., frequency =.79) (Bilodeau & Blick, 1965). Bilodeau et al. (1963) expected this third class of words to produce large numbers of intrusion errors, consisting of many different associates.

In their basic paradigm, Bilodeau et al. (1963) had subjects study words that were the second most common associates to the set of cue words representing the three classes just described. Then, given the words as cues, subjects were asked to recall as many of the studied words as possible. Based on their classification system, Bilodeau et al. (1963) were able to successfully predict the patterns of errors that would occur on the cued recall task. As predicted, the R1-dominant words produced the highest error rates, specifically high rates of intrusion for their most common associate. R2-dominant words produced the most accurate recall, and R3-n-dominant words produced high error rates with a wider variety of intrusions.

Several subsequent studies further explored this paradigm. Bilodeau and Blick (1965) examined the effects of delay between study of the list and the cued recall test. They found that the original pattern of results reported by Bilodeau et al. (1963)—the highest level of false recall for the R1-dominant words, followed by the R3-n-dominant words, with the lowest levels of false recall occurring for the R2-dominant words—was replicated at delays of 2 minutes, 20 minutes and 2 days. After 28 days, however, Bilodeau and Blick (1965) reported that subjects' cued recall protocols simply began to resemble free-association responses. This is hardly surprising, as the "cued recall" results themselves had a built-in component of free association. As subjects forgot the list words, free association responses dominated subjects' "recall".

Several later studies used similar experimental paradigms (Fox, 1968; Bilodeau & Fox, 1968), but with the same instructions that encouraged some mixture of recall and free association. In essence, these researchers seem to have been studying a combination of what today would be called conscious recollection and priming on a conceptual implicit memory test (e.g. Srinivas & Roediger, 1990). Although researchers drew conclusions about false responding in cued recall, we believe that virtually all of these experiments need to be repeated with instructions that warn against guessing, before the conclusions are accepted as demonstrating true errors of memory. The properties of false memories aroused in cued recall procedures still await systematic study.

FALSE RECALL ON FREE RECALL TESTS

The previous sections have dealt with errors induced on recognition and other cued tests. Retrieval cues such as strong associates and the "copy cues" (Tulving, 1976) used on recognition tests are powerful memorial cues. Although most of the literature produced by experimental psychologists documents the power of these cues in eliciting veridical memories, we have seen in the previous sections that these cues can also elicit false memories. This pattern provides further evidence for the claim that the factors that normally operate to improve memory also increase the probability of false memories (Roediger, McDermott, & Goff, 1997).

In this section we review evidence that false memories can be produced via associative processes in free recall of word lists, too. Further, we show that systematic errors can be produced (a) immediately after presentation of the list, and (b) when subjects are strongly discouraged from guessing. The beginnings of this research can be traced to a report by Deese (1959b). Deese was not interested in errors *per se* but rather in finding evidence for the associative nature of memory. In another paper that received much more attention at the time, and which has been cited much more frequently in the intervening years, Deese (1959a) showed that the degree to which items within a list were associatively related to one another correlated with overall recall of items in the list. Strong associative bonds within a list aided recall. Deese (1959a) also noted that intrusion errors sometimes occurred on recall tests and that there were no theories to explain why.

Deese (1959b) proposed that the associative nature of the list could be used to predict not only accurate recall, but also intrusions in recall. In order to try to find a correlation between intrusions in recall and list structure, Deese (1959b) needed to find a way to obtain substantial levels of intrusion in recall. To this end, he constructed 36 lists, each of which comprised 12 associates to a critical nonpresented word. For example, he presented subjects with *bed, rest, awake, tired, dream, wake, night, eat, sound, slumber, snore, pillow* (i.e. the 12 most commonly produced words when subjects are asked to free associate to the word *sleep*). He then measured the probability with which subjects would erroneously recall the critical nonpresented item (e.g. *sleep*) on an immediate free recall test. Although all his lists consisted of the 12 most common forward associates to the critical item, the lists differed in their backward association strengths to the critical item. That is, although the lists were constructed by collecting the words most frequently produced in response to the critical item on a free association task (i.e. the forward associates), the mean probability with which the list words (e.g. *bed, rest*) elicited the target (e.g. *sleep*) as an associate (i.e. the backward association strengths) differed across word lists.

Deese (1959b) predicted that if the associative structure of the list influenced errors (as well as correct recall), then systematic fluctuations in the associative structure might affect the probability of intrusions in the recall test. Specifically, he predicted that the backward association strength of the lists should correlate with the probability of obtaining intrusions of the critical items on free recall tests administered immediately after presentation of each 12-word list. Deese's (1959b) predictions were confirmed; Figure 1 in his paper shows that the probability of erroneous recall of the critical nonpresented item, which varied from 0% to 44% across lists, was highly correlated ($r = .87$) with the backward association strengths of the lists, or the mean probability with which the individual list words elicited the critical target item on a free association task.

Deese (1959b) concluded that the associative structure of a list was critical in determining accurate and false recall. Deese's report of intrusions in free recall did not arouse much interest for the next 25 years, and given the renewed enthusiasm for studies of false recall today, it is worth asking why. Probably most researchers saw the 1959b paper on intrusions as a minor addition to the more important 1959a paper, which showed how associative structure affected recall of list items. As already noted, experimental psychologists have traditionally been much more interested in correct performance, and errors typically have been considered a nuisance rather than an object of serious study. (As noted in the first few pages of the chapter, Deese [1965] himself failed even to cite the 1959b paper in his book on *The structure of associations in language and thought*.) However, Cramer (1965) did report a similar finding, although it was not the primary focus of her paper. She presented subjects with 26 words: 6 filler words and 4 sets of 5 associatively related words. The associative sets converged on four critical nonpresented words. Cramer (1965) reported that 51% of her subjects erroneously recalled at least one (of the four possible) critical words, and she did cite Deese (1959b) as a predecessor. However, despite a few desultory citations (e.g. Johnson, Hashtroudi, & Lindsay, 1993), not many researchers knew or cited Deese's (1959b) paper until the mid-1990s.

ROEDIGER AND McDERMOTT'S (1995) EXPERIMENTS

In the Spring of 1993, Endel Tulving mentioned Deese's (1959b) report to us. We looked it up and found what we considered to be surprising results: Although the levels of false recall were low to moderate for most of the associative study lists Deese had created, the levels for some of the lists were quite high. Deese (1959b) did not specify the instructions subjects had been given; there was no evidence they had been warned strongly against guessing. If subjects had perceived the recall task as a word association task (in which they simply generated associatively related words) more than as a task in which veridical recall was required, then the high intrusion levels observed for some lists might be expected, and so might the strong positive correlation of intrusions to word association norms. We hasten to add that we did not believe that Deese (1959b) had not measured explicit recollection; rather, we were simply puzzled by the high intrusion rates. Single-trial free recall often reveals very few instances of intrusions (at least for unrelated items), and subjects seem to set a high threshold and do not guess wildly. As Cofer (1973, p.538) put it, "subjects in recall experiments seem reluctant ... to produce material when they are uncertain that it is correct." (See also Roediger & Payne, 1985.)

If Cofer is correct, then the results from selected lists in Deese's (1959b) study are even more surprising. Therefore, the aim of our first experiment was to replicate and extend Deese's (1959b) high intrusion levels with certain lists. We presented six of the associative lists used by Deese to students in a Memory class at Rice University. These lists consisted of the 12 strongest associates to the words *chair, mountain, needle, rough, sweet,* and *sleep.* The students were asked to pay close attention to each list and, following presentation of each list, to recall as many words as they could without guessing.

Somewhat to our surprise, we replicated the basic phenomenon reported by Deese: Students erroneously recalled the critical nonstudied item as having been presented 40% of the time, on average. We also examined the output position of the critical nonpresented items and found that when subjects produced the critical items on the recall tests, items tended to occur towards the end of the recall protocols; 63% of the time the items appeared in the last fifth of subjects' recall. Further, we compared the level of false recall to the level of accurate recall as a function of serial position. Critical items were recalled with a probability equivalent to that of studied items that had been presented in the middle of the lists. This was a surprising finding that has been generally replicated (McDermott, 1996a; Roediger & McDermott, 1995, Experiment 2; Saldaña, McDermott, Pisoni, & Roediger, 1997; Schacter, Verfaellie, & Pradere, 1996c). If we take recall from the middle serial positions as an index of retrieval from long-term store, as in classic two-store models (Atkinson & Shiffrin, 1968; Glanzer, 1972), then the nonpresented items are recalled from long-term store with the same probability as items from the middle of the list.

Following the study and recall of all six lists, the students took a recognition test on which studied items, critical nonpresented items, and unrelated non-studied items appeared. For each word presented, subjects assigned a rating of *sure old* (4), *probably old* (3), *probably new* (2), or *sure new* (1). Collapsing across level of confidence, the probability with which subjects correctly endorsed the studied items as being "old" (.86) was no greater than the probability with which they mistakenly classified the critical lures as "old" (.84). Further, over half of the critical nonstudied items (.58) were assigned to the "sure old" category. The recognition results indicated that subjects seem to remember the critical nonpresented associate much as if it had actually been presented.

Encouraged by these results, in which Deese's false recall findings were replicated and extended to false recognition, we sought to examine further the nature of illusory memories. Among the questions asked in the second experiment were the following: What is the role of initial recall in producing the high levels of false recognition? (That is, did the preceding recall test cause the high levels of false recognition?) Second, what is the phenomenological experience of subjects when erroneously classifying the critical items as having been studied? (Do they really think they vividly remember the occurrence of the item from the presentation sequence, or does it just seem very familiar?)

To address the first question, we manipulated prior testing history on the recognition test. Subjects studied 16 lists in Experiment 2 but received an immediate free recall test following only half of the lists. Therefore, on the final recognition test, we could compare false recognition for lists previously tested and those not previously tested. On the basis of the testing effect, or the finding that accurate recall (and sometimes recognition) is enhanced by prior testing (Thompson, Wenger, & Bartling, 1978), we hypothesised that testing might solidify false memories, as well (see also Schooler, Foster, & Loftus, 1988).

As shown in Table 9.3 our results supported this hypothesis: Although the probability of false recognition on the lists that had not been followed by an immediate free recall test was substantial (.72), it was not as high as the probability for the lists that had been previously tested (.81). A similar finding was observed for studied items: The hit rate for lists not previously tested (.65) fell short of that for lists previously tested (.79). In addition to the obvious parallels in the effects of testing for studied and critical items, it is worth noting the similarity of magnitude for hits and false alarms in this paradigm: Subjects appear to treat critical lures as list items.

To address the issue of phenomenological experience of subjects, we utilised the remember/know procedure (Gardiner, 1988; Tulving, 1985; see Gardiner & Java, 1993, and Rajaram & Roediger, 1997, for comprehensive reviews). Subjects were given standard old/new recognition instructions but were also told

TABLE 9.3
Recognition Results From Roediger and McDermott's (1995)
Experiment 2

Item Type	Initial Test	Proportion of Responses		
		Old	Remember	Know
Studied	Yes	.79	.57	.22
	No	.65	.41	.24
Critical	Yes	.81	.58	.23
	No	.72	.38	.34

Probability of accurate and false recognition (and remember/know judgements) as a function of whether an initial recall test preceded the recognition test.

that for each item classified as old, they should indicate whether they could vividly recollect some specific aspect of the presentation episode of that item (by writing an R, for *remember*) or whether they simply knew the item had been presented earlier but lacked the ability to recollect the actual presentation (by writing a K, for *know*). The question of interest was whether subjects would ever claim to remember something specific about the instance of presentation of the critical items that had not been presented. Our hypothesis was that the great majority of critical items erroneously recognised would be classified as known, given that there was no presentation instance to remember. Subjects' false alarms would be based on some general feeling of familiarity with the items, not a recollective experience (e.g. Jacoby, 1991). Indeed, prior experiments had shown that false alarms are predominantly classified as known (e.g. Gardiner, 1988; Rajaram, 1993). To our surprise, subjects were quite willing to claim that they could remember the presentation of the critical items—they did so on 48% of the lists. Further, subjects gave remember responses to critical nonpresented items with the same probability as they claimed to remember items that actually had been studied (.49). Therefore, unlike in most prior work, we were able to elicit high levels of false remembering.

A final noteworthy finding from this experiment is that the testing effect was localised in remember responses. For both studied and critical items, the probability of know judgements did not change substantially as a function of prior testing (see Table 9.3). Instead, the enhancement seen in overall recognition was restricted to remember judgements. Despite the fact that subjects were specifically told to make their remember/know judgements with respect to the study episode (i.e. not to report whether they remembered writing the item on the previous free recall test), taking the test made subjects more likely to think they were recollecting the original study episode.

In summary, Roediger and McDermott (1995) expanded the work of Deese (1959b) and changed the basic paradigm he introduced into one that is becoming widely used to induce and assess false memories in recall and recognition. In general, we will refer to experiments in which related words are presented to elicit false recall and false recognition (often with metamemory judgements) as the Deese-Roediger-McDermott paradigm, or the DRM (pronounced DREAM) paradigm for short.[3] Obviously, the Roediger and McDermott (1995) experiments owed a debt to Deese (1959b), but the paradigm we introduced and which is in common use now is quite different from the one Deese used. Among other differences, it includes only lists intended to produce high levels of false recall, followed by recognition and metamemory judgements.

Next we review the studies that have explored false recall and false recognition in variants of the Deese-Roediger-McDermott paradigm. Most of the studies to date have manipulated various independent variables to examine their effects on the dependent variables mentioned earlier: probability of false recall, output position in false recall, probability of false recognition, confidence, and probability of remember responses. A few studies, however, have introduced new dependent variables, usually measuring metamemorial aspects of performance. First we review the various other metamemory judgements that have been examined, then we turn to a discussion of the many independent variables that have been manipulated, followed by discussion of the subject variables examined. Finally, we conclude this review section with a discussion of the few studies that have attempted to identify the neural correlates of illusory memory by using this paradigm. Although reviewing the literature in terms of classes of variables may not be as exciting as doing so in terms of theoretical implications, we justify our organisation by noting that at this early stage of inquiry it will be more profitable to try to gain an understanding of the basic phenomena to be explained. Later, after we have reviewed the evidence, we turn to its implications for some of the most popular theories of false memory.

ADDITIONAL METAMEMORY JUDGEMENTS IN FALSE RECALL AND FALSE RECOGNITION

In an attempt to explore further the enigmatic finding of high proportions of remember judgements to critical lures, Norman and Schacter (1997) asked subjects to justify their recognition judgements (remember, know, or new). Even when pressed to describe the aspect of the item's presentation that was remembered, subjects still frequently assigned remember classifications to the critical nonpresented items. However, the information provided by subjects in this condition was usually not specific to the individual item (e.g. the way the item sounded when spoken), but often referred to thoughts or associations accompanying the word (e.g. for the word *music*: "This word occurred in the list with *note* and *piano*; I remember thinking about the music I listened to this morning").

In a second experiment, Norman and Schacter (1997) attempted to quantify subjects' recollections of the nonpresented items by giving them a variant of the Memory Characteristics Questionnaire (MCQ) developed by Johnson, Foley, Suengas, and Raye (1988). Subjects were asked to specify for each item remembered whether they could recollect various sensory characteristics (e.g. sound) or spatiotemporal context (e.g. list position) of the items. Specifically, subjects were asked to rate (on a 7-point scale) the degree to which they remembered (1) the sound of the word; (2) the position the word occupied in the study list; (3) the word that had come immediately before or after the target word; (4) any reaction they might have had when studying the word; (5) a specific thought occurring during study of the word; or (6) associating this word with other studied words. Three variables (sound, list position, and specific thought) discriminated between studied and critical items in that subjects reported retrieving more such information for studied items than for critical items. Nonetheless, subjects did claim to be able to ascribe substantial detail to the critical nonpresented items.

Mather, Henkel, and Johnson (1997) obtained results that converge nicely on Norman and Schacter's (1997) basic findings. In their study, subjects were asked to rate (on a 5-point scale) the degree to which they recalled (1) the sound of the word; (2) feelings or reactions encountered when previously hearing the word; (3) any associations made when hearing the word; and (4) rehearsing the word. As in Norman and Schacter's (1997) data, both the sound of the word and feelings when hearing the word were given higher ratings for studied items than critical items. Also consistent with Norman and Schacter's (1997) data, the association rating did not discriminate studied from nonstudied items. The final variable, rehearsal at study, also did not discriminate between studied and non-studied items. This last finding is perhaps one of the most interesting in this study because it suggests that the locus of the false memory effect may not simply be an implicit activation of the critical item at study but rather that subjects are con-sciously, effortfully processing and rehearsing these nonpresented items during the study phase. We will return to this idea in a discussion of the possible mechanisms for the effect, later in the chapter.

The primary conclusion from the MCQ studies is that when subjects are asked about the specific perceptual features of test items, they can recall more such attributes for items that were heard in the DRM lists than for those often recalled but never presented. Still, they frequently make errors in recall and recognition by endorsing critical nonpresented items as having occurred in the list, and they also claim to recollect attributes of the items' presentations, albeit not at the level of studied items. It should be pointed out that the differences observed between studied and critical items on these measures are based on statistical aggregates: they are not substantial enough to allow for the classification of a memory as veridical or false on an item-by-item basis.

A final metamemory judgement that has received attention is that of voice attributions. In a variant of the basic DRM procedure, Payne, Elie, Blackwell, and Neuschatz (1996a) presented a long, 64-word list, constructed around six critical items. Items were always blocked according to list, but the voice in which the items occurred was manipulated. Subjects were shown a videotape of two people ("Jason" and "Carol") speaking the words in the lists. Subjects were then given three successive recall tests (an aspect of the experiment to be discussed later, in the repeated testing section). Following the third recall test, subjects were asked to assign voices to the words they had recalled (i.e. whether Jason or Carol had spoken the word during study), with the option of leaving blank any words to which they could not assign a voice. Consistent with the finding that subjects think they remember critical nonpresented items, they also claim to recollect the voice in which the items were presented: In Payne et al.'s experiment, subjects assigned a voice to 87% of the critical items they had recalled. The comparable rate for studied items was 94%. Although the probability for studied items was greater than for critical nonstudied words, subjects still showed a remarkable tendency to report the voice in which critical nonpresented words had been presented.

Payne et al. (1996a) had several different ways of presenting the lists; in one condition, all of the words in a given sublist (e.g. all words related to *sleep*) were presented by a single speaker. This condition allowed an examination of the likelihood that subjects would classify the critical nonpresented items as having been spoken by the person who spoke the words that corresponded to that critical item. Surprisingly, subjects classified the nonpresented items this way only 53% of the time. In contrast, the probability of correctly classifying the studied items to the appropriate speaker was 84% in this condition. These findings are something of a puzzle.

Using a slightly different procedure, Mather et al. (1997) found a much higher attribution figure on a recognition test. In their study, 76% of subjects claimed that the critical nonpresented item had been spoken by the speaker who had spoken the associated words. In Mather et al.'s experiment, however, subjects were not given the option of claiming not to remember the speaker of the item: They were told on the recognition test to choose whether the item had been presented by the female speaker, the male speaker, or not at all. Thus, the figures are not directly comparable. It would also be interesting to know in Payne et al.'s experiment how the remaining 47% of items were classified—were they attributed to the other speaker, or were most classified in the "don't know" category? Payne et al. did not present these data.

Regardless of the specific patterns of response classifications, the primary conclusion from these two studies is that subjects are quite willing to attribute a voice to the presentation of the critical nonpresented items (see also Saldaña et al., 1997). The extent to which these judgements are influenced by the voices that spoke the associated studied items is still something of an open question: Mather et al. (1997) conclude that it is a highly influential factor; Payne et al.'s (1996a) results, however, seem to suggest otherwise. Further work is clearly needed before any strong conclusions can be drawn.

In summary, several studies have examined a number of dependent variables in the DRM paradigm (or close variations of it). These variables include the probability of recall, probability of recognition, output position, and probability of remember responses. In addition, voice attributions and specific questions about the perceptual and cognitive aspects of the initial study phase have been examined. The majority of the results converge on the claim that although it is sometimes possible to distinguish between studied and critical items, the false memories created in this paradigm are extremely robust (often to the extent of being indistinguishable from true memories). In the following section, we review how important independent variables that have powerful effects on veridical memory influence false memories.

FACTORS AFFECTING FALSE RECALL AND FALSE RECOGNITION IN THE DRM PARADIGM

We begin this section with a discussion of the variables that have been examined in the encoding phase, followed by a review of the experiments with manipulations of retention interval, and conclude with factors in the test phase and how they influence false recall and false recognition in this paradigm. This organisation of factors in terms of encoding, retention, and test phases corresponds to standard experimental practice, but of course it must be borne in mind that manipulations of factors at a particular stage (e.g. retrieval) are not independent of earlier stages of processing (e.g. encoding). Still, for our purposes, this scheme provides a useful way to organise the literature.

Study Variables

Included in this section are variables that have been manipulated before and during study presentation. These variables include manipulation of instructions during the study phase and manipulations of the study material itself. Researchers have asked many fundamental questions about false recall by manipulating basic study variables within the DRM paradigm. We consider these studies here.

Instructional Manipulations at Study

An interesting but as yet little-examined question is whether these false memories are immune to a warning, or knowledge of the false memory phenomenon. Gallo, Roberts, and Seamon (1997) examined false recognition on a final test (given after presentation of a series of associative lists) as a function of the study instructions given to subjects. In the *uninformed* and *cautious* groups, subjects were given standard study instructions, similar to those used by Roediger and McDermott (1995); in the cautious group, however, test instructions also included clauses asking subjects to attempt to minimise false alarms and informing them that the test would include nonstudied associates of presented items. In a third condition, the *forewarned* condition, subjects were informed before the study phase of the specific memory illusion under investigation and were given a sample study list and corresponding test to demonstrate the effect. Subjects were told to attempt to minimise their false alarms to these critical nonpresented items on the subsequent recognition test.

Gallo et al. (1997) found that a vague warning to be cautious (given just prior to the test) reduced the hit rate but did not lead to a statistically reliable decrease in the critical false alarm rate, relative to the standard instructions. Numerically, the decrease was present, however: Critical false alarms occurred with a probability of .81 in the uninformed condition and .74 in the cautious condition, as can be seen in Fig. 9.4. (The instruction to be cautious did reliably attenuate the proportion of remember responses assigned to the critical items, in comparison to the uninformed group.) When subjects were explicitly forewarned, they were able to decrease substantially the proportion of critical lures erroneously recognised. False recognition was still substantial, however, even in the forewarned condition, in which subjects classified the critical lures as old .46 of the time. The primary conclusion from this experiment is that knowledge about the false recognition phenomenon is sufficient to reduce but not to eliminate the effect. A nonspecific warning to attempt to minimise false alarms did not reliably attenuate the false alarm rate of the critical nonpresented items, although strong conclusions about this effect cannot be made, in part because of the moderate (.07) yet statistically insignificant effect.

McDermott and Roediger (1997) have obtained data that point to a similar conclusion. In these experiments, the critical item around which the list was constructed was presented in half of the lists and not in the other half. All subjects were informed that the lists contained words that were highly associated to one critical item and that this item sometimes was present in the list but sometimes was not. Subjects were told to pay close attention to the lists and to make sure that they did not remember the critical item as having occurred when in fact it did not. We also gave our subjects a sample list, and explained to them that people often

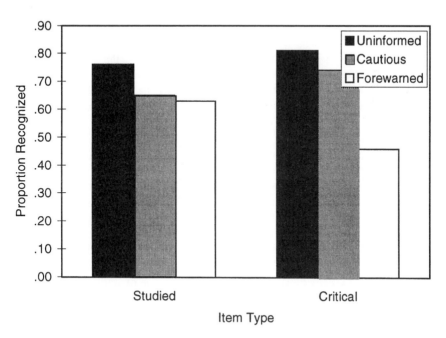

FIG. 9.4. Probability of accurate and false recognition as a function of instructional condition. Adapted from Gallo et al. (1997).

mistakenly recalled the critical item (in our example, *king*) when in fact it had not been presented and to be sure that they did not commit this error.

In our first experiment, 12 lists were presented, followed by an old/new recognition test. Although subjects were better than chance at determining the prior history of the items, they still classified nonstudied critical items as "old" 61% of the time. (When the item had been presented, the hit rate was 78%.) In both this experiment and in Gallo et al.'s (1997) experiment, one factor contributing to the false recognition effect may be in the delay between study and test; all lists were presented prior to the recognition test, so there was a moderate delay between study and test (due to the fact that all lists were presented, followed by one long recognition test). Therefore, in Experiment 2, McDermott and Roediger moved the test so that it occurred immediately following each list. That is, subjects were given a one-item recognition probe immediately following each 15-word study list. Here, too, subjects were better than chance at discriminating whether or not the item had been present in the list; nevertheless, they were far from perfect at this task (with .38 of the nonpresented items erroneously classified as old and .81 of the presented items correctly classified as old). By comparing results of McDermott and Roediger's (1997) two experiments, we can conclude that changing the task to a more direct source-monitoring task (by introducing an extremely short retention interval) made it easier for subjects to determine when the item had not been present in the list, although it did not improve their ability to correctly determine when the item had been present in the list.

Perhaps the most interesting aspect of all these data is the simple fact that despite an explanation of the phenomenon, an explicit warning not to make such errors, and an immediate test, false recognition of the critical lures was still robust. In sum, the warning studies existing so far show that although subjects may be able to reduce false alarms in this paradigm, they are by no means completely successful in doing so. Further work is needed to determine the extent to which warnings can influence study and test strategies so that subjects can most effectively reduce false recall and recognition.

A second instructional variable that has been manipulated at encoding is level of processing (Craik & Lockhart, 1972). Level of processing manipulations are usually instantiated by instructing subjects to think about some meaning-based attributes of the studied words (e.g. their pleasantness)—in the deep condition—or to think about an orthographic or phonemic attribute (e.g. the number of vowels in the word)—in the shallow condition. Relative to shallow processing, deep processing greatly enhances recall and recognition of studied items (Craik & Tulving, 1975). Read (1996) examined the proportion of recalled and remember responses (in the remember/know paradigm given after the recall test) as a function of study orientation for one of the lists most likely to induce false recall, the *sleep* list. Read (1996) postulated that even if there was no difference in level of recall of the critical nonpresented item as a function of level of processing, it seemed reasonable to expect differences in assignment of remember judgements to the critical intrusions. This hypothesis was based on Gardiner, Gawlik, and Richardson-Klavehn's (1994) results with accurate recognition, which show that elaborative rehearsal enhances remember judgements (and leaves know judgements unaffected) and that maintenance rehearsal enhances know judgements (but not remember judgements). Therefore, Read (1996) hypothesised that elaborative rehearsal should lead to enhanced recall and remember judgements for the critical nonpresented items, as well as for studied items, relative to the more shallow processing task of maintenance rehearsal. His results, however, failed to support the prediction: Although level of processing affected recall of studied items in the predicted direction, *sleep* was erroneously recalled with similar probabilities in the maintenance (.76) and elaborative (.73) conditions, and the remember responses were unaffected as well. However, Read also did not replicate Gardiner et al.'s basic finding of increasing remember responses for studied items, so it seems possible that there was not enough power in his experiment to detect differences.

Tussing and Greene (in press) examined the effect of level of processing on false recognition following the presentation of six 12-word associative lists. They found no differences in the probability of false alarms to the critical nonpresented words in their three encoding conditions: pleasantness rating, letter counting, and judging whether each word began with a vowel. However, caution is warranted in interpreting this null effect because the deep encoding condition (i.e. pleasantness rating) did not produce a higher hit rate than the two shallow encoding conditions.

Two studies have demonstrated level-of-processing effects on retrieval of the critical nonpresented items. Toglia, Goodwin, Lyon, and Neuschatz (1995a) found that deep processing (pleasantness judgements) enhanced recall of critical intrusions (as well as studied items) relative to the shallow condition (determining whether the word contains an "a"). Similarly, Thapar, McDermott, and Fong (1997) obtained large effects of level of processing such that judging the pleasantness of the list words produced higher levels of false (and accurate) recall than did counting the number of vowels in the words or determining their colour. This pattern was achieved on a final free recall test given immediately after study of the lists, and also after one- and seven-day delays.

The results of level-of-processing manipulations are inconsistent and puzzling. One possible explanation for the lack of effects reported by some researchers is that regardless of the overt study task, subjects naturally engage in a deep level of processing when presented with blocks of associatively related words. This interpretation would account for the lack of level-of-processing effects on studied items obtained in some of the experiments. We expect that the level of processing engaged in at study will be shown to affect studied and critical items similarly, as Toglia et al. (1995a) and Thapar et al. (1997) have found. Further experiments will be needed to provide conclusive evidence, however.

Study Material

We turn now to characteristics of the study material itself. Among the variables examined thus far are: number of associates comprising the study lists, rate of presentation of the studied items, list structure when multiple lists are presented together (i.e. whether blocking associates together results in differing rates of false recall compared to interspersing items from various lists), effects of repeating presentation of the study words, and dividing attention during the study phase. Finally, we consider whether some associative sets induce higher probabilities of false recall and false recognition than others and possible implications of such a finding. We consider first the very basic question: How does the number of associates in a list affect false recall?

Number of Associates.   Deese (1959b) found that the level of false recall in his experiment was well predicted by the mean associative strength of the list. That is, false recall following his 12-word lists correlated highly ($r = .87$) with the mean associative strength linking the list words to the critical nonpresented items. In their first experiment, Robinson and Roediger (1997) introduced a straightforward variation of list length. The lists were either 3, 6, 9, 12, or 15 items long. (Lists always contained the highest associates first; thus the 12-word lists were constructed by dropping the last three items from the 15-word list, etc.) Robinson and Roediger (1997) argued that on the basis of Deese's hypothesis, one might predict that shorter lists would produce higher probabilities of false recall because they have higher mean associative strengths. However, their results showed the opposite: the longer the list, the higher the probability of false recall of the critical nonstudied item (see Fig. 9.5). In a second experiment, list length was held constant by adding unrelated words to the number of associates in the lists from Experiment 1. In this way, the average associative strength of the lists to the critical nonstudied item was much lower than in Experiment 1; if mean associative strength determines false recall, then false recall should have been much lower in Experiment 2 than Experiment 1. However, by comparing results of the two experiments, Robinson and Roediger were able to determine that the filler words added to equate list length (in Experiment 2) did not attenuate the intrusion levels relative to Experiment 1, although recall of the presented associates was affected by this manipulation (see Fig. 9.5). This finding suggests that it is the total associative strength of the list, not the mean associative strength, that most accurately predicts false recall.

A second interesting finding to emerge from Robinson and Roediger's (1997) experiments is that the critical nonpresented item does not behave as though it were another (presented) item in the list, as Roediger and McDermott (1995) seemed to find. As the list length increased, the probability of recall of any individual studied item decreased, whereas the probability of false recall increased. The probabilities of false and accurate recall were therefore inversely related.

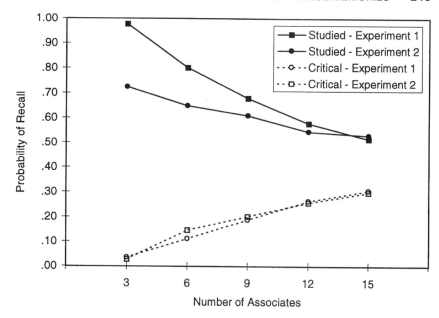

FIG. 9.5. Probabilities of accurate and false recall as a function of number of associates studied. Adapted from Robinson and Roediger (1997).

Presentation Rate. Another basic study manipulation is the rate of presentation of the study items. Predictions for the effects of presentation rate on false recall are difficult to make. If one believes that deeper processing promotes higher false recall, it might follow that slower presentation, which allows for more elaborative and relational processing, might enhance false recall. Conversely, it seems intuitive that the faster the items go by, the more difficult it might be to effectively encode each individual item; subjects might be left with a general feeling of the overall theme of the list but little retention of the specific items. The empirical evidence for presentation rate exists in the form of several unpublished studies, at least as of this writing (May 1997). Schwartz (1996, personal communication) presented items at either a 1-, 5-, or 10-second rate and found false recall was inversely proportional to presentation rate: the longer the study period, the lower the probability of false recall. Specifically, the level of false recall fell from .51 to .44 to .26 with the 1-, 5-, and 10-second rates, respectively. Toglia and Neuschatz (1996) also found differences in false recall as a function of study time. Specifically, they found a .72 false recall probability for a fast, 1-second rate, but that probability was sharply diminished (to .49) when the study rate was extended to 4-seconds. Therefore, the current data suggest that in general, the faster the rate of presentation, the higher the rate of false recall. Whether this claim will survive manipulations at the extreme is still undetermined. Robinson, Balota, and Roediger (1997) tested subjects at several rates under 100ms. Of course, veridical recall is quite poor at such rates, but the interesting finding was that (relative to probability of accurate recall), the probability of false recall remained quite high. Subjects recall very little, but what they do recall is as likely to be the critical nonpresented item as any of the items that were presented. This research is still being conducted with recognition procedures, so further comment is not warranted at this time.

Blocked/Random Presentation.   In a variation of the basic paradigm discussed here, McDermott (1996a) combined several lists to make one long list, in which the items converged around three critical nonpresented words. That is, the 45-word study list contained 15 items related to each of three critical items (e.g. *cold, sleep,* and *needle*). This type of list construction permits an examination of whether and how order of presentation of the studied words affects the probability of false recall. Specifically, to what extent does false recall differ as a function of whether items are blocked according to list or are randomly intermixed throughout the study phase? Opposing predictions can be made. One could argue that random presentation would lead to higher false recall because the overall list structure is more confusing, leaving subjects trying to organise the list subjectively but unsure of the exact items that were studied. The fact that quicker presentation enhances false recall would seem to bolster this prediction. Conversely, it could be expected that blocked presentation would lead to enhanced false recall because it would enhance relational processing and magnify the possibility of implicit associative responses occurring. For example, the probability that *point* would elicit *needle* as an IAR would be greater if *point* were presented in the context of other *needle*-related words (e.g. *thread, pin, sewing ...*) than if it occurred in proximity to other words unrelated to *needle*.

As can be seen in Fig. 9.6, McDermott (1996a) found that blocked presentation of the list led to higher false recall than random presentation. Indeed, in the blocked condition, after a single presentation of the list, the probability of false recall (.57) exceeded the probability of veridical recall (.38). Toglia et al. (1995b) have obtained this blocked/random effect in recall, and Mather et al. (1997) and Tussing and Greene (in press) have found the same pattern in recognition memory.

Repetition.   Tussing and Greene (in press) examined whether repetition of the study list affects the level of false recognition. On the basis of IAR theory, one might expect that the probability of false recall and false recognition would increase with repetition of the list because the probability of an implicit associative response of the critical nonpresented item would be enhanced with multiple presentations of the study words. However, when Tussing and Greene (in press) presented words from six associative sets (randomly ordered), they

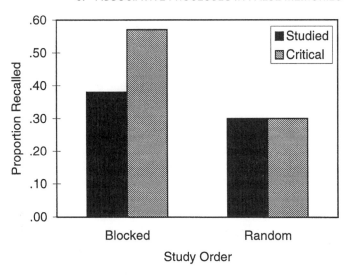

FIG. 9.6   Probability of accurate and false recall as a function of study order. Adapted from McDermott (1996a).

found no reliable difference between false recognition when the list items were presented once (.74) or three times (.67) (see also Shiffrin, Huber, & Marinelli, 1995).

McDermott (1995) presented three associatively related 15-word lists blocked together. As expected, repetition enhanced accurate recall (from .38 for once-presented lists to .61 for lists presented five times); however, repetition decreased the probability of false recall (.22 for repeated lists, compared to .57 for once-presented lists).[4] Explanations of this finding are not obvious, but it is reminiscent of the reduction in false recognition shown by Hall and Kozloff (1970; see Fig. 9.1). However, before we stretch too far to find explanations, it would be desirable to determine if the effect is replicable.

Dividing Attention.   A fifth study variable that has received interest is the effect of dividing attention during the study phase on later false recognition. This question is interesting because it speaks to the issue of the role of elaborative, relational processing in producing the phenomenon. If organisational strategies during the study phase are contributing to the effect (as would be suggested by the outcomes of the level of processing, study time, and blocked/random experiments), we would expect that dividing attention during the study phase would diminish false recall and recognition. In two experiments, Payne, Lampinen, and Cordero (1996b) found that dividing attention during the study phase does indeed attenuate later false recognition. This outcome can be considered as supporting Underwood's (1965) notion that IARs during study elicit false recognition, that IARs would be less likely to occur if attention is divided.

Characteristics of the Study Lists.   An interesting aspect of Deese's (1959b) original results, and one that is somewhat overlooked today, is that relatively few of his lists produced high intrusion rates. For example, the famous *butterfly* list (the 12 most common associates to the word *butterfly*) failed to elicit any intrusions in Deese's sample of 50 subjects. Roediger and McDermott (1995, Experiment 1) used six of Deese's lists, the ones that had produced the highest intrusion rates in his study. For our second experiment, we created 18 more lists and published all 24 in the Appendix of our paper; these lists have been used extensively in later research, both by ourselves and by others. We have since created 12 more lists, as have other groups of researchers; it is also clear that standard categorised lists of the Battig-Montague (1969) type can elicit high false recognition of high-frequency items from the category norms when these are omitted from the study list (Hintzman, 1988; Shiffrin et al., 1995).

In most of the research reported in this chapter, a set of materials is used (e.g the 24 Roediger-McDermott lists), and the data are aggregated over materials. However, from even a casual glance at the results, it is apparent that the materials vary dramatically in their effectiveness in producing false recall and false recognition. Some lists produce high levels of erroneous remembering and others practically none. Deese (1959b) showed that in his set of materials, the average tendency of the items in the list to arouse the critical item as an associate predicted intrusions in recall. As of this writing, we know little more than this. Our main point in including this topic is to draw attention to it and to how critical it is to understanding the phenomenon of false memories aroused by associative processes.

The central question is why some lists produce high levels of false recall and false recognition, whereas others do not. After all, the lists are constructed in the same way. What characteristics of lists and/or target words elicit the phenomenon? Can the "good" lists be altered in some way to reduce levels of false remembering? Can the same be done with the "poor" lists? Such knowledge would bring the phenomenon under experimental control. Do abstract materials or concrete materials produce the stronger effect? Can subjects (or experimenters) predict which lists will produce high levels of false recall and false recognition?

We know the answer to none of these questions at this point, although each is currently stimulating experimental inquiry. Stadler, Roediger, and McDermott (1997) have made a start by providing data that will be critical to answering these questions. Stadler et al. performed a norming study in which two large groups of subjects studied and recalled 18 of the 36 lists in the expanded Roediger-McDermott set (the 24 lists in their Appendix and 12 more developed by

McDermott). After all lists had been studied and recalled, subjects received a recognition test over the whole set. Therefore, we have norms on the effectiveness of each list in producing false recall and false recognition. (The recognition results are possibly contaminated by the prior recall test, although other evidence makes us think that this is probably not a critical problem; see Robinson & Roediger, 1997, Table 1). These norms are a starting place for asking questions about the effectiveness of individual lists in producing false memories. Stadler et al. found that false recall and false recognition are quite reliable across subgroups of subjects (with split-half correlations of around .80). However, probabilities of correct recall and recognition correlated only weakly with the probabilities of false recall and recognition (.20 and .15, respectively). False recall and false recognition were highly correlated across the 36 lists, $r =$ .76.

Although the Roediger-McDermott lists were created to produce high levels of false recall and false recognition, and in the aggregate they do, the variation among lists is substantial. For example, lists constructed around the words *window, sleep, smell*, and *doctor* all produced false recall at levels at or above 60%. Conversely, six lists constructed the same way, and with the same face validity in producing false recall, led to levels of false recall at or below 25%. The list associated with *king* produced only 10% false recall. The same general pattern held for recognition. Although overall the lists produce high levels of false recognition, the variability in materials is great: It ranged from 84% false recognition (for the *window, smell*, and *cold* lists) to relatively low levels of false recognition (for the *lion*, 33%, and *king*, 27%, lists). Again, the reasons for these wide differences are not apparent from a simple examination of the materials. We also hasten to add that even the materials producing "low" levels of false recall and false recognition do so with higher probabilities than one would find with unrelated materials. The systematic study of variables underlying the differential effectiveness of materials is of critical importance to understanding these phenomena, but the work on this issue is just starting.

Retention Interval

We turn now to look at the next stage, the retention interval, and the role it plays in erroneous remembering. We begin by considering a short delay, designed to eliminate the contribution of primary memory, and then turn to the studies that have examined the effects of longer delays (of the order of hours and days) in order to flesh out the time course of false recall and relate it to forgetting curves for studied items.

McDermott (1996a) asked whether a short, 30-second delay would affect the level of false recall. It is well documented that for studied items, such a delay eliminates the recency effect but leaves recall levels for the beginning and middle portions of the list unaffected (Glanzer & Cunitz, 1966; Postman & Phillips,

1965). On the basis of the finding that the proportion of critical items recalled approximates the proportion of studied items recalled from the middle of the list on an immediate free recall test, and the assumption that recall from this part of the list represents recall from long-term store, we might hypothesise that recall of the critical items represents recall from long-term store. If so, we might expect that a short delay would not affect critical item recall (because it has no effect on long-term store but only short-term store).

This prediction was borne out in McDermott's (1996a) data. As can be seen in the first two data columns of Table 9.4, recall of the critical nonpresented item in the delayed condition (.46) did not differ from recall in the immediate condition (.44). (As expected, the delay eliminated the recency effect but left recall of the pre-recency items unaffected.) Zechmeister and Zechmeister (1996) reported a similar experiment, in which a delay of 90 seconds was used. In their experiment, the short delay affected studied items in the predictable manner (i.e. in the recency portion of the serial position function); in addition, they found that false recall increase across the short delay (from .55 on the immediate test to .70 in the delayed condition). This finding parallels studies that have examined more substantial delays, which have shown that false recall and recognition tend to increase or remain stable, whereas forgetting occurs for the studied items.

In McDermott's (1996a) experiment, in which subjects took an initial test either immediately or after a short delay, all subjects returned two days later for a final free recall test covering all the studied lists (those lists not initially tested, as well as those tested in the immediate and 30-second delayed conditions). Although levels of recall differed on the final test as a function of initial test condition (a testing effect, which will be discussed in the following section), in all three conditions the probability of false recall exceeded that of veridical recall after this two-day delay. Collapsing across the three conditions, the probability of

TABLE 9.4
McDermott's (1996a) Results

Initial Test Condition	Type of Recall Test			
	Initial Tests		Final Free Recall	
	Studied	Critical NS	Studied	Critical NS
Immediate	.58	.44	.18	.23
Delayed	.50	.46	.15	.24
No Test	—	—	.04	.12

Proportions of studied items and critical nonstudied items recalled on the initial tests and the final free recall test as a function of initial test condition.

false recall was .20 and the probability of accurate recall .12. In a second experiment, McDermott compared recall on the final free recall test on the day of study presentation to recall on the same test given one day later. Although studied items were forgotten across the retention interval, there was a small but statistically significant rise in the proportion of critical items recalled.

In a similar experiment, Payne et al. (1996a) observed no change in false recognition over a 24-hour delay (although correct recognition decreased). It is not yet clear when false memories in this paradigm increase with delay and when they remain stable, but the primary conclusion to be taken from these studies is that false recall is extremely robust, either remaining constant or increasing over a time interval, during which memory for the studied events is diminishing. As a consequence, in either case (stability or increase in absolute proportions), there is an increase in false memories relative to veridical memories. These findings are consistent with research in the prose recall literature, in which false recall and recognition of schema-consistent prose passages increase over delays ranging from one week to a year (Barclay & Wellman, 1986; Spiro, 1980; Sulin & Dooling, 1974).

Variables Manipulated at Test

Testing Effects.   We turn now to test variables pertaining to false recall and false recognition. The aspect of the test phase that has been most closely examined is the testing effect, or the finding that performance on a test is enhanced if an initial test is taken relative to when there is no initial test. Roediger and McDermott (1995) reported that this effect occurs not only for studied items, which is well known, but also for critical nonpresented items (see Table 9.3). Although some researchers have replicated this effect (e.g Saldaña, et al., 1997; Zechmeister & Zechmeister, 1996), others have not consistently replicated the testing effect for critical nonpresented items (e.g. Norman & Schacter, 1997; Payne et al., 1996a, Experiment 2; Schacter et al., 1996c). Similarly, Roediger and McDermott's (1995) finding of a testing effect in remember responses has enjoyed limited replicability (e.g. Payne et al., 1996a obtained it, but Norman & Schacter, 1997, failed to replicate it).

In an effort to make sense of the discrepant findings in the literature, McDermott (1996b) performed a meta-analysis of all experiments examining testing effects on false recognition in the Roediger-McDermott paradigm. Collapsing across studied and critical items, in 17 of the 22 relevant comparisons, there was a numerical advantage for the condition in which an initial test had occurred. When broken down by item type, the mean probability of accurate recognition was .75 and .67 for lists previously tested and not tested, respectively; comparable probabilities for the critical items were .73 and .70. When subjected to Wilcoxon signed-ranks tests, these data show a reliable overall effect for studied items but not for critical items.

A similar analysis was performed to determine the generality of the testing effect on remember judgements. The mean probabilities of remember judgements for studied items were .55 and .44 for tested and nontested conditions, respectively; the comparable levels for critical items were .52 and .46. A Wilcoxon test showed a reliable testing effect for studied items; however, the test for critical items fell just short of significance.

In the aggregate, the results with respect to accurate recognition and remember responses support the findings of Roediger and McDermott (1995) in that prior testing enhances later recognition and recollection (as manifested in remember judgements) of the studied items; the effect on critical nonpresented items is less conclusive.

Why is the testing effect manifested in some experiments but not others? One possibility is that recognition is a relatively insensitive measure with respect to testing effects. Support for this hypothesis lies in the finding initially reported by Darley and Murdock (1971) that under conditions in which little or no testing effect is observed for a final recognition test, a robust testing effect is obtained on a final free recall test. Lockhart (1975; see also Jones & Roediger, 1995) later showed that when the testing effect is obtained in recognition, it is generally restricted to an enhancement of the last few items of the study list. The finding that a recall test enhances later recall but not later recognition is broadly consistent with transfer appropriate processing approaches to memory (e.g. Morris, Bransford, & Franks, 1977; Roediger, 1990): Practice in recalling information transfers well to recalling it again, but does not transfer as well to later recognition.

Given that testing effects are ubiquitous in free recall and inconsistent in recognition, we might expect testing effects for false memory to behave similarly (i.e. to be more easily obtained on free recall tests). McDermott (1996a) has obtained robust testing effects on final free recall. As shown in Table 9.4, on a final free recall test given after a 48-hour delay, the probability of false recall corresponding to a given study list was twice as great (.24) when a free recall test had followed the study presentation than when maths problems had been worked following the presentation (.12). In another series of experiments, McDermott (1996c) has shown that the number of initial tests taken (0, 1, or 3) strongly influences the later probability (on a final free recall test) of both accurate and false recall. In addition, the number of tests affected remember judgements (both accurate and erroneous) in the same way.

On the basis of these results with free recall, we might ascribe the fleeting nature of the testing effect on recognition to the relative insensitivity of the test. It is our opinion that the testing effect is a real phenomenon in the domain of false memory (see also Roediger et al., 1997 for more extensive discussion of this point).

Hypermnesia. A couple of studies have examined whether there is a false memory analogue of hypermnesia. If people are given several tests in immediate succession, will the probability of false recall increase across the tests, similar to the increase often found in the probability of accurate recall (Erdelyi & Becker, 1974; see Payne, 1987, for a review)? Payne et al. (1996a, Experiment 2) addressed this question by presenting subjects with 60 words, which were grouped according to six associative sets (of 10 items per set). Although hypermnesia was not obtained for studied items, there was a reliable increase in critical items produced across the three tests (.27, .28, and .35 on Tests 1, 2, and 3, respectively). Payne et al.'s results also suggested that this increase was not attributable to a relaxation of criterion across tests. In a follow-up experiment with a slightly different procedure, they obtained similar data in that recall of the critical nonpresented items increased across successive tests (.27, .30, and .33 across Tests 1 to 3); this time, they also obtained increases across tests for studied items, or hypermnesia.

McDermott (1996c) also attempted to find an analogue of hypermnesia in false recall. Unlike Payne et al. (1996a), however, McDermott obtained no reliable hypermnesia for critical nonpresented items. The discrepancy between her findings and those of Payne et al. is likely due at least in part to the nature of the study lists: McDermott gave successive immediate free recall tests following the presentation of each 15-word associative set, whereas Payne and his colleagues grouped the associative sets together, followed by a series of final tests. Because hypermnesia (in the standard sense, with studied items) is usually only obtained following long study lists (Roediger, Payne, Gillespie, & Lean, 1982), it is plausible that list length is the distinguishing factor between the two studies. Note, however, the point mentioned earlier that the number of initial tests taken in McDermott's experiment did influence later false recall and remember judgements. Therefore, despite no increase across the successive initial tests, the act of taking the tests did influence later memory for the original event (by enhancing later accurate and false recall).

Multitrial Learning. The experiments reviewed here have examined the role of repeated testing in the absence of a subsequent study presentation. One can also employ a multitrial learning procedure to ask whether subjects will be able to use successive study–test episodes to edit out their intrusions in recall. McDermott (1996a) showed that across five study–test episodes, when accurate recall was improving steadily, false recall dropped substantially (from .57 to .32 when the items were blocked according to associative set and from .30 to .20 when the items were randomly ordered). Remarkably, though, even after five attempts at learning the list, subjects still produced robust levels of intrusions. Subjects were able to reduce but not eliminate false recall. This finding is similar to the results of Gallo et al. (1997) and McDermott and Roediger (1997) in showing that the memory illusion is quite resistant to correction.

Dividing Attention.   In a final test variable, in which multiple tests were not used, Payne et al. (1996b) examined the effects of dividing attention during the test phase on recognition levels of the critical nonpresented items. Recall that these researchers showed that dividing attention during study attenuated false recognition. In the same experiment, a similar finding was obtained for the test phase. When subjects were required to monitor for the presentation of three consecutive odd digits (presented over headphones, during the visual recognition test), both accurate and false recognition levels were diminished.

These results are interesting in part because they differ from those of investigators exploring other illusions of memory. For example, Jacoby, Woloshyn, and Kelley (1989b) found that dividing attention at test reduced accurate recognition of items but did not affect the illusory memories they were studying (the false fame effect from studying nonfamous names). Therefore, they argued that the false fame effect arises from automatic processes. Applying the same logic to Payne et al.'s experiment, the illusory memories produced in the DRM paradigm would be attributed to conscious recollection because dividing attention diminished the false recognition levels. This conclusion is in agreement with the finding that recognition of the illusory items is accompanied predominantly by remember judgements.

In summary, the studies that have examined the effects of test variables have clearly shown that just as testing influences what is later accurately remembered, testing can affect the likelihood of producing a false memory as well. In addition, dividing attention has detrimental effects on memory for studied items and has similar effects on false recall of the critical nonpresented items.

Subject Variables.   Researchers are just beginning to explore how subject variables might affect false recall in the DRM paradigm. There are two basic questions that can be asked: How do subject populations differ in their susceptibility to (and patterns of) memory illusions? Within a subject population, are there any factors that are likely to predict susceptibility to the illusion across individuals? We begin this section by reviewing the brief literature on subject populations, and then consider the question of individual differences within the normal population of subjects.

Norman and Schacter (1997) examined false recall and false recognition in the DRM paradigm in older adults, noting that older adults are more susceptible to false recognition in Underwood's (1965) continuous recognition paradigm (using both synonyms and rhymes; see Rankin & Kausler, 1979), in Jacoby et al.'s (1989a) false fame paradigm (Bartlett, Strater, & Fulton, 1991), and in Loftus's (1993) misleading information paradigm (Cohen & Faulkner, 1989). On the basis of these findings, they hypothesised that older adults would similarly show higher rates of false recall and recognition after studying lists of associated words. Results confirmed this prediction. As shown in the top half of Table 9.5, age and item type interacted such that younger adults recalled more studied items

(.68) than older adults (.51) but recalled fewer critical nonpresented items (.36) than the older subjects (.49). (These data were obtained by collapsing across their two experiments.) The recognition data generally showed the same pattern, with younger adults manifesting higher hit rates and lower critical false alarm rates than the older adults, although the false alarm rate difference between subject groups was evident in only one of the two experiments.

In a similar study, Tun, Wingfield, and Rosen (1995) compared older and younger adults with respect to their probabilities of false recall in the DRM paradigm. Although older adults recalled fewer studied items than younger subjects on immediate free recall tests, the subject groups did not differ in their levels of false recall. It is presently unclear why Norman and Schacter obtained age differences, whereas Tun and her colleagues found none. On the basis of work in other paradigms (discussed earlier) and existing theories of the effects of ageing on frontal control systems in memory (e.g. Moscovitch, 1989, 1995) we suspect that further work will reveal that older adults will show inflated false recall relative to younger adults (in this paradigm, as well as others); however, more research in this area is clearly needed before definitive conclusions can be drawn.

The other subject population that has been examined at this point is amnesic subjects, who show quite a different pattern from the normal older adults. Schacter et al. (1996c) compared normal older adults to twelve amnesic subjects, six of whom exhibited Korsakoff's syndrome, and six of whom had varying etiologies (but all had damage to medial temporal and/or diencephalic structures). The recall data are shown in Table 9.5: Amnesics recalled fewer studied items (.27) than did controls (.52) as well as (nonsignificantly) fewer critical items (.29) than did controls (.33). Schacter et al. note, however, that interpretation of the nonstudied difference is complicated by differences between the groups in other false alarms. An examination of the final recognition test data supports the conclusion that amnesics' memory for the critical nonpresented items (.16), like their memory for the studied items (.16), was lower than older controls (.66 and .57 for studied and critical nonpresented items, respectively). In some sense, the amnesic patients do not have sufficient capability for conscious

TABLE 9.5
Recall as a Function of Subject Population and Item Type

		Item Type	
Reference	Subject Population	Studied	Critical
Norman & Schacter	Young	.68	.36
(1997)	Old	.51	.49
Schacter et al. (1996c)	Old	.52	.33
	Amnesics	.27	.29

recollection to remember the critical nonpresented items! These results lend support to the idea, recurring in this chapter, that many of the processes that support accurate memory seem to overlap with those that support association-induced false memories. It will be interesting to see how other memory-impaired subject populations (e.g. patients with dementia of the Alzheimer's type) will behave in this paradigm. Schacter, Norman, and Koustaal (in press) review what is known of the neuropsychology of false memories in the DRM paradigm, as well as in other paradigms.

We now turn to the idea that individual differences within the population of normal individuals might predict susceptibility to this memory illusion. Hyman and Billings (1998) explored a number of different measures and showed that in a different paradigm, the single characteristic that predicted false recall was performance on the Dissociative Experiences Scale (DES; Bernstein & Putnam, 1986). This scale contains questions such as "Some people have the experience of finding themselves in a place and having no idea how they got there. How often does this happen to you?" People who report that such incidents happen to them often tended to be more likely to produce false recall in Hyman and Billings' (1998) report. On the basis of this research, Winograd, Peluso, and Glover (1996) asked whether the DES (or some other measure) might correlate with false recall and recognition in the Roediger-McDermott paradigm. Results of their study show that the DES can reliably predict associative false recognition, $r = .34$.

Research into individual differences and subject variables is clearly just beginning; there is still much to be learned in this domain. We consider now the studies that have used the DRM paradigm to explore the neural correlates that might underlie false memories.

Neural Correlates

Schacter et al. (1996b) used positron emission tomography (PET) to explore the neuroanatomical substrates that underlie false recognition. On the basis of the finding (discussed earlier) that patients with medial temporal damage exhibit low levels of false recall, coupled with reports implicating this region in conscious recollection (Nyberg et al., 1996; Schacter et al., 1996a), Schacter et al. (1996b) hypothesised that false recognition, like accurate recognition, would involve (in part) medial temporal structures. This prediction was borne out in the data: Accurate and false recall were accompanied by similar patterns of hippocampal activation.

Of primary interest in this study were possible differences in regions underlying accurate and false recognition. On the basis of the finding that accurate memories sometimes contain richer sensory and perceptual detail than do false memories (Mather et al., 1997, discussed earlier in the chapter; Schacter et al., 1996c), Schacter et al. (1996b) predicted that auditory regions might be differentially active for studied and critical nonstudied items. (The lists in this study were presented auditorily and tested visually.) Consistent with this prediction, Schacter et al. found reliable increases in blood flow during recognition for the studied items in left temporoparietal cortex, an area that is generally thought to underlie phonological/auditory processing. No such activation occurred for the critical nonpresented items. Thus, this experiment was able to provide evidence that the neural bases of true and false memories, although similar, may be distinguishable in some instances.

A similar conclusion was reached by Johnson et al. (1997); using event-related potentials (ERPs), they found differences between studied and critical nonpresented items on a recognition test (however, see Düzel et al., 1997, who used a similar approach and failed to find any differences). Johnson et al. (1997) reported greater bilateral prefrontal activity for "old" responses given to studied items than for the same responses given to the critical nonpresented items. However, this result was obtained only when test items were blocked according to item type (old, critical nonpresented, or unrelated new items). When the test items were randomly intermixed (as is usually done in behavioural studies, and was done by Düzel et al., 1997), no differences were found between studied items and critical nonpresented lures. Johnson et al. suggested that researchers should be sensitive to the processing changes that accompany such changes in task design (see also McDermott et al., 1997).

Johnson et al. (1997) also attempted to explore Schacter et al.'s (1996b) finding of temporoparietal differences between old and critical items. Although the waveforms for hits and critical false alarms did not differ from each other, they did differ from correct rejection of the critical lures. On the basis of this finding, Johnson et al. suggested that the blood flow differences obtained by Schacter et al. in their comparison of studied and critical nonpresented items might have been driven by correct rejection of the critical items. This type of argument is clearly speculative but suggests that there is a great deal of work to be done before blood flow differences averaged across many old and new items can be confidently interpreted as definitive markers in distinguishing between true and false memories.

SUMMARY OF THE EMPIRICAL RESULTS: WHAT DO WE KNOW?

In the preceding pages we have reviewed evidence from a large number of studies from the past 30 years on the topic of false recall and false recognition produced by associative processes. In this section we summarise some of the primary findings that any theory will need to explain. Following this summary, we briefly review several of the main theories introduced for explaining false recall and false recognition, and note strengths and weaknesses that exist for each theory, based on the foregoing review of results.

1. False remembering induced by associative processes can be found in free recall, cued recall, and recognition. We suspect that every task measuring explicit memory will reveal systematic memory illusions, even when subjects are given strict instructions not to guess.

2. As the number of words associated to a target word increases in a study list, the probabilities of false recall and false recognition increase in direct proportion, at least up to 15 associates.

3. Blocking materials at study (placing associated words together in sublists) increases false recall and false recognition relative to randomly ordered presentation; this finding parallels the blocked/random effect for veridical recall.

4. Increasing the rate of presentation has opposite effects on false recall and accurate recall, at least through ranges of around 1 second to 10 seconds. Faster rates lead to lower levels of veridical recall but higher levels of false recall.

5. Increasing retention intervals leads to forgetting of studied material but often has little effect on erroneous recall. False memories either remain stable over relatively short intervals, or actually increase. "Forgetting" of false memories may obey different laws from normal forgetting of studied material.

6. False memories aroused by associative processes often have the feel of real (veridical) memories. Subjects report remembering the moment of occurrence of words that were not presented, the voice presenting the words, and other characteristics of the event. Subjects' phenomenological experiences are often quite similar to those for real memories, although in some cases differences are detectable.

7. Testing effects occur for false recall as well as for veridical recall: Recall of a nonstudied word on a first test increases the probability it will be recalled on a later test. The same is probably true for the effect of recall on false recognition, but the data for recognition are less consistent.

8. These false memories are also quite robust, durable, and resistant to correction.

9. Whereas older adults show poorer recall of studied events relative to younger adults, false recall does not show similar drops with age and may even increase. Conversely, amnesic patients with damage to medial temporal structures show poorer accurate recall and less tendency towards associative memory illusions. Within the normal range of subjects, performance on the Dissociative Experiences Scale correlates with the tendency to produce illusory memories.

Of course, many other results have been reviewed besides the nine listed here, but these nine seem relatively secure. Other findings, such as whether antonyms or synonyms produce false recognition effects similar to those produced by associates, or whether increasing level of processing has an effect on false recall or false recognition, are in conflict in the literature, and we must await further research for their resolution.

THEORETICAL IMPLICATIONS

Associative processes can induce people to remember words that were not presented in a list studied only seconds earlier. Given the traditional emphasis on how associations produce excellent retention, this finding may seem surprising and counter-intuitive. However, many different theories have been extended to explain errors produced by associative processes. We cannot review all of these theories here in detail; instead, we will confine our remarks to a brief evaluation of the main strengths and weaknesses of several approaches to explaining the facts listed earlier. These approaches often have been advanced independently of one another but are not mutually exclusive.

The Implicit Associative Response Hypothesis

Underwood (1965) argued that encoding of a word arouses to conscious awareness an associate of that word, the implicit associative response. This simple idea can go far in helping to account for many of the facts just listed. The facts that increasing list length and the blocking of items at presentation increase false memories in variations of the DRM paradigm can be handled naturally by assuming that more IARs are aroused during blocked presentation and when more items are studied. In addition, the realistic feel of these false memories can all be accounted for by assuming that IARs are aroused during encoding. The item seems to have occurred because the subject recently thought of it. On the other hand, one might expect that slowing the rate of presentation would increase (not decrease) the occurrence of IARs; however, false remembering increases with faster rates, contrary to this prediction. Finally, if the critical item occurred during encoding as an IAR, it might be expected to behave like other items in the list as a function of independent variables. However, in some cases it does not. For example, the falsely recalled item is not forgotten according to the same function as studied items. Although the implicit arousal of the falsely remembered item must, almost by definition, play some role in this phenomenon, the idea by itself seems too simple to account for all the reported effects. The IAR hypothesis must be complemented by other theories.

Automatic Spreading Activation Theory

Underwood (1965) assumed that implicit associative responses were consciously produced during encoding. However, another approach to explaining phenomena of false recall and false recognition is to assume that activation spreads throughout a large semantic network automatically and unconsciously, as in models such as those of Anderson and Bower (1973) and Collins and Loftus (1974). The "node" of an item such as *sleep* could be primed by having 15 related words recently presented, and this activation might trigger false recall and false recognition. Such a theory provides a natural account for such findings as the effect of list length on false recall and false recognition, and for the fact that blocked presentation of the list leads to greater false remembering than does random presentation. This theory is testable in that one could correlate amount of priming in tasks such as lexical decision or naming from these lists (on the target words, such as *sleep*) with the probabilities of false recall and false recognition. Do lists that produce considerable priming also produce high levels of false recall and false recognition? Individual lists could also be manipulated to produce greater or lesser priming, and false recall and false recognition could be examined to see if corresponding effects are observed.

One drawback to this theory, and some others discussed later, is that the simple concept of activation does not permit linkages to subjective experience. Subjects in the DRM paradigm have the strong sense of remembering the illusory items, but sheer activation would probably be expected to give rise to experiences of knowing, not remembering. However, if one combined Underwood's (1965) idea of the IAR—the conscious, if implicit, production of the response—with the concept of automatic spreading activation, then the combined theory may be capable of accounting for most of the results reviewed. For example, the fact that divided attention at study reduces false recognition in the DRM paradigm would be difficult to explain using just automatic spreading activation (why should dividing attention affect an automatic process?), but the hybrid theory could do so by postulating that part of the false recognition was due to conscious processes and part to automatic processes. Such a theory would resemble two process accounts of priming, with controlled and automatic components (e.g. Neely, 1977; Posner & Snyder, 1975). However, details of such an account as applied to false recall and false recognition remain to be worked out.

Feature Matching Theory

In the continuous recognition paradigm, Anisfeld and Knapp (1968) argued that matching of features between the test item and studied items caused false recognition. This idea has been systematically elaborated in some global memory models of recognition memory (see Clark & Gronlund, 1996, for a review). The assumption is that matching of meaning features is critical—if the meaning of the test item matches that of the studied items to a sufficient degree, subjects classify the item as having been studied. If we assume that items associated to a critical nonpresented item share many semantic features with the critical item, then when the critical lure is provided on the test, it will often trigger a false alarm from matching of features. This provides the basic account of false alarms.

Although we believe that global matching theories could account for most of the results listed earlier, we note several weak links. First, one might expect synonyms to produce high rates of false recognition relative to other related words (such as associates or antonyms). Although Fillenbaum (1969) reported 5% greater false recognition from synonyms than associates, the false recognition rate was still rather low (given that meaning features overlapped quite closely), and this effect was not obtained in other work (e.g. Anisfeld & Knapp, 1968, Experiment 1).

A second problem is that global matching models assume that a test item is encoded and produces some familiarity value that varies on a dimension of strength. Strong feelings of familiarity lead to judgements of "old" if the criterion is surpassed. Critical lures in the DRM paradigm would receive very high familiarity values and therefore produce high levels of false alarms. However, the sticking point is the rich phenomenological experience of subjects in reporting false memories. The memories do not merely seem quite familiar in some global sense, but subjects claim to remember considerable detail about the events. Know responses are usually thought to indicate general familiarity, but in the DRM paradigm, subjects claim to remember the nonpresented words. There may be solutions to this issue within global matching models, but in general the mapping from constructs in the models to subjective experiences of the rememberer has not been worked out. The same seems true of connectionist theories applied to false memory phenomena (McClelland, 1995).

Third, Brainerd et al. (1995) reported that under some conditions there is a reversal of false recognition, wherein presenting a related item makes false alarms to a critical lure less likely. Some conditions have been considered earlier in this review, such as several presentations of the related item before the critical lure (Hall & Kozloff, 1973) or presenting the related items immediately prior to the critical lure (MacLeod & Nelson, 1976). As Brainerd et al. (1995) point out, it is difficult to reconcile this finding with global matching models.

Fuzzy Trace Theory

Fuzzy trace theory can explain the false recognition reversal just described and has other features that make it an attractive account of false recall and false recognition, which has led several groups of researchers to adopt the theory to explain their results (Payne et al., 1996a; Schacter, et al. 1996c). However, a similar sort of difficulty exists for Reyna and Brainerd's fuzzy trace theory (see Reyna & Brainerd, 1995, for a review) as for global matching models. According to fuzzy trace theory, experiences are assumed to leave two traces: verbatim traces (or those with specific features) and gist traces (or ones that capture the meaning of events but lack perceptual detail). False memories such as those created in the DRM paradigm are attributed to remembering the gist of experiences. The theory can account for many phenomena, but again founders (in our opinion) on the subjective experience reported by subjects. Remember responses are given by subjects when they believe details of the original experience are available, whereas know responses arise from general feelings of familiarity. The most natural mapping in fuzzy trace theory is that remember responses should reflect specific traces and know responses should arise from gist traces. Yet false memories in the DRM paradigm are predominantly experienced as remembered rather than known. Further developments of fuzzy trace theory may explain how this pattern of results is possible, but would seem to do so only at risk of abandoning some of the main assumptions about the two classes of memory traces.

Source Monitoring Framework

Johnson's source monitoring framework is directly relevant to the issue of how false memories are created (e.g. Johnson & Raye, 1981; Johnson et al., 1993). From this viewpoint, when subjects report remembering a word that did not appear in a list, they may be experiencing source confusion. This explanation is similar to that invoked by IAR theory: Subjects may internally generate the critical word during study of the list and later confuse the private events of thought with the external presentation of words. Many of the findings listed earlier could be interpreted within the source monitoring framework. One advantage of the source monitoring framework is the great emphasis on the experience of the rememberer and how different encoding operations may affect source confusions. In addition, considerable attention is devoted within the theory to decision criteria whereby the rememberer decides if something actually happened or was only imagined.

In explaining false remembering arising from associative processes, the source monitoring account shares considerable territory with the implicit associative responses hypothesis. That is, in both cases the subjects' confusion is thought to arise from their failure to distinguish whether the event in question (say, the occurrence of *sleep* within the list of associated words) actually happened in the external world or was aroused internally. As such, the weaknesses attributed to IAR theory also must be dealt with here, viz., the findings in which the event that was assumed to be activated does not behave like other members of the list. For example, the implicit response is not forgotten over time according to the same function as other members of the list. Still, no theory handles that finding gracefully, and the source monitoring framework is attractive because it is able to explain many other false memory phenomena, such as those that arise from creating mental images (e.g. Garry, Manning, Loftus, & Sherman, 1996; Goff & Roediger, in press).

Attributional Analysis of Remembering

Jacoby's attribution theory of remembering (e.g. Jacoby, Kelley, & Dywan, 1989a) is also relevant to the issues at hand, and he has incorporated memory illusions, such as the false fame effect (Jacoby et al., 1989b) into his theory.

Inspired by attribution theories that arose in social psychology, Jacoby and his colleagues have argued that activation arising from memory can be attributed (and misattributed) to various sources. For example, in an experiment reported by Jacoby, Allan, Collins, and Larwill (1988), subjects heard words in a first phase of the experiment. In a later, ostensibly unrelated phase they listened to words through noise and tried to identify them. Words that had been heard in the first phase were identified more easily in the second phase than words that had not been heard. However, subjects attributed this ease of perception to the noise having been less loud on those trials involving repeated words. In this case, an effect of memory was misattributed to variations in perceptual conditions at testing.

In the case of false memories, the situation is typically reversed. Some event comes easily to mind (either from the environment or from some other source) while subjects are engaged in retrieving events from memory from some particular time and place from the past. Because they are engaged in remembering specific events, and because some idea comes to consciousness during this attempt, the subjects attribute the activated information to "having a real memory" from that time and place. In fact, however, the events are not being remembered—or at least it is not from the time and place from which the subject is retrieving; instead, the memories arise from some different source.

To explain the phenomenon of false recall and false recognition of associatively related material, one need only assume that during the course of being tested on a list, the associated word (e.g. *sleep*) comes easily to mind, just as do list words. Because subjects are actively engaged in remembering and an event comes easily to mind, the item is misattributed to having been in the study list and is therefore "remembered". Again, this account probably could be used to explain most of the findings described earlier. One potential difficulty for the approach (although not the rendition just outlined) is that many memory illusions adumbrated by Jacoby and his colleagues have been hypothesised to arise from automatic processes in memory (i.e. processes that would be expected to give rise to know judgements rather than remember judgements in Tulving's [1985] and Gardiner's [1988] remember/know paradigm). However, by extensions such as the one just outlined, the theory would seem capable of explaining illusions of memory that arise from consciously controlled processes, or remembering. If one assumes that when people are engaged in an attempt to remember, the events that come easily to mind will be attributed to past experiences and will have the experiential feel of past experiences; in this way, false remembering would be explained.

Again, as with the source monitoring framework, Jacoby's attributional ideas are appealing because they can potentially account for many memory illusions. Indeed, the source monitoring framework and the attributional analysis of memory share many features in common. In our opinion, these theories provide perhaps the most compelling means of explaining how false memories arise, both from associative processes (as in the paradigms under discussion here) and from other processes (such as interference effects), too.

CONCLUSION

The concept of association is central to an understanding of human memory. The contribution of the present chapter is to review evidence that strong associations, long known to facilitate remembering, can create memory illusions as well. The literature reviewed suggests that a non-occurring event that is strongly associated to other, experienced events will frequently be recalled and recognised as having occurred. Research on this issue enjoyed a flurry of activity in the 1960s and early 1970s, remained relatively dormant for a time, and now has returned to the fore as researchers become engaged in exploring the processes involved. We suspect that this development is a healthy one for the field. As noted, errors have often been considered a nuisance in the study of memory and thought to be useful only for correcting "hit rates" in recall or recognition by factoring out the "false alarms" assumed to arise through guessing. We suggest that this approach is no longer profitable, if ever it was. Rather, we should consider the study of sensing and perceiving as a model for studying remembering (Roediger, 1996). Psychologists interested in those topics have studied perceptual illusions for 150 years and realised that an understanding of veridical perception demands a parallel explanation of illusions. Perceptual illusions have been a fertile ground for developing and testing theories of perceiving; the time is ripe for the systematic study of illusions of memory, as well.

NOTES

[1]The baserate for recognition errors for words unrelated to the associate stimulus words was .04; the baserate for words unrelated to the synonym stimulus words was .02. Anisfeld and Knapp (1968) determined significance levels for associate and synonym critical words based on these values. The unrelated baserate value in Table 9.2 is a weighted average.

[2]Grossman and Eagle (1970) used separate baserate measures for each type of stimulus word. The false recognition baserate for items unrelated to the antonym stimulus words was .08; the baserate for items unrelated to the synonym stimulus words was .05; the baserate for items unrelated to the associate stimulus words was .08. Again, the baserate value in Table 9.2 is a weighted average.

[3]We thank Endel Tulving for suggesting the nomenclature of calling this the DRM (or DREAM) paradigm.

[4]The .57 and .38 values are taken from McDermott's (1996a) Experiment 2 and not from McDermott (1995). However, the comparison is a valid one because the study conditions and the population from which subjects were drawn did not differ for the two experiments; the only difference was the number of list presentations preceding the recall test.

ACKNOWLEDGEMENTS

We thank Lyn Goff, Steve Kanne, Kate Pfeifer, Mitch Sommers, and Jason Watson for helpful comments on earlier drafts of the chapter.

REFERENCES

Alba, J.W., & Hasher, L. (1983). Is memory schematic? *Psychological Bulletin, 93*, 203–231.

Anderson, J.R., & Bower, G.H. (1973). *Human associative memory.* Washington, DC: Winston.

Anisfeld, M., & Knapp, M. (1968). Association, synonymity, and directionality in false recognition. *Journal of Experimental Psychology, 77*, 171–179.

Aristotle (1966). De memoria et reminiscentia. Translated by J.I. Beare. Selection 65 in R.J. Herrnstein & E.G. Boring, (Eds.), *Source book in the history of psychology*, (pp.328–329). Cambridge, MA: Harvard University Press.

Atkinson, R.C., & Shiffrin, R.M. (1968). Human memory: A proposed system and its control processes. In K.W. Spence & J.T. Spence (Eds.), *The psychology of learning and motivation: Advances in research and theory, 2.* New York: Academic Press.

Barclay, C.R., & Wellman, H.M. (1986). Accuracies and inaccuracies in autobiographical memories. *Journal of Memory and Language, 25,* 93–103.

Bartlett, F.C. (1932). *Remembering: A study in experimental and social psychology.* Cambridge, UK: Cambridge University Press.

Bartlett, J.C., Strater, L., & Fulton, A.L. (1991). False recency and false fame of faces in young adulthood and old age. *Memory and Cognition, 19*, 177–188.

Battig, W.F., & Montague, W.E. (1969). Category norms for verbal items in 56 categories: A replication and extension of the Connecticut category norms. *Journal of Experimental Psychology, 80*, (3, Part 2).

Bernstein, E.M., & Putnam, F.W. (1986). Development, reliability, and validity of a dissociation scale. *The Journal of Nervous and Mental Disease, 174*, 727–735.

Bever, T.G., Fodor, J., & Garrett, M.A. (1968). A formal limitation of associationism. In T.R. Dixon & D.L. Horton, (Eds.), *Verbal behavior and general behavior theory.* Englewood Cliffs, NJ: Prentice-Hall.

Bilodeau, E.A., & Blick, K.A. (1965). Courses of misrecall over long-term retention intervals as related to strength of pre-experimental habits of word association. *Psychological Reports, 16*, 1173–1192.

Bilodeau, E.A., & Fox, P.W. (1968). Free association, free recall, and stimulated recall compared. *Behavior Research Methods and Instrumentation, 1*, 14–17.

Bilodeau, E.A., Fox, P.W., & Blick, K.A. (1963). Stimulated verbal recall and analysis of sources of recall. *Journal of Verbal Learning and Verbal Behavior, 2*, 422–428.

Brainerd, C.J., Reyna, V.F., & Kneer, R. (1995). False-recognition reversal: When similarity is distinctive. *Journal of Memory and Language, 34*, 157–185.

Bransford, J.D., & Franks, J.J. (1971). The abstraction of linguistic ideas. *Cognitive Psychology, 2*, 331–350.

Calkins, M.W. (1894). Association. *Psychological Review, 1*, 476–483.

Clark, S.E., & Gronlund, S.D. (1996). Global matching models of recognition memory: How the models match the data. *Psychonomic Bulletin & Review, 3*, 37–60.

Cofer, C.N. (1973). Constructive processes in memory. *American Scientist, 61*, 537–543.

Cohen, G., & Faulkner, D.L. (1989). Age differences in source forgetting: Effects on reality monitoring and eyewitness testimony. *Psychology and Aging, 4*, 10–17.

Collins, A.M., & Loftus, E.F. (1974). A spreading-activation theory of semantic processing. *Psychological Review, 82*, 407–428.

Conrad, R. (1964). Acoustic confusions in immediate memory. *British Journal of Psychology*, *55*, 75–84.

Coren, S., & Girgus, J.S. (1978). *Seeing is deceiving: The psychology of visual illusions*. Hillsdale, NJ: Lawrence Erlbaum Associates Inc.

Craik, F.I.M., & Lockhart, R.S. (1972). Levels of processing: A framework for memory research. *Journal of Verbal Learning and Verbal Behavior*, *4*, 671–684.

Craik, F.I.M. & Tulving, E. (1975). Depth of processing and the retention of words in episodic memory. *Journal of Experimental Psychology: General*, *104*, 671–684.

Cramer, P. (1965). Recovery of a discrete memory. *Journal of Personality and Social Psychology*, *1*, 326–332.

Cramer, P., & Eagle, M. (1972). Relationship between conditions of CrS presentation and the category of false recognition errors. *Journal of Experimental Psychology*, *94*, 1–5.

Darley, C.F., & Murdock, B.B. (1971). Effects of prior free recall testing on final recall and recognition. *Journal of Experimental Psychology*, *91*, 66–73.

Deese, J. (1959a). Influence of inter-item associative strength upon immediate free recall. *Psychological Reports*, *5*, 305–312.

Deese, J. (1959b). On the prediction of occurrence of particular verbal intrusions in immediate recall. *Journal of Experimental Psychology*, *58*, 17–22.

Deese, J. (1965). *The structure of associations in language and thought*. Baltimore: The Johns Hopkins Press.

Düzel, E., Yonelinas, A.P., Mangun, G.R., Heinze, H.-J., & Tulving, E. (1997). Event-related brain potential correlates of two states of conscious awareness in memory. *Proceedings of the National Academy of Sciences*.

Ebbinghaus, E. (1913). *Memory: A contribution to experimental psychology* (H.A. Ruger & C.E. Bussenius, Trans.). NY: Teachers College, Columbia University. Original work published 1885.

Erdelyi, M.H., & Becker, J. (1974). Hypermnesia for pictures: Incremental memory for pictures but not words in multiple recall trials. *Cognitive Psychology*, *6*, 159–171.

Fillenbaum, S. (1969). Words as feature complexes: False recognition of antonyms and synonyms. *Journal of Experimental Psychology*, *82*, 400–402.

Fox, P.W. (1968). Recall and misrecall as a function of cultural and individual word association habits and regulation of the recall environment. *Journal of Verbal Learning and Verbal Behavior*, *7*, 632–637.

Gallo, D.A., Roberts, M.J., & Seamon, J.G. (1997). Remembering words not presented in lists: Can we avoid creating false memories? *Psychonomic Bulletin & Review*, *4*, 271–276.

Gardiner, J.M. (1988). Functional aspects of recollective experience. *Memory and Cognition*, *16*, 309–313.

Gardiner, J.M., Gawlik, B., & Richardson-Klavehn, A. (1994). Maintenance rehearsal affects knowing, not remembering; elaborative rehearsal affects remembering, not knowing. *Psychonomic Bulletin & Review*, *1*, 107–110.

Gardiner, J.M., & Java, R. (1993). Recognising and remembering. In A. Collins, S. Gathercole, & P. Morris (Eds.), *Theories of memory* (pp.168–188). Hove, UK: Lawrence Erlbaum Associates Ltd.

Garry, M., Manning, C.G., Loftus, E.F., & Sherman, S.J. (1996). Imagination inflation: Imagining a childhood event increases confidence that it occurred. *Psychonomic Bulletin & Review*, *3*, 208–214.

Gillund, G., & Shiffrin, R.M. (1984). A retrieval model for both recognition and recall. *Psychological Review*, *91*, 1–67.

Glanzer, M., (1972). Storage mechanisms in recall. In G.H. Bower (Ed.), *The psychology of learning and motivation: Advances in research and theory*, *5*. New York: Academic Press.

Glanzer, M., & Cunitz, A.R. (1966). Two storage mechanisms in free recall. *Journal of Verbal Learning and Verbal Behavior, 5*, 351–360.

Goff, L., & Roediger, H.L. (in press). Imagination inflation: The effects of number of imaginings on recognition and source monitoring. *Memory and Cognition.*

Grossman, L., & Eagle, M. (1970). Synonymity, antonymity, and association in false recognition responses. *Journal of Experimental Psychology, 83*, 244–248.

Guthrie, E.R. (1935). *The psychology of learning.* New York: Harper & Row.

Hall, J.W., & Kozloff, E.E. (1970). False recognitions as a function of number of presentations. *American Journal of Psychology, 83*, 272–279.

Hall, J.W., & Kozloff, E.E. (1973). False recognitions of associates of converging versus repeated words. *American Journal of Psychology, 86*, 133–139.

Hartley, D. (1749). *Observations on man, his frame, his duty, and his expectations.* London and Bath: Richardson.

Hintzman, D.L. (1988). Judgements of frequency and recognition memory in a multiple-trace memory model. *Psychological Review, 95*, 528–551.

Hobbes, T. (1651). *Leviathan or The Matter, Forme and Power of a Commonwealth Ecclesiasticall and Civill.* London: Printed for Andrew Crook at the Green Dragon in St. Paul's Churchyard.

Hyman, I.E., & Billings, F.J. (1998). Individual differences and the creation of false childhood memories. *Memory, 6*, 1–20.

Jacoby, L.L. (1991). A process dissociation framework: Separating automatic from intentional uses of memory. *Journal of Memory and Language, 30*, 513–541.

Jacoby, L.L., Allan, L.G., Collins, J.C., & Larwill, L.K. (1988). Memory influences subjective experience: Noise judgments. *Journal of Experimental Psychology: Learning, Memory, and Cognition, 14*, 240–247.

Jacoby, L.L., Kelley, C.M., & Dywan, J. (1989a). Memory attributions. In H.L. Roediger, III & F.I.M. Craik (Eds.), *Varieties of memory and consciousness: Essays in honour of Endel Tulving.* Hillsdale, NJ: Lawrence Erlbaum Associates Inc.

Jacoby, L.L., Woloshyn, V., & Kelley, C.M. (1989b). Becoming famous without being recognized: Unconscious influences of memory produced by dividing attention. *Journal of Experimental Psychology: General, 118*, 115–125.

Johnson, M.K., Foley, M.A., Suengas, A.G., & Raye, C.L. (1988). Phenomenal characteristics of memories for perceived and imagined autobiographical events. *Journal of Experimental Psychology: General, 117*, 371–376.

Johnson, M.K., Hashtroudi, S., & Lindsay, S. (1993). Source monitoring. *Psychological Bulletin, 114*, 3–28.

Johnson, M.K., Nolde, S.F., Mather, M., Kounios, J., Schacter, D.L., & Curran, T. (1997). The similarity of brain activity associated with true and false recognition memory depends on test format. *Psychological Science, 8*, 250–257.

Johnson, M.K., & Raye, C.L. (1981). Reality monitoring. *Psychological Review, 88*, 67–85.

Jones, T.C., & Roediger, H.L. (1995). The experiential basis of serial position effects. *European Journal of Cognitive Psychology, 7*, 65–80.

Locke, J. (1690). *Essay concerning human understanding.* A.C. Fraser (Ed.), Oxford: Clarendon. [Republished in 1894].

Lockhart, R.S., & Murdock, B.B. Jr. (1970). Memory and the theory of signal detection. *Psychological Bulletin, 74*, 100–109.

Lockhart, R.S. (1975). The facilitation of recognition by recall. *Journal of Verbal Learning and Verbal Behavior, 14*, 253–258.

Loftus, E.F. (1993). Made in memory: Distortions in recollection after misleading information. In D.L. Medin (Ed.), *The Psychology of learning and motivation: Advances in theory and research.* New York: Academic Press.

MacLeod, C.M., & Nelson, T.O. (1976). A nonmonotonic lag function for false alarms to associates. *American Journal of Psychology, 89*, 127–135.

Mather, M., Henkel, L.A., & Johnson, M.J. (1997). Evaluating characteristics of false memories: Remember/know judgments and Memory Characteristics Questionnaire compared. *Memory and Cognition, 25*, 826–837.

McClelland, J.L. (1995). Constructive memory and memory distortions: A parallel-distributed processing approach. In D.L. Schacter (Ed.), *Memory distortion* (pp.69–90). Cambridge, MA: Harvard.

McDermott, K.B. (1995). [*Effects of repetition on associatively-induced false recall.*] Unpublished raw data.

McDermott, K.B. (1996a). The persistence of false memories in list recall. *Journal of Memory and Language, 35*, 212–230.

McDermott, K.B. (1996b). *Remembering words not presented in lists: The role of testing in producing a memory illusion.* Doctoral dissertation, Rice University, Houston, TX.

McDermott, K.B. (1996c). *Testing enhances the illusion of remembering.* Poster presented at the 37th Annual Meeting of the Psychonomic Society, Chicago.

McDermott, K.B., Ojemann, J.G., Akbudak, E., Snyder, A.Z., Conturo, T.E., Miezin, F.M., Ollinger, J.M., Petersen, S.E., & Raichle, M.E. (1997). An fMRI study of recognition memory using blocked and single trial designs. *Society of Neuroscience Abstracts.*

McDermott, K.B., & Roediger, H.L. (1997). False recognition of associates can be resistant to an explicit warning to subjects and an immediate recognition probe. Manuscript in preparation.

Melton, A.W., & Irwin, J.M. (1940). The influence of degree of interpolated learning on retroactive inhibition and the overt transfer of specific responses. *American Journal of Psychology, 53*, 173–203.

Mill, J. (1869). *Analysis of the phenomena of the human mind* (2nd edn). London: Longman, Green, Reader, & Dyer.

Miller, G.A. (1956). The magical number seven plus or minus two: Some limits on our capacity for processing information. *Psychological Review, 63*, 81–97.

Morris, C.D., Bransford, J.D., & Franks, J.J. (1977). Levels of processing versus transfer appropriate processing. *Journal of Verbal Learning and Verbal Behavior, 16*, 519–533.

Moscovitch, M. (1989). Confabulation and the frontal systems: Strategic versus associative retrieval in neuropsychological theories of memory. In H.L. Roediger & F.I.M. Craik (Eds.), *Varieties of memory and consciousness: Essays in honour of Endel Tulving.* Hillsdale, NJ: Lawrence Erlbaum Associates Inc.

Moscovitch, M. (1995). Confabulation. In D.L. Schacter (Ed.), *Memory distortion: How minds, brains, and societies reconstruct the past.* Cambridge, MA: Harvard University Press.

Neely, J.H. (1977). Semantic priming and retrieval from lexical memory: Roles of inhibitionless spreading activation and limited-capacity attention. *Journal of Experimental Psychology: General, 106*, 226–254.

Neisser, U. (1967). *Cognitive Psychology.* New York: Appleton-Century-Crofts.

Norman, K., & Schacter, D.L. (1997). False recognition in younger and older adults: Exploring the characteristics of illusory memories. *Memory and Cognition, 25*, 838–848.

Nyberg, L., McIntosh, A.R., Houle, S., Nilsson, L.-G., & Tulving, E. (1996). Activation of medial temporal structures during episodic memory retrieval. *Nature, 380*, 715–717.

Paul, L.M. (1979). Two models of recognition memory: A test. *Journal of Experimental Psychology: Human Learning and Memory, 5*, 45–51.

Pavlov, I.P. (1928). *Lectures on conditioned reflexes.* London: International Publishers.

Payne, D.G. (1987). Hypermnesia and reminiscence in recall: A historical and empirical review. *Psychological Bulletin, 101*, 5–27.

Payne, D.G., Elie, C.J., Blackwell, J.M., & Neuschatz, J.S. (1996a). Memory illusions: Recalling, recognizing, and recollecting events that never occurred. *Journal of Memory and Language, 35*, 261–285.

Payne, D.G., Lampinen, J.M., & Cordero, M.L. (1996b). *Remembrances of things not passed: Further evidence concerning false memories.* Paper presented at the 37th Annual Meeting of the Psychonomic Society, Chicago.

Posner, M.I., & Snyder, C.R.R. (1975). Attention and cognitive control. In R.L. Solso (Ed.), *Information processing and cognition: The Loyola Symposium* (pp.55–85). Hillsdale, NJ: Lawrence Erlbaum Associates Inc.

Postman, L., & Phillips, L.W. (1965). Short-term temporal changes in free recall. *Quarterly Journal of Experimental Psychology, 17*, 132–138.

Postman, L., & Underwood, B.J. (1973). Critical issues in interference theory. *Memory and Cognition, 1*, 19–40.

Raaijmakers, J.G.W., & Shiffrin, R.M. (1980). SAM: A theory of probabilistic search of associative memory. In G.H. Bower (Ed.), *The psychology of learning and motivation* (Vol. 14, pp.207–262). New York: Academic Press.

Rajaram, S. (1993). Remembering and knowing: Two means of access to the personal past. *Memory and Cognition, 21*, 89–102.

Rajaram, S., & Roediger, H.L. (1997). Remembering and knowing as states of consciousness during retrieval. In J.D. Cohen & J.W. Schooler (Eds.), *Scientific approaches to consciousness* (pp.213–240). Mahwah, NJ: Lawrence Erlbaum Associates Inc.

Rankin, J.S., & Kausler, D.H. (1979). Adult age differences in false recognitions. *Journal of Gerontology, 34*, 58–65.

Read, J.D. (1996). From a passing thought to a false memory in 2 minutes: Confusing real and illusory events. *Psychonomic Bulletin & Review, 3*, 105–111.

Reyna, V.F., & Brainerd, C.J. (1995). Fuzzy-trace theory: An interim synthesis. *Learning and Individual Differences, 7*, 1–75.

Robinson, K., Balota, D., & Roediger, H.L. (1997). [*Effects of fast presentation rates on associatively-induced false recall and false recognition.*] Unpublished data.

Robinson, K., & Roediger, H.L. (1997). Associative processes in false recall and false recognition. *Psychological Science, 8*, 231–237.

Roediger, H.L. (1973). Inhibiting effects of recall. *Memory and Cognition, 2*, 261–269.

Roediger, H.L. (1990). Implicit memory: Retention without remembering. *American Psychologist, 45*, 1043–1056.

Roediger, H.L. (1996). Memory illusions. *Journal of Memory and Language, 35*, 76–100.

Roediger, H.L., & McDermott, K.B. (1995). Creating false memories: Remembering words not presented in lists. *Journal of Experimental Psychology: Learning, Memory, and Cognition, 21*, 803–814.

Roediger, H.L., McDermott, K.B., & Goff, L. (1997). Recovery of true and false memories: Paradoxical effects of repeated testing. In M.A. Conway (Ed.), *False memories and recovered memories* (pp.118–149.) Oxford: Oxford University Press.

Roediger, H.L., & Payne, D.G. (1985). Recall criterion does not affect recall level or hypermnesia: A puzzle for generate/recognize theories. *Memory and Cognition, 13*, 1–7.

Roediger, H.L., Payne, D.G., Gillespie, G.L., & Lean, D. (1982). Hypermnesia as determined by level of recall. *Journal of Verbal Learning and Verbal Behavior, 21*, 635–655.

Rumelhart, D., & McClelland, J. (1986). *Parallel Distributed Processing.* Cambridge, MA: MIT Press.

Saldaña, H.M., McDermott, K.B., Pisoni, D.B., & Roediger, H.L. (1997). Recollection of illusory voices. Manuscript in preparation.

Schacter, D.L., Alpert, N.M., Savage, C.R., Rauch, S.L., & Albert, M.S. (1996a). Conscious recollection and the human hippocampal formation: Evidence from positron emission tomography. *Proceedings of the National Academy of Sciences, 93*, 321–325.

Schacter, D.L., Reiman, E., Curran, T., Yun, L.S., Bandy, D., McDermott, K.B., & Roediger, H.L. (1996b). Neuroanatomical correlates of veridical and illusory recognition memory: Evidence from positron emission tomography. *Neuron, 17*, 267– 274.

Schacter, D.L., Norman, K.A., & Koustaal, W. (in press). The cognitive neuroscience of constructive memory. Chapter to appear in *Annual Review of Psychology*.

Schacter, D.L., Verfaellie, M., & Pradere, D. (1996c). The neuropsychology of memory illusions: False recall and recognition in amnesic patients. *Journal of Memory and Language, 35*, 319–334.

Schooler, J.W., Foster, R.A., & Loftus, E.F. (1988). Some deleterious consequences of the act of recollection. *Memory and Cognition, 16*, 243–251.

Schwartz, B.L. (1996). *Intrusions during recall of related lists depend on access to gist information.* Poster presented at the 37th Annual Meeting of the Psychonomic Society, Chicago.

Shiffrin, R.M., Huber, D.E., & Marinelli, K. (1995). Effects of category length and strength on familiarity in recognition. *Journal of Experimental Psychology: Learning, Memory, and Cognition, 21*, 267–287.

Slamecka, N.J. (1968). An examination of trace storage in free recall. *Journal of Experimental Psychology, 76*, 504–513.

Spiro, R.J. (1980). Accomodative reconstruction in prose recall. *Journal of Verbal Learning and Verbal Behavior, 19*, 84–95.

Srinivas, K., & Roediger, H.L. (1990). Classifying implicit memory tests: Category association and anagram solution. *Journal of Memory and Language*, 29, 389–412.

Stadler, M.A., Roediger, H.L., & McDermott, K.B. (1997). Norms for word lists that create false memories. Unpublished manuscript.

Sulin, R.A., & Dooling, D.J. (1974). Intrusion of a thematic idea in retention of prose. *Journal of Experimental Psychology, 103*, 255–262.

Thapar, A., McDermott, K.B., & Fong, C. (1997). [*Effects of level of processing and retention interval on false recall.*] Poster presented at the 38th Annual Meeting of the Psychonomic Society, Philadelphia.

Thompson, C.P., Wenger, S.K., & Bartling, C.A. (1978). How recall facilitates subsequent recall: A reappraisal. *Journal of Experimental Psychology: Human Learning and Memory, 4*, 210–221.

Thorndike, E.L. (1903). *Educational psychology*. New York: Lemcke & Buechner.

Toglia, M.P., Goodwin, K.A., Lyon, M.L., & Neuschatz, J.S. (1995a). *False memories in list recall: The role of depth of processing.* Poster presented at the 7th Meeting of the American Psychological Society, New York.

Toglia, M.P., & Neuschatz, J.S. (1996). *False memories: Where does encoding opportunity fit into the equation?* Poster presented at the 37th Annual Meeting of the Psychonomic Society, Chicago.

Toglia, M.P., Neuschatz, J.S., Goodwin, K.A., & Lyon, M.L. (1995b). *Thematic abstraction and the creation of false memories.* Paper presented at the first meeting of the Society for Applied Research in Memory and Cognition (SARMAC), Vancouver.

Tulving, E. (1964). Intratrial and intertrial retention: Notes towards a theory of free recall verbal learning. *Psychological Review, 71*, 219–237.

Tulving, E. (1966). Subjective organization and the effects of repetition in multitrial free recall. *Journal of Verbal Learning and Verbal Behavior, 5*, 193–197.

Tulving, E. (1968). Theoretical issues in free recall. In T.R. Dixon & D.L. Horton (Eds.), *Verbal behavior and general behavior theory*. Englewood Cliffs, NJ: Prentice-Hall.

Tulving, E. (1976). Ecphoric processes in recall and recognition. In J. Brown (Ed.), *Recall and recognition* (pp.37–73). London: John Wiley & Sons.

Tulving, E. (1985). Memory and consciousness. *Canadian Psychologist, 21*, 1–12.

Tulving, E., & Pearlstone, Z. (1 966). Availability versus accessibility of information in memory for words. *Journal of Verbal Learning and Verbal Behavior, 5*, 381–391.

Tun, P.A., Wingfield, A., & Rosen, M.J. (1995). *Age effects on false memory for words.* Poster presented at the 36th Annual Meeting of the Psychonomic Society, Los Angeles, CA.

Tussing, A.A., & Greene, R.L. (in press). False recognition of associates: How robust is the effect? *Psychonomic Bulletin & Review.*

Underwood, B.J. (1957). Interference and forgetting. *Psychological Review, 64*, 49–60.

Underwood, B.J. (1965). False recognition produced by implicit verbal responses. *Journal of Experimental Psychology, 70*, 122–129.

Underwood, B.J. (1969). Attributes of memory. *Psychological Review, 76*, 559–573.

Vogt, J., & Kimble, G.A. (1973). False recognition as a function of associative proximity? *Journal of Experimental Psychology, 99*, 143–145.

Whitlow, J.W. Jr. (1992). Associationism. In L.R. Squire (Ed.), *Encyclopedia of learning and memory.* New York: Macmillan Publishing Company.

Winograd, E., Peluso, J., & Glover, T.A. (1996). *Individual differences in susceptibility to memory illusions.* Poster presented at the 37th Annual Meeting of the Psychonomic Society, Chicago.

Zechmeister, J.S., & Zechmeister, E.B. (1996). *False recall and recognition of list items following delay.* Poster presented at the 37th Annual Meeting of the Psychonomic Society, Chicago.

10 The Functional Imaging of Recall

Tim Shallice
University College London, UK

Paul Fletcher and Ray Dolan
Institute of Neurology, London, UK

To a neuropsychologist the amnesic syndrome testifies to the utility of contrasting episodic memory with semantic memory (Tulving, 1972). Double dissociations of a classical type—in that each of the complementary sets of tasks can be performed normally with the other grossly impaired—can be found between tasks dependent on episodic memory and tasks dependent on semantic memory. Thus amnesic patients can perform normally on semantic memory tasks (e.g. Meudell, Mayes, & Neary, 1980) while patients with gross impairments on tests of knowledge —semantic memory patients—can perform normally on tests of episodic memory, given that one confines testing to concepts that they still retain (e.g. Coughlan & Warrington, 1981). This classical double dissociation suggests but does not entail (see Shallice, 1988, Ch. 11), that episodic and semantic memory tasks are carried out—at least in part—by isolable subsystems.

It was therefore natural that, when functional imaging of memory processes began, an attempt should be made to contrast the regions activated by tasks requiring episodic memory with those involving other memory processes. Thus a group working at the MRC Cyclotron Unit, Hammersmith, examined the activation when PET scanning of normal subjects was carried out in two verbal memory tasks (Grasby et al., 1993). A task stressing long-term verbal episodic memory was compared with an otherwise analogous task stressing phonological buffer processes. In each scan where the task stressing long-term verbal episodic memory was employed the subject was presented with one 15-word list three times at two seconds per word and then allowed 27 seconds for recall. In the scans stressing phonological buffer processes nine five-word lists were presented

247

at the same rate, so that the same number of words were presented in the two conditions overall. Each five-word list was followed by three seconds for recall. That phonological buffer processes and long-term verbal episodic memory processes would be differentially involved in the two conditions follows from classical cognitive psychology studies of short- and long-term verbal memory (e.g. Baddeley, 1986; Glanzer & Cunitz, 1966) and amnesic and auditory-verbal short-term memory impairments (e.g. Baddeley & Warrington, 1970; Shallice & Warrington, 1970; Vallar & Papagno, 1986).

When activation in the supraspan condition was subtracted from that in the subspan condition, the regions significantly more activated were the perisylvian areas bilaterally. This may represent the greater use of the auditory-verbal short-term store in that condition, as this is known from both neuropsychological (Shallice & Vallar, 1990) and PET studies (Paulesu, Frith, & Frackowiak, 1993) to be located in this region of the left hemisphere. However, it might also arise indirectly from "verbal fluency" types of operations used in retrieval from episodic memory in free recall, as verbal fluency leads to a *reduced* activation in primary auditory areas (Friston et al., 1991). However, when the activation in the subspan condition was subtracted from the supraspan condition the pattern of activation was much more surprising. Four regions were significantly more activated—both frontal cortices and two more posterior regions also bilaterally, namely the retrosplenial regions (Brodmann's area 31/23) and a region high on the medial surface of the parietal lobe—the precuneus (Brodmann's area 31). Strikingly the hippocampus and other medial temporal lobe structures were not more activated in the supraspan condition.

Were the regions found to be activated in this study merely some form of complex artefact dependent on the particular task used? A clear answer came in a second PET study which attempted to analyse the putative (long-term) episodic memory processes involved in more detail (Fletcher et al., 1995; Shallice et al., 1994). In this study we used a capacity that functional imaging has which neuropsychology, for instance, lacks. This is to be able to examine encoding processes separately from the retrieval ones employed with the same material. We used the same type of general methodology as in the Grasby et al. study in contrasting episodic memory processing with another type of memory process while maintaining nonmemory processes constant as far as possible across conditions. However the contrasts we made were different from those employed in the Grasby et al. study. We contrasted (long-term) verbal episodic memory processes with other different memory processes at encoding and recall. For encoding we contrasted episodic memory processes with priming ones, and at recall we contrasted them with semantic memory ones.

To carry out an effective PET study using a parametric or subtraction design one needs to ensure that noncritical processes are matched across conditions, and that the scan period is occupied as continuously as possible with the relevant process. Thus in a memory retrieval experiment high levels of retrieval need to be attained. But as memory encoding was to be examined on a single trial in one condition, we used category–exemplar paired associates (e.g. *poet → Browning*) where a fairly good recall performance (>80%) can be obtained from a single encoding trial for a list of 15 pairs.

The design employed at encoding was quite complex. Amnesic patients can have normal priming processes (Graf, Squire, & Mandler, 1984; Warrington & Weiskrantz, 1970). Therefore priming processes are probably separable from episodic memory ones (see e.g. Tulving & Schacter, 1990) and activation found in an encoding condition need not necessarily involve episodic memory but could just result from processes that give rise to priming. However, it has been shown that in dual-task paradigms a more demanding secondary task, which reduces the amount encoded in episodic memory, leaves priming processes unaffected if there is no structural overlap between the primary and secondary tasks (Baddeley et al., 1984; Jacoby, Ste-Maine, & Toth, 1993; Parkin, Reid, & Russo, 1990). We therefore employed a visuo-motor secondary task in which a joystick had to be moved from the central position to one of four boxes (0, 90, 180, 270°), when the relevant box lit up, which it did at a 1.35-second rate. There were two types of visuo-motor task. In the easy condition the boxes were illuminated in order. In the difficult condition they were illuminated at random.

The memory task involved presenting the paired associates at a one per three-second rate. There was a control condition in which categories analogous to those used in the memory condition were presented and the subject merely had to repeat each word. In the easy dual-task situation, four regions were significantly more activated in the memory condition than in the repetition condition after corrections for multiple comparisons were made. Two of these regions behaved in a related way in the difficult dual-task situation. These were the superior temporal gyri bilaterally and the left anterior cingulate cortex. Indeed the anterior cingulate was significantly more activated with a difficult than an easy dual-task condition.

For two regions, however, there was a significant difference between the memory and control conditions with an easy dual task but not with a difficult one, and moreover the difference between the degree of activation in the two memory tasks in the two regions was also significant. These were the left dorsolateral prefrontal cortex (Brodmann's area 46) and the retrosplenial area of posterior cingulate cortex (Brodmann's area 31/23). As the difficult dual-task manipulation led to a significant fall in the amount recalled, the logic of the experiment is that these two regions play a major role in encoding into episodic memory.

The retrieval experiment was considerably simpler. The key contrast was between an "episodic memory" retrieval condition and a "semantic memory" retrieval condition. In both conditions, a series of category labels were presented. However, in the "episodic memory" condition the subject had to recall the exemplars presented one with each category label five minutes earlier. In the "semantic memory" condition, which used different but equivalent categories, the subject had to give *any* exemplar when each category label was presented. In addition there was a repetition condition where the category labels only had to be repeated. Three regions—the left anterior cingulate and both the left and the right thalamus—were significantly more activated in both the semantic and episodic memory retrieval tasks than in the repetition condition. However, three regions—the right prefrontal cortex and the left and right precuneus—were significantly more activated in the episodic memory retrieval condition than in repetition and also in the semantic memory retrieval task (see Fig. 10.1).

The first striking aspect of these results concerns the replicability of the regions involved. If one compares the findings of the Grasby et al. study with this study, both studies contrasted long-term verbal episodic memory processes with other types of memory process, but in the Grasby et al. study the contrasting memory processes are auditory-verbal short-term memory (phonological buffer) processes; in the study just described the contrast is with priming and semantic memory processes. Yet the same four regions—the left and right prefrontal cortex and two medial structures (retrosplenial cortex and precuneus)—are selectively activated in the episodic memory tasks in both studies. More striking still, the four regions involved divide into two involved at encoding (left prefrontal and retrosplenial) and two at retrieval (right prefrontal and precuneus).

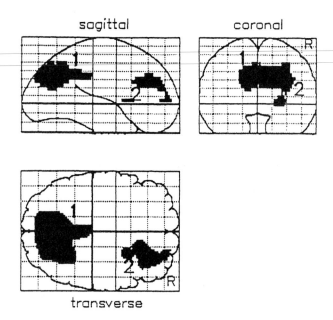

FIG. 10.1.   Regions significantly more activated in the episodic memory retrieval condition than in the semantic memory retrieval condition, using Statistical Parametric Mapping procedures (Friston et al., 1991) (from Fletcher et al., 1995; Fig. 6, p.409).

This chapter will be primarily concerned with the nature of the processes involved in the two regions activated at retrieval. The critical involvement of the left dorsolateral prefrontal regions for episodic memory encoding was also shown in a study being carried out at the same time (Kapur et al., 1994) in which it was found that the one region significantly more activated by deep encoding than by shallow—with the consequent benefits for effective episodic memory encoding—was the left dorsolateral prefrontal cortex.

As far as the retrosplenial cortex is concerned, an important pathway from the dorsolateral prefrontal cortex to the hippocampus goes via this region (Goldman-Rakic et al., 1984) and lesions to it can give rise to an amnesic state (Rudge & Warrington, 1991; Valenstein et al., 1987). It can therefore be viewed as a way-station in dorsolateral prefrontal modulation of input to the hippocampus.

THE EFFECT OF IMAGEABILITY ON RECALL

At retrieval two regions were significantly more activated in episodic memory recall. Post-hoc questioning of subjects indicated that they had used imagery in that condition, and two earlier studies have also suggested that episodic retrieval of visual images may be a critical process (Grasby et al., 1993; Roland et al., 1990). To test this hypothesis in a further experiment (Fletcher et al., 1996) word pairs were presented to the subject that were either imageable (e.g. *lake* ® *stream*) or abstract (e.g. *come* ® *go*). As imageable pairs are easier to learn, interpretation of any direct comparison of the two types of retrieval material (given that they gave rise to equal levels of recall) would, however, be liable to the interpretation that the imageable material would be the more novel, and Raichle et al. (1994) have shown that as material becomes better learned and hence less novel frontal activation, in particular, declines. We therefore added another factor—the semantic distance between stimulus and response. As this increased, so the amount of training necessary to obtain equivalent recall levels would increase. Thus we had a means of telling if the factors of amount of training/decrease in novelty did in fact have an effect on degree of activation.

Subjects showed large differences in the amount of imagery reported at recall between the two main types of pair. As predicted, the precuneus was significantly more activated with the imageable than the nonimageable pairs and this effect remained the same when the semantic distance factor was partialled out in an analysis of covariance. Thus the explanation of its role in the previous experiment as being activated in episodic memory retrieval processes that involve the recall of visual images was supported.

Since 1994, there have been many more studies of the role of the second region activated in the recall part of the previous study—the right prefrontal cortex. It, rather than the left prefrontal cortex, has been found to be activated in a large range of retrieval tasks including sentence-recognition (e.g. Tulving et al., 1994), other forms of cued recall (e.g. Cabeza et al., 1995), and word-item completion (e.g. Squire et al., 1992) where, though, the role of episodic memory is less clear (see Graf et al., 1984) as well as in a variety of nonverbal tasks (see Nyberg, Cabeza, & Tulving, 1996 for review). Only in one experiment, that of Petrides, Alivasatos, and Evans (1995), where the degree of learning was not well controlled across conditions, was no lateralisation found between the frontal lobes (see Nyberg et al., 1996).

What is the role of the right prefrontal cortex in memory retrieval? One possibility suggested by the Toronto group, when they obtained the first evidence of a specifically right frontal activation in episodic recognition processes, was that it arose from the subject being in what Tulving (1983) called "retrieval mode" (Tulving et al., 1994). That this is unlikely to be the complete explanation can be seen from a further aspect of the experiment on the effect of imageability on paired associate recall.

On the initial analyses neither of the two factors investigated—the imageability of the pairs and the semantic distance between stimuli and responses—had any effect on the degree of activation of the right prefrontal cortex. However, the region showed up strongly after the application of a different form of analysis—a principal components analysis in which one attempts to determine which regions are consistently activated together across scans. The area that loaded highest on the first factor was the right prefrontal cortex. However, this factor loaded in a very surprising way across scans (see Fig. 10.2). Both for imageable and nonimageable words, regions loading on this factor showed a strong U-shaped curve across semantic distance. As the semantic distance increased so their activation declined while there still remained a semantic relation between stimuli and responses (i.e. from *king* → *queen* to *train* → *whistle*). However, for the pairs where there was no semantic relation (e.g. *puppy* → *hurricane*) which took a greater number of trials to learn, these regions were as strongly activated as for the closest pairs, which had only been presented once. It is difficult to see how a process like being in retrieval mode could produce such a grossly nonlinear pattern.

Why might this occur? The theoretical perspective we have used derives from the Norman and Bobrow (1979) theory of memory retrieval (see also Conway, 1991; Morton, Hammesley, & Bekerian, 1985; Shallice, 1988). Norman and Bobrow's essential insight was that a retrieval cue alone provides an insufficient specification to guide retrieval search. Retrieval also depends on the retrieval task, which can be cognitively posed in a form somewhat distant conceptually from the contents of the traces, records, or whatever where the memories are stored. Thus an operation is required that produces from the combination of the retrieval task and the retrieval cue a specification of that region of the memory store where an appropriate memory trace/record relevant to the retrieval task might lie. Moreover the abstractness of this process means that candidate memories may be produced that are in fact inappropriate, so verification processes are required.

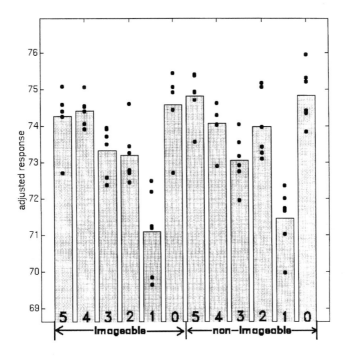

FIG. 10.2.   Activation at a right medial frontal pixel for paired associate retrieval of different levels of semantic distance. 0 = random, 5 = closely related (from Fletcher et al., 1996, fig. 4, p.1591).

In an extensive protocol analysis of the recall of everyday autobiographical memories Burgess and Shallice (1996) showed that everyday memory retrieval is indeed error-prone and that there are a number of types of thought process—so-called *recall specifications, hypotheses,* and *conscious memory search,* decisions to search for particular types of experience (more general and more specific)—which are clear conscious signs of the formation of descriptions. We also showed that a variety of verification processes are present in the protocols. Turning to the confabulatory disorders that can arise following neurological conditions such as anterior communicating artery aneurysms and frontal head injury, we showed that the patterns of confabulation found across patients fitted well with three types of basic deficit—the impairment of the descriptor process, the impairment of verification processes, and the impairment of mediator processes in which the verification processes operate through more general cognitive analysis of the implications of a retrieval.

If such processes exist why would they come into play as the semantic distance of the paired associates is varied? In fact in paired associate learning one can learn that an item is in the response set in part independently of the particular S–R association. Thus a common error is for the subject to produce an item in the response set other than the appropriate response for the presented stimulus.

In the present experiment this is not a problem when there is a semantic relation between stimulus and response, as an item in the response set semantically linked to the stimulus is most unlikely to be the appropriate response for any other stimulus. Thus when such a response comes to mind a further check that it has not come from some other stimulus in the set is unnecessary. In the random pair condition, however, no such guarantee is available and so a further check would be valuable. Thus extra monitoring and verification processes would be important specifically in the random pair condition. Also in the closest pair cases (e.g. *king* → *queen*) the response could arise just due to a word association process, so again an extra checking process would be useful. Thus extra verification processes would be expected at both extreme ends of the semantic distance scale. This provides a plausible possible explanation for the right dorsolateral frontal activation.

ORGANISATION AND RETRIEVAL

A final experiment shows that the right prefrontal response at retrieval is more complex than the previous discussion suggests. Organisation is known to be a key variable in ensuring high levels of recall (Mandler, 1979). In a study of the neuropsychological correlates of organisation in which categorised lists were presented in a variety of forms, namely either blocked or random at input and blocked or random at retrieval, the groups that were significantly impaired compared with normal controls were the left frontal group and the left tempero-hippocampal group (Incisa Della Rocchetta & Milner, 1993). Moreover, when the left frontal group was compared to all the other subject groups combined, significant differences occurred only in the condition where presentation type was blocked and recall was free. This suggested to the authors that deliberate and strategic retrieval processes are left frontally localised, as well as deliberate and strategic encoding processes. In fact there were no significant interactions between lesion groups and memory procedure. We therefore decided to examine the localisation of the use of organisation at retrieval and at encoding (Fletcher et al., submitted). Indeed at encoding, organisation processes seemed to be specifically linked to activation of left dorsolateral prefrontal regions, as would be expected from the Incisa Della Rocchetta and Milner findings.

For retrieval we contrasted retrieval from an organised list with retrieval of paired associates. The organised list was a set of four items from four related categories, e.g. four types of *bread*, four types of *fish*, four types of *fruit*, and four types of *meat*. The list was presented once five minutes before scanning and the retrieval cue for each word during the scan was the word "next". In the control condition 16 different categories were used in each list, corresponding to categories from four different lists in the internally generated retrieval condition.

Again, a single presentation trial was given, but this time recall was cued by each category label presented at a three-second rate. Two word repetition tasks were used as repetition controls for the two retrieval conditions.

Both retrieval tasks by comparison with their respective repetition control conditions showed a wide swathe of significantly greater activation through the right prefrontal region. There was no significantly greater activation in the left prefrontal cortex. However, there was also a surprising double dissociation. The retrieval of the organised list produced significantly great activation in the right dorsolateral prefrontal cortex, but for the retrieval of the control paired associates it was significantly greater in the posterior ventral prefrontal cortex (see Fig. 10.3).

There is no support for retrieval of an organised structure involving the left frontal cortex. Why, however, should the double dissociation in the right frontal lobe occur? Retrieval of a 16-item list from a 4 × 4 hierarchy requires continuous monitoring of where in the structure one is and whether one has generated the appropriate four items from a category. A subject will, for instance, know that only three of one particular category have so far been retrieved. By contrast, paired associate recall, where items are exemplars elicited by category cues, is, by extrapolation from the earlier discussion, a situation where monitoring and verification are less critical. Thus the greater right dorsolateral activation with the internally generated retrieval is not too surprising; it stresses verification processes more.

Why, though, might the posterior ventral right prefrontal region be more strongly activated by the paired associate condition? One possibility is that in the organised list retrieval condition, the recall specification conditions change only four times, namely as the subject moves to the next categories; when retrieval is of within-category items, the same recall specification conditions operate for a maximum of four responses. In the paired associate condition, however, the recall specification conditions change with each retrieval cue. Thus one possibility is that the paired associate condition stresses the description/recall specification process more.

The attribution of the greater activation in the right posterior ventral prefrontal region to the stressing of the recall specification process is highly speculative. However, the double dissociation within the right prefrontal region between two different verbal memory retrieval conditions, just like the U-shaped relation in the earlier experiment, suggests that the control processes involved in retrieval are complex. Moreover the continually surprising nature of the findings on verbal recall using functional imaging suggests that this technology is of great promise for isolating the relevant subprocesses involved in these complex control operations, where so far relatively little progress has been made by either experimental psychological or neuropsychological procedures. Functional imaging indeed provides a very promising tool for investigating control processes in general.

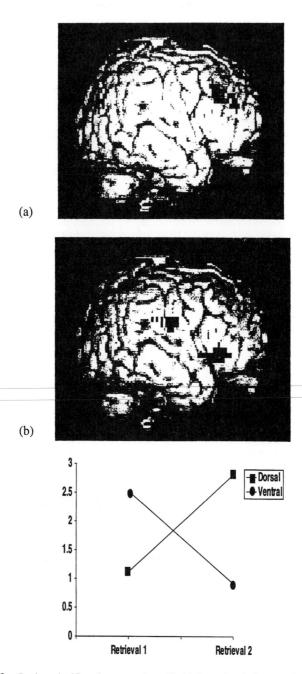

(a)

(b)

FIG. 10.3. Regions significantly more activated in (a) the retrieval of an organised structure and (b) paired associate retrieval (from Fletcher et al., submitted).

REFERENCES

Baddeley, A.D. (1986). *Working memory.* Oxford: Clarendon Press.

Baddeley, A., Lewis, V., Eldridge, M., & Thomson, N. (1984). Attention and retrieval from long-term memory. *Journal of Experimental Psychology: General, 113,* 518–540.

Baddeley, A.D., & Warrington, E.K. (1970). Amnesia and the distinction between long- and short-term memory. *Journal of Verbal Learning and Verbal Behaviour, 15,* 575–589.

Burgess, P.W., & Shallice, T. (1996). Confabulation and the control of recollection. *Memory, 4,* 359–412.

Cabeza, R., Kapur, S., Craik, F.I.M., McIntosh, A.R., Houle, S., & Tulving, E. (1995). Functional neuroanatomy of recall and recognition: A PET study of episodic memory. *Journal of Cognitive Neuroscience.*

Conway, M.A. (1991). *Autobiographical memory: An Introduction.* Milton Keynes, UK: Open University Press.

Coughlan, A.K., & Warrington, E.K. (1981). The impairment of verbal semantic memory: A single case study. *Journal of Neurology, Neurosurgery and Psychiatry, 50,* 1110–1116.

Fletcher, P.C., Frith, C.D., Grasby, P.M., Shallice, T., Frackowiak, R.S.J., & Dolan, R.J. (1995). Brain systems for encoding and retrieval of auditory-verbal memory: An in vivo study in humans. *Brain, 118,* 401–416.

Fletcher. P.C., Shallice, T., Frith, C.D., Frackowiak, R.S.J., & Dolan, R.J. (1996). Brain activity during memory retrieval: The influence of imagery and semantic cueing. *Brain, 119,* 1587–1596.

Fletcher, P., Shallice, T., Frith, C.D., Frackowiak, R.S.J., & Dolan, R.J. (submitted). The functional roles of prefrontal cortex in episodic memory. II Retrieval.

Friston, K.J., Frith, C.D., Liddle, P.F., & Frackowiak, R.S.J. (1991) Comparing functional (PET) images: The assessment of significant change. *Journal of Cerebral Blood Flow Metabolism, 11,* 690–699.

Glanzer, M., & Cunitz, A.R. (1966). Two storage mechanisms in free recall. *Journal of Verbal Learning and Verbal Behavior, 5,* 351–360.

Goldman-Rakic, P.S., Selemon, L.S.D., & Schwartz, M.L. (1984). Dual pathways connecting the dorsolateral prefrontal cortex with the hippocampal formation and parahippocampal cortex in the rhesus monkey. *Neuroscience, 12,* 719–743.

Graf, P., Squire, L., & Mandler, G. (1984). The information that amnesic patients do not forget. *Journal of Experimental Psychology: Learning, Memory and Cognition, 10,* 164–178.

Grasby, P.M., Frith, C.D., et al. (1993). Functional mapping of brain areas implicated in auditory-verbal memory function. *Brain, 116,* 1–20.

Incisa Della Rocchetta, A., & Milner, B. (1993). Strategic search and retrieval inhibition: the role of the frontal lobe. *Neuropsychologia, 31,* 503–524.

Jacoby, L.L., Ste-Marie, D., & Toth, J.P. (1993). Redefining automaticity: Unconscious influences, awareness and control. In A. Baddeley & L. Weizkrantz (Eds.), *Attention: Selection, awareness and control* (pp.261–282) Oxford: Clarendon Press.

Kapur. S., Craik, F.I.M., Tulving, E., Wilson, A.A., Houle, S., & Brown, G.M. (1994). Neuroanatomical correlates of encoding in episodic memory: Levels of processing effect. *Proceedings of the National Academy of Science USA, 91,* 2008–2011.

Mandler, G. (1979). Organisation and repetition: Organisational principles with special reference to rote learning. In L-G. Nilsson (Ed.), *Perspectives on memory research.* Hillsdale, NJ: Lawrence Erlbaum Associates Inc.

Meudell, P., Mayes, A., & Neary, D. (1980). Amnesia is not caused by cognitive slowness. *Cortex, 16,* 413–419.

Morton, J., Hammersley, R.H., & Bekerian, D.A. (1985). Headed records: A model for memory and its failure. *Cognition, 20,* 1–23.

Norman, F.A., & Bobrow, D.G. (1979). Descriptions: An intermediate stage in memory retrieval. *Cognitive Psychology, 7*, 44–64.

Nyberg, L., Cabeza, R., & Tulving, E. (1996). PET studies of encoding and retrieval: The HERA model. *Psychonomic Bulletin and Review, 3*, 135–148.

Parkin, A.J., Reid, T., & Russo, R. (1990). On the differential nature of implicit and explicit memory. *Memory and Cognition, 18*, 507–514.

Paulesu, E., Frith, C.D., & Frackowiak, R.S.J. (1993). The neural correlates of the verbal component of working memory. *Nature, 362*, 341–345.

Petrides, M., Alivasatos, B., & Evans, A.C. (1995). Functional activation of the human ventrolateral frontal cortex during mnemonic retrieval of verbal information. *Proceedings of the National Academy of Science USA, 92*, 5803–5807.

Raichle, M., Fiez, J.A., Videen, T.O., MacLeod, A.K., Pardo, J.V., Fox, P.T., Petersen, S.E. (1994). Practice-related changes in human brain functional anatomy during nonmotor learning. *Cerebral Cortex, 4*, 8–26.

Roland, P.E., Gulyas, B., Seitz, R.J., Bohm, C.J., & Stone-Elander, S. (1990). Functional anatomy of storage recall and recognition of a visual pattern in man. *Neuroreport, 1*, 53–56.

Rudge, P., & Warrington, E.K. (1991). Selective impairment of memory and visual perception in splenial tumours. *Brain, 114*, 349–360.

Shallice, T. (1988). *From neuropsychology to mental structure*. Cambridge, UK: Cambridge University Press.

Shallice, T., & Vallar, G. (1990). The impairment of auditory-verbal short-storage. In G. Vallar & T. Shallice (Eds.), *Neuropsychological impairments of short-term storage*, Cambridge: Cambridge University Press.

Shallice, T., & Warrington, E.K. (1970). Independent functioning of the verbal memory stores: A neuropsychological study. *Quarterly Journal of Experimental Psychology, 22*, 261–273.

Shallice, T., Fletcher, P., Frith, C.D., Grasby, P., Frackowiak, R.S.J., & Dolan, R.J. (1994). Brain regions associated with the acquisition and retrieval of verbal episodic memory. *Nature, 386*, 633–635.

Squire, L.R., Ojemann, J.G., Miezin, F.M., Petersen, S.E., Videen, T.O., & Raichle, M.E. (1992). Activation of the hippocampus in normal humans: A functional anatomical study of memory. *Proceedings of The National Academy of Science USA, 89*, 1837–1871.

Tulving, E. (1972). Episodic and semantic memory. In E. Tulving & W. Donaldson (Eds.), *Organization of memory*. New York: Academic Press.

Tulving, E. (1983). *Elements of episodic memory*. Oxford: Clarendon Press.

Tulving, E., Kapur, S., et al (1994). Neuroanatomical correlates of retrieval from episodic memory. *Proceedings of the National Academy of Sciences, 91*, 2012–2015.

Tulving, E., & Schacter, D. (1990). Priming and human memory systems. *Science, 247*, 301–306.

Valenstein, E., Bowers, D., Verfaellie, M., Heilman, K.M., Day, A., & Watson, R.T. (1987). Retrosplenial amnesia. *Brain, 110*, 1631–1646.

Vallar, G., & Papagno, C. (1986). Phonological short-term store and the nature of the recovery effect. Evidence from neuropsychology. *Brain and Cognition, 5*, 428–442.

Warrington, E.K., & Weiskrantz, L. (1970). Amnesia syndrome: consolidation or retrieval? *Nature, 228*, 628–630.

11 Three Dimensions of Spatial Cognition

Barbara Tversky
Stanford University, CA, USA

SPATIAL KNOWLEDGE

Our knowledge of the spatial world comes not just from vision, but also from hearing, touching, smelling, and from the feedback from our own bodies. From hearing, we can know where to look; from seeing, we can know where to reach. Spatial knowledge, then, is multimodal, and in part, supra-modal. Knowing the location of our bodies in space is essential for survival, as is knowing other critical locations, such as our homes. Spatial knowledge serves as a basis for thinking about other things, such as time, or mood, or ability, or ideas (e.g. Clark & Clark, 1977; Lakoff & Johnson, 1980). This is evident in uses of language that are so entrenched that to call them metaphoric seems overly poetic: "We're behind schedule"; "He's down in the dumps"; "She's at the top of the heap"; "That field is waiting for someone to enter".

Our knowledge of space is not like geometry or physical measurement. Rather, our knowledge of space seems to be constructed out of the things that are in space, not out of space itself. Moreover, our knowledge of space is not absolute or metric; rather it is relative, primarily, as we shall see, to other things in space as well as to a more global reference frame.

Bodies and the Surrounding World

One of the first aspects of space that we confront is our own bodies. Our bodies have three axes, that formed by our heads and feet, that formed by our fronts and backs, and that formed by our left and right. The head/feet axis is asymmetric, as

259

is the front/back axis. In addition, the front/back axis separates the world we can readily see and manipulate from the world that we cannot easily see or manipulate. The left/right axis of our bodies has no salient asymmetries. Our bodies exist in and interact with the world, which also has three axes; first, a vertical axis that is asymmetric due to gravity, and has a natural origin in the ground. Gravity has profound effects on the way things in the world look, for example a long vertical axis and vertical symmetry for many natural objects, and the way they behave, for example moving or even growing downwards or sideways more easily than upwards. The world we experience also has two horizontal axes with arbitrary origins, such as Greenwich. Experientially, their origins are in our incidental and varying viewpoint in the world. For the most part, these horizontal axes define the world we navigate. From our viewpoint, the world in front of us has a weak asymmetry in that things that are nearer appear larger and clearer than things that are far; the sideways horizontal axis has no essential asymmetries (parts of this analysis derive from similar analyses of Clark, 1973; Fillmore, 1975; Levelt, 1984; Miller & Johnson-Laird, 1976; and Shepard and Hurwitz, 1984). Thus, space as we perceive and experience it is not equipotential or arbitrary as it might be in a formal abstract treatment; rather space as we perceive and experience it is anchored, asymmetric, and biased.

These facts about the space of our bodies and the world they interact with form the basis for our conceptions of the spatial world. In the following pages, I will describe their implications for three different domains of spatial thinking. The first domain is the three-dimensional world around our bodies that we seem to keep track of effortlessly as we move about the world. Accessing objects in different directions from our bodies is biased in ways accounted for by the asymmetries of our bodies and by the relation of our bodies to the world. People keep track of the things around them by constructing a mental spatial framework derived from the body axes. The second domain is the primarily two-dimensional world that we navigate, which is thought to be captured by "cognitive maps". People's memory for the plane of navigation is systematically distorted. Those distortions indicate that people remember locations relative to each other and to a reference frame. The third domain is the two-dimensional plane of diagrams and charts; the issue of interest is the way space in graphics is used to convey abstract meanings. As for the other phenomena, so for this one, the reference frame naturally adopted yields biases.

SPATIAL FRAMEWORKS: THE WORLD AROUND OUR BODIES

Learning from Description

As we move about the world, we seem to keep track of the relative locations of our surroundings effortlessly, so that we know where things are relative to our bodies without having to look at them. As noted earlier, space is not uniquely visual. It is accessed by many modalities, and by language as well. In fact, it seems likely that one of the earliest uses of language was to describe the spatial world, to inform others how to find their way to water or food and how to avoid danger. Franklin and I (Franklin & Tversky, 1990) wanted to know whether this ability to keep track of surroundings under navigation could be tapped by language alone as well as by experience. The vivid imagery experienced by many in reading suggests that language can instil a rich mental world that can be mentally traversed and revised as the described situation changes.

In a series of experiments designed to capture those phenomena in a laboratory setting (Franklin & Tversky, 1990), participants read narratives describing themselves in settings such as an opera house or barn surrounded by objects such as a bouquet of flowers or a bucket beyond their head, feet, front, back, left, and right. After learning the environments, participants were reoriented to face another object and queried by direction terms such as "head", "front", and "left", for the objects currently lying in those directions. Participants performed this task quickly and accurately. However, the times to access objects varied considerably depending on the directions of the objects from the body. Many participants reported imagining themselves in the environments and imagining themselves looking at the specified direction to find the object, a position consonant with classical work and theory in imagery and mental transformations, a pattern we termed the *Mental Transformation* pattern (e.g. Finke & Shepard, 1986; Kosslyn, 1980; Shepard & Podgorny, 1978). According to this theory, responses should be fastest to identify objects directly in front of the observer, next fastest to those displaced 90 degrees, that is, those to left, right, head, and feet, and slowest to objects displaced by 180 degrees, that is, the object behind. These subjective reports notwithstanding, the pattern of retrieval times did not correspond to the Mental Transformation pattern. In particular, time to retrieve objects behind, requiring a 180-degree mental transformation, were shorter than times to retrieve objects to left and right, requiring 90-degree mental transformations.

For the upright observer, the times to retrieve objects in various directions from the body corresponded to the *Spatial Framework* analysis. According to this analysis, readers construct mental spatial frameworks from extensions of the axes of their own bodies and associate objects to them. Accessibility of the axes depends on the relative salience of the axes in context. For the upright observer, the head/feet axis is most salient because of its asymmetries and because it is aligned with the only asymmetric axis of the world, the axis of gravity. The front/back axis is second because of its asymmetries, and the left/right axis is slowest because it has no essential asymmetries. The obtained retrieval times corresponded to this pattern. When the observer in the scene is described as reclining and turning from front to back to side, no axis of the body is aligned with gravity. In this case, only the asymmetries of the body should determine retrieval times. Like the head/feet plane, the front/back plane is asymmetric, but in addition it separates the world that can be perceived and manipulated from the world that cannot be easily perceived and manipulated, so it should be more salient. In fact, when the observer is described as reclining, retrieval times to front/back are faster than those to head/feet.

These findings have been replicated and extended in several variations of the described scenes, including third-person rather than second-person descriptions (Bryant, Tversky, & Franklin, 1992), central objects as well as central persons (Bryant et al., 1992), external as well as internal perspectives (Bryant et al., 1992), multiple viewpoints in a scene (Franklin, Tversky, & Coon, 1992), and probing for directions from objects rather than probing for objects from directions (Bryant & Tversky, 1992). The basic pattern has also been found in experiments describing the room as moving rather than the person as turning in the scene (Tversky, in press). In that case, participants take twice as much time to reorient when the room rather than the observer is described as turning even though these transformations are formally identical. Because the two situations, that of the room turning and that of the observer turning, are formally identical but psychologically different, this result is not readily accounted for by a propositional model.

Learning from Experience

In the previous experiments, environments were instilled by discourse, not by actual experience with an environment. From a description of space, it is necessary to construct a mental representation of space, but from direct experience of space, it may not be necessary to construct a mental representation—memory may suffice—or a different sort of mental representation might be constructed. To investigate this, Bryant, Lanca and I (Bryant, Tversky, & Lanca, 1996) put participants in environments where they were surrounded by objects on all sides. Participants learned the environments from experience, from looking around themselves at the objects in the scene. At testing, they were either provided the objects in the specified directions from memory as before, or they answered while they were in the environments and could actually scan the scene.

This design—responding from memory versus responding from perception—allowed testing of another tenet of the classical view of imagery, that imagery is like internalised perception (Kosslyn, 1980; Shepard & Podgorny, 1978). According to the view that imagery is like internalised perception, the patterns of retrieval times should be the same for responding from memory as those for responding from perception. In fact, they were not. When participants responded from perception of the scene, their retrieval times corresponded to what we termed the *Physical Transformation Model*. Participants were fastest to respond to objects directly in front, next fastest to respond to objects displaced by 90 degrees, to head, feet, left, or right, and slowest to respond to objects located behind, displaced by 180 degrees. This pattern is exactly what the *Mental Transformation Model,* derived from prior work on imagery and mental transformations, predicted for the original task. However, when participants responded from memory of the scene, their retrieval times corresponded to the Spatial Framework model. Thus, the mental representations constructed from experience are functionally different from the mental processing that underlies responding while looking, but functionally the same mental representations as those constructed from descriptions.

Interestingly, when participants responded from perception of the scenes, they quickly learned the scenes. As they learned the scenes, they ceased scanning them and began to respond from memory, without looking. When participants ceased looking, their response times corresponded to the Spatial Framework model. Thus, even when perception is available, it may be more efficient to rely on memory.

Neither Imagery nor Propositions

These findings are difficult to accommodate within either a classical imagery account or a classical propositional account. The general pattern of retrieval times in memory to different directions from the body does not depend on the degree of displacement from frontwards, and the pattern of times from memory does not correspond to that from perception. Both these findings contradict the classical imagery position. On the other hand, propositional accounts do not naturally predict biases in directions nor do they predict slower reorientation when an environment rather than an observer is described as moving. Rather than depending on our internalised perceptions of space, the patterns of times in these tasks depend on our long-standing conceptions of the space of our bodies as they interact with the space of the world. In order to keep track of the objects surrounding us as we navigate the world, we construct schematic mental representations. The components of these mental representations are a framework, in this case, mental extensions of the natural axes of the body, and elements, tokens for the surrounding objects. Furthermore, the axes are biased in ways corresponding to our mental conceptions of the spatial world.

COGNITIVE MAPS: THE WORLD WE NAVIGATE

Now we turn to mental representations of the primarily two-dimensional plane of navigation, a domain of knowledge captured by the term "cognitive map". One prevalent view of cognitive maps is that they are like images, fairly veridical mental representations of the true state of things, preserving even metric information about the world. The well-known experiments of Kosslyn, Ball, and Reiser (1978) are taken as support for that view; in those experiments, times to scan between two points on a mental image of a memorised map correlated with actual distances between the points on the map. This view is appealing for its simplicity: internal representations are like external ones, and distances are captured metrically (Kosslyn, 1980; Shepard & Podgorny, 1978). The view can be easily refuted by demonstrations of systematic errors or biases in memory, but to find systematic rather than random errors requires careful construction of experimental tasks. Evidence for systematic errors in memory and judgement for maps and environments has accumulated.

As we navigate the world, we see the world from different viewpoints and different distances. In addition, some knowledge of the whereabouts of things in the world comes from maps and descriptions in addition to or instead of direct perception. Given multiple views and multiple information sources, encoding exact metric positions from each experience does not seem to be the best way to remember space, nor does it seem to be what our cognitive apparatus does. Rather, we seem to remember elements relative to each other and to a frame of reference. Elements may be landmarks, roads, cities, countries, depending on the situation, and frames of reference may be the canonical axes, relatively large environmental features such as highways, borders, rivers, and mountain ranges. In correspondence with this analysis, errors and biases in memory for maps and environments can be divided into those due to other elements and those due to reference frames (Tversky, 1981, 1992, 1993, 1996a).

Other Elements: Landmarks

When someone asks us where we live, we often answer relative to the nearest salient geographic feature we think our interlocutor is likely to know (Shanon, 1983). To a European, I might answer "California", to a New Yorker, I might answer "near San Francisco", to a local, I might answer "on Stanford campus". Thus, our information about regions is organised around landmarks. At the same time that they help to organise spatial knowledge, landmarks also distort spatial conceptions in ways that are inconsistent with any metric representation of space. Specifically, people judge distances to a landmark to be less than distances to an ordinary building (Sadalla, Burroughs, & Staplin, 1980). That mental distances are asymmetric defies any metric account of mental representation (Tversky, 1977), in particular the traditional view of cognitive maps.

Other Elements: Alignment

Using other elements of a spatial scene as a reference object can distort judgements of location as well as distance. According to the Gestalt principle of proximity, people mentally group together similar elements in a visual scene. Similar geographic elements, like North and South America, are likely to be mentally grouped. Consistent with this analysis, when asked to judge which of two maps of the Americas is the correct one, a significant majority of those questioned picked the incorrect map in which South America had been moved more directly "below" or more aligned with North America (Tversky, 1981). In actuality, South America is for the most part west of North America, but people group them and judge South America to be relatively more east than it actually is. The same error arises for North America and Europe and South America and Africa; a significant majority of viewers pick the incorrect map in which Europe and Africa have been moved southwards relative to North and South America. The error also occurs for judgements of directions between cities and for artificial maps, indicating that it is based in processes underlying organisation of spatial scenes.

Frame of Reference: Hierarchical Organisation

In remembering locations of elements, we use reference frames as well as other elements as organisers. A readily available reference frame for spatial elements is the larger spatial region in which the element is embedded, for example, states for cities. Stevens and Coupe (1978) asked students in San Diego to draw a line indicating the direction between San Diego and Reno. Most participants indicated that Reno was east of San Diego when, in fact, it is west of San Diego. Stevens and Coupe reasoned that rather than remembering the directions between all pairs of cities, people organise geographic knowledge hierarchically. They organise cities into states and remember the relative directions between states. When queried about directions between pairs of cities, they infer that information from the directions of the states in which the cities are contained. Because California is generally west of Nevada, people infer that Reno is west of San Diego. Stevens and Coupe demonstrated effects of hierarchical organisation on artificial maps as well as real-world examples.

Since then, others have demonstrated effects of hierarchical organisation in other tasks. Wilton (1979) and Maki (1981) have shown that reaction times to judge north–south or east–west directions between pairs of cities are faster when the cities are in different geographic units aligned with the directions, even when distances are closer than pairs of cities within the same geographic unit. Hirtle and Jonides (1985) found that people underestimate distances between pairs of locations within the same conceptual group relative to pairs of locations between conceptual groups. For example, students at the University of Michigan underestimated distances of pairs consisting of two campus buildings or two town buildings relative to the distances between pairs consisting of one campus and one town building. Thus, hierarchical organisation has been demonstrated to affect time and errors to make judgements of both distance and direction for natural and artificial stimuli (see also Chase, 1983; Hirtle & Mascolo, 1986; McNamara, 1986, 1992; McNamara, Hardy, & Hirtle, 1989).

Frame of Reference: Perspective

The next investigation seems to have been inspired by the famous cartoons of the New Yorker's view of the world, where Manhattan is large and differentiated, and the world in any direction from it is shrunken and hazy. In point of fact, this is how we see; the things that are closer to us loom larger and are more distinct than the things that are far away and appear telescoped together. Holyoak and Mah (1982) investigated the effects of mental perspective on distance estimates. They asked students in Ann Arbor to imagine themselves as either in New York or San Francisco, and then to make judgements about the relative distances between pairs of cities more or less equidistant across the country. Those with an east coast perspective judged the distance between New York and Pittsburgh to be relatively larger than those with the west coast perspective, whereas those with the west coast perspective judged the distance between San Francisco and Salt Lake City to be relatively larger than those with the east coast perspective. The students who were given no perspective and presumably adopted one from Ann Arbor gave estimates intermediate between the east and west coast perspective participants.

Frame of Reference: Rotation

A natural frame of reference for geographic entities is the north–south–east–west framework provided by the canonical axes. Geographic regions, however, may also induce their own local frame of reference from their own shape. In perception of objects, people extract the longer axis, often assuming symmetry around it, and further assume that the axis is aligned with vertical or horizontal (Rock, 1973). When the frame of reference induced by a region is not perfectly aligned with the external frame of reference provided by the canonical axes, the two seem to be mental-rotated more in correspondence. Thus, for example, South America seems to be tilted relative to north–south on a world map. Consistent with this, when students were asked to place a cutout of South American into a north–south east–west frame, they tended to position it upright (Tversky, 1981). Similar distortions occur for artificial maps and for judgements of directions between pairs of cities or roads in regions that are not quite aligned with the canonical axes for both real and artificial environments.

Organisation of Space

In organising spatial knowledge, people appear to extract the major elements or figures, be they buildings or roads or cities or countries. The locations and orientations of these elements are not remembered directly but rather relative to each other and relative to certain natural reference frames, such as those provided by larger geographic units or those provided by the canonical axes. The effects of the reference objects and frames are distorting; they anchor the element in question, drawing it closer in distance or orientation. It may then be impossible to put together all the parts into a consistent whole, that is, the result need not be consistent with any metric representation. Cognitive maps can be impossible figures (Tversky, 1981), although the more constraints imposed, the less the error as the constraints are often uncorrelated (Baird, Merril, & Tannenbaum, 1979). Thus, the term "cognitive map" is misleading; it implies a unitary mental representation that is Euclidean. Because spatial knowledge does not necessarily conform to metric assumptions and because knowledge of space comes from many different modalities—verbal, visual, kinesthetic, and more—a cognitive collage seems a more appropriate metaphor than cognitive map to capture people's knowledge of space (Tversky, 1993).

These systematic biases and errors are not restricted to the domain of space. Analogous biases and errors can be found in memory and judgements in social, political, and other abstract domains (e.g. Nisbett & Ross, 1980; Quattrone, 1986; Taylor, 1989; Tversky & Gati, 1978; Tversky & Kahneman, 1974). For example, people perceive members of groups far from their own to be more similar to each other than members of their own groups, an effect analogous to the effect of perspective on distance estimates for near and far locations (Quattrone, 1986). People prefer to say that red is like magenta than vice versa (Rosch, 1975) and prefer to think that a son is like a father than a father like a son, an asymmetry effect like that of estimating distances to landmarks or ordinary objects (Tversky & Gati, 1978). The prevalence of these biases across domains of thought suggests that decomposing a domain of knowledge into elements and larger units, and structuring elements with respect to other elements and with respect to reference frames, is the result of general cognitive processes and not restricted to spatial thinking.

GRAPHICS: THE CONSTRUCTED WORLD BEFORE OUR EYES

Graphics, on paper, wood, stone, sand, clay, or bone, are ancient human artifacts, far more ancient than written language. They have been used to portray animals, environments, tallies. Although the oldest extant map, a clay tablet from Mesopotamia, dates back more than 4000 years (Wilford, 1981), visualisations of inherently nonvisual relations are a recent invention, beginning with economic and political graphs in the late eighteenth century by Playfair and Lambert (Beniger & Robyn, 1978; Tufte, 1983). With increased contact among diverse language communities and with advances in graphic technologies, graphics are increasingly prevalent in more aspects of our lives, from signs in public places to graphical user interfaces. An interdisciplinary set of researchers has begun to study diagrammatic reasoning (e.g. Glasgow, Narayanan, & Chandrasekeran, 1995).

Elements and Spatial Relations: Elements

Studying the graphic inventions adopted across time and space, by different cultures, eras, and ages, reveals some universals that seem to be rooted in cognition (Tversky, 1995). Graphics consist of elements and the spatial relations among them. In depictions, the elements are the people or animals or objects portrayed; in writing, the elements are letters or pictographs; in graphs, the elements are lines, dots, numbers, and letters. Most writing systems began with icons as elements. The icons bore resemblance to what they represented but became schematised, conventionalised, and often symbolic with time and use (Coulmas, 1989; Gelb, 1963). For objects and some activities, it is relatively easy to construct icons that are readily interpreted. However, for abstract concepts, selecting icons is less natural and often relies on "figures of depiction" such as metonymy, where a concrete associate to a concept stands for the concept.

Spatial Relations: Levels of Preserving Spatial Information

These observations about icons have been noted many times. What is less obvious is how space, usually the space among elements, is used to convey meaning. The basic metaphor underlying meaning in graphics, as well as gestures and similar uses of space in communication, is that distance in space reflects distance in some abstract concept or dimension. The mapping from the conceptual dimension to space can preserve information from the conceptual dimension at different levels: at the nominal or categorical level, where only the separation into groups is meaningful; at the ordinal level, where the order of elements is meaningful; at the interval level, where the distances among elements are meaningful; and at the ratio level, where the ratios of the distances are meaningful.

A simple example of using space meaningfully at a categorical or nominal level is the separating of letters belonging to different words with spaces. Precursors of modern alphabetic languages did not always do this. Rows and columns also use space to group similar items together and separate them from dissimilar items. A simple example of an ordinal spatial device is an ordered list—children in order of age, baseball players in order of batting average, groceries in order of encounter in the grocery store. Indenting successively subordinate entries in an outline is also a meaningful ordinal use of space. Hierarchical trees, such as an organisation chart of a company or an evolutionary tree, are other examples of using space to convey ordinal information. In such trees, only one dimension, the vertical or horizontal dimension conveying time or power for example, is meaningful, depending on how the tree is rooted. The sequence on the perpendicular dimension is not interpretable. A simple example of using space meaningfully at the interval level is the x–y graphs found commonly in newspapers, magazines, and textbooks. Those graphs with a meaningful zero, such as plots of money, may preserve information at a ratio level. Pie charts are another ratio spatial device.

Spatial Relations: Directionality

In addition to spatial proximity, direction in space is often used to convey meaning. Consistent with its asymmetry both in the body and in the world, the horizontal dimension seems to be neutral, but consistent with its asymmetry in the body and in the world, the vertical dimension is not. For the vertical dimension, more, better, and stronger are associated with up; and less, worse, and weaker with down, in space as in language—remember top of the heap and feeling low—and in gesture—think of thumb's up and high five. This bias was evident in a survey conducted of tree diagrams that appear commonly in scientific texts, diagrams of evolution, of geological ages, and of linguistic families. For the diagrams of evolution, 17 out of the 18 texts with such diagrams found in texts in the Stanford main library portrayed human beings at the top of the chart. For the geological charts, 15 out of 16 portrayed the present era at the top. Thus, for both these topics, there is a strong tendency to place the present time, the best time so far, and people, the best species so far, at the top. For the linguistic trees, 13 out of 14 displayed the proto-language at the top. For linguistic trees, then, in contrast to biology and geology, the present time is at the bottom and the past at the top. However, at the top is the proto-language, the idealised language from which the others derived. The same holds for family trees, where the ancestor establishing the family sits firmly at the top.

Children's Use of Space to Convey Abstract Concepts

In order to learn how space is used spontaneously to convey nonspatial concepts, we asked children from different language cultures to use space on paper to express concepts of time, quantity, and preference (Tversky, Kugelmass, & Winter, 1991). The basic task for the children was as follows. The child and the experimenter sat side-by-side in front of a square piece of paper, thus sharing the same perspective. The experimenter put a dot sticker down in the centre of the page, stating that this stood for the time for eating breakfast (for example). The child was asked to put down stickers for the time to eat lunch and the time to eat dinner. One of the quantitative tasks asked about the amount of candy in a handful, the amount in a bag of candy, and the amount collected on Halloween. One of the preference tasks asked about a food loved, a food neither liked nor disliked, and a food that was disliked. Each child was first warmed up with a spatial task, representing the positions of tiny dolls in front of the child, and then given two temporal, two quantitative, and two preference tasks.

The children ranged in age from kindergarten through college. The task was simplified for the high school and college students. Participants included large samples of Hebrew-speaking Israelis, Arabic-speaking Israelis, and English-speaking Americans. Both Hebrew and Arabic are written from right to left, so this allowed us to examine the effects of writing direction on graphing direction. However, the right to left tendency is stronger in Arabic than in Hebrew for several reasons. In Arabic, letters are connected and formed from right to left, whereas in Hebrew, letters are not connected and most are drawn from left to right. In Arabic, at least until late in elementary school, numbers go from right to left, whereas in Hebrew, numbers go as they do in English, from left to right. Finally, Hebrew-speaking Israelis are more likely to have early exposure to a language written from left to right than are Arabic-speaking children.

There were several questions of interest. First, what information would the children's mappings preserve? Next, what direction would be used to represent increases? Third, is there a general graphing schema; that is, would the mappings be content-free? For information preserved, older children's mappings preserved more information than younger children's. Some of the youngest children treated the separate times, quantities, and alternatives as exactly that, as separate groups not on a single dimension. Their dots did not form a line; rather, they were placed seemingly randomly on the page. Most of the children did put the dots on a line, preserving order. To test for preservation of interval, in a separate study, we chose new examples where scale differences were blatant, for example, break-fast, morning snack, and dinner. We also elicited and then demonstrated the use of interval mapping for a spatial array. Despite these manipulations, only at about fifth grade did a large portion of the children preserve interval in their mappings. With age, then, children's use of space to map nonspatial relations preserved more information about the relations.

In contrast to information preserved, the use of the different directions to indicate increases showed no effect of age. For indicating time, there was an effect of language. A large portion of English-speaking children mapped time as increasing from left to right and a large portion of Arabic-speaking children mapped time as increasing from right to left. Hebrew-speaking children were in between. This was expected. Interestingly, the directionality of time did not change with age, suggesting that even college students did not bring their knowledge of graphing to this task, but rather treated each task for what it was, a request to use space to express a nonspatial relation.

Although writing culture affected direction of indicating increases for time, it had no effect on indicating increases for quantity or preference. Across cultures and ages, approximately equal numbers of participants indicated increases in quantity or preference as going from left to right, right to left, and down to up. The only direction that was not used to indicate increases was up to down. This finding is consonant with the observation that the vertical dimension has a natural asymmetry but the horizontal one does not. Increases are indicated as going upwards, or leftwards or rightwards, but not as going downwards. There are some "negative" relations that increase upwards; inflation and employment are examples. But these cases preserve the direction of the numbers even if they do not preserve the direction of the valence of the relation.

These findings indicate that children from diverse language cultures use space to express nonspatial relations in much the same way that graphic inventions do, suggesting that these graphic inventions and conventions are based at least in part on natural cognitive biases rooted in people's conceptions of space. Distance in space is used to convey distance on nonspatial relations, and the vertical dimension of space, but not the horizontal dimension, is used asymmetrically so that upwards is associated with more and with positivity. Not all uses of space to convey other meanings are culture-free; the direction of representing time is affected by the dominant direction of writing. This may be because time is frequently incorporated into writing, as in "the meeting will be between 2 and 4". Cross-cultural research on inventions of writing by pre-schoolers (Ferreiro & Teberosky, 1982; Levin & Tolchinsky Landsman, 1989) and inventions of arithmetic notation by children and throughout history (Hughes, 1986) illustrate similar uses of space to convey nonspatial meanings, and other ones as well.

IN CONCLUSION

Knowledge of the world begins with the world of our bodies and the world we inhabit and interact with. The spatial world and the things it contains are three-dimensional, but unlike mathematical abstractions, the three dimensions of our phenomenal world are not perfectly symmetric or equipotential. Gravity defines the vertical axis of the world. It imposes a major asymmetry in the world, with profound effects on the way things appear and the way things behave. In contrast, the two horizontal axes of the world are arbitrary and symmetric except with respect to a particular viewpoint in the world. From a particular viewpoint, the axis perpendicular to it is symmetric, but the axis defined by the viewpoint has a weak near/far or front/behind asymmetry. For our own bodies, the head/feet and front/back axes have strong asymmetries of both appearance and behaviour, whereas the left/right axis does not. These enduring facts about our bodies and the spatial world are incorporated in our enduring conceptions of space. I have discussed their implications for three domains of spatial knowledge, the knowledge we have of the three-dimensional space around our bodies as we move about; the knowledge we form of the two-dimensional spaces we navigate formed from navigation or maps or language, spaces that are often too large to be seen from a particular position; and the two-dimensional space of external graphic devices that we construct to represent, remember, and conceptualise information.

The analysis revealed similarities in the mental organisation of each of these domains. In each, space is conceived of as consisting of elements, not empty space. Elements are organised with respect to one another and with respect to a frame of reference. Selection of reference elements and reference frames is flexible and is determined by the particular demands of the situation. For keeping track of objects surrounding the body, the elements are the objects and the reference frame integrating them is a mental structure consisting of extensions of the three body axes. For keeping track of landmarks in an environment, the elements are the landmarks and the reference frame may be natural or conceptual features of the environments, such as rivers, roads, boundaries, categories, or the canonical directions. For graphic displays, the elements are the entities represented, numbers, words, objects, or functions, and the reference frame may be the sides of the page. In short, both perceptual and conceptual features of the situation determine selection of reference objects and frames (e.g. Tversky, 1996b; Tversky & Schiano, 1989). Once selected, reference objects and reference frames have biasing effects on memory, judgement, and information retrieval. For retrieving information in the space around our bodies, those directions primary in conceptual organisation are faster to retrieve. In judgements of direction, orientation, distance, and location of landmarks in the space of navigation, reference objects and frames serve as anchors and draw elements closer, leading to distortions that cannot be reconciled by metric models, mental or otherwise. In graphic displays, the vertical upwards direction in space is more likely to be chosen than the vertical downwards as the positive pole in mapping asymmetric abstract dimensions.

Not by coincidence, spatial language has the same character as mental conceptions of space. Spatial language is relative, it concerns elements, it relates elements to each other and to reference frames, all chosen to suit a situation (e.g. Levinson, 1996; Talmy, 1983; Tversky, 1996b). Language and gesture also reflect the spatial biases that are evident in memory and judgement, both literally and metaphorically (e.g. Clark & Clark, 1977; Lakoff & Johnson, 1980).

Although consistent with our enduring conceptions of space, these biases are not consistent with accounts based on imagery. Central to the classic accounts of imagery (Kosslyn, 1980; Shepard & Podgorny, 1978) is that features of images of objects and of transformations of objects bear resemblances to features of perception of objects and of perceiving transformations of objects. For features, for example, larger parts are faster to find on images than smaller parts, and the same part is faster to find on a large image than a small one. Similarly for transformations, mentally scanning an image increases with distance in the world, and mentally rotating an image increases with angle of separation. This has led to the notion, supported more recently by neuropsychological evidence (Kosslyn, 1994) that imagery is like internalised perception. Indeed, the demonstrations of imagery just described are consistent with exactly that view. Nevertheless, this view of imagery cannot account for all mental representations of the visual or spatial world, those discussed in detail here and many others as well. They differ systematically from perception and they do not preserve metric properties. Nor do these diverse phenomena fit comfortably into a classical propositional account, as a propositional account does not incorporate spatial biases in any natural way. These pervasive phenomena of spatial thinking across diverse domains can be explained in terms of the analysis developed of how people conceive of the spatial world and their place in it.

ACKNOWLEDGEMENTS

This chapter represents a draft of a paper presented at the Second International Conference on Memory, Padua, Italy, July 1996. I would like to thank my collaborators in some of the research, Nancy Franklin, Holly Taylor, David Bryant, and Diane Schiano, for years of stimulating discussion. Some of the research reviewed here was supported by the Air Force Office of Scientific Research, Air Force Systems Command, USAF, under grant or cooperative agreement number, AFOSR 89-0076, NSF-IST Grant 8403273 and NSF Grant BSN 8002012 to Stanford University. Preparation of the manuscript was facilitated by funds from Interval Research Corporation.

REFERENCES

Baird, J., Merril, A., & Tannenbaum, J. (1979). Studies of the cognitive representations of spatial relations: II. A familiar environment. *Journal of Experimental Psychology: General, 108*, 92–98.

Beniger, J.R., & Robyn, D.L. (1978). Quantitative graphics in statistics. *The American Statistician, 32*, 1–11.

Bryant, D.J., & Tversky, B. (1992). Assessing spatial frameworks with object and direction probes. *Bulletin of the Psychonomic Society, 30*, 29–32.

Bryant, D.J., Tversky, B., & Franklin, N. (1992). Internal and external spatial frameworks for representing described scenes. *Journal of Language and Memory, 31*, 74–98.

Bryant, D.J., Tversky, B., & Lanca, M. (1996). Retrieving spatial relations from observation and memory. Manuscript submitted for publication.

Chase, W.G. (1983). Spatial representations of taxi drivers. In R. Rogers & J.A. Sloboda (Eds.), *Acquisition of symbolic skills* (pp.391–405). New York: Plenum Press.

Clark, H.H. (1973). Space, time, semantics and the child. In T.E. Moore (Ed.), *Cognitive development and the acquisition of language* (pp.27–63). New York: Academic Press.

Clark, H.H., & Clark, E.V. (1977). *Psychology and language.* New York: Harcourt, Brace, Jovanovich, Inc.

Coulmas, F. (1989). *The writing systems of the world.* Oxford: Blackwell.

Ferreiro, E., & Teberosky, A. (1982). *Literacy before schooling.* London: Heinemann.

Fillmore, C.J. (1975). *Santa Cruz lectures on deixis.* Bloomington, IN: Indiana University Linguistics Club.

Finke, R.A., & Shepard, R.N. (1986). Visual functions of mental imagery. In K.R. Boff, L. Kaufman, & J.P. Thomas (Eds.), *Handbook of perception and human performance* (Vol. 2, Ch. 37, pp. 1–55). New York: Wiley-Interscience.

Franklin, N., & Tversky, B. (1990). Searching imagined environments. *Journal of Experimental Psychology: General, 119,* 63–76.

Franklin, N., Tversky, B., & Coon, V. (1992). Switching points of view in spatial mental models acquired from text. *Memory and Cognition, 20,* 507–518.

Gelb, I.J. (1963). *A study of writing.* Chicago: University of Chicago Press.

Glasgow, J., Narayanan, N.H., & Chandrasekaran, B. (1995). *Diagrammatic reasoning: Cognitive and computational perspectives.* Cambridge, MA: MIT Press.

Hirtle, S.C., & Jonides, J. (1985). Evidence of hierarchies in cognitive maps. *Memory and Cognition, 13,* 208–217.

Hirtle, S.C., & Mascolo, M.F. (1986). The effect of semantic clustering on the memory of spatial locations. *Journal of Experimental Psychology: Learning, Memory and Cognition, 12,* 181–189.

Holyoak, K.J., & Mah, W.A. (1982). Cognitive reference points in judgments of symbolic magnitude. *Cognitive Psychology, 14,* 328–352.

Hughes, M. (1986). *Children and number: Difficulties in learning mathematics.* Oxford: Blackwell.

Kosslyn, S.M. (1980). *Image and mind.* Cambridge, MA: Harvard University Press.

Kosslyn, S.M. (1994). *Image and brain.* Cambridge, MA: MIT Press.

Kosslyn, S.M., Ball, T.M., & Reiser, B.J. (1978). Visual images preserve metric spatial information: Evidence from studies of image scanning. *Journal of Experimental Psychology: Human Perception and Performance, 4,* 52–76.

Lakoff, G., & Johnson, M. (1980). *Metaphors we live by.* Chicago: University of Chicago Press.

Levelt, W.J.M. (1984). Some perceptual limitations on talking about space. In A.J. van Doom, W.A. de Grind, & J.J. Koenderink (Eds.), *Limits in perception.* Utrecht, The Netherlands: VNU Science Press.

Levin, I., & Tolchinsky Landsmann, L. (1989). Becoming literate: Referential and phonetic strategies in early reading and writing. *International Journal of Behavioural Development, 12,* 369–384.

Levinson, S. (1996). Frames of reference and Molyneux's question: Cross-linguistic evidence. In P. Bloom, M.A. Peterson, L. Nadel, & M. Garrett (Eds.), *Space and language* (pp.109–169). Cambridge, MA: MIT Press.

Maki, R.H. (1981). Categorization and distance effects with spatial linear orders. *Journal of Experimental Psychology: Human Learning and Memory, 7,* 15–32.

McNamara, T.P. (1986). Mental representations of spatial relations. *Cognitive Psychology, 18,* 87–121.

McNamara, T.P. (1992). Spatial representations. *Geoforum, 23,* 139–150.

McNamara, T.P., Hardy, J.K., & Hirtle, S.C. (1989). Subjective hierarchies in spatial memory. *Journal of Experimental Psychology: Learning, Memory and Cognition, 15,* 211–227.

Miller, G.A., & Johnson-Laird, P.N. (1976). *Language and perception.* Cambridge, MA: Harvard University Press.

Nisbett, R.E., & Ross, L. (1980). *Human inference: Strategies and shortcomings of social judgment.* Englewood Cliffs, NJ: Prenctice-Hall.

Quattrone, G.A. (1986). On the perception of a group's variability. In S. Worchel & W. Austin (Eds.), *The psychology of intergroup relations* (pp.25–48). New York: Nelson-Hall.

Rock, I. (1973). *Orientation and form.* New York: Academic Press.

Rosch, E. (1975). Cognitive reference points. *Cognitive Psychology, 7,* 532–547.

Sadalla, E.K., Burroughs, W.J., & Staplin, L.J. (1980). Reference points in spatial cognition. *Journal of Experimental Psychology: Human Learning and Memory, 5,* 516–528.

Shanon, B. (1983). Answers to where-questions. *Discourse Processes, 6,* 319–352.

Shepard, R.N., & Hurwitz, S. (1984). Upward direction, mental rotation, and discrimination of left and right turns in maps. *Cognition, 18,* 161–194.

Shepard, R.N., & Podgorny, P. (1978). Cognitive processes that resemble perceptual processes. In W.K. Estes (Ed.), *Handbook of learning and cognitive processes* (Vol. 5, pp.189–237). Hillsdale, NJ: Lawrence Erlbaum Associates Inc.

Stevens, A., & Coupe, P. (1978). Distortions in judged spatial relations. *Cognitive Psychology, 13,* 422–437.

Talmy, L. (1983). How language structures space. In H. Pick & L. Acredolo (Eds.), *Spatial orientation: Theory, research, and application* (pp.225–282). New York: Plenum Press.

Taylor, S.E. (1989). *Positive illusions.* New York: Basic Books.

Tufte, E.R. (1983). *The visual display of quantitative information.* Cheshire, CN: Graphics Press.

Tversky, A. (1977). Features of similarity. *Psychological Review, 84,* 327–352.

Tversky, B. (1981). Distortions in memory for maps. *Cognitive Psychology, 13,* 407–433.

Tversky, B. (1991). Distortions in memory for visual displays. In S.R. Ellis (Ed.) & M.K. Kaiser & A. Grunwald (Associate Eds.), *Pictorial communication in virtual and real environments* (pp.61–75). London: Taylor & Francis.

Tversky, B. (1992). Distortions in cognitive maps. *Geoforum, 23,* 131–138.

Tversky, B. (1993). Cognitive maps, cognitive collages, and spatial mental models. In A.U. Frank & I. Campari (Eds.), *Spatial information theory: A theoretical basis for GIS* (Vol. 5, pp.14–24). Berlin: Springer-Verlag.

Tversky, B. (1995). Cognitive origins of graphic conventions. In F.T. Marchese (Ed.), *Understanding images* (pp.29–53). New York: Springer-Verlag.

Tversky, B. (1996a). Memory for pictures, environments, maps, and graphs. In D. Payne & F. Conrad (Eds.), *Intersections in basic and applied memory research* (pp.257–277). Mahwah, NJ: Lawrence Erlbaum Associates Inc.

Tversky, B. (1996b). Spatial perspective in descriptions. In P. Bloom, M.A. Petersson, L. Nadel, & M. Garrett (Eds.), *Language and space* (pp.463–491). Cambridge, MA: MIT Press.

Tversky B. (in press). Mental models of spatial relations and transformations from language. In C. Habel & G. Rickheit (Eds), *Mental models in discourse processing and reasoning.* Philadelphia, PA: John Benjamins Publishing Company.

Tversky, A., & Gati, I. (1978). Studies of similarity. In E. Rosch & B.B. Lloyd (Eds.), *Cognition and categorization* (pp.81–98). Hillsdale, NJ: Lawrence Erlbaum Associates Inc.

Tversky, A., & Kahneman, D. (1974). Judgments under uncertainty: Heuristics and biases. *Science, 185,* 1124–1131.

Tversky, B., Kugelmass, S., & Winter, A. (1991). Cross-cultural and developmental trends in graphic productions. *Cognitive Psychology, 23,* 515–557.

Tversky, B., & Schiano, D. (1989). Perceptual and conceptual factors in distortions in memory for maps and graphs. *Journal of Experimental Psychology: General, 118,* 387–398.

Wilford, J.N. (1981). *The mapmakers.* New York: Knopf.

Wilton, R.N. (1979). Knowledge of spatial relations: The specification of information used in making inferences. *Quarterly Journal of Experimental Psychology, 31,* 133–146.

Author Index

Subject Index